Traveling Around the World with Mike and Barbara Bivona

Part One

Mike Bivona

iUniverse LLC
Bloomington

TRAVELING AROUND THE WORLD WITH MIKE AND BARBARA BIVONA PART ONE

iUniverse books may be ordered through booksellers or by contacting:

iUniverse
1663 Liberty Drive
Bloomington, IN 47403
www.iuniverse.com
1-800-Authors (1-800-288-4677)

ISBN: 978-1-4917-1041-8 (sc)
ISBN: 978-1-4917-1040-1 (hc)
ISBN: 978-1-4917-1039-5 (e)

Library of Congress Control Number: 2013917955

Printed in the United States of America.

iUniverse rev. date: 06/05/2014

Contents

Prologue – Traveling Around the World with Mike and Barbara Bivona – Part One

In 1998, my wife Barbara and I began writing for the Long Island, New York, Ballroom Dance Newsletter, "Around the Floor." The columns covered our travels around the world and the many dancing experiences that we enjoyed. The stories that appeared in our columns were quite condensed from the full actual events. So I thought it would be fun to present the articles as they appeared in the newsletters and then tell the full stories as originally experienced. The result was my book *Dancing Around the World with Mike & Barbara Bivona* – 2010. I so enjoyed writing about our dancing experiences that I decided to write this book, but with less emphasis on dancing and more about the places we've traveled to, the people we've met, and some of the history of the lands we've visited. As some, but not all, of the stories originated from our condensed columns, I will present those articles, when appropriate, before telling about our full experiences of the places we visited. In planning this publication, I thought that limiting the book to around 300 pages would be a more enjoyable read; to accomplish this, I will probably have to write three books or more. So, here is Part One of our wonderful journeys to places around the world.

Although I will be 80 years old next year, Barbara and I will still continue to travel and to add our adventures to future volumes.

Acknowledgements

I would like to thank my lovely wife, Barbara, for the use of her wonderful articles that I was able to expand into our actual travels, and for her patience in tolerating my absence when I would isolate myself for endless hours to write about our experiences. Also, I would like to thank the many people we've met in our journeys that became part of my stories and whose kindness helped enrich our lives.

Chapter One – How I Got Hooked on Traveling

I was born in the East New York section of Brooklyn, NY, on May 18, 1934. My first home was 681 Liberty Ave., between Cleveland and Ashford streets. My father, Luciano Joseph Bivona, came to the United States from Sicily, Italy, with his mother, Angelina, to join his father, Victor Bivona, when he was 12 years old. My mother, Margaret Concetta Compietelli, was born in the U.S.; her folks migrated from the Naples area of Italy. Our neighborhood consisted of predominantly Italian immigrants with American-born offsprings. The language heard throughout the neighborhood was Italian and broken English. So, in my early years, although I was born in the U.S., I spoke English with an Italian accent. A picture of the busy two-way street with a trolley car in front of my birthplace transporting passengers, and a fire station on the next street is from the Brian Merlis Collection at WWW.Brooklynpix.com. It's presented with his permission:

When I was five years old, we moved a few blocks away to 545 Liberty Avenue. Our new home was on the second floor of a two-family building. There was a social club storefront on the street level. It was considered a better location than my birthplace, which was on the top floor of a three-story building that hosted an Italian deli and Nick's Barber Shop on the ground floor. At the age of seven, after I was hit by a car and suffered a fractured skull on the busy avenue, my parents decided to move to a safer part of East New York. My new home was at 589 Cleveland Street on the corner of the Blake Avenue pushcart street market. It was the first time that we lived in a mixed ethnic neighborhood. There were Italians, Jews from Russia and Poland, African Americans, and a handful of Irish families. We only lived on Cleveland Street a few years, and then moved to 2244 Pitkin Ave, between Van Siclen and Hendrix Streets, which was under the Eighth Avenue overhead elevator train line, still in the East New York section of Brooklyn. So, at age ten, I had lived in four different homes and felt like a gypsy. I have to assume that moving so often at such a young age must have installed some sort of a traveling bug in my system. Our latest home was the second floor of a three-level house; a picture of the corner building with a billiard parlor on the street level, and the Lyric Movie Theater across the street. The picture is from the Brian Merlis Collection at WWW.Brooklynpix.com and is presented with his permission:

Our new community had a mix of Italians, Germans, Jews, Irish, and African Americans living and playing together without too much friction. It was while I lived in this section of Brooklyn that I first took public transportation out of my neighborhood on what I considered at that time to be a faraway journey.

My first memorable adventure with traveling began when I was 15 years old. I was required to join everyone in my neighborhood and go to the 75th Police Precinct for a smallpox vaccination. That is where I bumped into Police Officer Maloney who was the cop that patrolled our neighborhood and on many occasions told me to "Move along and don't loiter." After I had received my smallpox shot, he approached me and told me to follow him, which I did without hesitation. He led me to the gym where boys my age were playing basketball, boxing, and lifting weights. He asked me if I would like to join the basketball team; I said okay, and that is when my experience with organized sports began. I wasn't very good at the game, so he suggested that I try baseball, and offered to loan me a ball and glove to encourage me to give it a try, but only if I promised to practice. It wasn't difficult to find boys my age to practice with, and after a couple of weeks, I told officer Maloney that I was ready to join the Police Athletic League (PAL), which he managed for our district. By the end of the season, I was playing shortstop and batting third, which made me a very happy and important teenager. Our team ended the season in second place in our division, which pleased officer Maloney to no end. The following year, we won our division's championship, and in addition to the shiny brass trophies and medals that we received, we were rewarded with a trip to the St. George Hotel's swimming pool in downtown Brooklyn, which was a short train ride from where I lived.

At that time, it was the largest hotel in New York City, boasting 2,600 rooms and rising 30 stories high with a rotating light beacon at the top that lit the sky at night. It was a collection of buildings constructed between 1895 and 1929 that eventually occupied a full city block. The hotel was bounded by Clark Street, Pineapple Street, Hicks Street, and Henry Street. It was so large that the Clark Street-Brooklyn Heights subway station operated from below the hotel with a direct entrance into the hotel. So where is there a reward in going to a hotel? For the teenagers on our team, leaving our neighborhood and going to such an enormous world renowned hotel, was a once in a life-time experience, and that in itself was reward enough for us; our activities the rest of the day was a bonus.

During excavation for its foundation, underground saltwater springs were discovered. They tapped into them and the largest indoor saltwater pool in the world was created, with a continuous flow of free natural seawater. Although the hotel no longer exists, the building that made up the complex has been recycled and now accommodates dormitories for local universities, a large gym, a small pool that is a remnant of the original, and business offices. It has the distinction of being the first "Landmarked Neighborhood Building" in New York.

Our trip to the train station of Clark Street-Brooklyn Heights on the IRT Broadway-Seventh Avenue Subway Line was my first journey out of my neighborhood into a city atmosphere. My only other experiences with faraway places were Coney Island Beach, which required taking multiple trains, and to movie theatres, which required taking trolley cars or buses. What a thrill it was exiting the train and entering the hotel's station; it looked like a palace. Starry eyed by the rounded, beautiful tiled mosaic walls that were decorated with sailing ships and shiny panels reading "Clark Street-Brooklyn Heights," we followed the mosaic tiles pointing and directing us to the St. George Hotel entrance. The station was busy with an abundance of people traveling in every direction. I entered my first elevator-lift and was amazed at how quickly it got us to our destination above the train station and into the hotel. The following is a poster advertising the St. George Pool that is similar to the ones that were discreetly placed throughout the station and aboveground walkways:

There was so much splendor and activity around us that I had trouble absorbing all of the surroundings. The ornate Art Deco lobby of the hotel looked more like the entrance to a royal palace. Red-coated bellhops greeted and directed us through an arcade lined with pinball machines and aquatic pictures of swimming champions on both sides of the hallway. I recognized two of my movie heroes: Johnny Weissmuller and Buster Crabbe; both played Tarzan in many adventure films that I had seen. There were shops throughout the arcade similar to the ones found today in many large upscale hotels. In those bygone days, top-of-the-line shops in the Brooklyn neighborhood that I lived in were to be found only in a female's daydreams.

We entered the swimming pool area and were given a set of swim trunks, a towel, and a locker key on an elastic band that could be secured on a wrist or ankle. All of our swimsuits were black, which matched the one-piece suits that the girls at the pool wore. From a distance, the people in the pool looked like members of a penguin colony, with tuxedoed birds jumping in the air, moving about the pool area, and swimming and diving in every direction.

We followed our leader to take mandatory showers in a huge room with private stalls. Although I had lived in four different dwellings up until that time, none of them had anything that resembled a full standup shower. The closest thing we had was a bathtub with a shower hose attached to a spout, so our shower consisted of a sit-down event after a bath. I must have spent half an hour in the shower stall, enjoying the stinging water hitting my body and soaping myself over and over again. Our coach came into the room and had to order me out of my newfound temple.

The swimming pool was somewhat of a miraculous place for me. Looking at it from the overhead observation deck made it look like a mini-river to my boyish eyes. It measured 40 by 120 feet, with a 10-foot diving board abutted by three lower boards located at the 10-foot-deep end of the pool. At the shallow end, which was three feet deep, a waterfall splashed into the pool making rhythmic sounds that seemed to complement those of the bathers. Mosaic aquatic wall designs of fish and boats, separated by alternating mirrors and a series of supporting pillars faced with translucent green ceramic tiles, made the place seem infinite.

We were reminded by our guardian that we were on our "good behavior" and that any rowdiness would result in our being kicked out of the premises. Those words worked magic as our anxiety at being in such an incredible place was starting to show in our restlessness. We spent several hours swimming, diving, racing, and enjoying ourselves at a place we only imaged existed in Esther Williams's movie films. After we had exhausted ourselves in the pool, our leader escorted us to an air-conditioned gym where we continued depleting our energy until our actions became sluggish from fatigue. The only exposure I had to air conditioning was when attending a movie house in my neighborhood. I never dreamed that other places had the same comfort. I remember saying to myself, "Soon they'll probably have air conditioning in cars and houses," HO HO HO . . . We ended our excursion with a mandatory return to the shower stalls, much to my delight, but we were only given five minutes to complete our final wash; it would be many years before I set foot in a shower stall again, and that was when I joined the U.S. Air Force three years later.

For our good behavior that day, our coach took us to see an incredibly large television set in the air-conditioned lounge area of the hotel; it was probably about 60 inches, but to my inexperienced eyes, it seemed like the size of a full movie screen. Television sets were just beginning to appear in homes on very small black and white 12-inch screens. The sets were expensive and not easy to locate, so much so, that three years later when I joined the Air Force in 1952, we still didn't have a TV set in our home, nor did I know of anyone in my neighborhood that had one. We ended the amazing day being physically and mentally exhausted. Physically from the swimming and the gym workouts, and mentally from seeing sights that were to us out of a Buck Rogers comic book or one of his science-fiction movies.

Needless to say, the experience set my mind in the direction of leaving my neighborhood in Brooklyn and dreaming about faraway places. The next stimulus came a year later when I was 16-years old. I somehow managed to become a pseudo cowboy and spent lots of time at a horse-riding academy on Linden Blvd, which was about a half a mile from where I lived. The owner, Jake, asked me if I would like to work at his horseback-riding concession during the summer at Coney Island; I immediately said yes and my next influential experience to distant places began. My job at the riding concession consisted of holding a horse or pony's reins while walking riders, mostly children, around a small track. I did this for ten hours a day, seven days a week, in fair weather from the beginning of June till the end of September.

When we weren't busy, I was able to rotate shifts with other riding attendants, which gave me lots of time to explore Coney Island. One of the fringe benefits of working near the boardwalk was that when other concessionaires got to know you, their wares and goodies were free in exchange for helping them clean up or doing odd chores. I had many free hotdogs, ears of corn-on-the-cob, BBQ steak sandwiches, French-fries, and cokes at Nathan's Famous hot dog stand. I was able to ride the *Cyclone, Parachute Jump, Wonder Wheel,* and many others, free of charge. One of my most enjoyable benefits was lying on the beach while meeting pretty girls who thought I was the king of the midway because I worked at carnival-land. One of my less pleasurable events was when I returned home in the evening. I had to strip down and leave my clothing in the hallway, and immediately jump into the tub-shower to try to remove the aroma that I carried home from working at the stable. After a couple of weeks, my father and I agreed that it would be okay for me to sleep in one of the backrooms of the stable for the remainder of the season. This made life a lot easier for me and my sister Anne who was responsible for washing my clothing in addition to her other household chores. My mother passed away when I was 13 years old, and the household burden went to my older sister; what she didn't need added to her agenda was taking care of my ripe clothing. I didn't waste any time in buying an extra pair of dungarees so I could alternate my outfits while living at my temporary residence in the backroom of the pungent-smelling stable. It was odd that no one that worked at the carnival complained that I didn't meet the cleanliness standards of my family. I guess we all shared a common fragrance. There was a convenient Laundromat at Coney Island that I used when the mood came over me, to get the stiffness out of my Levi's, which wasn't very often. As a matter of fact, I do remember sleeping with my clothes on occasionally, which didn't bother me or my friends.

Sleeping at Coney Island gave me an opportunity to explore the never-ending fascinating places along the boardwalk, including Surf Avenue, Steeplechase Amusement Park, and the Bowery. The island is a peninsula in the southernmost part of the Borough of Brooklyn, and is landlord to one of the world's most beautiful beaches. It extends from the exclusive private neighborhood of Seagate to its west; Brighton Beach and Manhattan Beach to its east; and the Gravesend neighborhood to the north. It became a resort after the Civil War as excursion railroads and the Coney Island and Brooklyn Railroad streetcar lines reached the area in the 1860s. With easy access to the beach area came major hotels, horseracing, amusement parks, and less-reputable entertainment, such as the Three-card Monte Street Hustle, a variety of gambling establishments, street hucksters, and prostitution. At the beginning of the 20th century, Coney Island turned from what was considered an upscale resort to an accessible location for day-trippers from the five boroughs of New York City, seeking to escape from the summer's heat by using the magnificent beach that extended from West 37th Street at Seagate, through Coney Island, Brighton Beach, and on to the beginning of the communities of Manhattan Beach, a distance of approximately two and one-half miles. The Riegelmann Boardwalk ran the whole length of the beach and had a number of amusement and refreshment stands on and around the boardwalk. Between 1880 to the end of WWII, Coney Island was the largest amusement area in the world, attracting millions of visitors a year. Within that time period, it contained three competing amusement parks: Luna Park, Dreamland Park, and Steeplechase. In addition, it had many independent smaller amusement parks and concessions lined up on Surf Avenue, the Bowery, and the surrounding streets.

The first park to open was Steeplechase Amusement Park in 1897. A disastrous fire required that it be rebuilt in 1907 to a somewhat fireproof park, which was still operating when I worked there; unfortunately, following an illustrious run, it was closed in 1964. Diminutive pictures of Coney Island and Steeplechase Park follow; in the first picture, the *Merry-go-round* is in the forefront, the *Cyclone Ride* to its left, and the *Parachute Jump* and *Wonder Wheel* are in the background:

The following picture is of Steeplechase Park's reopening in 1908; the entrance was on the wood-planked Bowery Walk:

The attractions in the park that I remember so well are the *Ferris Wheel,* the *One Ring Circus,* and my favorite, the two *Horse Race Tracks,* which consisted of a high track and a lower track. Each had four horses seating two riders each, racing along guided rails parallel to each other. The high track was a slightly longer course, approximately 1,700 feet with a higher starting point, and traveled one lap around the exterior of the *Pavilion of Fun* building. The 1,600-feet-long inner track with a lower starting point ran under the colonnade roof on the side of that building. The riders' horses were drawn up on a cable to an elevation of 22 feet at the start of a race, and quickly dropped downward along a 15% grade track to gain speed. The riders then rode across a miniature lake, while their momentum carried them upward again to a height of 16 feet above the beach; they then descended through a tunnel and raced upward over a series of jolts until they reached the finish line. Heavier riders usually had the advantage of winning, as their weight moved the horses down the ending slopes at a faster pace than their lighter competitors. At the end of the ride, racers were led to the *Pavilion of Fun's Insanitarium* and *Blowhole Theater.* Riders would enter a stage on their hands and knees through a low doghouse where a cowboy, a tall farmer, and a dwarf clown awaited and guided them through an alley called *Comedy Lane.* While the hosts distracted the victims, a system of compressed-air jets would blow men's hats and toupees off of their heads and send women's skirts flying upward to their shock and embarrassment. The clown's job was to prod the man's buttocks with an electric stinger; when his girlfriend would reach out to help the stunned guy, the clown would shoot a blast of air under her dress and watch it soar as the audience roared with laughter. The mortified couple would hurry by six-foot-high playing cards, a tree with six-foot-long hotdog branches, and a dwarf clown who swatted them with slapsticks. Finally, the couple would reach a moveable floor known as the *Battleship Roll.* Piles of barrels on either side of the walkway would begin to shake and appear to be falling down on them as they scrambled for safety and escaped into the audience. The exhausted racers then had the option to leave or, at no charge, sit in the audience and enjoy the next group's embarrassing encounters with the clowns. Some girls would repeat their performances several times during the day wearing colorful undergarments that they would change each time, as if to tell the audience, who's laughing now!

I wrote extensively about the *Race Track Ride* because it was the most popular attraction in Steeplechase and the ride that I most often either participated in or watched as a spectator in the comfortable seats of the theater. The list of rides and their purpose at the park could fill two books; therefore, I'll only list some that I enjoyed while spending my memorable summer working in *Fantasyland.* In Steeplechase, there was the *Mixer,* a large revolving platform, 30 feet in diameter with room for up to 24 people. As it spun faster and faster, it catapulted riders into its surrounding scoop-like bowl. There was a one-of-a-kind

Chicken Carousel that had 38 chickens and 14 ostriches instead of horses. The ride was as popular as its sister, the *Horse Carousel,* which thrilled children of all ages who rode on the enormous backs of carved animals. Another carousel, the *El Dorado*, was a special attraction and ride as it contained a menagerie of animals on three platforms arranged in ascending tiers, each revolving at different speeds. Its crow's watch-like canopy rose to a height of 42 feet and was illuminated with 6,000 lamps that enhanced the appearance of its horses, pigs, cows, and other barnyard animals. Watching riders enjoying themselves on the backs of the strange-looking animals was one of the funniest scenes in Coney Island. I had two other favorite places at the park where I spent many a relaxing hour; they were the fenced Private Beach in front of Steeplechase, which was for the use of its paying customers or special freeloaders like me, and the world's largest outdoor salt water pool, which held 670,000 gallons of water. Free ocean water fed the 270-foot long and 90-foot wide outdoor mini-manmade lake that housed two large bathing platforms on either side of its length. The pool could accommodate over a thousand bathers who took advantage of swimming, diving, jumping, or just relaxing in or hiding from the sun. I was proud to brag that I had swum in the world's largest indoor salt-water pool at the St. George Hotel, and the world's largest outdoor salt-water pool at Steeplechase Park; oddly, both were in the Borough of Brooklyn. The park also had many rides and swimming places for small children, in addition to the multitude of imaginative assorted fun and thrill rides. Unfortunately, after my short excursion to the Steeplechase Park, it was closed in 1964. Till this day, I don't think there is an amusement park that can compare to the sophistication and variety of the rides that Steeplechase had in its heyday.

The second major amusement park to be built in Coney Island was Luna Park. It lasted from 1903 to 1944 until it disappeared in a roaring fire that destroyed the park beyond repair. While it existed, the Park owners claimed in one year to have had almost five million visitors using their astonishing themed attractions, such as *A Trip to the Moon and Back* in a rocketship, *Shoot the Chute*, which was a flat-bottomed boat that slid down a ramp inside a waterfall into a large lagoon, and *The Helter Skelter*, which was a ride with a slide built in a spiral around a high tower; users climbed up the inside of the tower and slid down the outside, usually on a mat or canvas sack. Unique to the park were rides on live elephants and camels. So innovative were the rides at the park that it's thought that many of Disney World's parks themes are an extension of Luna Park's.

Although Luna Park was not part of my summer experience, I did get to visit the new park a couple of years ago. In May of 2010, a new Luna Park resurrected on 8th Street and the ocean side of Surf Avenue directly across the street from the original. Mayor Bloomberg of New York City proudly headed the opening ceremony dedicating the new Playland to the people of the five boroughs of New York City: Brooklyn, Queens, Bronx, Staten Island, and Manhattan. He dedicated the new Playland to the millions of visitors from around the world who would come and enjoy its amazing fun-rides. The mayor said, "I can't wait to stand in line at Nathan's Famous hotdog stand, which is located just a few blocks away, for a serving of my favorite soul food, a foot-long hotdog, and curly French potatoes."

The rides for the new park were made by the world's leading amusement park manufacturer, Zamperla of Venice, Italy. Some of the modern rides are the *Air Race,* where riders pilot their own planes around a control tower pole while they spin, flipping head over heels in barrel rolls. The *Surf's Up* ride allows riders to balance on a surfboard and ride a 90-foot wave. The *Tickler,* which is modeled after the original one at Luna Park, rotates cars in circles as they speed over the coaster's tracks twisting and turning. The *Electric Spin* is a combination spinning ride and coaster where riders sit facing outward on a spinning platform that travels back and forth along a U-shaped track. There are over 20 rides at present with plans to expand the park and possibly come pretty close to rivaling its namesake. The new park's grand entranceway is decorated with crescent moons and is similar to the one that I saw as a young boy and that millions of visitors from around the world passed through in the first half of the 20th century. A promotion poster authorized by Newkai was taken from Wikipedia Commons and is presented below:

Another popular amusement area was throughout the streets of Coney Island, where many independent concessioners had rides and attractions. Some popular ones were shooting galleries, miniature horse races, the strongman bell challenge, guess your age games, guess your weight games, throw the ring games and win a doll, toss a penny into a hole and win a prize, a pony and horse ride (my job), girlie shows, bars and grills up and down almost every street along Surf Avenue, bumper cars, and, of course, the many eating establishments from upscale dining at Steeplechase Park to Nathan's Famous hotdog stand, Nedick's juice and hotdog stand, soft custard ice cream stands, and on and on . . . It certainly was a never-ending place to spend an hour, a day, a week, or a month, eating, drinking, and enjoying fun-and-thrill rides. One of my favorite part-time jobs when not attending the ponies was collecting tickets at the girlie shows, which were only a couple of blocks from where I worked. I had a deal with the ticket-takers to watch their booths while they took breaks; my reward was free entry to the girlie shows, even though I was underage. I certainly met lots of interesting people at those joints.

One of my biggest problems that summer was keeping relatively clean, especially after a couple of days tending to the ponies at the stable. My problem was solved in a place called Ravenhall Baths, which was next door to Steeplechase and bordered their property on West 19th Street. It had an outdoor swimming pool, probably the second largest in the world, which was almost as large as the one at Steeplechase, with showers, steam rooms, a gym, lockers, and lunch counters. On rainy days when we couldn't show our ponies and the swimming pool was closed, I would use my special "freeloading" privileges and meet my buddies who worked at the baths. I would shower and use the facilities as if I was a member, to get myself in hygienic and presentable condition. There were Brylcreem hair dispensers in the washrooms for their customers' use, which I made good use of, as it was strong enough to keep my red-curly-unruly hair under control. After being made presentable for public display, we would usually mosey along to Steeplechase where we used our "freeloading" privileges to enter the indoor *Pavilion of Fun* facilities to help pass the time of day, while relaxing and having a great time. After its first fire in 1907, the pavilion was rebuilt as a glass-and-steel indoor amusement park. It covered five acres with such exotic rides as *The Pipe,* which was a covered slide where riders would climb to the top of the stairs and speed down inside the pipe, crashing into the cushioned pavilion floor. *The Human Pool Table* was a large flat surface made up of 24 large rotating discs that revolved in opposite directions challenging players to move from one surface to another without falling and becoming entangled with each other. *The Human Roulette Wheel* spun until passengers sitting on it were flung to the perimeter, and *The Human Zoo* ride forced visitors to descend a spiral staircase until they found themselves in a cage, where they were offered peanuts and monkey talk by onlookers. These attractions and others were more than enough to keep young teenagers busy until dinnertime or until the sun came out and our jobs resumed.

I am proud to boast that I frequently enjoyed three rides at Coney Island that are now on the National Register of Historic Places. According to Wikipedia, they are *The Wonder Wheel*, which was built in 1918; its steel Ferris wheel has both stationary cars and rocking cars that slide along a track. It holds 144 riders, stands 150 feet tall, and weighs over 2,000 tons. At night, the steel frame is outlined and illuminated by neon lights. Today it's part of Deno's Wonder Wheel Amusement Park. *The Cyclone* roller coaster ride was built in 1927, and is one of the nation's oldest wooden coasters still in operation. It is a favorite of roller coaster aficionados, and boasts of being 85 feet high with a 60-degree drop. It is owned by the City of New York and is operated by Astroland Amusement Park in Coney Island. Lastly, *The Parachute Jump* which originally was the *Life Savers' Parachute Jump* at the 1939 New York World's Fair and was the first thrill ride of its kind, rising over 270 feet into the sky. Patrons were hoisted up into what seemed to be clouds and then were allowed to drop, using guy-wired parachutes. Although the ride has been closed since 1968, it remains a Coney Island landmark and is sometimes referred to as "Brooklyn's Eiffel Tower." Between 2001 and 2004, the jump was completely dismantled, cleaned, painted, and restored, but unfortunately remains inactive. After an official lighting ceremony in July 2006, *The Parachute Jump* was slated to be lit year round using different color motifs to represent the seasons. However, the idea was scrapped when New York City started conserving electricity in the summer months.

Well, as all good things must come to an end, my Disneyesque journey ended and I prepared to return back to the reality of my old neighborhood in East New York. Some of the concessionaires were moving south for the winter and asked if I would like to join them. This was a difficult decision to make for a young boy who was fascinated with traveling to unknown places. The thought of roaming feely with circus-type people, and all the pretty girls who never seemed to tire of rubbing my red-wavy hair, was very tempting. After much thought (about two minutes), I wisely declined. My friends threw me a going-away beach party on my last night in Playland. Lulu from the girly show, Johnny from Steeplechase, Frankie from the bathhouse, my boss from the pony ride, and many other acquaintances came to say goodbye to the young redhead. We roasted hotdogs, potatoes, and marshmallows, while friends played their guitars, harmonicas, jaw harps, and tambourines, and sang "You are my Sunshine," "Life's a bowl of cherries," "So long it's been good to know you," and other popular songs of that time. Before the festivities ended, it seemed as if everyone in Coney Island came to say goodbye. I've always been amazed at the Coney Island sights at night. It seemed as if all the attractions put on their Sunday best, all dolled-up and showing off their brilliance in the form of colorful flickering lights. The *Wonder Wheel,* in the daytime looks like a large circle with no personality, but when the sun sets, all of a sudden it becomes bright and illuminated, a sparkling circular presence, outshining all the other attractions as it turns and its multicolored lights change positions with each other, giving the appearance of being the main source of energy in the park, and that every other display revolves and is energized by it. Directly behind it was *The Parachute Jump*, which seems to be an inanimate object in the daytime; at night, it lights up the sky and resembles a rocketship ready for takeoff into outer space. Its brilliant sparkling lights make it the highest focal point in the park.

It was the last time that I would experience Coney Island's brilliant night views, the unique mixed scents from its tenants, the invigorating saltwater air, the beige sand nestling between my toes, the smiling faces of my jolly friends, and the camaraderie of the most amazing collection of rainbowed personalities to be found on this planet. I forced myself to hold back the tears that were forming in my mind and would soon escape through my eyes; my young macho persona allowed me to leave before the cascade began. That evening and my summer adventure in Coney Island ended with lots of hugs and kisses, some tears from the gals, and promises from everyone to keep in touch . . . if not in this life, then we surely would meet in the next one. I left looking at the dark ocean meeting the blackened sky and knew that one day its horizon and its mysteries would unfold for me, for I was, without a doubt, hooked on traveling. It wouldn't be for another two years, when I was 18 that my next journey would begin. I enlisted in the U.S. Air Force, where my assignments would take me from Upstate New York through many beautiful western states and finally to Asia, visiting Formosa (Taiwan), Korea, and finally settling in Japan for two years.

Chapter Two – From New York to Japan

It was in the middle of the Korean "Conflict-War" in 1952 that I decided it was time for me to enlist in the military and help bring the war to a successful conclusion. By the time I decided to join the regular military, I had a good understanding of what being in the Army was about. When I was 16, I lied about my age and joined the New York Fighting 69th National Guard Regiment and knew from my experience with the renowned Army regiment that I didn't want to be a soldier in the U.S. Army. The experience turned me off because of the rigorous drilling and weapon handling that is required to become one of the world's finest infantrymen. So, I zeroed in on the U.S. Air Force, as the possibility that flying around the world and realizing my dream of visiting faraway exotic places had a better chance of becoming a reality. I enlisted in the Air Force for four years, hoping that I would be assigned to a job that would have me flying to some of the places that I had dreamed about.

My first assignment was at Sampson Air Force Base near the City of Geneva, in Upstate New York, for three months of basic training, from early October 1952 to the beginning of January 1953. The base is located in the New York "Snow Belt" and has for its neighbors the City of Rochester (40 miles), Niagara Falls (70 miles), and Seneca Lake in its backyard. The base was formerly a naval submarine training center, where the lake's depth of 600 feet and 38-mile length allowed vessels the opportunity to practice in simulated ocean conditions. Seneca Lake is the largest of the glacial Five Finger Lakes, which are Canandaigua Lake, Honeoye Lake, Keuka Lake, Hemlock Lake, and Seneca Lake. The naval base was converted to an Air Force training center during the Korean War. Unlucky me, I got to be stationed at probably one of the coldest places in the U.S. When the cold wind hit the semi-frozen lake in the winter, the temperature at the base dropped to below zero, which was always followed with icicles forming in my nostrils when we did our daily morning outdoor calisthenics.

We were billeted in open barracks (no partitions) with 70 men in each building. Our new home was heated by a coal furnace, which blew hot air into the barracks like a wind storm, creating an annoying howling and whistling sound, and causing no end of bloody noses due to the unfiltered dry hot air heat. After being assigned our bunks, a bulky, muscular, buck sergeant (three stripes) named Fargo began instructing us on the proper military way to make a bed. By the expressions on my fellow recruits' faces, I could see that they agreed with me: "Are we children? We know how to make a bed without supervision." Well, Sgt. Fargo had other ideas; he said, "There is only one way to make a bunk, and that is the military way. If you don't make it right, it's 50 pushups, and if you don't make it right three times, then there will be no blankets or sheets on your bunks for the next day." He got everyone's attention and we learned how to make hospital corners and tight sheets and blankets in a very short time. To pass the tightness test, he would bounce a quarter in the center of the blanket; if it didn't bounce six inches, you failed the test. That event was the beginning of what we in the military called "Chicken Sh . . ." The popular term means, "Expending an inordinate amount of time doing 'minutia manure' tasks for the benefit of no one in particular."

After the bedtime orientation, we gathered outside in the freezing temperature and marched at quickstep to the supply room for uniform fittings. We were asked what size shirts, pants, jackets, shoes, and hats would fit our undisciplined bodies? After all the guess work, when we put on our uniforms, we looked like a bunch of misfits; nothing seemed to fit. When we returned to our barracks, it resembled a comedy of errors play, with the players trying to swap their issued wardrobes with one and another, hoping by some miracle that a proper-sized garment would result in the exchange. The only item that fit everyone properly was something called "long johns," which were thermal underwear that seemed to immediately attach to one's skin. Our crowning moment on the first day was at the barber shop. I was asked how I would prefer my curly-red-hair trimmed. I said "Long in the back and short in the front." I didn't get the last word out of my mouth before the barber removed all the hair from my head except for about half an inch, which made my nose seem that it was a transplant from Cyrano de Bergerac's face.

The three months of basic training couldn't go by fast enough. As fall turned into winter, the weather became intolerably cold, especially when we had to camp outdoors for days at a time. The fierce winds would hit the partially frozen lake and blanket us with ice mists that would chill my body with no escape or relief. But, like all good soldiers, we managed to survive and lived to tell our family and friends how we almost froze to death while in the service of our country, in Upstate New York. Our daily routine at 6 A.M. was to "rise and shine" to the sounds of a bugle coming through the loudspeakers that were strategically placed throughout our building to make the loudest and most annoying sounds. I was privileged to awake a half hour earlier as I was assigned to coal duty and had to shovel the black chunks of rock into the furnace so that my fellow airmen would awake to a relatively warm environment. We were given a half an hour to dress and assemble outside in the below-zero temperature so we could quickly march to the mess hall for a gourmet military breakfast. We marched at quickstep and then ran in the cold morning air until icicles formed under my wool mask, around my eyebrows, and into my nose; it felt as if the ice in my nose was going to spread and puncture my brain. We drilled for an hour and then, as a reward, trotted to the mess hall and took our place on the "chow line," which gave us a chance to defrost and enjoy the aroma of the hot coffee and bacon that enveloped the gigantic dining room. Breakfast became the most important event of the day; after an hour drilling and nearly freezing our butts off, the hot coffee, bacon and eggs, biscuits, and more hot coffee was something everyone looked forward to as a reward for surviving the bitter weather.

A most memorable experience in boot camp was my first weekend pass. The closest city was the small town of Geneva. It was a short distance from our base, but the city of choice for most of us was Rochester, which was a bustling city with a population of over 300,000 people. It was only a little over an hour bus ride from our base. It was rumored that their USO Club had beautiful female volunteer hostesses who were willing to talk and dance with soldiers. It was over two months since we had any contact with women, so we were all anxious to get on the bus and see what the club and the City of Rochester and its environs had to offer. The USO (United Service Organization) was founded in 1941 and was a "Home away from home" for American servicemen around the world. It gave them a quiet place to talk, write a letter, get a free cup of coffee and a snack, attend social dances, and enjoy the entertainment of the many Hollywood celebrities who volunteered their time for the benefit of the servicemen and women in the military. The organization is sponsored by the Salvation Army, Young Men's Christian Association (YMCA), Young Women's Christian Association (YWCA), National Catholic Community Service, National Travelers Aid, and the National Jewish Welfare Board. These not-for-profit organizations combined their efforts to raise money to support the everyday activities that benefited millions of servicemen and women during WWII. The organization was disbanded after the Second World War and reestablished during the Korean Conflict.

Getting to Rochester was easy; making it even more enjoyable was the fact that the USO was near the bus terminal. When we entered the large hall, we were treated to coffee and cake by pretty young girls that welcomed us as if we were family members returning home from the war. The first order of the day was to find a place to sleep for two nights. We were given a list of nearby hotels, motels, and boarding houses that had discount prices for servicemen. My two buddies, Frank and Johnny, and I chose a nearby hotel that allowed the three of us to share a room at a very reasonable price. The small L-shaped room had two single beds and a pullout couch. After over two months of sharing an open barracks with 70 soldiers who made the most unimaginable sounds in their sleep, the hotel room seemed like a quiet prince's palace.

It was in the middle of December and near the Xmas holiday, so the city was decorated for the festive occasion. Everyone we met was in the spirit of the season, which resulted in our getting free drinks and many free meals in the restaurants and bars that we visited. Especially nice was the dance hall at the USO Club. It was also decorated for the occasion; a large 12-foot local pine tree was harvested, its fragrance filled the hall bringing rushing memories of the many days spent at my grandparents' house decorating their freshly cut trees and inhaling the same aroma that was in abundance in the hall and around the neighborhoods of Rochester. We were invited to a holiday dance on Saturday night at the USO Club, which gave us an opportunity to dress for the first time in our formal blue uniforms, wearing our handsomely boxed visor hats and mirror-shined black dress shoes, minus our winter long johns. We were welcomed by the pretty volunteers whose numbers magically grew to match the amount of men present at the party; approximately 100 pretty, shiny faces were there to share the holiday spirit with us. We spent the night dancing, talking, spiking our soft drinks, and listening to the girls tell us how much they appreciated our being in the military and our willingness to put our lives at risk for their benefit.

We were fortunate to meet many of the friendly people of the city who invited us to share their homes and dinner tables; it's not surprising that today the city is considered one of the ten best places to live in the U.S. I thought at the time that living there in the future could be an option that I should keep in mind and explore when the proper time came for me to settle down.

We returned to Sampson AFB after a well-deserved weekend and continued our military drillings and studies, and, in the blink of an eye, our basic training was over. On graduation day, we joined hundreds of other flights in formations on the parade field and marched past the officers' grandstand, saluting, while a dozen F84 Thunder Fighting Jets (training planes) flew overhead leaving their thunderous noise and jet streams in the sky as they passed and welcomed us as bona fide members of the U.S. Air Force. What a feeling; I had a new stripe on my sleeves (Private First Class), I was part of a group of men that had successfully completed three grueling months of boot camp, and a part of the best flying organization in the world. A big graduation bonus was that we were leaving the freezing weather behind; but I did hold onto my winter long johns that had served me so well, just in case my next tour of duty was in Alaska.

Well, my next assignment wasn't Alaska, but it was close. It was Francis E. Warren AFB, in Cheyenne, Wyoming, about fifteen hundred miles away, and probably one of the coldest places in the winter months in the U.S. Our mode of transportation was a C-54 Skymaster, a military transport plane that dated back to WWII and was developed from the four-engine prop Douglas DC-4 Airliner. A picture of the beautiful lady follows:

About 50 airmen from the graduating flights who were going to Francis E. Warren AFB gathered together on the airstrip and nervously waited to board the shining lady. I was the only one from my flight going to Cheyenne and felt uneasy about leaving my buddies behind. I was scared and excited at the same time. It was my first experience with air flight and I couldn't wait for the thrill of taking off and getting airborne, just as I had seen so many of my movie star war heroes like John Wayne and Errol Flynn do in their wartime movie roles. We boarded the aircraft and sat side by side on both sides of the craft, along the length of the plane. Shoulder to shoulder, teenagers trying to act grownup, but scared as hell, especially when the flight sergeant told us that there was a parachute under each position, just in case. His only instruction for their use was "Put this thing on, buckle the front, tie the top and bottom, and then jump out this door; after you exit, count to ten and pull this ring"; that was the extent of our visual and verbal instructions for the use of the life-saving device.

The four engines roared and in short order, we were airborne. We flew over Michigan, Illinois, Iowa, and Nebraska. "Nebraska-Nebraska-Nebraska," the sound of a state that I will never forget. I call it a sound instead of a name because after hearing it in so many sentences the words got garbled. The saga began when our leader said, "We've developed ice on our wings and are going to have to land in Nebraska; put on your parachutes and make ready in case we have to bail out." I thought, "Is this guy nuts?" I didn't know the first thing about jumping out of an airplane, no less in freezing weather. We scrambled for our chutes and somehow got them on and checked by our brilliant flight sergeant. He then remarked, "Don't worry men; the worst thing that can happen if you jump is that you freeze up and remain in the sky and if you're lucky you might even come down as a snowflake." He then said, "If we don't make a crash landing in the cornfields, we will be landing at Offutt Air Force Base in Omaha, Nebraska, in approximately ten minutes." There wasn't a peep from the 50 grownup soldiers, only stillness; the only thing that could be heard was the silence and my heart pounding through the inside of my ears. The brilliant one then said, "Hold on men, we are going to be losing altitude pretty fast, so if you have to pee, do it now, but don't leave your seats."

We landed and, due to the additional weight from the icing, the plane thudded and bounced along the runway until it came to a sliding stop. The runway was lit with torches to light our way and probably to melt some of the snow from its surface. When the C-54 finally ended its flight and shut off its huge noisy engines, the silence in the plane became even louder. It seemed that everyone was in suspended animation; we were frozen in place and didn't dare move for fear of waking up and discovering that we were dead. We finally thawed out, removed our parachute armor, grabbed out duffle bags, and got the hell out of the shiny lady as quickly as we could. Looking back at the plane, I could actually see icicles hanging from the wings and caked on the fuselage. Our plane was dwarfed by SAC's humongous fighting machines, the B-29s, B-50s, and an assortment of other sophisticated flying equipment. Our unexpected landing was at Offutt Air Force Base, headquarters of the Strategic Air Command (SAC) and the very place where the first two bombers, the B-29 Superfortresses, Enola Gay and Bockscar, which dropped atomic bombs on Hiroshima and Nagasaki, Japan, were built.

Two busses were waiting for us. We rushed in quickstep to board and were on our way to Wyoming in short order. The whole maneuver was so efficient that I got the feeling that the routine must have been done many times before. It would have been nice if our brilliant flight sergeant would have mentioned that what was happening was part of our military training; it certainly would have taken a lot of pressure off the 50 teenager-grownups.

We traveled the remaining part of the day and the following night, making only necessary pit stops before arriving at Francis E. Warren AFB late the following morning. How do I begin to explain the shock of getting off the warm bus and walking into severe cold air?

The temperatures we left behind at Sampson AFB were springtime in comparison to the Wyoming January winter greeting we encountered. The surprise of the zero degrees weather, the mounds of snow along the roads and paths, and the ferocious winds pounding at me like a sledge hammer, made me wish that I was back home in Brooklyn in our heated, cold-water flat. The elevation of the base is over 6,000 feet, which accounts for the fact that the Cheyenne, Wyoming location is probably one of the, if not the, windiest places in the U.S. When the original fort was built in the late 1800s, the buildings were constructed in a triangular shape with the main point facing the prevailing winds to reduce damage to the structures. Talk about going from the frying pan into the fire (pun intended); the base had to be the coldest place I could ever imagine and is probably why I love staying in Florida for six winter months every year in my senior days to escape the cold weather in Long Island, N.Y.

There was some redeeming information that our new flight sergeant gave us. He pointed out where we would be spending most of our classroom time learning new communication skills; thank God, the classes were all indoors. He also informed us that reveille was at seven o'clock in the morning, and that our classes started an hour later. No outdoor marching, running, or drills were required before or after classes. He politely escorted us through the valley of snow to our pre-WWI barracks; it was identical to the one we had left behind at Sampson AFB. He then gave us some much-needed good news; our classes didn't start for another week because most of the training staff were still on holiday vacations, so after orientation we had the rest of the day to ourselves, unsupervised. As we were falling out, the sergeant called me aside to inform me that due to my experience with coal furnaces, I was elected as the Barrack Coal Marshal. I was trapped again, the major difference from my last assignment was that I didn't have to shovel any coal; my job was to make sure that it was shoveled by someone else.

I can't express the feeling of euphoria and gratitude that I felt when hearing the bugle call at 7 A.M. the next morning, waking up, and then deliberately going back to sleep with no fear of retribution. It was the first time in over three months that I actually had time to myself with nothing to do. So my buddies and I, Tim and Phil, went to a late breakfast at 9 A.M., and spent the rest of the day exploring the base by shuttle bus. A strange sight throughout the base was a network of wires and ropes with pulleys that went from each barrack to the Mess Hall. In inclement weather, before paths could be cleared, food would be transported from the kitchen by a pulley system to the individual buildings. Seeing that procedure in operation was like imagining a mother with multiple umbilical cords feeding her children, it really looked weird.

Our bus driver freely gave us some information about the base:

> Francis E. Warren AFB was named after Wyoming's first governor, who served as a U.S. Senator for over 37

> years. At the age of 19, he was awarded the Congressional Medal of Honor for heroism during the Civil War. He was also the father-in-law of the General of the Armies during WWI, Black Jack Pershing, who as a captain was stationed at the fort prior to it becoming an air base. Other well-known figures stationed here were General Billy Mitchell (the Father of the Air Force), General Mark Clark, who served in WWI, WWII, and as the Supreme UN Commander during the Korean War. Some other amusing information is that entertainers Neil Diamond and Chris LeDoux grew up on the base. The base is currently a training center and is the proud host of the United States ICBM Missile Headquarters.

While touring the base, I noticed a civilian walking along the white snow background wearing royal blue pants. There was only one person in the world that I knew of that owned such a pair of pistol-pocket, royal blue, tapered cuffed pants; it was my hometown buddy, Paul Maggio. What a small world; I hadn't seen him since we enlisted together back in Brooklyn. He was called up before me and was sent to Lackland AFB in San Antonio, Texas for motor pool management. He was stationed at our base for further training and was to be reassigned at a later date to a permanent post. What a lucky break; we now had someone who could tell us where the best places were for entertainment. He took us to the PX (Post Exchange) and introduced us to the greatest little coffee shop in the world, which boasted of having the best cream-filled donuts on our planet. He told us that the nearest civilized city was Cheyenne, the capital of Wyoming, with a population of about 30,000 residents. It was at that time probably the smallest-big city in the U.S. by population. We made plans to join him and visit the most popular place in the little city, the Trolley Car Diner, the next morning for their special breakfast. And special it was: stacks of hotcakes, mounds of bacon, and, for a morning dessert, "apple pie a la mode." I didn't know such a treat existed as pie with vanilla ice cream on top. Till this day, it's still one of my favorite desserts, except occasionally I'll substitute blueberry pie with lots of vanilla ice cream. Well, that was the extent of what was exciting in the smallest-big city in the U.S. Paul told us that for real entertainment and lots of girls, we would have to travel 100 mile to Denver, Colorado. He walked us through the rest of the town. There was a movie house, a couple of diners, a few retail stores, and lots of cowboys riding horses. It seemed that the preferred method of transportation by the locals was on horseback rather than motor vehicles. I was excited to be in horse country and made a mental note to get as much riding in as possible, weather permitting.

After goofing off for a week, we began our classes. The essence of our training was to study Morse code, teletype operations including code identification, typing, telegraph, facsimile operations, and orientation to something quite new for that time, computer applications and procedures. After intense studying and practical application of the various communication methods, our military title became Communication Specialist.

We didn't waste any time in making plans to visit Denver. It was a short distance from our base, but transportation by bus and train were infrequent and unreliable due to the severe weather conditions in the area. The cost to use those methods was also very expensive for our small pockets. So three of my buddies and I decided to buy a 12-year-old 1941 Chevrolet Sedan for $200. With the addition of the beat-up Chevy to our lives, we gained an incredible amount of freedom in choosing where we could travel. We developed a rotation system where each of us had a choice as to what destination our new baby would transport us. As we traveled around the military base on our new wheels, the WAFs (Women in the Air Force) all of a sudden noticed that we existed. We were so busy dating the girls that getting to Denver became difficult. As our classes were from Monday through Friday from 8 A.M. to 4 P.M., we had lots of time to study and practice during the week, which gave us ample time to travel the countryside on weekends. Due to the severe weather conditions in the winter months, we had to be very careful in deciding our travel plans, as unexpected blizzards were always waiting to cause grief to inexperienced travelers, which we were. So we spent lots of time on the base at the servicemen's club socializing with the gracious WAFs, sometimes driving them around town, visiting the movie house and the ever-popular Trolley Car Diner. When weather conditions were favorable, we would drive for two hours to Denver to visit dancehalls and get to know the civilian cowgirls that seemed to be a part of the fixtures at the halls throughout the city.

Denver is the capital of Colorado and at that time had a population of over 200,000 people and was probably one of the most beautiful cosmopolitan, small-town places in the U.S. Although it was a large city, its neighborhoods had a small-town feeling. The people were very friendly and treated servicemen with respect and expressed much gratitude for our commitment to the war effort. The city is surrounded by the beautiful snowcapped Rocky Mountains to the west and the High Plains to the east. Considering that it's only a couple of hours car ride from Cheyenne, the climate is quite different. It boasts of having 300 days of sunshine a year, with a semi-arid climate resulting in mild temperatures and moderate humidity. It has four distinct seasons and although it can get heavy amounts of snow, the abundance of sunshine makes it a comfortable place to visit, and absolutely a great place to live, even in the winter months that we visited.

Our favorite dancehall in Denver was the Palomino Club. It was a large country western hall that had the best combo band music in the area for dancing, mixing country music with swing and cha-chas. The 3,000-square-foot palace was always filled with dancers from end to end. It had a large-enough dance floor that allowed us plenty of room to express ourselves and socialize with the ever-so-willing cowgirls. Lots of pretty young ladies attended the dancehall, always dressed in western outfits of every imaginable color, with high-heeled boots to match; some even sported cowboy hats. The girls were always happy to dance with GIs and actually considered it an honor to spend time with us. There was also an electric bull on the premises. For two dollars, anyone, male or female, could try their luck on the rocking-vibrating monster that had fierce, threatening large horns and bright red-lighted eyes. Once, and only once, did my buddies and I each try to show how macho we were. Each of us in turn mounted the iron monster, but none of us lasted for more than a few seconds; off we went, head over heels, landing on not-so-soft hay. The disengagement was called "up and out," and entitled us to a free, large glass of tap beer and a complimentary cushion to ease our pain. For some reason, the girls got friendlier than usual after we were thrown from the big bull; they comforted us and graciously showered us with sympathy and lots of hugs.

In our last week of training, I came down with pneumonia. I spent two weeks in the hospital eating lots bacon (a sure cure in those days) and other fatty foods to line my lungs and protect them from cold air (how remedies have changed). A sure cure for pneumonia in those days was to eat lots of greasy food, keep windows closed to keep the cool air from coming into a room, and get lots of rest. How little we knew. Because of my mandatory rest period, much to my dismay, my group shipped out two weeks before I did. They all went home on furlough before leaving for Oakland, California, and then overseas where they hopefully would help bring the Korean War to a speedy conclusion. The upside for me was that in addition to eating lots of bacon, ham, and eggs, I was able to see springtime come alive in Cheyenne. The dismal snowbound city turned into a green, snowless, massive pasture, with grass, flowers, and horses and cowboys visible in every direction.

For a week, until it was my time to leave, I was the only one left in my barracks. My friend Paul Maggio and I decided to do a little horseback riding just as we did in the good old days in Brooklyn. We rented two beautiful mares; mine was a brown and white pinto, and his was a charcoal lady with a bright white mane and tail. We had an hour to ride and reminisce about the time we spent at the horse stables with our teenage friends. We walked the girls for a while and then got daring; we decided to do some trotting and then cantering. When we got the feel of the ladies, we galloped at full speed to see which horse was fastest. Little did we know that a sheriff was keeping an eye on us through his binoculars. He came after us blowing a hand-held horn. We slowed down and waited for him to approach. I thought he was a bandit and was going to start shooting. Flashing his badge, he told us that we were breaking the law. Paul said, "What law?" He said, "You boys were galloping the horses and anything over a canter is downright cruel to animals and could get them pneumonia, so you broke the law." He wrote us five-dollar tickets for speeding and told us to get the horses back to the stables before they caught their death from sweating and being overheated in the cool spring air. Well, that was a new experience for us. I'm sure that in our lifetimes we will get tickets for speeding cars, but I don't think we will ever again get a citation for speeding horses.

When my departure day came, Paul drove me to the Cheyenne train station in the jalopy, which he had bought from us. I had an overnight train ride back to New York City and spent the next two weeks visiting with family and friends. After saying my goodbyes, I was faced with deciding how to get to my new assignment, which was 3,000 miles away at Oakland Naval Station, in Oakland, California. I could either fly and get there the same day or take a four-day, three-night train ride. Since my last flying experience, airplanes were not my choice of transportation. So my father and I headed for Pennsylvania Station, in Manhattan, where I boarded a locomotive train to California, hoping that it would be a more pleasant and interesting journey than my previous long-distance train ride from Cheyenne. After boarding the train, I looked back and saw my father waving; he had tears in his eyes complemented by an enormous smile on his face. At the last moment, he rushed to the train and handed me the food basket we had both forgot about that my grandmother had prepared for me with much love and good homey advice about avoiding non-Italian women.

The trip was a tedious one, four days and three nights, many with me being the only passenger in my economy-class car. Sitting and sleeping on seats that semi-reclined for that period of time was one of the most uncomfortable traveling experiences I have ever had. The only salvation was the sandwiches my grandmother Tootsie made, consisting of eggplant, meatballs, and potatoes-eggs. As we got closer to the Golden State, the train filled with other servicemen who made the ride a little more tolerable. We discussed military matters, especially how we were looking forward to going overseas and the many new and exciting experiences that awaited us. How foolish young minds are; truly, "Youth is wasted on the young." The thought of getting wounded or even killed hardly entered our minds.

I joined my fellow Communication Specialists who were still waiting to get their overseas assignments and were just passing the time of day goofing off until the information was available. When our orders finally came, we had to wait another week and then it was off to Korea, which is where we figured we were going all along. We were able to get weekend passes so my Chevy buddies and I headed for San Francisco, which was on the opposite side of the San Francisco-Oakland Bridge. We took a shuttle bus across the enormous two-leveled suspension bridge to our destination. When in a new city the best place for servicemen to get oriented is usually the USO, so that is where we headed. The facility was very similar to the one in Rochester, N.Y., with a large open area for dancing and socializing, and friendly hostesses to meet and assist us in any way they could. Our first concern was where we could find inexpensive lodging. A pretty volunteer named Guinevere gave us some choices, but strongly recommended a hotel near Fishermen's Wharf, which had lots of places in the neighborhood for us to dine and hang out. So we took a cable car to the pier area. I couldn't figure out what the fuss was about San Francisco's cable cars; everyone I told that we were going to San Francisco advised me not to miss a ride on the special cars. I found that the only difference between them and the trolley cars we had on Liberty Avenue in Brooklyn was that they were painted a bright red and ours were a dull yellow and a mixture of some other ugly, nondescript colors. On the way to the pier area we passed the foot of the Golden Gate Bridge. The sun reflecting off of the huge, single-level structure actually made the bridge look as if it were painted gold. It's actually painted orange; the name of the structure is in honor of the mid-1800s Gold Rush and that mining era. I thought the San Francisco-Oakland Bridge (Bay Bridge) was a more significant structure. It has two levels and seemed to travel a longer distance than the Golden Gate Bridge. We also passed the fabled Chinatown neighborhood, which is home to the largest group of Chinese people outside of Asia. The change in scenery from the traditional American cut-out houses in the area that were lined up along each other, compared to the colorful oriental homes and shops, made me feel that we had left our homeland and entered a foreign country. The Green Dragon Gate that welcomes guests to enter their Asian world, was not only a work of art in its formation and oriental design, but seemed to relay a message that the people abiding within were proud of their accomplishments and of who they were. We located the hotel that the hostess recommended and were directed to a nice suite with two beds and two pullout bunks, which was far superior to the open barracks' sleeping facilities that we had at the Naval Station. What was especially nice was an 18-inch black and white television set that required 10 cents for an hour of entertainment.

The weekend went by fast with us enjoying Italian cuisine at the Pompeii and Alioto restaurants on the wharf and the many bistros that served Dungeness Crabs that we couldn't seem to get enough of. Fishermen's Wharf gets its neighborhood character from the city's early days during the Gold Rush when Italian immigrant fishermen settled the area and netted the delicious crabs. Today it is still home to an active fishing fleet with colorful boats lining and adding character and charm to the Bay Area. We also did lots of bar-hopping and carousing with the local ladies. But, as all good things must come to an end, when our time expired, we packed our bags and headed back to the Naval Base in Oakland.

A Robert Burns quote states: "The best laid plans of mice and men gang aft agley." Well, my buddies left for Korea and I found myself at the naval hospital having my appendix removed. Either I ate too much meatloaf at the Mess Hall or the Dungeness crabs decided to get revenge for my devouring so many of their kind. Whatever; I spent the next two weeks in the hospital and had to wait another two weeks before I received my travel orders. I soon found out that my position was filled in Korea and my new assignment was Nagoya, Japan, for further assignment. I was on my own again; my buddies from boot camp and communication school were scattered all over the world at their permanent posts, while I didn't have the faintest idea where my final destination would be. Being that I was in the Air Force, you would think that my next mode of transportation would be by plane, but that's not how the military works. Lucky me, I would get to spend the next two weeks aboard the *USS General J. C. Breckinridge* troopship with over 5,000 Army and Marine soldiers. I was one of the few airmen on the ship, which made me stand out like a sore thumb. The Army and Marine uniforms were brownish, mine was blue, UGH! To get an idea of how crowded the ship was, I'll compare it to the *Jewel of the Sea* cruise ship, which I recently had the pleasure of sailing on to the Baltic countries of Finland, Norway, Sweden, Estonia, and Russia. The ship is 1,100 feet long and accommodates approximately 3,600 passengers and over 1,000 crew members. The troop ship was 622 feet long and had almost twice as many passengers as the modern-day cruise liner. Oddly, on our Baltic trip, I met a former Marine who had sailed on the *Breckenridge* about the same time as I did. It took him over 50 years before he ventured on another ship; that's how bad his memory was of how crowded and uncomfortable the conditions were on that vessel.

Our first stop was Pusan Harbor, in South Korea, to deliver supplies and troops to reinforce our fighting forces. It took a couple of days to unload the supplies and approximately 5,000 soldiers. Watching the endless lines of men disembarking was a depressing scene that I still carry with me today. I wondered which of my young comrades would join the ranks of the already 35,000-plus dead and 198,000 wounded soldiers in Korea. Fortunately, an armistice was signed at the end of the month that I arrived on July 27, 1953. Although the document was signed, it took many months for the North Koreans to stop fighting and to abide, somewhat, by the terms of the agreement. Hundreds of weary soldiers boarded the ship for R&R (Rest and Rehabilitation) in Tokyo, Japan, which was our next port-of-call.

We arrived in Tokyo Harbor, carefully docked at a huge pier, and unloaded the happy soldiers, including me, at the enormous port where a military information center was set up for our convenience. After waiting in line for hours, I was informed that I would be taking an overnight train that evening from Tokyo to Nagoya, approximately 200 miles away. It was good to get my land-legs back and feel steady again on solid ground after spending two weeks on the troop ship. A big surprise was that I was assigned to a sleeping car with a soft private bunk bed, private toilet, and lots of room to spread out, a big improvement from the accommodations on the *Breckinridge.*

Nagoya AFB was the headquarters of the 5th Air Force. I was excited, hoping that somehow I would stay at the base where so many planes were available to help me with my travel plans to faraway places. I stayed at the base for over one month, which gave me an opportunity to spend time in the large city of Nagoya, which at that time had a population of about one million people. The city was heavily bombed during WWII by our B-29s; their main target was the Mitsubishi

Aircraft Engine Works. It has been estimated that general firebombing destroyed over 100,000 buildings with over 500,000 people being displaced. Considering that it was only eight years after the end of the war, there wasn't a trace of any destruction to be seen throughout the large metropolis. Considering the devastation that our forces caused its residents, it was really surprising that they went out of their way to be very friendly and polite to U.S. servicemen.

My orders finally arrived; I was to return to Tokyo for further assignment, but this time the mode of transportation was a C-47 twin-engine-prop transport, a smaller, two-engine version of the one that I was supposed to fly from New York to Wyoming, but instead was forced to land in Nebraska. The plane had the same seating arrangements as her bigger sister the C-54. About 30 men sat side-by-side around the inner parameter of the aircraft. One big difference during the flight was that we all had to put on our parachutes, and the flight sergeant didn't have any prepared speeches to scare us with, probably because some of the passengers were officers. This time we were given explicit instructions on the proper use of our parachutes in case of an emergency, and the proper protocol for jumping in an orderly fashion from the aircraft.

Needless to say, I was shocked when I arrived at an Army base in a god-forsaken swamp on the outskirts of Tokyo and told to make myself comfortable in a large tent with folding cots. There were ten cots in the tent with nine of them already occupied by other airmen who were also waiting for what would hopefully be their final orders. Sleeping on the cots was a once-in-lifetime experience. Mosquito nets were provided to protect us from the flying cannibals that seemed to be everywhere, in sizes that put some of them in the class with small birds. After my first uncomfortable night sleeping on a cot that seemed to be made out of concrete, I awoke the next morning to the throbs and pain of my right arm that was bitten unmercifully. The blood-suckers used my right arm for their BBQ when it rested on the net during my overnight slumber. I was beginning to wonder if joining the military wasn't a mistake. Aside from being in the hospital more times in one year than in my whole life, my first air flight resulted in a forced landing. My two-week experience aboard the *Breckinridge* in sweltering July heat and swelling seas had me seasick for most of that trip. I was being shipped from one military base to another with no final destination in sight, and the prospect of staying in a mosquito-infested swamp for an undetermined period of time was really giving me doubts about my decision-making abilities.

Fortunately, I only remained in the hell-hole a couple of days before receiving orders to relocate to the city of Tokyo. I was taken by jeep to the heart of the city and dropped off at the eight-story New Kaijo Building, which was located across the street from the Imperial Palace. I stared at the building, frozen in disbelief that it was going to be my residence for the next three years. What a turn of events, hopefully for the better. Its large square lobby had a dining hall (not Mess Hall), a PX, barber shop, and reception desk. After producing my orders to the sergeant manning a large mahogany wooden welcoming desk, I was directed to an elevator that took me to the eighth floor where my future home awaited me. It was a nice-sized room that I would be sharing with two other airmen. A picture of the New Kaijo Building follows:

The New Kaijo Building is in the middle of the picture with the Airmen's Club across the street on the left and the Imperial Palace's moat in the foreground.

My new home had regular single beds with thick comfortable mattresses, private standup lockers and a personal room boy. It was the policy of the U.S. that servicemen had to use the locals as valets, probably to provide jobs for them and to get money into their economy. Our room boy, Shunsuki, made our beds, took care of our laundry, shined our shoes, and did other menial tasks for us, all for ten dollars a month from each occupant. After the horrible swamp experience, I thought that I had died and gone to heaven; little did I realize that the fun was just beginning.

My work assignment was on the same boulevard just two city streets away in the Meiji Building, another high-rise structure facing the Imperial Palace. A photo of the building follows:

The Air Force's main communication center in Asia was located in the building; I was thrilled at becoming an integral part of that elaborate system and finally having a place that I could call home for the foreseeable future, in a cosmopolitan city like Tokyo, which was quite different in size and sophistication from my previous assignments. Although I was born and bred in Brooklyn, N.Y., which is one of the largest of the five city boroughs with a population of over two million people, my experience there was mostly a neighborhood one, consisting of family and mostly Italian-American friends. Tokyo was a whole different place; it was a mirror of Manhattan, N.Y., which I visited briefly on special occasions, such as seeing the latest movies on the new large Cinemascope screens, and working at part-time jobs for short periods of time when I was a younger teenager; I say younger due to the fact that I was only 19 when I arrived in Japan and anxious to end the teenage phase of my life. A nice touch to my new experience was our dining hall. On most military installations, the procedure was to wait on line with tray in hand and have food plopped onto silver compartmentalized trays. Not so at my new home in the New Kaijo Building: we sat at tables for four, with menus, and waiters from the local population who took our orders as if we were in a restaurant, and politely served while smiling and nodding throughout the event. The icing on the cake was that we had open seating so we could eat whenever it was convenient for us within certain time frames.

At the end of my first month in Japan, an armistice was signed with North Korea. There were celebrations throughout Tokyo that lasted for over a week and included fireworks displays by the Japanese and the combined United Nations' military, with lots of hoorays and hugs between soldiers and the locals; tears of joy flowed freely as we all tried to comprehend that the horrific war-conflict was over. What a wonderful experience witnessing a war coming to an end and the resultant relief that came with it from the anxiety of possibly being shipped to the fighting zones in Korea, where our boys died by the tens of thousands. It took a few months before the fighting actually stopped; as a matter of fact, some of the bloodiest encounters between the North Koreans and the United Nations' forces took place during that period, each trying to occupy as much territory as possible before concluding the terms of the treaty. In the meantime, our military was making arrangements to ship soldiers back to the States. For the next couple of years, fighting troops from the United Nations passed through Tokyo on R&R leave before returning to their homes for discharge. But, as the treaty was tenuous, a large number of soldiers remained in Korea and a substantial number in Japan as backup support in case of another military surprise from the North Koreans or the Chinese. What is astonishing is that today, March 31, 2013,

60 years after the ending of the Conflict, we are again faced with a belligerent North Korea that is threatening to bomb the U.S. with nuclear weapons of destruction.

As the war was over, we were given a choice of staying in Japan for our three-year tour of duty or returning to the States a year earlier. I chose to take the shorter tour, and being that the Conflict was over, personal travel became less restrictive, and I was able to travel to many exciting places throughout the country. In addition to the many religious shrines and small towns that I was fortunate to visit, one of my favorite trips was to Mt. Fuji, which was just over 60 miles from Tokyo.

Although there are many mountains in Japan, most of them are ranges. Mt. Fuji, however, stands alone as it soars into the sky to 12,385 feet making it the highest point in the country and one of the most picturesque and recognizable scenes in the world. The snow-capped mountain cone has been worshiped by the Japanese since ancient times, and is a well-known symbol of the country's magnificent landscape. The last eruption of the active volcano occurred over 300 years ago and luckily, it has been dormant since then. On a clear day, the mountain can be seen from Tokyo. Depending on the weather, its view changes dramatically. In the winter, the mountain is covered with snow and looks like a white pyramid that sometimes blends into the sky and becomes invisible. In the summer, its pale blue crest wears a pronounced crown of snow that joins a light mist, producing the picture that is world renowned as one of Japan's unique symbols. On a clear day at sunset, the mountain turns into a bright red figure almost hypnotizing the viewer, as it is impossible not to remain fascinated with one of nature's true wonders. There are only about 100 days a year that the mountain can be seen as a mist cloud visits the icon for the rest of the year, making it invisible to the naked eye.

So, after watching the mysterious wonders of the mountain for over one year, I decided that it was time to get a closer look at the surreal structure. Mt. Fuji is open to explorers only during July and August of each year when the weather is mild and much of the snow is gone. So my friend Mieko and I boarded the metro bus and took a roughly three-hour trip to its base. What a difference looking up at the skyscraper rather than looking at it from a distance made. I wasn't too sure that I wanted to challenge the huge mountain, but being that hundreds of people of every age were waiting on line to begin their journey, I decided, what the hell, why not give it a try? There is a Japanese proverb: "You're crazy if you never climb Fuji, and you're crazy if you climb it twice," which kept creeping into my thoughts, but being invincible at age 20, away we went up the mountain. My companion and I knew right away that we had made a mistake. There are ten rest stations on the mountain; we started at the bottom while most people remained on the bus and began at station five, so by the time we reached that popular rest stop, we were exhausted. Most people were just starting their climb, while it took us eight strenuous hours to get from the bottom to the fifth station. We devoured some noodle soup and rice and took a quick nap before we foolishly resumed our climb. At the first stop, we bought walking sticks as souvenirs; the tradition was to have them stamped at each station, which we did for a hefty price. After cherishing the walking aide for my remaining time in the country, it was confiscated from me at the embarkation security station before I left the country; it suspiciously was on the list of Japanese treasures that were not allowed to leave the country; I'm sure that today it's resting over someone's fireplace with a fairytale to go along with the prized possession.

Onward and upward we went beyond the fifth station where all traces of vegetation disappeared from that point on. Our destination was the eighth station, which we reached after midnight. We bought a snack and then tried to find a place to sleep in something called a hut where it seemed hundreds of climbers were already squeezed in on straw mats sleeping throughout the cold building. What an experience; we didn't make reservations, so we had to plead and generously pay an attendant to give us a spot on a mat among snoring and smelly climbers, so we could get some desperately needed rest. We had been climbing for almost 15 hours with less than 2 hours sleep, had little to eat, were freezing and lightheaded from the high altitude, and began to wonder if we were in complete control of our mental faculties.

Daylight woke us with renewed energy; we were able to make it to the crest in time to see the most spectacular sunrise imaginable; it seemed that the sun occupied the whole of my vision in its roundness and soft bright redness. As the morning progressed, that soft redness became a hot flame in the sky and on our bodies, as the return trip down the mountain was on the side of the *Rising Sun*. Traveling down a desert of volcanic ash and gravel, which spread out as far as we could see, made the journey feel as if we were walking on hot coals, as the sun's reflections brightened the path we had to travel. The path ended at the fifth station, where we quickly got on line for the next bus to take us back to the comfort of familiar surroundings, a hot shower, and a steak dinner. The Japanese proverb proved to be true: "You're crazy if you never climb Fuji, and you're crazy if you climb it twice." After our experience, our mountain-climbing days were surely over. It certainly was a love-hate experience. We loved the challenge of climbing the majestic mountain from the bottom, but hated the unsanitary huts and eateries that were not priced for excellence but overpriced for the convenience of being at a place where you had no choice but to use their services.

Being billeted in the heart of Tokyo put me close to movie theaters, restaurants, great shopping, and the famous Ginza Market; they were all walking distances from my home in the New Kaijo building. One of the most popular entertainment venues in Tokyo was the Ernie Pyle Theater, named in honor of the famous American correspondent who was killed in the Pacific during WWII. The theater was originally called Takarazuko Gekijo but was rechristened the Ernie Pyle Theater to pay tribute to the fallen battlefield journalist who wrote from a foot soldier's point of view, and had a great following in the military and back home in the U.S. It was a 2,000-plus-seat theater that the GIs would fill to the rafters to see free shows by beloved American entertainers such as Bob Hope, Louis Armstrong, and Bing Crosby. It was also the main movie theater for both Americans and Japanese, where they could enjoy the latest Hollywood movies at reasonable prices.

One of my favorite pastimes was shopping at the outdoor Ginza Market on Sundays, when time permitted, with my special friend Mieko. A picture of her is below modeling with two of her friends; she is the beautiful girl on the right:

It's difficult to describe the outdoor market where we spent many pleasant hours *hondeling* with merchants. There were hundreds of street-vendors selling everything from rubber bands to household furniture. Restaurants, nightclubs, and bars lined every street with music filling the air and exotic food aromas tempting passersby to enter their establishments for food, drinks, and other delights; it was a neighborhood where anything could be purchased if money were no object. There were also many department stores selling famous and not-so-famous designer clothes. The largest and most popular was the Mitsukoshi Department Store, which is known as "The Harrods of Tokyo," housing such upscale shops as Tiffany & Co. and Barney's Fifth Avenue. It was with the street peddlers that I learned the art of bargaining and trying to outsmart the experts. After many instances of negotiating up and down the dollar scale, when I bought something at a discounted price, I somehow always felt that my prize wasn't such a bargain after all, and that I was probably out-foxed by the more experienced merchants. But it was a great way to spend the day outdoors with Mieko while sampling the food at the many stands and enjoying the music and camaraderie of the good-natured merchants and other bargainers.

When I had been stationed in Tokyo a little over a year, I was asked if I would like to work in the Imperial Palace as a liaison between the Japanese meteorologists and their counterparts in the Air Force. I jumped at the opportunity to work with the locals, especially being that my hours would be from 8 A.M. until 4 P.M., instead of the exhausting rotating shifts that had kept me in a state of confusion since joining the communication team. The assignment also added my third stripe; I became a sergeant and was able to eat in the noncommissioned officers' dining hall, which entitled me to a lower bow from the Japanese staff (the lower the bow, the more honorable the person). Every morning I was picked up by jeep and driven to the communication station on the palace grounds, which made my head swell and gave me an exhilarating feeling of importance.

The 284-acre Imperial Palace complex was not only in the heart of Tokyo but was also the heart of Japan. The Imperial Family resided in their temporary quarters on the palace grounds at that time as their original residence was destroyed by allied bombing during WWII and wasn't restored to its former splendor until 1968 long after I left the country. The Japanese take their monarchs very seriously and run their lives, to a great extent, by the preaching and dictates of the emperor. The fact that I was working in the Imperial Palace made me a very honored and special person to the Japanese people that I came into contact with and their bows become lower and lower as they recognized me as the "Imperial American."

The palace grounds were surrounded by a moat, a gray-stoned wall, and beautiful stone bridges running across the moat from the outside boulevard. Oriental spire rooftops gave the complex the appearance of a heavenly place, especially since the grounds are slightly elevated from the street level. Passing over the bridges, you can't help noticing the abundance of royal white swans guarding the palace and hissing and trumpeting their presence while reminding guests that they are entering hallowed grounds and to act accordingly. Entering the gated stronghold over the Nijubashi Bridge, which means double bridge due to its reflection in the water that makes it look like there is also a mirrored bridge below, leads to the interior of the walled stronghold.

Entering in early spring when cherry blossom trees are in bloom and the surrounding gardens are showing off their multi-rainbow treasures, gave me the feeling that I was entering a beautiful floral wonderland; the colors were breathtaking and the fragrance soothing to my soul. The magnificence of the four royal gardens within the palace walls is a testament to the passion and respect that the Japanese have for floral beauty and creativity. The Outer Garden is open to the public and is an inviting resting place for visitors to bring their lunch and enjoy the surrounding beauty of the landscape and the tranquility of the area. The Fukiage Garden is where the Imperial Palace royal residents live and where the offices of the Imperial Household Agency are located. The East Garden is the home to many training centers for traditional crafts and occupations and the Kitanomaru National Garden houses the castle tower and the outer defensive positions of the former Edo Castle. In 1952 the garden was cleared and became the Kitanomaru Park, which would eventually boast of having such illustrious tenants as the Tokyo Museum of Modern Art, 1963; the Tokyo Science Museum, 1964; and the *Nippon Budokan Center*, 1964, which translated is the Japan Martial Arts Hall. The gardens are separated by moats, walls, and very large boulders. I enjoyed having lunch at the Outer Garden but especially liked walking through the East Garden, which was also open to the public. It is encompassed by a dense forest and a collection of trees with at least one representative from each of Japan's 47 prefectures. This garden was designed as a place for quiet meditation and rejuvenation. It featured well-tended paths lined with azaleas, zigzag bridges to confuse evil spirits, as they can only walk in straight lines, and ponds full of koi fish. Among the buildings in the East Garden were an Archery Hall, Kendo and Judo Hall, the Music Department, the Imperial Stables, and the Imperial Guard House. Some special attractions in the gardens were an extraordinary 350-tree Bonsai Garden behind the imperial residence, a 400-year-old crabapple tree, and a 500-year-old juniper tree, which I was able to see on one of the two days a year that the restricted palace gardens were open to the public. On January 2 and on his birthday, December 23, the emperor made public appearances; I was fortunate to see Emperor Hirohito when he presented himself several times during his January appearance.

While working on the hallowed grounds, I was asked many times what the U.S. Air Force was doing in the Imperial Palace. Since the grounds of the palace were more stable than the surrounding area and buffered by a moat that encircled the complex, it was one of the few places in Tokyo where seismographic equipment that measured the earth's tremors could be installed without picking up the too many vibrations from the outside automobile traffic and the heavy building equipment that was at work throughout the city. The seismographic equipment was the property of the U.S. and required a representative to be present to make sure that it was being used in accordance with the rules of the treaty between the two countries.

A picture of the Imperial Palace, the Nijubashi Bridge (double bridge), and the protective moat follows:

There were about 20 Japanese personnel working at the station, which gave me an opportunity to get to know and socialize with them. About once a month one of my new friends would invite me to their home for dinner and to meet their family and friends. Sitting down on a mat and eating on a low table with chopsticks took some getting used to. After a few tries, I was able to adjust my body so that my legs wouldn't fall asleep and cause me any embarrassment due to the fact that I had to get up many times, interrupting dinner to exercise my limbs, much to the surprise of my hosts, who couldn't understand why Americans couldn't eat in what they considered a most comfortable position. A culture shock was that the women served the men their meals while they ate in separate rooms. After the meal the women would join us for tea, social discussions, and a question and answer session. They invariably would produce a written list with questions about the United States, and would meticulously record the answers exactly under their questions on their lists. A question that came up often and seemed to puzzle them was, "How was it possible that the country that defeated the Japanese Empire could have done so badly in defeating the inferior Koreans?" It was a good question for which I had no valid answer so I would respond, "I don't know."

One of the benefits of having Japanese friends who went out of their way to welcome me into their homes was that I was introduced to lots of delicious homemade food, which 50 years later is still one of my favorite delights. Since I spent so much time with the locals, I did manage to pick up some of the language pretty well, but writing and reading was a puzzlement to me, as I didn't have much time to study the intricate pictured language.

A picture of me standing in front of one of the smaller buildings at the Palace follows:

My favorite method of transportation while stationed in Japan was the metro train system. It has an astonishing procedure for handling the incredible volume of passengers that relied on it for their daily commute. Everyone waits on the station's platforms in lines designating where the train doors will be. When a train arrives and the doors open, the orderly platform dwellers would file one at a time, very politely, into the train; when the cars seemed full, then the remaining passengers on the platform would push the people in front of them into the cars, ever so civilly, until there wasn't an inch of unoccupied space left. When the lines were unusually long, there were platform attendants wearing white gloves that gently shoved riders into the cars. Well, that was when I was there from 1953–55, when the population of the city was ten million; currently the population has more than doubled, and I can't imagine the organized chaos that must take place when riding the metro today.

Just before my tour of duty ended, I was approached by a Japanese electronics company that was recruiting Americans for their communication and organizations skills. They were paying sign-up bonuses of $2,000, which was almost a year's salary to me in those days, to stay on and work for them in the electronics field. The offer included additional training in the new computer industry and a salary that was tempting, to say the least. But the call of my grandmother's meatballs and spaghetti was stronger than the financial offer, so I declined. Many of my Air Force buddies took the offer; some even married local girls and settled in Japan while others eventually relocated to the U.S. as representatives of the electronics companies.

Saying goodbye to my buddies and the Japanese personnel I worked with was difficult. I was given a going-away party by the airmen in my group, which was also attended by the officers in our communication center. The party was at the Airmen's Club across the street from our quarters. About 25 of my friends chipped in and gave me an unforgettable going-away bash that lasted till the club closed at 1 A.M. A 17-piece "Glen Miller" copy-band provided music throughout the evening, while we drank and danced the night away. I was lucky to have a second going-away party by my Japanese coworkers at the Imperial

Palace. The event was more subdued, but we did have a couple of hours of good sushi, lots of sake', and lots of farewell handshakes and hugs.

When my tour of duty was over, I relocated to Yokohama AFB to await transportation back to the states on the ever-so-faithful *General J. C. Breckinridge* transport ship . . .

This chapter ends my first journey outside of the United States. Some of the following chapters will be extensions of the stories that were published as condensed articles in the newsletter *Around the Floor.* In addition, I will write about many of our trips around the world that were not connected with our dancing experiences.

Chapter Three – Dancing in Buenos Aires – Learning the Tango

~*~

AROUND THE FLOOR: OCTOBER/DECEMBER 1999
TRAVELING AROUND By Barbara Bivona

Mike and I were drawn to the Argentine Tango after we saw the first of many Tango shows that appeared on the American stage, which originated in Argentina. So, when an ad appeared for a trip to Argentina to study Tango dancing, Mike booked it before I could say no. The trip was sponsored by Daniel Trenner of West Medford, Massachusetts. He called it *Puente al Tango* (Bridge to Tango); his mission was to bring the true Tango form from Buenos Aires to North America and the rest of the world. His unique tours had been so successful that he extended his "Puente" to Canada and Europe. A deciding factor for our joining him was the ratio of one instructor to every two students, so no one in our group of 40 was ever left without someone to help break down and explain the dance patterns. Our days consisted of four hours of Tango lessons, divided into a two hour master class by the most renowned dancers in the Tango world, a one-hour practice session, and an hour interview and performances by the master teachers, who spoke about their love and personal experiences with the romantic dance. We learned about the history of Tango from one of the original Tango dance styles, *Canyengue*, and how its evolution resulted into the current dance form. At night, we were picked up around ten o'clock and taken to a *milonga*, which is the Argentine name for a tango club. Dances at these places are done in sets of three or four tangos, followed by a set of Argentine waltzes or a *milonga* dance (tango walk), with brief intermissions between each dance. The sets are the basis of the *milongas* and are danced at every ballroom, with occasional meringues and mambos in between. We occasionally even danced quickstep and swing, as both dances are becoming popular in Buenos Aires. I danced with our teachers and the local *tangueros*, which was a bit intimidating at first because I am trained to do figure tangos; the locals dance the salon tango, which has less movement and is done in a smaller area due to the crowded dance floors that are so prevalent in the clubs. It was a whole different ballgame, but we soon learned to catch the ball. The dances lasted until about 5:30 A.M.; however, Mike and I didn't, so we usually called it quits between 2:00 and 4:00 A.M. and happily returned to our hotel quite exhausted from the day's events. Each morning, after a late breakfast, we had an opportunity to spend a few hours walking around the city, visiting local restaurants, wonderful shops, and parks, before returning to our classes and nighttime dancing.

Included in the trip was a beautiful Broadway-type Tango show in which some of our teachers performed. In addition, Daniel Trenner hosted a party at his apartment one afternoon, which lasted until ten at night. We enjoyed his huge rooftop terrace that overlooked the beautiful cupolas of Buenos Aires where we were treated to a three-piece tango band for our dancing pleasure. What made the afternoon special was the professional tango exhibition performed by local tango aficionados. The elite of the Tango world were present and politely asked many of us to dance; what a wonderful experience to be floating on a strategically located rooftop in the heart of one of the most beautiful cities in the world, being led by world famous dancers, to the music of the seductive Argentine Tango. My OH MY!! A lifetime dream come true!! . . .

We talked, lived, and danced Tango for eleven days, and remained in Buenos Aires for a few extra days after our group left so we could do some sightseeing. We went to the mausoleum of Eva Peron, the famous antique and street fair in San Telmo, and, of course, we went to the City of Caminito, made famous by a song of the same name by the immortal singer, Carlos Gardel. Daniel helped us to realize a dream. We loved to Tango before we went to Argentina. We fell in love with it in Buenos Aires.

END OF ARTICLE

~*~

Many of our friends have enjoyed themed vacations for years. Some of the places that they have visited and can't stop talking about are trips to Montana for fishing, skydiving and bird watching; touring the Grand Canyons, and the other numerous national parks; visiting Rio De Janeiro and New Orleans for Mardi Gras, and my all-time favorite dream vacation, but not yet realized, spending a month in Venice, Italy to learn how to paint its beautiful sea and landscapes. When our friends would tell us about their wonderful journeys, my mind would spin and wonder if any of our traveling passions would ever materialize. Our opportunity for a themed vacation came when an advertisement appearing in the catalogue "Bridge to the Tango," published by Daniel Trenner of West Medford, Massachusetts arrived in our mail. The picture of tango dancers and the description of the upcoming trip to Buenos Aires took my breath away. The adventure was for 11 days of intensive studying and training with instructors whose ages ranged from early twenties to late seventies. The experiences and memories of the older instructors ranged from the beginning of the 20th century, when tango was in its infancy and danced mostly in brothels, through the reign of the infamous dictator Juan Peron and his wife the ever-popular Eva. The younger instructors, fortunately, were far removed from the hard times and challenges their ancestors experienced and were mostly concerned about the rapture and passion of their profession as tango aficionados and teachers. Part of the advertisement, which appears below, shows the excitement of two dancers embraced in the tango and gave the purpose of the tour and descriptions of the instructors that were the participants in that wonderful journey. The brochure also includes some exciting comments from former students who went on a tour, which added to the flavor, expectation, and romance that occupied my mind.

I showed Barbara the flyer; we didn't waste any time reviewing the itinerary inch by inch, over and over again. She didn't know that I had already booked the trip. The more we delved into the details, the more excited we became. Famous tango dancers, such as Gustavo Naveira, Olga Besio, and Omar Vega were to be our mentors and instructors. Even tango dancers we saw so many years ago in the "Tango Argentino" Broadway show were part of the group.

When I first told Barbara that I had already booked the trip, she didn't say a word; she thought I was joking. When I convinced her that it was for real, the hugs and kisses that followed are still felt by me today when we dance the tango. What a surprise birthday present for her, and what a chance for us to really get the feel of the tango, which we loved so much, in the country where the passionate dance originated. A copy of one of the pages of the travel brochure, "Bridge to the Tango," which captured our imaginations, follows. It is reproduced with the permission of Daniel Trenner.

TOURS AND EVENTS

9th Dancer's Journey to Buenos Aires

Roberto and Vanina

"Never in my life have I experienced such uninterrupted joy, fun and excitement"

—TD, Oregon

" Ten days with Bridge To The Tango introduced me to the Tango community and culture of Buenos Aires, now I feel part of it! Bravo!"

—TD, Oregon

"I can't say enough about Jeff and his professional approach, he does an outstanding job".

—LG, Arizona

"With Bridge To The Tango you experience the very best. When you can have butter, why would you settle for margarine?"

—SM, Missouri

OUR PURPOSE

During our first tour to Buenos Aires in 1993, social tango and the great surviving milongueros were hard to find. Our job was to reveal this unpublicized world of clubs, or 'milongas'. Eight years later, our mission has changed. Tango's revival has given birth to a growing sprawl of events and schools, an intimidating maze to be navigated by a foreigner. Our staff dance year-round in Bs. As., and are in constant touch with the changing scene. From your first moment in BsAs, you will experience the best and most interesting clubs and teachers.

THE MASTER TEACHERS

An encounter with the living legends of Argentine Tango is at the heart of your trip. In our private studio spaces we organize daily group lessons and interviews with some of the most famous people in tango. Over the years our faculty has included: Pepito & Suzuki Avellenada, Juan Bruno, Eduardo Arquimbau, Esther and Mingo Pugliese, Gustavo Naveira & Olga Besio, Rodolfo & Maria Cieri, Nito and Elba Garcia, Facundo and Kely Posadas, Puppy Castello & Graciela González, Teté Rusconi & Maria Villalobos ,Teté & Sylvia Ceriani, Tommy O'Connell, Mariano 'Chico' Frumboli, Eduardo Cappusi & Mariana Flores, and many others.

OUR STAFF INSTRUCTORS

Our staff instructors are a cornerstone of our organization. They help gender balance the classes, providing one-to-one learning that enhances your experience and raises your learning curve, no matter what your level. They also go social dancing with you at night. Every staff instructor is a bilingual professional tango dancer, chosen not just for their tango but for their great personalities. Some of our staff have been working with us for many years, helping create a very relaxed and friendly environment. They have included: Lorena Ermocida (TangoX2), Omar Merlo (TangoX2), Pablo Pugliese, Gabriel Guerberoff, Florencia Taccetti, Luciana Valle, Damien Essel, Marcelo Solis, Valencia Batiuk.

OUR KEY STAFF

Jeff Anderson, Program Director for the past 3 years, has received rave reviews for his thoroughness and presence. He is a masterful translator and has an encyclopedic knowledge of rare and interesting things about tango in Buenos Aires. An actor, playwright, singer, and classical pianist, he lives in Buenos Aires, where he is exploring the creative possibilities of tango improvisation for performance.

Gabriela Entin and Robert Blank are our year-round staff in Buenos Aires. Gabriela has been Daniel's Administrative Assistant for 11 years. Robert, from Germany, has been living in Buenos Aires and working with us since 1994.

Zoraida Fontclara and Diego Alvaro are our "dance captains" since 1995. They coordinate the relationships between instructors and participants. They are internationally known teachers and performers, and run the famous mid-day classes and dances at the *Confiteria Ideal* in Buenos Aires.

Brooke Burdett, another American living the tango in Buenos Aires for the past 4 years, serves in a host of special roles for *Bridge to the Tango*. She also travels internationally, teaching and performing tango.

Now the fun began. I had booked a March tour, which is summer/early fall in Buenos Aires, so we had to prepare the proper clothing for that time of year. We had to arrange for air transportation and research the best exchange rate for the dollar. Exchange rates can be very tricky; there can be a difference of ten to twenty percent if the right choices aren't made. Many travelers use their hotels or exchange stores to convert their dollars to local currency, which can be a very costly mistake. We found that our Citibank ATM card was the fastest and least-expensive way to convert dollars. There are many Citibank outlets in Buenos Aires: no lines, no forms to fill out, no passport problems; you can just walk into a bank as you would in the U.S., go to the ATM machine, use your card, and, behold, the local currency is in your hand at a very favorable exchange rate. We also had to educate ourselves to whatever sightseeing was available within our time frame, the history of Argentina, and to any additional tango dancing opportunities in Buenos Aires.

Our tour had an optional airfare in coach with not much of a discount. The flight was ten hours and, considering that we had to be at the airport two hours prior to take off, we decided to explore flying business or first class so we could use the especially comfortable lounges reserved for those classes. American Airlines was the primary airline going to Argentina; its price for first class was more than our tour price. So we opted for business class, which worked out to be a couple of hundred dollars per person more than coach. As luck would have it, they were running a special promotion for our time slot, which included the use of The Admiral Club's first-class lounge at the airports. This turned out to be a blessing in disguise. Foreign flights require that passengers check in two hours prior to scheduled take-offs. Our plane was delayed for an additional hour, which meant killing three hours at the airport. What a difference having the use of The Admiral's Lounge made, as they served free coffee, Danish pastries, nuts, and pretzels, and also had comfortable large and spacious seats, with no crowds, plenty of reading material, private restrooms, several television sets, and finger sandwiches. Not a bad way to spend three hours. Since then, whenever financially possible, we try to fly business or first class if the airline's lounge is included in the price. We left for Buenos Aires from Miami, Florida. Luckily, we were wintering in Florida at the time, which made it convenient for us to take an airport limousine from Boca Raton, where we were staying, to the airport, without worrying about parking or the safety of leaving a car for two weeks at one of the airport parking lots.

Business Class on our ten-hour trip was exceptionally more enjoyable than our previous experiences with flying coach. There was more than adequate room for our carry-on bags in the overhead compartments and a separate area for hanging clothes or storing golf bags. After settling in, we were offered champagne, wine, refreshments, and finger snacks. The seats were spacious and reclined completely for sleeping, and were almost as comfortable as a standard bed. This became especially important as our flight left around midnight for a scheduled arrival at 10:00 A.M. By the time we boarded and got organized, a good night's sleep was a welcome friend.

The seats were two abreast with large windows, which gave us the feeling of spaciousness and made getting a good night's sleep a pleasant reality. The restrooms were larger than what we were used to when flying coach and were restricted to passengers in our section, which cut down on waiting time and the activity that is so prevalent around the service areas on planes. Snacks were served without the usual annoying waiting period due to our section having fewer people to accommodate. Private television was available with a choice of several current movies to choose from, which was nice; it certainly was better than not being given a choice of movies, as is common when flying coach. Breakfast was served upon request. It was an event; we chose our meals from a menu, which included a good variety of hot or cold breakfast delights. Ten hours "flew by" very quickly, due mostly to the comfortable seats and the relative quiet in our restricted area, which allowed us to sleep without too many interruptions.

While resting on my comfortable seat/lounge, I took the opportunity to read about the history of Argentina and to see if there were any places of interest that we might include in our sightseeing. I bought the *Lonely Planet City Guide to Buenos Aires,* by Wayne Bernhardson. While at home, we had done extensive research on the Internet, so reading the information in the travel guide became easy and familiar to us. Although Argentina dates back to 1536, when Spanish explorer Pedro de Mendoza made camp in Buenos Aires, the romantic history of Argentina actually began at the turn of the 20th century with the introduction of tango dancing and a singer/song writer named Carlos Gardel. To appreciate the passion that the people have for the Argentine tango, a brief history of tango and its first and foremost hero, Carlos Gardel, is in order.

The tango originated in the streets around the capital of Argentina, Buenos Aires, in the 1890s, and was considered a vulgar dance practiced in houses of ill repute and other unsavory places. It combined gaucho (cowboy) verse with Spanish and Italian music. Carlos Gardel was also considered to have been born and nurtured in the streets, but not in Argentina. He was born to a single mother, Berthe Gardes, in Toulouse, France, in or around 1890. Today, being a single mother carries very little social stigma, and in many cases, women travel that journey by choice preferring not to be tied down with a permanent partner, while enjoying the experience of motherhood. But in the late 19th century, Berthe and her young son were a disgrace to her family and community. When Carlos was three or four years of age, Berthe's lover paid for her and her son to relocate from France to Argentina.

They arrived in the capital alone and abandoned, and were immediately destined to live in the poor neighborhoods of Buenos Aires. So we have the arrival of the tango and Carlos at the same time, late in the 19th century, and the same place, Buenos Aires. These two forces were to become engaged in one of the most passionate dances of all time. It began in the lowest of places, brothels and tenements, and found its way into the homes of the rich and famous. Around the world it travelled—New York, Paris, and Italy—making music, inspiring dancers, and finally the grand finale: acceptance of its passion in motion pictures.

Today, wherever tango music is heard, a picture or the sound of Carlos's voice is in close proximity. He has become almost mystical. When he died in an unfortunate plane crash in June 1935, it is said that a Cuban woman committed suicide in Havana, while a woman in New York and another in Puerto Rico tried to poison themselves, all over the same man whom they had never met but with whose voice and music they were enamored. Below is a picture of Carlos Gardel playing the romantic lead in one of his few movie appearances:

Gardel with Mona Maris in the film "Cuesta Abajo", Paramount 1934

When listening to Carlos's music in Spanish, I always regretted not understanding the language, so I did some research and am presenting one of his famous songs, LA CUMPARSITA, written by Gerardo Rodriguez in 1917, with Spanish and the English translations side by side:

LA CUMPARSITA Lyrics & Music: Gerardo Hernán Matos Rodriguez

LA CUMPARSITA

La cumparsa de miserias sin fin...
Desfile...
Enfermo de aquel ser
enfermo...
que pronto ha de morir
de pena;
por eso es que en su lecho
solloza acongojado,
recordando el pasado
que lo hace padecer.

Abandono a su viejita
que quedó desamparada
y loco de pasión,
ciego de amor,
corrió tras de su amada,
que era linda, era hechicera,
de belleza era una flor.
Que admiró su querer,
hasta que se cansó
y por otro lo dejó.

Largo tiempo después,
cayó al hogar materno
para poder curar su enfermo
y herido corazón,
y supo que su viejita santa,
la que el habia dejado
el invierno pasado,
de frio se murio.

Hoy ya solo, abandonado
a lo triste de la suerte,
ansioso espera su muerte
que bien pronto ha de llegar...
Y entre la triste frialdad
que invade al corazon,
sintio la cruda sensacion
de su maldad...

Entre sombras
se le oye respirar
sufriente...
al que antes de morir sonrie
porque una dulce paz le llega;
sintio que desde el cielo
la madrecita buena,
mitigando sus penas,
sus culpas perdono...

THE LITTLE MASKED PARADE

The masked parade of endless miseri
promenades
around that sick
being...
that soon will die
of sorrow;
That's why in its bed
cries mournfully
remembering the past
that makes it suffer.

He abandoned his mother
who remained deserted
and mad with passion,
blind with love,
he ran after his beloved one,
she was pretty, she was bewitching,
she was a flower of beauty.
She admired his love,
until she got tired of him
and left him for another man.

A long time later,
He went back to the maternal home
to be able to cure his ill
and injured heart,
and learned that his holy mother,
the one that he had left
last winter,
died of cold.

Today all alone, abandoned
on the sad side of luck,
he anxiously awaits his death
that should arrive soon..
And within the sad coldness
that invades the heart,
he feels the raw sensation
of his wickedness..

Among shadows
his suffering breathing
is heard
he smiles before dying
because a sweet peace comes to him;
he feels that from the heavens
his good mother,
mitigating her griefs,
has forgiven his faults...

Our plane arrived at the Aeropuerto Internacional Ministro Pistarini de Ezeiza, simply known as Ezeiza (EZE), Buenos Aires, at 10:00 A.M., exactly on time and with no unusual surprises. The airport was located only 29 miles from our hotel, the Continental on San Roque Boulevard, downtown, in old Buenos Aires. Our luggage arrived at the airport unharmed, which was another surprise, so we promptly took a shuttle bus to our hotel. We were surprised at how light the traffic in Buenos Aires was, considering its population of approximately three million residents. It appeared that most motorists obeyed the traffic laws. We arrived at our hotel and considering that it was rated a four-star hotel, we got another surprise, but this time an unpleasant one. We learned that foreign hotels are not rated the same as in the U.S. Although the hotel was not up to the American standards that we expected, it was located in a great part of the city, and was only two blocks from Avenida Florida Blvd, which boasts every type of retail store imaginable: leather goods, women and men's designer clothing shops, shoe stores, etc. Also, the Avenue has every type of restaurant that exists: Italian, Spanish, American, French, South American, Russian, etc. We tried as many restaurants as possible in our short stay in Buenos Aires and, of course, Barbara tried as many of the shops as she could. Her only complaint was that she didn't have enough time and money to visit them all. Some memorable sights on the Avenue were street dancers dancing the tango at will, women wearing colorful designer dresses, men sporting Latin type hats, with suits and ties. The views gave the avenue a very sophisticated Bohemian-European-Manhattan atmosphere.

Hearing tango music while walking along the busy streets was absolutely enchanting; people just stopped and began dancing whenever their fancy dictated. Of course, Barbara and I also enjoyed a few impromptu tango steps while we walked along, joining the others in the pleasure and the feeling of our surroundings.

Our hotel was only a short walk from the historic area of San Telmo. It is one of the oldest neighborhoods in Buenos Aires, and was one of the wealthiest areas in the city until yellow fever took its toll. The wealthy abandoned their dwellings and the area became a haven for scoundrels and the immigrants of that era. Still unspoiled by the rampant modernization that seems to be going on all over Buenos Aires, San Telmo has become an artist's quarter, where bohemians find large spaces to rent at low rates, very much like Greenwich Village,

New York, after WWII, when our GIs found inexpensive lifestyles while attending local universities. It was here in the late 1800s that the tango was born in the brothels and houses of ill repute, and it was in neighborhoods like this, in Buenos Aires, that Carlos Gardel grew up and turned the tango into the nation's, and the world's, most popular music and seductive dance. Most of the nightlife of Buenos Aires is concentrated in this district, as well as some of the most interesting restaurants and bars. As street dancing is popular in this neighborhood, Barbara and I took advantage of the great music heard everywhere to practice some of our tango steps.

Considering the location of these wonderful places and their close proximity to our hotel and the "Confiteria Ideal," where we would spend most of our time being taught tango and listening to great lecturers, the fact that the hotel didn't meet American four-star standards became less important. We spent very little time in the hotel, and only used our room to get some much-needed sleep after long days at the dance sessions and *milongas* (clubs). Fortunately, the hotel had a restaurant with large viewing windows looking out on the street level, which became a great comfort station for drinking delicious dark Argentinean coffee and for "people watching." It's amazing how European the people looked; the men were inclined to wear European-cut suits and the ladies dressed in a very sophisticated and stylish manner. The viewing of the street activity and the beautiful Argentineans was very relaxing as we enjoyed an espresso or cup of local coffee. Breakfasts were included in our tour price, so we were able to begin our day by admiring the passing people traffic, as we leisurely enjoyed our extensive meals.

Arriving at our hotel in the morning gave us an opportunity to unpack and settle into our hotel suite. It had a bedroom and a separate sitting area with window air conditioners. Although the hotel and rooms were quite old, they were quaint and very comfortable. Our group leader, Jeff Anderson, welcomed us at the reception area set up for our group. Fortunately, he would be at our disposal for the entire trip. Jeff told us that some of our tour group were going to the Avenida Florida Boulevard for lunch, and then to a local shoe store to look at leather dancing shoes that were handmade by a local shoemaker on site. We joined some of our new friends for lunch, which we rushed through, because we couldn't wait to order new dancing shoes from the local shoemaker. Barbara and I were fitted by a pleasant assistant and we were hypnotized watching the shoemaster, Joseph's, precision as he created a pair of dancing shoes in about a half-an-hour. The shoes were made of the finest soft Argentinean leather, almost tissue-like to the touch. When our shoes were ready two days later, we tried them on and were surprised that they fit perfectly. Needless to say, we would wear them at every dancing opportunity, as our happy feet enjoyed the feel of the soft, tissue-like leather caressing them; they didn't even require a breaking-in period.

We spent our first evening getting acquainted with our new friends at a cocktail reception. Our new acquaintances were from around the world: Germany, Italy, Canada, and many parts of the U.S. Later that evening, at about 10:00 P.M., we were off to our first *milonga* at the Club Gricel. We were escorted to the club in a small bus by our fantastic staff instructors who began their routine of catering to our every wish and to our safety. The club had a typical nightclub atmosphere and held a comfortable two hundred people. There was a DJ in attendance playing a variety of music for dancing, but most of the dancing and music was tango. There is no such thing as a "no smoking" area in the clubs in Buenos Aires, so a smoke cloud filled the place and made it very uncomfortable to see and breathe, especially since the club wasn't air conditioned, which is not uncommon in the city. But, the music and dancing made up for these shortcomings. The men were all dressed in suits, as is the custom, and the women wore pretty, short-sleeved dresses with slits on the sides that showed off their sexy legs. Considering it was summer/early fall in Buenos Aires, there was surprisingly a lot of sweating going on in the club. It's probably one of the reasons that the *milongas* start late in the evening and continues into the early morning, as it does cool down quite a bit between those hours.

The tradition at the dances is that, if a man wants to dance with a particular female, he makes eye contact and then nods his head. If the woman accepts the invitation, she will nod her acceptance; if she doesn't want to dance, she will turn her head away. It is customary for men to ask women to dance, even if the women are escorted by other men. Using eye contact takes away the embarrassment and doubt that goes along with verbally asking someone to dance. It's really a neat way to enjoy an evening without all the uncertainties that go along with approaching strangers and asking them to join you in a romantic dance. Our instructors made sure that everyone in our group had a partner to dance with. Many of us enjoyed dancing with the locals once we got the knack of "eye contact" and its meaning. The dancing routine was that three tangos would be played, with about a minute intermission between each to talk and get acquainted with your partner. This also allowed dancers a chance to decide whether or not to continue dancing with the chosen person. If the partners decided to continue dancing, then, when the music resumed they would continue dancing in the "line of direction" (counter clockwise), being very respectful of the other dancers around them. No kicks, fans, or other dangerous moves were allowed on the dance floor because they could interfere or cause collisions with other dancers. Occasionally other dance music was played, more or less as an intermission between tangos. The students took advantage of these dances to show off their swing, cha-cha, mambos, etc. It is strange that the Argentines do not dance any other dances than the tango and its variations. Our night ended about 2:00 A.M., and we left exhausted from the excitement of our new experience and the incredible amount of dancing we had done. Many of the students stayed until closing at 5:30 A.M. God Bless them!

The next morning, which was Saturday, we woke up at about 9:30 A.M., and rushed to enjoy a buffet breakfast. The selection included many hot and cold dishes, which we devoured to replenish our energy, which had been exhausted the night before. In the early afternoon, we had our first tango lesson at one of the most picturesque salons in the city, Confiteria Ideal, which has been featured in many movies, such as the 1997 *Tango Lesson*, written by and starring Sally Potter and one of our dance instructors, Gustavo Naveira; the 1998 movie *Tango*, written by Carlos Saura and starring Carlos Rivarola, Cecilia Narova, and Mia Meastro; and the 1998 movie *Evita*, written by Tim Rice, Alan Parker, and Oliver Stone, and starring Madonna and Antonio Banderas. The Confiteria was built in 1912 as a café-bar-nightclub and still carries the look of the turn of that century's Art Deco architecture, with its ancient wood flooring, dark wood furniture, opulent marble staircase, and an ornate two-person elevator. Some of the world's famous people, such as Maurice Chevalier, Marie Felix, Dolores del Rio, Vittorio Gassman, Robert Duvall, and many local and foreign dignitaries, have enjoyed the food and dancing at this one-of-a-kind romantic establishment.

The emphasis on our first lesson was the relationship between dance partners and their responsibility toward each other. To emphasize the importance of each one knowing and respecting the other's movements, we were taught some of our partner's steps. The men danced the women's part and the women did the leading. Talk about confusion, yet it was very helpful in learning how difficult it is for a woman to dance backwards and to respond quickly to the male's lead. I learned to do *ochos* (figure eights), *cortes* (kicks), and many other sophisticated tango steps while dancing backwards; it was quite different and very easy to confuse the steps. It took a while, but the men seemed to get the routines down pretty well and translated their experience into holding and leading the ladies with a lot of consideration and appreciation for their role in the tango. In Argentina, it is not uncommon to see people of the same gender dancing together. They are taught to dance both parts, as leaders and as followers. We practiced for about two hours and then had a one-hour intimate interview session with a master teacher of the tango. Our teacher shared with us his joys and heartbreaks with the tango, and how dancing saved his sanity during his youth through the troubled political times in Argentina. After the session, we had an additional hour of practice with our partners, the dance instructors, and other students—male and female. It took a bit of getting used to dancing with a member of the same sex, but it worked out well and we gained important knowledge—not only in dancing the tango, but applying what we learned to other dances.

After the session, members of the tour paired and enjoyed dinner at one of the many local restaurants, which was followed by walking around San Telmo and enjoying a street fair that was taking place. At about 10:00 P.M., we again boarded our bus for a night at Salon El Pial, another local *milonga*; however, fortunately, this club was air-conditioned. We danced the night away and returned back to our hotel about 2:00 A.M., again leaving many of our group to dance on until closing at about 5:00 A.M.

After several lessons, our instructors concentrated on the meaning of improvisation, which is the essence of the dance. "It's easy enough to learn the many steps in the Argentine tango, but the fun and passion of the dance is to improvise and to introduce new steps and feelings into your dance routines. To hear the music; to feel the music; to express the proper attitude; when this synergy is accomplished, then improvisation causes passion to radiate from the dancers' bodies and movements resulting in a 'dance of love.'" At one of the sessions Dan Trenner interjected: "And isn't this why we all traveled from around the world to Buenos Aires, to learn and experience the 'dance of love'?" Everyone smiled and agreed with his interpretation, that if the dance is properly performed, the result will be a romantic expression of love through tango dancing.

The rest of our trip was the same every day: a morning buffet breakfast, dance lessons for about four hours at different venues, lectures by master tango dancers, an afternoon nap when possible, dinner at a local restaurant, dancing at a different *milonga* till the wee hours of the morning, and then returning to our hotel, exhausted and exhilarated from the day's activities.

An exceptional day was a visit to our tour leader's apartment for a private rooftop dance party at his *La Cupula*, which is a spectacular turn-of-the-century penthouse. Buenos Aires is often described as the "Paris of the South," and the view from the penthouse roof validated that belief. We got the same feeling when we visited Paris. The views were similar and absolutely magnificent; their church steeples, cupolas of every size and shape, and the brilliant effect of the sun's rays shining off the gold trim of many of the cupolas and steeples were mirror images of the architecture in each city.

The party was exciting as a trio band consisting of a guitar, bass, and bandoneon played beautiful tangos, which gave us an opportunity to meet and dance with many of our instructors, master teachers, and local dance aficionados. A buffet was set up with local finger foods and an open bar kept everyone refreshed and somewhat immune from the afternoon heat of the sun. There were several tango exhibitions by our teachers, some local dancers, and teachers with students. It gave us an opportunity to dance on the rooftop with our instructors and made me feel as if I were dancing in the sky on a cloud. The afternoon turned into evening as we socialized and caressed our partners and our newfound friends to the sounds of tango music. We drifted from the party and walked the enchanted streets of the magical city back to our hotel to prepare for another evening of tango dancing at a local club.

One of the places we wanted to see while in the city was Eva Peron's burial place in the Recoleta Cemetery. The cemetery is in the trendy Recoleta section of the city, where there is an artisan market and the dwellings of the wealthy residents of Buenos Aires. The cemetery is enclosed by a high wall, but some of the high monuments and statues can be seen from the outside. However, the message is clear: "private privileged property." Traditionally, only the wealthy and powerful members of the aristocracy were buried at this cemetery, with Eva Peron being an exception. The remains of Eva are secured in a modest *Familia Duarte* subterranean vault, which irritates the upper class to no end, as she was considered anything but an aristocrat. Her embalmed remains (embalming is not usual for the people of Argentina), rest there after being transported from South America to an obscure cemetery in Milan, Italy, where her husband, Juan Peron, lived, and then back again to Buenos Aires after his death. Her family tomb is modest, but the floral arrangements at and around the tomb are breathtakingly beautiful: fresh, colorful, and by no means humble. When entering the cemetery, one is overwhelmed with the aboveground splendor of monuments, mausoleums, and statues, ranging from modest to grand scale mini-cathedrals. Many mini-buildings have gates and/or glass doors; their coffins and stairwells can be easily seen from outside, as if the viewers were being asked to look at the splendor within. The overall cemetery reminded me of the aboveground cemeteries in New Orleans, only on a much grander scale.

Only a few blocks from Eva's tomb we found the tomb of her husband, Juan Peron, in the less-exclusive graveyard of Chacarita Cemetery, which is not on the elaborate scale of the Recoleta Cemetery, but is the home of many famous people who were not of the aristocracy. The cemetery was established in 1870 to accommodate the countless victims of the yellow fever plague. It has only a few tombs and statues to match the splendor of Recoleta, one of the most visited being Buenos

Aires's "songbird," Carlos Gardel, who is held in a near-saint status by many Argentineans who feel a quasi-religious devotion to him. Plaques from people around the world cover the base of his life-sized statue, which is embroidered with flowers placed by the steady procession of people paying their respect to the great tango singer; the abundance of beautiful flowers that decorated his tomb enhanced the overall appearance of a rather dreary cemetery.

The day before our dance tour ended, we had some free time to go shopping and sightseeing, and to leisurely walk around the nearby neighborhood. We chose to return to the leather shop to buy a spare pair of their handmade soft-leathered dancing shoes, to be used on special dancing occasions. Our last class and farewell *milonga* was at the Sunderland Club, where we had a cocktail party, danced with our partners, other students, beautiful local women, handsome men, and some of our master instructors. I actually danced with two male instructors and enjoyed the dancing very much, even though dancing the female part was quite difficult, but with the expert guidance that I had, I was able to dance and enjoy the follower's part. One of our master teachers, Mingo Pugliese, and his dance partner-wife, Ester, approached us and said they liked our styling and passion for the dance. He said, "Michael, all of the teaching, demonstrations and lectures that you were a part of mean nothing if you do not develop the proper 'Attitude.' There is no dance, if you do not have the right romantic 'Attitude' when doing the tango." He praised our attitude and told us to "Continue dancing for the love of it, and to have a happy and passionate life with the tango as I and my wife have."

The next morning we had our farewell breakfast and said good-bye to the many new dancing friends whom we had shared our wonderful themed vacation with. We extended our stay for three additional days, and accomplished all the sightseeing that we had planned. The cemetery visits to see the final resting places of Eva and Juan Peron and Gardel will always be etched in my mind. We spent many hours just walking around the city, visiting neighborhoods, and talking to as many locals as possible. Fortunately, Barbara has a great understanding of the Spanish language, which helped us to just relax and meet people on a comfortable level.

There was a special place that we wanted to visit, and put a whole afternoon aside to satisfy our curiosity; it was the few blocks called "Caminito" in the La Boca district. We have been in love with the word *Caminito* for years as it's the name of one of our favorite Argentine tango songs, sung by our favorite singer, Carlos Gardel. In the song, *Caminito* means "little path," and is the road to his lover. The last stanza of the song goes something like this: "Little path covered with thistle, the hand of time erased your tracks. I would like to fall beside you and let time kill us both." As with many tango love songs, the words are very dramatic and often fatal. So, with Carlos's music ringing in our ears, we headed for the area so dramatically described in the song.

When approaching the small area, the variety of bright colors that the buildings are painted caused my eyes to dilate: bright yellow, shocking greens, many shades of blue and all the shades of red; these colors were on the sides and fronts of the buildings, steps, and trim. Even the light posts were painted in rainbow colors. Although there were menageries of colors, they somehow blended to express the story behind that small area by the waters of *La Boca*, which mean mouth, as in mouth of the Riachuelo River. Millions of foreign immigrants entered Argentina between 1880 and 1930, turning Buenos Aires from a small town into a bustling metropolis. Many Italians migrated from Genoa to La Boca and settled in the Caminito area so they could work in the nearby shipyards, as they had in their home town of Genoa. They were poor and took scraps of metal or other discarded usable materials from the shipyards to build their homes in Caminito and the surrounding area. The material's finishes were ugly, so they decided to paint them with whatever leftover paint they could find at the shipyards. Although today no one lives in Caminito, the area is a testimonial to the ingenuity and hard work of its original settlers. The buildings are occupied by shops and restaurants, and are considered an open-air museum, representative of the time when La Boca was the melting pot of Argentina.

Tango music filled the air throughout the area, giving motion to street performers, tango dancers, and musicians. Barbara and I immediately joined other tango lovers and showed off some of the wonderful routines that we had learned from our accomplished dance instructors. The whole scene seemed to be out of an *Alice in Wonderland* story; the street dancers were dressed in formal attire, men wearing tuxedoes, while the ladies showed off their open-back, short, beautiful dresses. We felt part of the exotic kaleidoscope; how much better could it get?

We found a second-floor restaurant and sat on the terrace overlooking the square where we could view the surreal colorful scene and enjoy a hearty lunch. We ordered pizza with cheese and pepperoni, which was a house specialty, and polished it off with a bottle of very sweet white Argentine wine, while we watched the street fill with tourists. By the time we finished our lunch, the streets were packed with people shopping, dancing, or just browsing the stores. We joined the crowd and couldn't help buying some tango paraphernalia. I bought a great ceramic picture, 10 × 14 inches, depicting two tango dancers with a Caminito sign in the background; Barbara bargained with a shopkeeper for a beautiful multicolored shawl and two fans with tango dancers and Caminito's colorful buildings in the background. With our arms filled with our purchased prizes, we bid farewell to Caminito and its rainbowed past and present, which is still etched in my mind as a fond memory of love and romance in the place where tango was born.

While looking out the window of the plane that was carrying us home to the U.S., and watching the beautiful city of Buenos Aires fade into the distance, Mingo Pugliese's words were echoing in my mind: "You must have the right romantic 'Attitude' to truly enjoy the tango, but what's more important, you must have the right 'Attitude' to fully enjoy life."

While doing the tango at various dance halls, Barbara and I have been approached on many occasions by people watching us dance and have been told that when dancing we seem to be telling a story of love and seduction. It makes us feel fulfilled to have people enjoy our dance routines, and I often smile when I think of Mingo's advice. Maybe, in some way, we captured what he was telling us. In any case, we thank you Mingo for helping enhance our love and passion for the tango. Some years later, we were at the weekly *milonga* of the "Argentine Tango Lovers of Long Island" in Westbury, Long Island, and the dance master teaching the tango and performing a show was none other than Mingo's son, Pablo. What a wonderful experience; certainly "six degrees of separation" were in play, our being taught by the senior Puglieses in Argentina, and then by their famous son, thousands of miles from Buenos Aires in a local Long Island club—what are the odds? He loved the story we told about our experience with his parents, and spent most of the evening telling us how much he loved the tango and his beloved Argentina.

Chapter Four – Paris and the Moulin Rouge

~*~

AROUND THE FLOOR: JANUARY/MARCH 2000
TRAVELING AROUND by Barbara Bivona

Mike and I decided to spend a week in Paris before meeting up with our tour group from the Smithsonian Institute for two weeks of exploring the Amalfi Coast area of Southern Italy. We kept putting off a trip to France because we had heard such negative reports about the French people's attitude toward Americans. However, the call of the Eiffel Tower, the Louvre, and Notre Dame was strong, so, putting aside our concerns, we flew off to Paris for a week of adventure. The French people surprised us; it seems that the main problem they have with Americans is that we do not communicate well with them. The people we met didn't speak English, and we, unfortunately, didn't speak French. But once we discovered a European language that they understood, things got more comfortable for us. I have a working knowledge of Spanish, and Mike understands and speaks some Italian. The French understand one or the other of these languages and readily spoke to us when necessary. An example of this was one day, while trying to navigate a course on foot to the Champs Elysees with a walking map, I discovered that I was holding the map upside down and, after a very long walk, realized we were about two miles in the opposite direction. We asked a passerby to help us get to the Champs Elysees in English with no luck, but Spanish and some sign language did the trick; she understood us, walked us to the Metro, and made sure we got onto the right train.

Mike found an ad for the Argentine show *Tango Pasion* that was traveling around the world and, fortunately for us, was performing in Paris; we bought tickets and rushed to see the show that evening. The Parisian ladies were dressed in their finest silks and jewels, and the men wore suits and ties. The audience reacted very unexpectedly to the performance, with cheers, bravos, and enthusiastic applause. By the end of the show, the cheering rivaled an Army-Navy football game.

We wanted to go to the Moulin Rouge nightclub, but the cost for an evening of dinner, dancing and a show was astronomical: $440.00 USD. We decided to pass on the show, but Toulouse-Lautrec kept calling us. So we decided, what the heck, this was a once-in-a-lifetime experience, so why not go for it? Our seats were at the edge of the elevated dance floor. The orchestra was wonderful; they played Cha-Chas, Rumbas, and cheek-to-cheek music. After drinking a bottle of Parisian wine, we felt like we were in heaven. Suddenly, the orchestra played an Argentine Tango. The dance floor cleared. Can't anyone Tango here? We didn't get up because we didn't want to be alone on the dance floor with a thousand people watching us. My heart was pounding. I wanted to Tango, but not as the only couple on the stage. Slowly, dancers drifted on the floor. No one could do an Argentine Tango, but they swayed to the music and enjoyed themselves. Now we were safe. We could dance and be inconspicuous in the crowd. As we danced to a few measures of the Argentine Tango, we became aware of the crowd thinning around us and soon we were alone on the stage dance floor. Our worst fears: we were the show! We moved toward the middle and performed our well-learned routines. When we finished, the French gave us a rousing Army-Navy cheer.

END OF ARTICLE

~*~

The unedited version of this story began many years before our trip to Paris. Our daughter, Laurie Jo, graduated from college and decided to backpack through Europe with one of her friends so that they "could find themselves." I wasn't aware that she was lost, but being that she had saved enough money by working odd jobs during her stay at the university, plus the many monetary gifts she accumulated during her lifetime, we couldn't refuse or interfere with her dream of being on her own and finding her identity while traveling through Europe with her closest friend Claire. So we gave her our blessing and away she went with her traveling companion. Their main travels included London, England; Amsterdam, Holland; Paris, France; Rome, Italy; parts of Switzerland; and, lastly, Athens, Greece. In Athens, they spent time with my nephew, Dennis, who lived in that city. He escorted them to some of the wonderful Greek Islands and, as they stayed a few days in my nephew's home, they were able to experience, somewhat, what living in a major European city was like. In all their other travels they stayed at pensions; she told us they were not great residences, but at her age, backpacking and living in extremely modest hotels while traveling through Europe was a once-in-a-lifetime adventure, so why not join the hundreds of other lost souls in search of themselves and fit in?

After spending a month traveling through many European countries, she returned home to us a different person. She told us of the wonders that she had seen and the people she had met, many of them young, exploring backpackers from around the world. It seems that they all had one thing in common, "they were all lost and trying to find themselves." I was happy that her trip was a success and all she had dreamed it would be. We asked her what place she enjoyed the most and she said, without a doubt, Paris. The people were friendly, the sightseeing awesome, and the other backpackers she met were in abundance with everyone hanging around, drinking espresso, and sharing their personal stories. The Parisians seem to encourage young people, and have many public facilities to accommodate them, such as public toilets, parks with ample seating areas, and many sidewalk cafés. Her choice of Paris as a preferred place to see remained in the back of our minds and, when we booked a trip with the Smithsonian Institute to tour the Amalfi Coast area in Southern Italy, we researched the possibility of visiting Paris first.

Our Smithsonian Institute trip was to begin in Naples, Italy, and would travel into the surrounding areas, and finally return to Naples. So we had to figure out the best way to go from New York City to Paris and from Paris to Naples. We decided that while we were in Italy, why not make a stop in Barbara's favorite city, Rome? So, a flight from Rome to New York City was contemplated. We decided the best way to travel from New York City to Paris was with Delta Airlines. We had many frequent flier miles and were able to book a business class passage to

Paris; that was easy. However, Paris to Naples was another matter. The only convenient airline was Alitalia and a one-way ticket from Paris to Naples was almost one-third more than a round trip from Paris to Naples. So we booked a round-trip fare and used it to get to Naples. Unfortunately, we couldn't get a refund for the unused portion. We figured we could get from Naples to Rome by train, which is what we did. Next, we booked a flight from Rome to New York's Kennedy Airport with Delta Airlines on a return flight, and were able to use our frequent flier miles to complete our journey in business class.

We were excited and nervous, as we had never traveled to Europe on our own, all of our previous trips were with tours; so we began serious in-depth research with a passion. We decided to spend a week in Paris before our trip to Italy, and made a list of the places we wanted to see, including places we had seen in movies and fantasized about. We kept talking about the movies: *An American in Paris* (1951), with Gene Kelly, Leslie Caron, Oscar Levant, and Nina Foch singing and dancing to George and Ira Gershwin's lyrics and music; *April in Paris (1952)*, with Doris Day and Ray Bolger, and the great musical *Gigi* (1958), with Leslie Caron, Maurice Chevalier, Louis Jourdan, and Eva Gabor, about life in Paris in the late 1800s and the passion of being a part of Paris at that time. Doris Day's song, "April in Paris," and Maurice Chevalier's singing of "Gigi" were ringing in my ears and bringing back all the warm memories from watching those great musicals about *Paree.* So we compiled our "Wish List," humming the songs we remembered from those great musicals about the "City of Love." We began making a list of the places we wanted to see and that's when the fun began: the Eiffel Tower, Notre Dame, Arc de Triomphe, the Louvre Museum, the Moulin Rouge, the Latin Quarter, the Sorbonne, the Pantheon, the Catacombs, and, hopefully, Versailles. Wow, what a wish list! Hopefully, we would get to see most of them. Also, a walk along the "Avenue des Champs-Elysees" would be a must.

We booked our business-class flight on Delta Airlines, which happened to be running a special that included the use of their first-class lounge Crown Room at JFK Airport, which we took advantage of without giving it a second thought. What a difference comfort makes! We were able to lounge around for over two hours in pure luxury, enjoying drinks, snacks, sandwiches, magazines, newspapers, and the use of very sophisticated clean restrooms. The most memorable comfort was the lack of noise that we were used to hearing when waiting in a coach lounge. We had an evening flight and were pleased when we were handed menus to choose our dinner; we were famished and enjoyed the selections offered. After dinner, we had a drink and then used the reclining seats to relax, sleep, and spend a very restful night dreaming to the hypnotic hum of the jet engines. Our sleep was broken at about 7:00 A.M., French time, by our stewardess; it was breakfast time and we were given menus to select our hot or cold choices. Considering that France is six hours ahead of Eastern Standard Time in New York, we really weren't in the mood for any food, but we forced ourselves to have some coffee and Danish. The flight took about eight hours, so we landed the following day around 9:00 A.M., French time, at Charles de Gaulle Airport, which is located just north of Paris. With the help of a French policeman, we were fortunate to get a cab and were taken to the Hotel Ambassador Opera on Haussmann Boulevard. We chose this hotel because friends of ours had just returned from Paris and said it was an American four-star hotel, away from the hustle and bustle of the tourist areas on the Left and Right Banks of the Seine River. It sounded perfect, so we booked our stay at the contemporary-style, air-conditioned, boutique-type hotel. Well, that is why I thought we chose this hotel, but even before we unpacked, my wife was on the phone asking the concierge where the Galeries Lafayette and the Le Printemps department stores were located. Much to her delight, they were only a couple of blocks away on the same boulevard. I contemplated tying her up to stop her from leaving the room and running down the boulevard to also explore the covered shopping streets, which were within walking distance of our hotel. But, being that it was early morning Eastern Standard Time, we decided to take a nap and plan our day when we awoke.

After refreshing ourselves, we explored the eight-story hotel, which had just been refurbished and seemed to sparkle. Air conditioning should never be taken for granted in Europe. Many hotels do not have that comfort and many more have air conditioning, but ration it during the daytime and evenings. Fortunately, Hotel Ambassador had a friendly policy and we were cool throughout our stay. The hotel had several restaurants and an up-to-date gym on the eighth floor, with large windows overlooking the city and an incredible view of the Eiffel Tower. We had our breakfast/lunch at their "16 Haussmann Restaurant," which was quite casual, and had high ceilings, large windows, and a wooden deck overlooking the busy Boulevard. If I had a valium pill, I would have slipped it into Barbara's drink, as she was *kvetching* and bobbing in her chair and rushing me to finish my meal. Finally, we finished eating and immediately exited the hotel and headed toward her targets, the covered shopping streets on and along Haussmann Boulevard and, of course, the Galeries Lafayette and Le Printemps department stores. It's amazing that when we prepared our "Wish List," there was never any discussion about shopping being our first priority.

Choosing to travel in September is always a good choice in Europe. The weather in many cities is usually in the high 60s to mid-70s, which is ideal for walking through neighborhoods for sightseeing and shopping. Barbara, evidently, had all of this figured out when we planned our trip. Boulevard Haussmann was a shopper's delight, very similar to the covered Ginza Market in Tokyo, Japan. Every imaginable vendor was represented, selling wares from their stands, which were decorated in very colorful patterns, giving one the feeling that they were inside a rainbow looking out. It didn't take long for us to zero in on some nice, inexpensive ballroom dancing CDs that would be difficult, if not impossible to find in the states. Especially precious were the CDs of French singers Edith Pilaf, the tragic songbird who sang, "La Vie En Rose"; Maurice Chevalier, "the French Al Jolson," singing "Bon Soir, Good Night Cherie"; and the exotic and heroic American, Josephine Baker, singing songs in French, such as "Easy to Love," "The Loveliness of You," and "Goodnight, My Love." I enjoyed walking along the Boulevard and talking to the friendly French people we met along the way, while zigzagging through the streets leading up to the main events, which were the Galeries Lafayette and Le Printemps department stores. They are neighbors on the Boulevard and were built in the mid and late-19th century. They sprawl through several buildings and are considered the greatest emporiums ever built. When they were constructed, they were among the first department stores and soon revolutionized Europe's way of retailing. Needless to say, we left a considerable amount of unbudgeted funds in these beautifully decorated palaces. While shopping under one of their enormous stained-glass roofs, it gave us the feeling that we weren't spending money but were having a grand time on a merry-go-round at a circus, trying to capture the brass ring. Unfortunately, in this case we were the brass rings, and they certainly caught us. Loaded down with packages, we headed back to the hotel. I still had jet lag, or maybe I was hallucinating, but I could have sworn that Barbara was hopping, skipping, and singing while walking ahead of me, with her conquests dangling from her extended arms.

Later that evening we decided to walk along the Boulevard to find a local restaurant and have dinner. Through our many years of traveling around the world, we learned that some of the best restaurants are to be found by walking around local neighborhoods. That night was no exception. After walking about five minutes, we looked into a storefront window restaurant that had no more than a dozen tables, and observed a person holding what looked like a boat oar, stirring what looked like food in a very large vat. Indeed, it was a boat oar, and he was stirring the evening's special dinner, paella. Being that we both loved that Spanish delight, we sat down at a window table drooling in anticipation of a delicious meal. We ordered a pitcher of white sangria and were told that the evening's special could be ordered in a number of different ways. The price depended on the ingredients chosen by us, so Barbara, being a shellfish lover, ordered her meal with clams, mussels, lobster, and sausage; an abundance of saffron rice was mixed with peppers, peas, and some other green vegetable. I've never developed a taste for shellfish, so I ordered my meal with sausage, pork, and lots of vegetables in my rice. *Voila!* The meal was spectacular; we both agreed that the Spanish cuisine we devoured in France was the best we had ever eaten, including the paella we enjoyed in Spain and Portugal.

The next day we got up early and decided to walk along Boulevard Haussmann, with a walking map of the area that our pleasant concierge, Pierre, gave us. He also gave us very explicit instructions on how to get to the Eiffel Tower. After strolling down the Boulevard for what seemed to be an eternity, we realized that the Eiffel Tower seemed to be disappearing in the distance. We stopped a young lady and tried to explain our predicament, but unfortunately, she didn't speak English. We showed her the Eiffel Tower on the map and with Barbara's language skills in Spanish, told her where we were headed. She immediately turned the map around, as Barbara was holding it upside down, resulting in our walking in the opposite direction. Needless to say, we were embarrassed, but the young lady smiled and walked us two blocks out of her way to the Art Nouveau entrance of the Metro Train System. She graciously pointed to the train number we had to take to get to our destination. The Metro needs some explaining, as it's quite different from what we New Yorkers are accustomed to. To describe it briefly, it's first-class travel with very clear station signs and a very comprehensive color-coded Metro Map that can get you around underground Paris with little difficulty. When we went to buy a ticket to our destination, the clerk gave us a pamphlet in English, which explained the various tickets that were available for traveling around the great city. We bought a weekly pass (*coupon he'bdomadaire*) that was good for our entire stay. The station resembled New York's Grand Central Station, and with its comprehensive color coding, we had no trouble finding the track that our train ran on. We arrived at our destination, which not only had its name tiled on the platform wall, but also had some of the main attractions that were above ground. Considering that the population of Paris is over two million people and the metropolitan area about ten million, the trains were exceptionally clean, not too crowded, and the people very polite—quite a difference from what we were accustomed to when riding the subways in New York City where the train platforms are dirty, the trains crowded and not very clean. We were so excited when we exited the train that we ran up the moving escalator to the street level. What a sight to see! The best-known monument in the world, the Eiffel Tower, the symbol of Paris, was right in front of us. After taking a dozen pictures, we took an elevator to the top of the 1,000-plus-foot structure and hypnotically gazed at the magnificent city of Paris. The visibility was endless; we were told that on a clear day, seeing 35 to 40 miles was possible. It was certainly one of the most beautiful cityscapes in the world that we have seen. It was lunch time, and where else to enjoy some French cuisine but at one of the Tower's restaurants. We tried to get into the "Jules Verne Restaurant" at the upper platform of the tower; however, reservations were required weeks in advance. But, the "Altitude 95" restaurant on the first platform was a good second choice. We took the elevator to that level and had a wonderful lunch while absorbing a spectacular view of the city. We made a mental note, that if we could, we would try to get reservations at the "Jules Verne Restaurant" for dinner so we could see the City of Lights in the evening in its entire splendor.

Where to next? Paris consists of 20 different neighborhoods, called *arrondissements,* that are either on the Left or Right banks of the Seine River, so we figured, being that we were already on the Left Bank, that the best approach to sightseeing the magnificent city was to walk along the River and stop and explore whatever stimulated our interest.

We checked our "Wish List" and decided that the first stop would be *le Panthéon* and then on to Notre Dame. The stroll along the Seine River was breathtaking to say the least; the effect of the three bridges crossing the Seine River is surreal, especially the Pont Neuf Bridge, which has twelve arches; seven arches joining the Right Bank and another span of five arches connecting *lle de la cite* (this is the island that hosts the Notre Dame Cathedral) with the Left Bank. It also boasts an equestrian statue of King Henry IV, who was responsible for its construction. The activity on the stone bridge was bustling with people socializing and trading all sorts of small wares. The sun shining off the water, the arches and bronze statues, and the beautiful 14th century towered palaces and ancient buildings in the background had the effect of a glorious dream-like beaming halo above and around the bridge.

Next was *le Panthéon*, which is the burial place for some of the great souls of the Nation: Hugo, Zola, Rousseau, Voltaire, and many others. Originally, it was built as a majestic church and dedicated to the city's patron, St. Genevieve. When we entered, Barbara was immediately drawn to Foucault's Spinning Pendulum; she moved so fast that I thought she had spotted a designer store. Since her college days, she has turned her studies in astronomy and geology into a passion. I had no idea what Foucault's Pendulum was, and quite frankly, wasn't too interested, but my curiosity was piqued when I was told that it was in perpetual motion; I was fascinated by how it could keep moving without something being coiled. We located a docent who was lecturing about the pendulum and became fascinated and enthralled while she told of the history and its purpose. I was hypnotized by the slow movement, swaying to and fro beneath the dome of the former church, tracing its invisible path against the hour table below. On the ground, a large white ring surrounding the area of oscillation is marked with a series of numbers that reflects a period of 24 hours. A short video display was also available relating its story; it told visitors to "Imagine for a moment that your feet were no longer touching the ground and consider that the pendulum's plane of oscillation, which also doesn't touch the ground, remains unchanged with respect to the stars, even as the earth rotates; this is proof that the Pantheon moves around the pendulum and not vice-versa."

Interesting—I'm still trying to figure it all out, but I enjoyed watching the hypnotic motion of the pendulum, which made me relax, while trying to absorb all the information about its purpose. We exited the Panthéon and walked down its enormous steps to the street, which was crowded with pedestrians and people having outdoor late lunches or early dinners in the Latin Quarter of the Left Bank.

It was a short and pleasant walk to the *Pont Neuf Bridge* where we crossed over to the *Ile de la Cite,* where the Notre Dame Cathedral was located. On the way, we stopped at a street-side café and had some wonderful espresso coffee, while admiring the Parisians and tourists busily moving about the Latin Quarter. The appearance of the Parisians were very similar to what we had seen in New York City, very serious in their demeanor and dress, the men wearing suits with ties and carrying briefcases, the fashionable ladies dressed the same as their New York sisters and just as beautiful to behold. All were very determined looking and seemed to be in a rush to get to their destinations, as we were, so off we went to the historical Notre Dame Cathedral.

Crossing the beautiful *Pont Neuf Bridge* and absorbing the Notre Dame Cathedral was mind boggling; one of the noblest monuments in the Western world, its presence and French Gothic beauty dominates the Seine River, the *Ile de la cite,* and Paris itself. The location dates back to a Roman Temple to Jupiter, which was replaced by a Christian basilica, then a Romanesque church, and finally the Cathedral as it stands today. The building was being renovated, so there was scaffolding around most of the upper portion, but the construction did not hide the famously grotesque gargoyles, the soaring elegance of the flying buttresses, the sculpted portals, the bell tower, and the many waterspouts. Looking at the Cathedral, I envisioned *Quasimodo* swinging from apse to gargoyles and ringing the famous Cathedral's bells, rising up and coming down while holding the bell's ropes, as his heart pounded and burst for the fair maiden, *Esmeralda*. I reflected on Victor Hugo's historical romance story, which was made into one of the most memorable movies of my youth, *The Hunchback of Notre Dame* (1939), starring Charles Laughton, Maureen O'Hara, and the evil Claude Frollo played by Cedric Hardwicke. Every time I hear "Notre Dame," memories of *Quasimodo* swinging and jumping from place to place flash wildly through my mind.

The interior of the Cathedral's graceful columns were impressive and were dominated by three rose windows located to the west, north, and south of the structure. Their colors were spellbinding and beautiful to behold as the sun glittered through, accomplishing its designer's intention: to create unparalleled multiple colorful kaleidoscopes from all directions. The vastness of the holy place and our fatigue from our travels shortened our visit; we would have liked to spend at least a few more hours at the numinous venue. It was time to call it a day. Jet lag was still playing havoc with our minds and bodies, so we exited the incredible piece of French history, walked across the bridge to the Left Bank, hailed a taxicab, and returned to our hotel, where we had a quick dinner and retired after a rather long and exciting day. Before closing our eyes for the night, we decided that we would spend the next day at the Louvre Museum and explore the surrounding area of the Right Bank.

First thing the next morning we visited our concierge, Pierre. We had done some research before we began our trip and decided that we had better get some insider information about the *Musee du Grand Louvre* to guide us through the multitude of exhibits, architecture, and surrounding gardens. Considering that the museum displays about 300,000 works of art, and warehouses an even greater number, whatever advice Pierre could give us would be greatly appreciated and put to good use. He suggested that we spend at least two hours exploring the outside of the museum and asked what exhibits we were interested in seeing. We had previously decided that the Egyptian Exhibit was a must, as Barbara's interest in geology was attracting us to the mystique of the ancient Egyptians. He suggested that we spend from one to two hours at that exhibit and then explore whatever struck our fancy as we got the feel of the museum. He also suggested that we get a box lunch or eat at one of the many restaurants in the gardens, which would give us an opportunity to enjoy the beautiful Carrousel and *Tuileries Gardens* adjoining the museum. The information certainly gave us a sensible plan; we thanked Pierre and immediately went to the Metro and took the train to our next adventure. The system of turnstile revolving doors (Iron Maidens) that the Metro has for entering with passes is impressive. One inserts a prepaid pass into a slot, which opens an Iron Maiden turnstile (named after a medieval torture device), then enters while retrieving the pass, and walks through. It's that simple and practical, and considering the system has been successfully in place for over a decade, it was surprising that so many American transportation centers were still using the antiquated coin method for entrance to their train systems. We decided to have breakfast at a sidewalk café in the Latin Quarter and chose one right outside of the train station's exit where viewing the colorful pedestrians rushing to their destinations made the experience a more enjoyable one.

We crossed the footbridge to the Louvre Museum area where we were overwhelmed with the panoramic view that was bewildering in its complexity and beauty. To see so many places for the first time and to be intimately familiar with them in my mind's eye was an experience in *déjà vu.* There was a panoramic view from the high vantage point, where we were standing, of the American architect I.M. Pei's glass-paneled Pyramid in the courtyard. It was engulfed by rising waterspouts and a glimmering pond; the Arc du Carrousel in the near background; the Place de la Concorde; the Arc De Triomphe de L'Etoile; the Grand Arch de la Defense; the Louvre Museum and the surrounding gardens; combined they were a once-in-a-lifetime scene not soon forgotten. Although it was our first trip to the museum, most of the structures were implanted in our minds from movies and pictures that we had seen. We took about an hour taking pictures and admiring the amazing amount of statues, figures, friezes, and every other conceivable outdoor works of art. We had to close our eyes and quickly enter the museum, or we would have spent the whole day admiring the variety of masterful artwork around and on the buildings.

We got a tour guide booklet with maps from the information center that directed us to the *Ancient Egyptian Art Exhibit.* After getting quite lost, we finally found the exhibit and spent the remainder of the morning studying and admiring over 3,000 years of Egyptian history and artifacts, ranging in size from four-inch statuettes to larger-than-life-size statues. Barbara was enthralled with the whole experience, especially the information and displays about its famous rulers: Amenhotep III, Akhenaten, Ramesses II (the Great), and our favorites, Tutankhamen (King Tut) and of course, Cleopatra. A painted relief of Cleopatra in the time-honored guise of a bare-chested male pharaoh giving a sacrifice to the goddess Isis absorbed our minds and imagination. We were amused, as she certainly didn't look like the Cleopatra played by the beautiful actress Elizabeth Taylor, whose appearance we usually associate with Cleopatra. As I watched Barbara, who was fascinated and absorbed with the excavation exhibits, I could picture where her imagination was taking her: probably right to an Egyptian dig, maybe King Tut's, where she would be shoveling earth, examining stones and making a great discovery. It was past lunchtime and we both decided to take Pierre's advice and have lunch in the outside gardens.

We strolled to the Tuileries Garden (*Jardin des Tuileries*), which extended from the Louvre to the Place de la Concorde. We walked the central alley path, which was lined with shady clipped chestnut trees, manicured lawns, and ornamental ponds at each end, surrounded by a multitude of beautiful flowers, dancing fountains, and statues. We stopped at the first restaurant and ordered some sandwiches and drinks to go. We luckily located two empty chairs, which were strategically located at one of the ponds, and quickly placed them so we could enjoy the view of the gardens, statues, and a surprising sight of children and adults at play around the pond. It's interesting to note that there were chairs throughout the park for the convenience of the public, which can be placed wherever one wishes to sit. Children were sailing and chasing their boats around the pond. Many of them had motorized remote-controlled boats, which they were having fun racing, but most were just enjoying a playful casual sail or just horsing around with their friends and most likely their parents. Taking in the whole sight of trees, flowers, statues, ponds, children, and some grownups at play, with people promenading around was what we needed to end our perfect day at the Louvre. It was our time to "stop and smell the roses." We enjoyed our sandwiches, took many great photographs, and decided to head back to our hotel, as it was becoming overcast and threatening rain. Instead of taking the Metro back, we decided to take a city bus, which was, according to a helpful policeman, nearby and would drop us off close to our hotel. Unfortunately, it started to rain as we were waiting for our transportation and we got pretty wet. But we figured what the heck—we were in Paris and the ride to our destination seemed a short one. So, drenched, we boarded the bus, inserted our Metro pass into the open machine, as we saw other passengers do, and away we went to our comfortable hotel.

The weather cleared so we decided to walk and discover a new restaurant, and whatever other surprises we might find along the way. Our first stop was to the concierge, Pierre, to get directions to the closest bistros. He said for us to go outside and walk in whatever direction we chose, and we would certainly find a restaurant that would satisfy our appetites. We did just that, and found a quaint Italian restaurant around the corner from the hotel. We entered and were greeted in French, seated, and given wine and meal menus. We were surprised that both menus were in French so we asked for English menus, but the waiter didn't understand us. I tried some Italian to no avail, but Barbara's Spanish did the trick. He told us that they didn't have an English menu and further explained that we were in a kosher restaurant, as were the other restaurants on that street. We decided to stay and try our luck by ordering pasta with eggplant and a bottle of local wine. The restaurant had about 20 tables, and while we were enjoying our wine and waiting for our meals to be served, a gentlemen and companion came in and sat at the table next to ours. They nodded hello, sat down, and lit cigarettes. UGH! The waiter saw that we were uncomfortable and asked them if they would mind sitting at the far end of the restaurant. They rose and sort of apologized to us and politely moved to their new table. Of course, we didn't understand French, but we assumed that the conversation went along those lines. The pasta and eggplant were absolutely delicious and the French wine, as usual, complemented the meal. We enjoyed the meal so much that we went back to the Italian-Kosher-French restaurant again before we left Paris. Before retiring for the evening, we decided to return to the Louvre Museum the next day to see the painting of *Mona Lisa*, the statues of *Venus De Milo,* the *Winged Victory of Samothrace,* and if possible, the *Stele* (stone) of *Hammurabi's Code* (the first written laws), which was written between 1795 and 1750 BCE.

We were out of bed early the next morning and decided to enjoy another breakfast at a street side café on the Right Bank. We entered the Metro station, went to the Iron Maidens, inserted our passes, and were surprised that the turnstiles didn't open. After several tries with no luck, we approached the cashier booth and tried to explain our predicament. He spoke some English, and asked if we had used the passes on a bus? I will never know how he knew, but I said "Yes" and he shook his head and said, "No good." It seems that the passes we had were only good for use on the train system of the Metro, and inserting them into the bus's turnstile voided them. I thought to myself, now we are in for it—what an opportunity for the notorious anti-American French to "zing" us. However, to our surprise, he took our passes, issued new ones (at no charge), and asked, "Where are you going?" I said, "The Louvre Museum." He exited his change booth and escorted us through an Iron Maiden, using our new passes, and directed us to the track that our train would be arriving at. We thanked him profusely as he disappeared from sight. What a pleasantly surprising experience to begin our day!

After having another delightful outside breakfast on the Right Bank, and enjoying the promenade of Parisians going about their daily routines, we rushed to the Louvre Museum, hoping to accomplish our goal of seeing all the exhibits we had discussed the night before. In my mind's eye, I couldn't get the beautiful gardens out of my head and hoped that we would be able to spend some extra quality time in them after finishing our tours. We were able to see all the exhibits and I was constantly reminded of the great baseball player and manager, Yogi Berra's, famous quote: "It seemed like *déjà vu* all over again." We recognized most of the displays and were familiar with their history from school studies, movies, magazines, and posters, with many of them at one time or another being incorporated into my daydreams, especially *Venus De Milo.* We were satisfied with what we had accomplished and exited the great museum in the middle of the afternoon. We headed straight for the *Tuileries Gardens* and strolled through the Central Valley path, again admiring all of man and nature's bounty. We ended up at the eastern end and entered the Garden Carrousel (*Jardin du Carrousel*), which is at the front of the Louvre. Its beautiful flowers and trim yew hedges complemented the oddly static buxom female nude bronzes by the sculptor Maillol that seemed to blend in with the foliage as if they were a part of one another. We left the grounds in anticipation of getting back to our hotel in time to refresh and dress for the Argentine show, *Pasion del Tango* (Tango Passion), for which we were able to get tickets through our concierge, Pierre. He advised us to dress well for the theatre as Parisians usually dressed up nicely when they attend shows. Barbara was ecstatic; she could wear and show off a new outfit that she had purchased at the Galleria Lafayette with complementing shoes. I wore my suit and tie that I had to go out and buy, under protest, for the event.

We took a taxicab to the Theatre des Champs-Elysees, which was not on the famous Boulevard, but nearby. It is one of the few major examples of Art Nouveau remaining in Paris. The theatre is known for its contemporary music, dance, and opera, unlike the traditional and more conservative venues, such as the Paris Opera House, which was featured in the plays and movies, *Phantom of the Opera.* We were pleasantly surprised at how fashionably dressed the ladies were; many of the gentlemen actually wore tuxedos, but most wore suits and ties; good thing I was persuaded to purchase a tie. We did fit in pretty well with the locals. An observation we made was that the Parisians appeared very reserved. Although they seemed to speak in a normal manner, with much feeling, they didn't seem to laugh out loud or smile much in public. It did seem that many of them smoked cigarettes and cigars, and no matter how we tried to avoid the smoke, we couldn't because there was always someone smoking in the public areas. We entered the auditorium and were ecstatic when we read the program. Music by some of our favorite composers was part of the show, including Carlos Gardel, whose music we were introduced to in Buenos Aires and loved to dance to. We had spent endless hours listening to his smooth, deep soul love and melancholy songs. Part of the show also included the compositions of Astor Piazzolla, the father of modern tango or *Nuevo tango.* These two great tango icons had a chance meeting when Piazzolla was a teenager and Gardel was touring New York City. Gardel was impressed with the boy's talent with the bandoneon, his love for tango music, and some of his early compositions. He wanted Piazzolla to join his world tour, but the young prodigy's father thought he was too young to be traveling with a group of musicians whose reputation was known to be rowdy. Divine intervention played an amazing part in Piazzolla's life, as Gardel and all the members of his band were killed in an airplane crash while on that tour in South America. Piazzolla is considered one of the most important tango composers of the 20th century. He was born in Mar del Plata, Argentina, in 1921, to Italian parents, but spent most of his childhood with his family in New York City, where he was exposed to jazz and the music of J.S. Bach. He returned to Argentina at the age of 16, and played in nightclubs and with various orchestras. His early compositions combined tango with jazz, and then graduated to a fusion of tango with a wide range of other Western influences, such as baroque music from the 17th and 18th centuries. One of his first popular pieces, "Adios Nonino," was being presented in the evening's show. This composition established a standard structural pattern for his works: a formal pattern of "fast-slow-fast-slow-coda," with the fast sections emphasizing gritty tango rhythms and harsh, angular melodic figures. The slower sections usually make use of the smooth string instruments and bandoneon. His operetta, *Maria de Buenos Aires*, and other compositions established him as one of the world's foremost tango classical music composers of the 20th century.

The curtains parted and an ensemble of beautiful dancers wearing the colors of tango (black and red) appeared; men wore a variety of black outfits and high-heeled Latin-style shoes, and the women showed off every color of the rainbow, which were incorporated into their Latin-styled dresses and pants. The first dance was to the music of Carlos Gardel and Julian Plaza's "Mi Buenos Aires." It was a beautiful fast tango performed by several couples doing their own interpretations of the tango. The music was fast and required precise coordination and confidence between the partners, especially when the girls performed kicks between the men's legs. This type of music is not considered romantic and it's not sensual in sound, but it did allow the dancers to show off their skills at a very fast pace, with precision in their kicking, swaying, and body balancing; the style is considered an aerobic interpretation of the tango.

My favorite tango song, and very popular with dancers, was played halfway through the show: "La Cumparsita," by G.M. Rodriguez. The romantic dance was performed by one couple, slowly, with minor rhythm changes. The dance told a story of seduction, the meeting, flirting, pursuing, and finally, a conquest of the sexes. It was done to perfection, so much so that Barbara and I found ourselves applauding wildly, but we seemed to be the only ones that appreciated the performance. The last three pieces of music played out of the 19 performed were by Astor Piazzolla, one of which was previously mentioned, "Adios Nonino." His music is not usually of the romantic sexy type of tango we picture when envisioning "the Great Lover, Valentino" romancing his conquests. His pieces are fiery and complicated, as previously mentioned, a fusion of many types of Western music that have come down through the ages. His music gave the dancers an opportunity to show off their dancing skills at a very fast to slow pace, with precision being almost robotic in its accuracy. His music ended the show, and the Parisians, who up until that point didn't seem to be enjoying the show, as their applause didn't seem to be spontaneous or generous, arose in unison, and blew the roof off of the theatre with their applauding, cat calling, and whistling. Of course, the entertainers did a couple of encores, which received additional appreciation from the audience with some pretty loud sounds; I think we began to fall in love with the Parisians at that point. We left the theatre and had some difficulty finding a taxicab, as it was pretty late in the evening, so we walked toward Champs-Elysees and finally hailed a cab. The driver was the first Frenchman that we thought was downright obnoxious, but I closed my eyes and changed the location of the taxi to New York City and felt right at home. Being in a good mood, I rewarded him with a very gracious tip because he reminded me of the cabbies of our hometown. Before retiring, we decided that the next day we would explore the *Arc de Triomphe* and the Champs-Elysees; we would also ask Pierre about getting us tickets to the Moulin Rouge, where I would finally get to see some exotic in-the-flesh Can-Can girls dancing.

The next morning we went straight to Pierre and asked if he could get tickets for the famous Moulin Rouge show that evening, preferably with seats as close to the stage as possible. He said that he had a cousin who worked at the box office and that he would contact him immediately. He told us to have some coffee and return in 15 minutes when he would have the information for us. We decided to have breakfast at the hotel and returned to Pierre's desk when we finished. He had all the information we needed. Did we want to see only the show? Did we want to see the show and have drinks? Or did we want to have a sit-down dinner with wine at a good location? He gave us the price of each in American dollars, which put us in a state of shock. We certainly wanted to see the entire show with dinner included, but the price was $440.00 for the first evening show, which we thought was prohibitive. We told him we had to talk it over and went back to our room to discuss and investigate the pricing. We checked our travel guides and spoke to some other guests at the hotel that we met during our stay. All said that the prices we were given seemed to be the going price, being that the American dollar did not have a favorable exchange rate at that time. Well, the images in Toulouse Lautrec's paintings and posters of the Moulin Rouge's beautiful women were flashing through my mind, and the music from the movie resounded in my soul, so we told Pierre that we would like to see the show that evening, including dinner and wine. He told us that the price also included transportation to and from the cabaret, which certainly made the price a little more palatable.

We hurried to the Metro for another rendezvous with an "Iron Maiden" and had no difficulty finding the track that our train would arrive on to take us to the *Arc de Triomphe* station. Although I was anxious to see the sights we had planned for the day, my mind was really focusing on the evening show at the Moulin Rouge. That changed when we exited the train station; the sight of the *Arc de Triomphe* completely filled my eyes and absorbed every thought in my mind. It was so overwhelming! Not only was I viewing the magnificent structure, but I immediately saw the image of Adolf Hitler reviewing his troops, in a show of arrogance, and marching through the *Arch* on that horrific day in history during WWII, when his army occupied that great city. I shook the view from my mind's eye and thought of the more recent and happier events of Lance Armstrong as he rode through the *Arch* after his stupendous accomplishments of winning the *Tour de France* race seven times. The race's participants traveled through the Alps for over 2,000 miles; Lance Armstrong accomplished these feats after his miraculous struggle and recovery from cancer. Unfortunately, his seven wins have been stricken from the books due to his substance abuse, but the excitement of his winning was etched in my mind, especially when viewing the *Arch*. After clearing my mind, we attempted to cross the square in front of the monument. This turned out to be a big mistake as we were almost run down by insane car and scooter drivers. After we had crossed, an American tourist who watched our obstacle course maneuvers told us that there was an underground crossing that would have been a safer choice. It would have been nice if we had met him before attempting our suicide mission.

We were immediately attracted to the grave of the *Unknown Soldier* from WWI, whose body was retrieved from Verdun in the region of Lorraine and buried beneath the *Arch* with a large and decorative flat headstone. Flowers in the shape of a horseshoe surrounded the site. Each evening at 6:30 P.M., a flame of remembrance is rekindled during a small formal ceremony in memory of the fallen heroes of that war.

The *Arc de Triomphe* was commissioned by Napoleon in 1806 to commemorate his army's victories, but it remained unfinished until after his death. It was completed in 1836 during the reign of Louis-Philippe. The design of the structure was based on the *Arch of Titus* in Rome, but is three times larger (164 feet high and 148 feet wide). Surprisingly, it was built in the same proportions as its little sister in Rome. It is the highest triumphal arch in the world, and is adorned with many reliefs, most of them commemorating Napoleon's victories. So impressive are the faces in the sculptures that they seem to be staring back at you from their high vantage points. We climbed the steps to the viewing platform where I was amazed at the view. I thought that our previous experiences with the panoramic views of Paris could not be matched, but here it was, another marvel of French ingenuity. The integration of architecture and the beauty within the overview of the city was beyond belief; one has to see this sight to understand the complexity of the decision-making by the city's fathers, and of the German generals who disobeyed Hitler's orders to destroy the magnificent city in WWII. Fortunately, their decisions not to have the city destroyed saved the "City of Lights," and left most of the city unscathed by the war, so that future generations could still marvel at the beautiful architecture and the talent of the French people who were responsible for the wonderful sights that everyone on the viewing platform was enjoying.

Looking in all directions, you can see twelve avenues emanating from the "star" (center), as well as all the other phenomenal views of Paris. Looking eastward, down the Champs-Elysees toward the Louvre, there is the *Place de la Concord,* the *Tuileries Gardens,* and the *Arc de Triomphe du Carrousel,* with the statue of four gilded bronze horses mounted at the top, shining in the sunlight as they are being driven by their leader (probably Napoleon), in all their military glory. Further down across the Seine River, the Eiffel Tower beamed in its height and splendor, and the golden dome, *Invalides* (Napoleon's resting place), sparkled in the sun. In the opposite direction, in the business district, seeing *La Grande Arche de la Defense,* the newest of Paris's arches and the surrounding avenues entering the "star" (roundabout) was too much to absorb all at once. We took a multitude of pictures and then descended the 200-plus steps to the street level. We decided to take the more cautious path out of the square and actually enjoyed the walk through the underground tunnel without being concerned about being run over by oncoming traffic and becoming part of the Champs-Elysees's pavement. As I walked down the road, I looked back at the *Arch* and recalled another happy occasion that took place at this monument. When WWII ended, some of the soldiers of the victorious allied armies marched through *L'Arc de Triomphe* led by the towering figure of French General Charles de Gaulle. I remembered the event from my childhood, when seeing movie newsreels and newspaper photographs of that historic day.

We decided to have a late lunch at a sidewalk café on the Champs-Elysees. The scene from our outdoor table on the street and the procession of people reminded me of a similar view in Rome of the *Via Veneto,* where some of the most fashionable women in the world parade their stylish wares. Of course, the French women cannot be outclassed by any of their foreign sisters, so there they were on the avenue promenading so stylishly in what I'm sure were the latest in women's fashions and designs. What a beautiful sight! After lunch, we decided to walk back to our hotel and enjoy the beautiful day while window shopping and exploring the neighborhoods. However, after walking some distance, we decided to take a taxicab back to the hotel and hopefully get some sleep before our night out at the Moulin Rouge. Barbara was apprehensive about going into an area that had a reputation for its rowdiness and of being a red-light district, but I assured her that the reputation was exaggerated, and being that we were traveling by bus with lots of other people, that the excursion would be a safe one.

A small bus holding about 20 people picked us up at the hotel and away we went to experience one of my fantasies, which was imbedded in my mind by the images of Henri de Toulouse-Lautrec's paintings and posters of exotic French girls doing the naughty Can-Can dance. The *Moulin Rouge* (French for Red Mill or windmill) is a cabaret, situated in the red-light district of Pigalle on Boulevard de Clichy on the Right Bank. Recognized by a large red imitation windmill on its roof, it went from a high-class brothel, where it's said that the striptease originated, to a fashionable spectacular cabaret, visited by the very best in French society. One of my favorite memorable movies was the 1952 *Moulin Rouge,* adapted from the book of the same name by Pierre La Mure, and starring Jose Ferrer and Zsa-Zsa Gabor. The musical was about the 19th century painter, Henri de Toulouse-Lautrec, played by Jose Ferrer, and his struggle with a deformity due to a leg injury as a child, which he had difficulty dealing with and which resulted in his drinking, carousing in the red-light district, and patronizing the Moulin Rouge. His reckless lifestyle eventually caused his early demise. The film's musical score, which immediately hit the top ten charts, was by George Aurie. I remembered seeing the film on my newly purchased color television set and couldn't believe my eyes; I was actually seeing a movie, in color, in my own living room. Color television is certainly here to stay, I thought; it was probably one of my better lifetime predictions.

We entered the cabaret and were escorted to our table, which was right at the edge of the raised stage. I was in a position where the only way I could see the performers was by raising my head upward . . . lucky me. We were seated at a table with six other people from various parts of the world, but the table was situated so that everyone had an unobstructed view of the stage. Our waiter broke open a bottle of white French wine and allowed me to sample it before pouring. I have always been tempted to swish the wine sampling around in my mouth and then gargling, just for the fun of it, but Barbara saw the look in my eye and said, "Don't you dare!" What a mind reader she is. The dinner was adequate and the coffee and desserts just fine, but I couldn't wait for the show to start. Finally, the long-legged international ensemble of girls appeared—slightly dressed, or should I say almost undressed, and performed an exotic Can-Can routine. When the show ended, I was not disappointed and after a couple of glasses of fine French wine, was quite content with our experience at the Moulin Rouge, even though it cost a small fortune. After the show, there was general dancing on the same raised stage that the Can-Can dancers performed on. We did some shuffling to foxtrots and waltzes with about 50 other couples, and then they played a slow, seductive Argentine tango. The stage cleared and we were the only ones left on the dance floor in front of 1,000-plus patrons. We decided to leave the dance floor as we didn't want to be the only ones dancing in front of such a large crowd, but soon other couples came into the arena, so we began to dance the sexy Argentine tango, which was being played by an amazingly talented seven-piece band. I noticed that no one really knew how to do the dance and soon all of the dancers cleared the floor to watch us; we had become the show. Not being bashful, we began to perform our routines: slow balancing, leg rubs, leg kicks, *cortes,* and all the other seductive moves we had learned through so many years of lessons and practice. The only problem we had was that the band wasn't ending the dance after the usual three minutes, so even though I felt that we could dance the whole night away, we came to our final step where Barbara kicks her leg between mine and leans way back. The music ended and the applause and howling was incredible. I had that same feeling as the night we attended the *Tango Pasion* show; we were again at an Army/Navy football game with lots and lots of wonderful cheering. We took our bows and left the brightly lit stage and returned to our table to be greeted by people surrounding us and asking where we learned to tango. Considering that the crowd was of international origin, the scene became quite hysterically amusing, as we didn't understand a word that was spoken by many of our admirers; we just smiled and nodded our heads. A person approached us, I think he was the manager, and asked if we would perform another tango. I was ready, but Barbara was very reluctant. I sort of forced her onto the dance floor while the emcee announced our performance. The music began and we again fell in love with the dance and each other. The music was slow and we took advantage of the tempo to do many of our caressing sways and smooth kicks. This time we did lots of reverse slow dragging dips mingled with sways, which pleased the crowd as their applause and howls were stimulating and, if the band hadn't stopped playing, "We would have danced all night." Again, we bowed and acknowledged the audience's appreciation by taking several more bows. When we returned to our table, two beautiful showgirls were waiting for us, one with a bucket of ice and the other with a bottle of champagne. We were startled by the presentation and even more so by the double-cheek kisses we received (especially on my part) from the gorgeous young girls. A shapely blond-headed Can-Can dancer (the other one was a redhead), said in perfect English, "Compliments of the management and Moulin Rouge." They popped the cork and poured us the bubbly. I suggested that they also share the wine with our table guests, which they did and we toasted each other in our various languages: Good Luck, Arigoto, and Gracias. We received two more double-cheek kisses; I got two great hugs, lucky me, and then the two gorgeous girls disappeared (sigh).

We left the "Rouge" and accepted the handshakes and pats on the back that many of the patrons so generously gave us. We boarded our bus and while resting, I kept saying to myself, "What a night." I never expected in my wildest dreams to have an evening so filled with excitement and camaraderie with people from around the world. Who would have imagined that we would be part of the night's program? We decided before retiring that we would spend the next day taking a boat ride on the Seine River and then explore the Left Bank. We kissed, said goodnight, and away I went into my tango-dream-world.

Below is a picture of Barbara and me doing an Argentine tango at the Fox Hollow Country Club in Woodbury, New York (not at the Moulin Rouge). The picture was taken by my son, Stephen Bivona, and I'm proud to present it here:

The next morning, we jumped out of bed, showered, dressed, and then I waited for an additional half hour until Barbara added finishing touches to her beauty. When she was satisfied that we were presentable enough to face the outside world, we left and went directly to the Metro for another rendezvous with an Iron Mistress. We paid the maiden so often I was beginning to think of her as more of a mistress than a maiden. After inserting our train passes, she smiled, opened her arms, and allowed us into the railway station. Our ride was short; we got off the train at the Tuileries Station and quickly exited. It didn't take us long to find another wonderful sidewalk café to enjoy our treat. We relaxed and had a leisurely brunch, knowing as we watched the wonderful procession of tourists and Parisians parade by, that we had plenty of time before we boarded our sightseeing boat for a morning cruise down the famous Seine River. We didn't rush our feast and just laid back and enjoyed the special sights and the clear Parisian morning air that surrounded us.

We boarded our glass-covered ship, *le Bateau Mouches*, which was only an arm's length from the Eiffel Tower. The ship carried over 300 passengers, but was laid out so that everyone had a decent view of the waterway. We immediately found a seat that would give us a good view of the sights on the Seine River. Fortunately, the weather was cooperating with our plans as it was one of those days where, "On a clear day, you could see forever." Our boat was equipped with a text display and an audio announcement system synchronized to the boat's movement that provided commentary, in several languages, on the passing sights through respective earphones. The system informed us that the Seine River has been Paris's source of protein since the days the *Parisii* tribe first established a fishing village on the *Ile de la Cite*, between 250 and 200 BCE. Since the days of the Roman Empire, it prospered through extensive river trading beginning in Northern France and linking the Loire, Rhine, and Rhone Rivers, extending almost 500 miles, and finally flowing out to the English Channel. The area around the *Ile de la Cite* boasts some of the world's oldest and most majestic historical monuments, which we were about to see from the vantage point of 80 feet above sea level, which is quite different from our previous experiences from high structures with panoramic views; we enjoyed looking at one building at a time as we traveled along the river. It enabled us to study the structures and neighborhoods from quite a different perspective—not from on high but from the street level.

Our voyage began at the Eiffel Tower and passed the *Grand Palais, Concorde, Louvre, Musee* d'Orsay, *Notre Dame*, and my favorite, the *Statue of Liberty.* Wait a minute, "What was the Statue of Liberty doing on the Seine River in Paris?" The information came forthwith from our high-tech electronic docent. In 1889, Americans living in Paris donated a small replica of the New York Statue of Liberty (there are numerous other replicas around the world) to the city of Paris in appreciation of France's gift of the original statue to the United States. The statue is identical in detail to her big sister, except it is about one-fifth the size (36 feet, not including a pedestal of about the same size) of the New York version. What a glorious sight it was to see the world-renowned symbol of freedom proudly displayed by one of the countries that was instrumental in our success during America's Revolutionary War. The Lady was located on its own *Isle de Grenelle,* next to the *Pont de Grenelle Bridge* that connects the Right and Left Banks or 15th and 16th Arrondissements.

One of the highlights of the cruise was experiencing the same places and seeing the same landscapes that inspired many of the 19th century artists beautiful paintings. The 19th century Impressionist artists—Édouard Manet, Camille Pissaro, Edgar Degas, Alfred Sisley, Claude Monet, Berthe Morisot, and Pierre Auguste Renoir—all loved painting the surrounding landscapes, with or without people. The Impressionist art movement started as a group of Paris-based artists began publicly displaying their paintings in the 1860s; the movement got its name from Claude Monet's painting, *Impression, Sunrise.* We traveled some of the same routes that his famous boat-studio floated by, while he painted the activity on the river and its landscapes, which are beautifully reflected in his celebrated painting of his boat on the river in *Le bateau Atelier (*Floating Boat Studio).

One of Monet's best friends was Pierre Auguste Renoir, with whom he worked closely during the 1860s. Renoir also loved boats, landscapes, nature, and portraits; they became painting buddies for many years, copying each other's styles just for the fun of it and defying anyone to tell the difference. It's amazing that all of these talented artists arrived in Paris at about the same time, knew each other, learned from each other's styles, and produced, in my opinion, some of the most beautiful paintings in existence. My favorite is one of Renoir's people paintings the *Bal au Moulin de la Galette Montmartre* (Dance at Le Moulin de la Galette), which is an open-air scene of a popular dance garden on the *Butte Montmartre.* Evidently, I'm not the only one that loves the painting, as it recently sold for $78 million.

What a fulfilling day of sailing along a magnificent waterway, and to actually see so many of the places that were stored in my memory come alive, with an added bonus of having the electronic docent's dialogue not only refresh my recollection of many of the sights and stories, but to add and fill in information that I had forgotten or wasn't aware of. What a wonderful learning experience. We disembarked and headed for the fabled Latin Quarter for a late lunch.

I wondered why an area in France was called the Latin Quarter. I checked my French dictionary and found that it derived its name from the world-famous Sorbonne University, where Latin was the common language for all students during the Middle Ages, and hence, the name Latin Quarter. We found a quaint sidewalk café with lots of pedestrian traffic on the *rue Mouffetard Street,* which is a primary artery where shops, international restaurants, student bars, and cafés were in abundance. We enjoyed a wonderful French soufflé, a glass of wine, good conversation, and my favorite: watching the girls, oops, I mean, people, go by. We spent a couple of hours walking around the neighborhood exploring the shops and admiring, up close, the incredible architecture and designs on the buildings. I was interested in the friezes on the building, while Barbara was more interested in what was inside them. We decided it would be nice just to spend the rest of the afternoon walking around and having dinner at a local restaurant.

For some reason, Barbara was pushing me toward the bridge that led to the Right Bank, and although I was enjoying the left side of the Seine River, I acquiesced as usual, and we meandered over to the Right Bank. As we were crossing the footbridge, she began walking at a quicker pace and I began wondering what she knew that I didn't. Something was drawing her like a magnet to the *rue du Faubourg St-Honore* street, and then I knew. The great fashion houses of the world were represented in the stores along this street. Her secret designer city map identified all the stores in the area and the high-end clothing sold at each location; they were listed alphabetically in directory order. She didn't tell me, but she had memorized most of the list to be used when the occasion arose. She had all the information needed for her to spend the day in paradise. She said, "The entire world looks to Paris as the Grande Dame of Haute Couture and although Milan, London, and

New York provided serious competition, the French designers were still every American girl's dream when it comes to clothing." I felt my wallet and bank account deflating at a very rapid pace. I didn't recall my wife as such a *connoisseur* when it came to clothing, but then I realized, of the eleven closets in our home, she occupies seven. She gave me a cryptic history of some of the designer clothing and of the latest fashions as we visited each store, which featured designs by Hermes, Pierre Cardin, Louis Feraud, Yves Saint-Laurent, and Gianni Versace. She even knew that the popular Gucci had its Paris address in the neighborhood. Well, we spent the rest of the afternoon visiting many boutiques and buying some of the latest female fashions. Barbara bought me a Gucci tie, which, to this day, I've only worn once. I was surprised when my wife told me that she was buying all the goodies with money she saved for the occasion—lucky me. Our afternoon ended in time for dinner, so we decided to eat at a local French restaurant and experiment with more exciting French cuisine. After dinner, we entered what was becoming the "tunnel of love" due to its easy access and very clear train station directories; we inserted our passes for passage through an Iron Mistress, and returned to our hotel. Before retiring, we decided that our last day in the City of Lights would be spent at the *Chateau de Versailles,* which was a short distance from Paris.

We were up early in the morning and picked up our passes from Pierre to avoid the long lines that he warned us would be at Versailles. As usual, he gave us explicit directions about using the Metro and RER (Reseau Express Regional), which was the train line that would get us to Versailles, which is located on the outskirts of Paris. Our plan was to see the Chateau first and then spend some leisurely time in the gardens. When we arrived, we were awestruck at the size of the palace and its gardens, which seemed to extend as far as the eye can see. We immediately entered the Chateau through a marbled courtyard and into the main palace. Fortunately, audio headgear was available that explained in detail those parts of the palace that we were interested in visiting; we put the equipment to immediate use. The audio docent boasted of the palace being one of the largest in the world with more than 700 rooms, 2,000 windows, 1,250 fireplaces, 67 staircases, and more than 1,800 acres of parks and gardens. In its royal heyday, the palace had entertained princes, courtesans, and ministers and required an army of servants to cater to their needs. Among the main attractions are the royal apartments, which were so opulent it's difficult to comprehend that people occupied them comfortably. An amusing story is that the royalty used the rooms in the winter, but had to abandon them intermittently in the summer months when the stench from their toilets became unbearable. The toilet facilities were hidden behind decorated paneled doors, and although the servants serviced them regularly, when summer approached "all the king's men" and women left until the air cleared and it was aromatically safe to return.

The rooms, noticeably the *Salon de Venus* and the *Salon de Diane,* preserved the austere, marble décor of the 17th century. An interesting statue of Louis XIV (the Sun God) as a Roman Emperor caught our attention and certainly reflected his future plans and ambitions. It's interesting to note, that with all his dreams of a glorious and spiritual reign, one of the things he is most remembered for today is his design of "high heels" for shoes that gave him more height, as he was unhappily only five feet three inches tall. Currently, some women's high-heeled shoes are called French heels or Louis heels.

One of the most fascinating rooms in the palace was the Hall of Mirrors where the Treaty of Versailles was signed by the Allied and Associated Powers (mainly France, Britain, Italy, and the United States) with Germany in 1919 following WWI. This was the room where, due to the harsh terms of the treaty, seeds for WWII were planted. It's interesting that the magnificent Hall of Mirrors serves as a corridor between the Imperial War Room and the Peace Room, certainly an appropriate place to sign the Peace Treaty finalizing WWI.

Exiting the palace, we both had stiff necks from viewing all the beautiful and decorative ceilings throughout the Chateau. We entered the garden area, where we were overwhelmed with the size of the grounds; how would we begin to explore and enjoy 1800 acres plus additional small palaces in one day? Well, the answer was simple. We boarded a little glass-sided train that ran through the gardens, making stops at the Grand Trianon and Petite Trianon Palaces and other points of interest. It allowed us the opportunity to appreciate the adventure, while sitting down and giving our feet and necks well-deserved rests.

The garden's beauty is beyond description; when admiring them from the main palace's upper floors, the panoramic view is breathtaking; it appeared as a multicolored painting. When looking at the gardens from the ground level, the perspective changes to one of individual beauty and artistic accomplishments. The grounds are laid out geometrically around a main axis, creating pathways and circular and semi-circular pools called basins. Everything is symmetrical and staggered on several levels. Trees were pruned to create a veritable design of vegetation. Closer to the Main Palace were flowerbeds that complemented the designs' features, especially when viewed from the upper floors of the main palace. One of our favorite sites was the *Neptune Fountains* and its water-jetting scene; it seemed as if music was being played by the jetting water hitting the pond. While walking around the fountain, the sound of the music changed, and if one listened closely, and with a little imagination, a familiar melody can be created in one's mind. The *Orangerie Garden* is a gardener's delight. It was started in 1684 to protect the oranges and oleanders in cold weather. Six grassy lawns are defined around a large round basin by double hedges of boxes with multicolored flowers between them. What else can be said about the most beautifully created and maintained gardens in the world? It's no wonder that the king's head gardener and botanist, Le Notre, took 40 years to complete the formal gardens, fountains, jet waterfalls, statues, water flowers, Grand Perspective, and Grand Canal.

Our first stop on the glass train was the Grand Trianon Palace, built by Louis XIV as a hideaway for him and his family from the hectic court, which he had moved from Paris to the Chateau to escape from the unruly Parisians. After the demise of the French Monarchy, the Grand Trianon (called so after the Petit Trianon was built nearby by Louis XV) was occupied by Napoleon from 1805 to 1815 and today is used by the French president when entertaining foreign officials. As a matter of fact, the "Treaty of Trianon" between the Allied countries and Austria-Hungary concluding WWI was signed at the palace. Hungary lost over two-thirds of its empire at the signing, which resulted in territorial adjustments establishing Romania, Czechoslovakia, and the Kingdom of Serbs, Croats, and Slovenes. Although the gardens at the palace are not as elaborate as those of its big sister, the floral arrangement and decorations are certainly worth mentioning. The orange trees, floral flowerbeds, and the smell of jasmine combine to give a calming effect that sort of slows one's pace down to a slow stroll. It was getting late, so we didn't have an opportunity to explore and spend more time in the magnificent garden, but hurried on to the beautiful pink-marbled Grand Trianon Palace. Our audio equipment came in handy, as we only stopped at places of interest and received all the information necessary to satisfy us. It's worth mentioning that Louis XV used this palace and its beautiful botanical gardens to rendezvous and stroll through the menagerie with his mistress, Madam de Pompadour. The madam eventually tired of the palace and convinced the king to build her a palace of her own. He agreed, and the Petit Trianon Chateau went to the drawing board. The Petit Trianon Chateau has a colorful romantic history. The idea for the Chateau was conceived by Madam de Pompadour, but she never lived to see its completion. Instead, it was subsequently occupied by her replacement, the king's new mistress, Madame du Barry. Upon his death and the accession to the throne by the 20-year-old Louis XVI, this Chateau and the surrounding park were given to the new king's 19-year-old wife, Queen Marie Antoinette of Austria, whom he married when she was 14 years old. Our audio docent informed us that she used the palace to escape from the formality and burden of her royal responsibilities. She further alienated herself by making it difficult for anyone to enter the palace without her permission, which she gave very sparingly; this policy also applied to her husband, the king. She immediately began redecorating the Chateau to her own taste, with no cost spared, to make her feel at home in the "Little Chateau." In contrast to the formal, symmetrical French gardens that Versailles was renowned for, she commissioned a complete overhaul in her gardens, featuring meandering paths, hills and streams, and on an island, a small neo-Classical *Temple of Love,* commemorating her marriage to the king. A mock farming village, called *Le Petit Hameau* (The Little Hamlet), completed the rustic area of the Versailles grounds.

Le Petit Trianon is considered one of the most beautiful buildings in France. The exterior of the palace is simple and inviting. On the inside, it's difficult to determine the original decorating from Marie

Antoinette's intrusion. The extensive woodwork and carvings are from the original building, but the most impressive site is her boudoir featuring mirrored panels, which can be raised or lowered to hide the windows. Her bedroom is quite simple, with more attention paid to securing her privacy than to artistic design. Time was limited, so we exited and were frustrated that we couldn't explore more of the beautiful palace and the awe-inspiring grounds. Exhausted, we headed for the train station for our return trip back to Paris. We promised each other that we would return to the magnificent palace in the future, and spend considerably more time exploring man and nature's combined successful creations.

We arrived at our hotel in time to refresh, and quickly walked the few blocks to our favorite Italian-French-Jewish kosher restaurant. As it was our last night in Paris, we ordered an expensive bottle of wine; I intentionally went through the ritual of wine tasting at a very slow pace to savor the moment. We again ordered pasta smothered with eggplant; its taste was out of this world, which encouraged us to savor the flavor and our last moments in Paris.

We arose early in the morning to catch our flight to Naples, Italy, to meet our Smithsonian Institute tour members and continue our adventure. As I looked out the window of the plane, I could see Paris in all its glory. We both promised her we would return. She smiled at us, and as we gained altitude and distance, she disappeared from our sight, but not our minds or hearts. No doubt, we will surely meet again, and without a doubt, dance a tango once more, at the Moulin Rouge.

Chapter Five – From Paris to Italy

Looking down at Naples through the plane's window, I couldn't help but reflect that my mother's parents came from this city at the end of the 19th century. How times have changed. We were flying, at our leisure, by choice, to Italy for an extended vacation. My ancestors fled Italy in desperation to the U.S. in search of a better life, leaving behind generations of family history, traditions, and their loved ones. I imagine that when they boarded the ship to the "Promised Land," their dreams of a better life, decent jobs, peace, and security swelled their hearts with joy, while their tears reminded them of what they were leaving behind. Here we were two generations later, visiting the very country that my grandparents fled because they were unhappy with their circumstances because they could not visualize a future that offered any relief from their stagnant lives. What a difference: our visit was one of pleasure and relaxation; their exodus was one of desperation, hardship, and hope for a better life. Fortunately, the sacrifices they made by leaving their homeland for an unknown country resulted in most of their dreams becoming realities beyond their expectations, and fortunately for us their dreams became our realities.

We were able to locate the representative of our tour by the huge sign displayed at the arrival waiting area: "Smithsonian Amalfi Coast Tour." What a relief to see our contact waiting for us. All the anxiety and uncertainty of arriving at a new destination, especially in a foreign country, that traveler's experience, disappeared at the sight of that very large sign. Our escort, Concetta, was standing under the sign with what seemed to be an equally large smile on her face. She directed us to the area where our specially tagged luggage would be gathered by her assistant, while we waited. This was another nice experience: no searching for luggage, especially in a foreign airport where finding one's baggage is one problem, but communicating with someone if the baggage is misplaced or lost is, without a doubt, a nightmare. The assistant retrieved our luggage and placed it in a holding area, along with the baggage of several other tour members. Within an hour, we were on a small bus and on our way to our home for the next few days: the Bellevue Syrene Hotel, in Sorrento, *Italia.*

The hotel occupies a prime location at the seaside; it's on a clifftop overlooking the Bay of Naples with a view of *Isola de Capri.* It's also next to the reconstruction of a Pompeiin villa, which depicts a fascinating insight to the region's ancient history. The hotel's foundation was a Roman villa dating back to the 2nd century BCE, and after several reconstructions, it was transformed into the Bellevue Syrene Hotel. The name "Syrene" refers to the sirens from Homer's Odyssey, but certainly can be indicative of the serene atmosphere of the hotel and its surroundings. Getting to the hotel in our small bus was quite an experience. The driver had to maneuver up a winding hill that could not accommodate our bus and a passing vehicle coming from the opposite direction at the same time. The Italian drivers have a unique system of horn blowing, utilizing every inch of the road while praying. Traveling up the winding road leading to our hotel, our driver would blow his horn when coming to a curve in the road. If there was no horn response from a vehicle coming from the opposite direction, then he would proceed up the winding hill. If there was a horn response, then by some magical signal, one of the vehicles would squeeze over to the side of the road allowing the other to pass. As passengers, we did lots of praying, but the driver's unique skill in handling the bus got us to our destination safely. This whole scenario reminded me of some years ago when we were touring Rome, on a normal-size bus, and the driver couldn't make a left turn into a side street because a small car was parked close to the intersection blocking the passage. He exited the bus and volunteered three male pedestrians to help him lift, with small jerking movements, the small vehicle onto the sidewalk until there was enough room for the bus to pass. When he passed the car, the driver exited again and he and his three helpers jockeyed the car back to its original place on the street.

Italian drivers are without a doubt unique, and creative in the maneuvering of their vehicles.

The hotel in Sorrento adjoins the Piazza Vittoria that complements its 18th century architecture, which, fortunately, has not been damaged through the hotel's many restorations. Its 18th century antique frescos blended into the surroundings, enhancing its original style and justifying the hotel's listing as one of Italy's historic places. Especially attractive are its terraces that face the Bay of Naples, offering breathtaking views of the pristine blue-green water and the various boat occupants that combine to make a picture-perfect scene. There is a small elevator that provides access to the beach area and to a magnificent spa midway down the cliff. The spa includes a Roman bath built into the rocks on the side of the cliff, a pool with hydro massages, and a relaxing sauna. We put all of the health-related venues to good use as soon as we showered and changed into our bathing suits.

Before dinner, we had a cocktail party for our group of 30-plus travelers and met our Smithsonian coordinator, docent, and driver. The tour leader-docent, Fran, briefly gave us an overview of our schedule for the Amalfi Coast trip and took the opportunity to have each member introduce themselves. She reminded us that this was primarily an outdoor tour and that we should be prepared for some strenuous walking and climbing. Just what Barbara wanted to hear! Her geological antenna was up, as she couldn't wait to explore and dig—an amateur geologist's dream.

After the meeting, we proceeded to dinner at the hotel restaurant and were seated at a window with a view of the Bay of Naples, Mt. Vesuvius at a distance, fishermen attending their catch of the day, and beautiful glimmering islands in the distance. We were fortunate to share a table with two members of our tour, Shirley and Dallas Peck, from the great southern state of Virginia. Dallas was the Director of the U.S. Geological Survey and one of the world's foremost geologists, specializing in volcanic eruptions—which happens to be one of Barbara's passions, in addition to her digging holes and discovering rocks. We became fast friends and spent most of the trip with them, enjoying their camaraderie and their wonderful ability to tell amusing and fascinating stories, such as:

> They were both widowed and working for the U.S. Geological Survey (U.S.G.S.). As he was the director of the organization, he had a privileged parking spot: number one in the parking field. After seeing Dallas at some business functions and learning he was a bachelor, Shirley, a secretary at U.S.G.S., decided that he was the man for her, so she arrived very early one morning and parked her car in his parking space. She was immediately called into the personnel director's office and reprimanded for her poor judgment, and told to move her vehicle immediately to her usual place in the vast area at the back of the parking field. The next morning, arriving early again, she parked in his number one spot for the second time; this time Dallas told the security guard that he wanted to meet the perpetrator who had the audacity to park in his sacred spot, so he could personally discharge that person. So the redheaded Shirley, with a smile on her pretty face and dressed for the occasion, entered Dallas's office to get her discharge papers. Instead, after salivating for a few seconds, he told the security guard to leave and asked Shirley if she would like a cup of coffee.

The rest is history: her gamble paid off and a year later, they were married.

After dinner, our tour group met for additional orientation with Fran who discussed what to expect the next day on our visit to the ruins of the ancient city of Pompeii. She related in detail the history, excavation, salvaging, and reconstruction of the one-time great city. The Smithsonian Institute's tours usually have an instructor with credentials accompanying them, which makes traveling to historic places all the more interesting. The hour-long lecture and distribution of material covering various topics of interest to the members of the tour also gave us an opportunity to ask questions and to really delve into the next day's planned activities. After the meeting, we retired for the night in anticipation of awakening to an exciting journey the following day.

After breakfast, we boarded our tour bus for the short trip to the ancient city of Pompeii. While looking at the remains of this once great city, it's impossible to absorb or comprehend the complexity of the destruction immediately. It required much thought and imagination to envision the city as it once was before its earthquakes and volcanic eruptions. While we were pondering the unbelievable site, Fran wisely recommended that we purchase an inexpensive book that was for sale at the entrance of the city square, which had overlay pages. The pages had the sites as we were experiencing them; when applying overlays of the pages, we could see how the buildings and streets probably looked prior to the time of their destruction beginning on August 24, 79 CE. The cobblestoned streets seemed to be intact, laid out in the usual Roman straight line crisscross grid formation, making it easy to envision what the original city streets looked like. Walking on the stones of the streets where ancient Romans traveled enhanced the feeling of being a part of the city thousands of years ago. The literature we received the previous night described how the "volcano collapsed higher roof-lines and buried Pompeii under many meters of ash and pumice." Pompeii, along with its sister city, Herculaneum, and other smaller cities located at the base of Mt. Vesuvius all experienced the same fate: total destruction. Fran guided us through the remains of the Forum, the *Macellum* (great food market), the *Pistrinum* (mill), the *Thermopolium* (a bar that served beverages), and the *Cauponae* (small restaurant). We also visited an amphitheater and two smaller theaters, but everyone's favorite was *The Lupnara*, from the Latin world *lupa* for prostitute, which was a two-story brothel. Its rooms displayed frescoes depicting the services being offered to customers. Our group seemed to have spent more time in this building than we did on the whole day's outing. But it was lots of fun and amusing, to say the least. The most memorable sights were the mummified bodies of the Pompeian's that were immortalized by the layers of molten ash from the volcano, which kept their remains almost intact, going about their daily routines, unaware of the calamity that was to befall them. The populations of the combined cities at the base of Mt. Vesuvius were estimated to be about 30,000 to 40,000 people. Fortunately, most of them escaped during the first signs of the impending destruction, as they had a similar earthquake scare in the year 62 CE, in which much of the infrastructure of the city was destroyed. Still, it is estimated that thousands of people perished, many leaving permanent monuments of themselves in the form of well-preserved skeletons. Fran's in-depth knowledge and explanations of the sites we visited made the whole experience exciting and helped us to envision what life was like during the heyday of this great ancient city, and of the day of its demise.

Considering that the event occurred almost 2,000 years ago, I asked Fran where all the detailed information about the destruction of the city came from. She had a ready answer: "Pliny the Younger, who was the 16-year-old nephew of Pliny the Elder, was eyewitness to the two-day catastrophic volcanic eruption of Mt. Vesuvius that destroyed and buried the cities at the base of the volcano." She didn't go into detail about his two famous letters, as they were quite long and covered the event in great detail, but she gave us enough information so that we had a good understanding of what happened on those horrific days. Fran also distributed material to those of us who were interested in the details of Pliny's letters, which I was happy to receive. The contents of the two letters were written by the young man who witnessed an eruption column estimated to be 20 miles tall, from his perch on a hillside in the town of Misenum, across the bay from Mt. Vesuvius. I couldn't wait to read the details of what else he witnessed.

When we returned to our hotel in the late afternoon after a very fulfilling day, I read all the fascinating material that she gave me, and learned that Pliny the Younger, in addition to writing his two famous letters about the horrible event that took place in 79 CE, was also a prolific writer, poet, author of many books, and a natural philosopher of ancient Rome. He was counsel to Emperor Trajan, a Roman Senator, and held many high government offices throughout his life. His second letter about the eruption was written some 25 years after the event, focusing on his uncle's brave mission of discovery and rescue on those eventful days.

His uncle, Pliny the Elder, personified Roman intellect. He is regarded with the highest honors for literature, next to Homer, Cicero, and Virgil. His writing included *History of His Times*, a 31-book collection extending from the reign of Nero to that of Vespasian; the *Naturalis Historia,* a 160-volume encyclopedia, into which he collected much of the knowledge of his time; and 20 books on the *History of the German Wars.* In addition to being a renowned author, he was a naturalist or natural philosopher, and a naval and military commander of some importance. It was in his capacity as the Commander of the Roman Fleet at Misenum and his innate curiosity about nature that brought his life to a sudden end. During the volcanic eruptions, he took some of his ships to investigate and observe the phenomenon personally and to also rescue some of his friends from their perilous position on the shore of the Bay of Naples in the town of Stabiae. His nephew's second letter states:

> The eruption can be compared in appearance to a stone pine tree; for it shot up to a great height in the form of a tall trunk, which spread out at the top as branches. Occasionally it was brighter and occasionally darker and spotted, as it was either more or less filled with earth and cinders. Several earth tremors were felt at the time of the eruption and were followed by a very violent shaking of the ground, the ash was falling in very thick sheets and the sun was blocked out by the eruption, and daylight hours were left in darkness. Also, the sea was sucked away and forced back by an earthquake (a phenomenon now called a tsunami).

It was under these conditions that the Elder ventured out to "search, investigate, and rescue." The Younger continues:

> He set off across the bay, but encountered thick showers of hot cinders, lumps of pumice and pieces of rock which, altering the shoreline and water depths, blocked his approach to the shore and prevented him from landing at his destination. The prevailing southerly wind also stopped him, but he continued south to Stabiae, where he landed and took shelter with Pomponianus, a friend. Pomponianus had already loaded a ship with possessions and was preparing to leave, but the wind was against him. Pliny the Elder and his party saw flames coming from several parts of the mountain, which would later destroy Pompeii. After staying overnight, the party decided to evacuate in spite of the rain of ash and because of the continuing violent conditions threatening to collapse the building they occupied. Pliny, Pomponianus, and their

> companions made their way back toward the beach with pillows tied to their heads to protect them from falling rocks. By this time, there was so much ash in the air that the party could barely see through the murk and needed torches and lanterns to find their way. They made it to the beach but found the waters too violently disturbed from the continuous earthquakes for them to escape safely by sea. It is here that Pliny the Elder died.

He is remembered in vulcanology, where the term "plinian" (or plinean) refers to a very violent eruption of a volcano marked by columns of smoke and ash extending high into the stratosphere. The term ultra-plinian is reserved for the most violent type of plinian eruptions. What an amazing piece of history: eye witnessed, written, and forwarded down through the ages so that we could understand and learn from that unfortunate event. With some imagination, while reading this material, I was transported back in time. I felt that I was a part of those two horrendous days, if only briefly, that occurred almost 2,000 years ago.

After dinner, our group met for our evening orientation with Fran. She discussed what we would be seeing the next day at Herculaneum, the second-largest city to be destroyed by the eruptions. After exploring the city, time permitting, we would then have an opportunity to scout around the base of Mt. Vesuvius. We retired to our room early after an exhausting day in the field, which gave us an opportunity to read the material that Fran had distributed at the lecture about the city of Herculaneum.

We woke early the next morning, and had our usual delicious hot and cold buffet breakfast before boarding our bus for the short ride to Herculaneum. The city was established around the end of the 8th century BCE by the Oscan tribes from the Italian mainland. Although Pompeii and Herculaneum were destroyed by the same eruptions, the condition of Herculaneum after its partial excavation was quite different than its sister city. Whereas most of Pompeii's building's roofs were destroyed during the event, the buildings in Herculaneum remained almost intact. The reason is that the first eruption began spewing ash and volcanic stones into the sky. When it reached the boundary between the troposphere (extending 6 to 12 miles above the earth's surface) and the stratosphere (30 miles above the earth's surface), the top of the cloud flattened, leading Pliny to describe it as a "stone pine tree." The prevailing winds blew towards the southeast, which caused the volcanic material to fall on the city of Pompeii and the surrounding area, causing the roofs in the city to collapse under the weight of the falling debris. Herculaneum lay to the west of Vesuvius, and was only mildly affected by the first phase of the eruption. Fortunately, the first event caused most of the inhabitants of the small city to evacuate, which, in turn, resulted in less loss of life than in Pompeii. It's believed that the loss of life in Pompeii was in the thousands and its smaller sister city in the hundreds. According to the U. S. Geological Survey's research:

> The amazing good state of preservation of the structures and their contents is due to three factors: (1) by the time the wind changed and ash began to fall on Herculaneum, the structures were already filled with debris; thus, the roofs did not collapse. (2) The intense heat of the first pyroclastic flow carbonized the surface of organic material and extracted the water from them, and (3), a deep dense volcanic tuff formed an airtight seal over Herculaneum for almost 1,700 years.

Excavation began at the modern city of *Ercolano* (a modern version of the original city's name) in 1738; however, excavation ceased once the nearby town of Pompeii was discovered, which was significantly easier to excavate due to the reduced amount of debris covering the site, 16 feet versus 60 feet. In the 20th century, excavation resumed in the city and, as it was submerged in a mass of volcanic mud that sealed and preserved wood and other materials, much of what was discovered was in situ (its original place and form). Although the city was much smaller than Pompeii, its intact remains make it a more dramatic sight; tourists walking around and exploring gave us a good idea of what the original living city must have looked like. Some of the excavated city lies about 60 feet below the modern city of *Ercolano,* giving the site a panoramic effect of a "before and after" picture of what the city looked like in all its glory in 79 CE and its current condition as a tourist destination in the 21st century. In the meantime, the monster Mt. Vesuvius was still lurking in the background, smirking at the people who had the audacity to build on the very site it destroyed almost 2,000 years ago. Many of our group discussed why people would build a new city at the very place that once was destroyed by a natural disaster, especially when the monster was still a living and breathing threat. We couldn't come up with a logical explanation, undoubtedly, because we were not native Italians and didn't possess their passion for the land and country.

Fran guided us through what seemed to be a living city, with buildings, marbled floors, frescos, and furniture in situ. The most famous of the luxurious buildings, to date, is the *Villa of the Papyri.* It was given its name due to the 1,800 carbonized scrolls that were discovered in the early excavations, which are now located at the National Library in Naples for further evaluation. The villa was the seashore retreat for Lucius Calpurnius Piso Caesoninus, Julius Caesar's father-in-law. It stretches down toward the sea in four terraces. He was a literate man who patronized poets and philosophers, which explains the enormous library that was located in his villa, including the 1,800 scrolls. The most gruesome site of the city was the *fornici* (storehouses), where about 300 skeletons were excavated, all in their sleeping positions as they met their terrible demise. One interesting skeleton is called the "Ring Lady," named for the unusual rings still remaining on her displayed fingers extending from her mummified body.

Although Herculaneum had only a quarter of the population of Pompeii, with about 5,000 residents, it was considered a wealthier resort, where the royalty lived and played; it even had a-state-of-the-times sports stadium. The large *Palaestra* (stadium) was where a variety of ball games, wrestling matches, and other sports activities were staged and enjoyed by the populace. It was startling to see only a few of the estimated 20 peristyle columns of the sports arena; the remaining columns are still preserved under solidified volcanic mud beneath the city of *Ercolano.* One has to wonder how much of the ancient city will never be uncovered and will remain buried and a continued mystery, beneath its modern counterpart.

After lunch, we gathered for our planned visit to Mt. Vesuvius. Unfortunately, there were heavy dark rain clouds over the monster, so Fran decided to detour to the *Phlegraean Fields* instead, which lies mostly underwater just west of Naples along the Bay. The field's name literally means burning fields, and refers to the highly volcanic nature of the area, certainly a great place to stop and explore remnants of earthquakes and volcanic eruptions. Our destination was the town of *Pozzuoli,* where the *Solfatara Crater,* the mythological home of the Roman god of fire, *Vulcan,* is located. *Solfatara* is a shallow volcanic crater, and although dormant, its ground is hot to the touch and emits jets of steam and sulfuric fumes. The name comes from the Latin, *sulpha terra* (land of sulfur). Fumaroles, which are vents in a volcanic area that emit steam and hot gases, and boiling pools of mud made the site surreal. When we reached the crater, Barbara and Dallas got so excited that they both raced ahead of our group, as if they were sprinting in a race. I thought that they were going to jump into the mud pools and enjoy an unexpected bath, but they were saved by the yellow tape that cordoned off the boiling mud baths to prevent such ventures. The smell of sulfur was so overwhelmingly obnoxious that most of our group remained at a distance, including me and Shirley; our reaction was to cover our noses and let out "eeew" sounds, while Barbara and Dallas inhaled the odor and responded with "ahhs." The smell was, without a doubt, the combination of rotten eggs, plus some indescribable offensive mixture of chemicals. The less adventurous members went into the 16th century *Sanctuary of San Gennaro,* built at the site of his martyrdom, which was near the entrance to the crater. Inside was a stone believed to have been stained with his blood that turns bright red and liquefies on his annual celebration in Naples. We then spent some time enjoying and taking pictures of the Greek and Roman ruins in the nearby surrounding area, which were, surprisingly, in disrepair. Due to the overwhelming stench of the place, we coaxed Fran to terminate the visit to Vulcan's home and head back to Syrene for well-deserved rests, aromatic baths, and showers to get the unpleasant smell of the place out of our nostrils and clothing. After much persuasion, but some resistance, Barbara and Dallas finally decided to join the group for the return trip. On the bus ride back, Fran went over some details for the following day's trip to the *Isle of Capri* and handed out literature, including street maps, about the history and geography of the "Magnificent Island in the sun." She then told us that we were free to have dinner on our own that evening. The four of us decided to have a relaxing evening in the town of Sorrento, which was a short walk from our hotel. The slow bus ride back to our hotel was a well-deserved respite, and gave me an opportunity to reflect on what I had seen over the last couple of days. Although it's exciting to go from textbook experiences to the actual places where ancient history existed and was written, visiting Mt. Vesuvius, Pompeii, and Herculaneum was bittersweet. All of the sites dealt with death and destruction, and I was happy that we were leaving behind those memories and continuing on to, hopefully, more pleasant adventures.

After refreshing ourselves, we met at the Piazza del Vittoria outside the hotel and strolled to *Corso Italia,* the main street in Sorrento, enjoying the sights along the narrow streets and the many touristy shops along the way. The town was buzzing with tourists, so we searched for a sidewalk café with available seating and good views of the promenade of tourists shopping in the varied shops and enjoying the abundance of restaurants. One restaurant in particular caught our attention; it was an English pub populated by English-speaking tourists enjoying themselves playing the game of darts, and for a moment, I was transported from Italy to England. It was strange, but we all had the same experience. The predominant language heard while walking and viewing the shops and restaurants was English; it seemed that most of the tourists and locals spoke that language. We were pleased to find a sidewalk café playing local Neapolitan love songs, where the waiters spoke Italian, and English only when necessary, giving us back the feeling of being in Italy. Both girls ordered gnocchi potato pasta with marinara sauce, and raved it was the best pasta and sauce they ever had. Dallas and I ordered pasta with local buffalo mozzarella spread over the top, complemented with eggplant in a meat sauce that was absolutely out of this world. We nursed our dinner with wine, espresso, and desserts so we could linger on and enjoy the music and festivities that were taking place in the square. Musicians were serenading the tourists and dancers were displaying their local talents and showing off their bright and colorful Neapolitan outfits. Some dancers came to our table and coaxed us to join them in their revelry; Dallas wouldn't budge, but the rest of us ran out to join the dancing. We formed a circle with Barbara and Shirley at my side and danced to a Neapolitan *Tarantella,* which is a quick-motioned dance with lots of turns and kicks. We truly "could have danced all night," but the half hour we did was out of a fairy tale, with dancing and singing, and then singing and dancing some more. The whole experience was reminiscent of my family's parties when I was a young boy. Relatives would gather to celebrate a worthy occasion and, invariably, ended up singing and dancing in a circle led by my lively grandmother, Angelina, and my beautiful mother, Margaret. When the dancing in the square ended, the music continued and everyone around the square joined the chorus and sang *"Torna A Sorriento"* (Return to Sorrento). Few of us knew all the words, but humming the tune gave us the same wonderful exhilarating feeling. I loved the song so much that I had to find out what the lyrics were. After some passionate research, I came up with Italian and English versions, which were written by the brothers, Giambatista and Ernesto De Curtis, in 1902, as follows:

TORNA A SURRIENTO (De Curtis)
(Italian)
Vide 'o mare quant'è bello!
Spira tantu sentimento,
Comme tu a chi tiene mente,
Ca scetato 'o faie sunnà.
Guarda, gua', chistu ciardino:
Siente, siè' sti sciure arance;
Nu profumo accussì fino
Dinto 'o core se ne va . . .

E tu dice: "I' parto, addio!"
T'alluntane a stu core,
Da sta terra de l'ammore . . .
Tiene 'o core 'e nun turnà?
Ma nun me lassà,
Nun darme stu turmiento!
Torna a Surriento,
Famme campà!

Vide 'o mare de Surriento,
Che tesoro tene 'nfunno;
Chi ha girato tutto 'o munno
Nun l'ha visto comm'a ccà.
Guarda attuorno sti Sserene,
Ca te guardano 'ncantate
E te vonno tantu bene . . .
Te vulessero vasà.
E tu dice: "I' parto, addio!" ***ecc.***

TORNA A SURRIENTO (Come back to Sorrento)
(English)
See the beauty of the waters!
How it plucks the very heartstrings!
'Tis like you, whose glance seduces,
though awake, to think we dream!
Look, O look upon this garden,
smell the scent of orange blossoms,
scent so sweet it winds its tendrils
round about the inmost heart . . .

Yet you say: "Farewell, I'm leaving?"
You'd desert these loving arms
and this very land of love . . .
Could you mean not to return?
Go not away from me,
break not my heart with sorrow!
Come back to Sorrento,
that I may live!

See the waves that lap Sorrento,
'tis in truth a jewel they cherish;
those who've never traveled far have never
seen its like in all the world.
See these sirens round about you,
gazing at you with enchantment
loving you so much and longing
to bestow a fleeting kiss.
Yet you say: "Farewell, I'm leaving!" ***etc.***

We ended the festivities singing another Neapolitan favorite, *"Funiculi Funicular."* This song has always puzzled me. Everyone enjoys the liveliness of the music, but there seems to be lots of confusion as to the lyrics. While I was in the mood, I decided to research this song as well.

It was written in 1880 by Peppino Turco and set to music by the Italian composer Luigi Denza. It was written to commemorate the opening of the first funicular on Mt. Vesuvius. The Italian version, with an English translation follows:

FUNICULI FUNICULA (Denza) ***(Italian)***
Coro:
Jammo, jammo, ncoppa, jammo ja, *(rip.)*
Funiculì funiculà funiculì funiculà,
ncoppa jammo jà, funiculì funiculà.

Solo:
Aissera, Nanninè, me ne sagliette,
tu saie addò? *(rip. dal Coro)*
Addò, sto core ngrato chiù di spiete;
Farme non pò! *(rip.)*
Addò, llo fuoco coce ma si fuje.
Te lasso stà. *(rip.)*
E non te corre appriesso, non te struje,
Sulo a guardà. *(rip.)*

Jammo, jammo, ncoppa, jàmmo jà *(rip.)*
Funiculì funiculà funiculì funiculà,
Jammo, jammo, jà, funiculì funiculà!

Coro:
Jammo, jammo, ncoppa, jammo jà, *ecc.*

Solo:
Se n'è sagliuta, oïe Nè, se n'è sagliuta,
La capa già; *(rip.)*
E ghiuta, pò è tornata, e po' è venuta . . .
Sta sempe ccà! *(rip.)*
La capa vota vota attuorno, attuorno,
Attuorno a te, *(rip.)*
Llo core canta, sempe no taluorno,
Sposammo, oïe Nè! *(rip.)*

Jammo, jammo, ncoppa, jammo jà *(rip.)*
Funiculì funiculà funiculì funiculà,
Jammo, jammo, jà, funiculì funiculà!

Coro:
Jammo, jammo, ncoppa, jàmmo jà *(rip.)*

Solo, poi tutti
Funiculì funiculà funiculì funiculà, *ecc.*

FUNICULI FUNICULA ***(English)***
Chorus:
Come on, come on, to the top we'll go! *(rep.)*
Funiculi, *etc.*
To the top we'll go, funiculi.

Solo:
I went up this evening, Nanetta,
do you know where? *(rep. by Chorus)*
Where your hard heart can't reach
with scornful wiles! *(rep.)*
Where the fire burns, but if you run
you can escape it. *(rep.)*
It doesn't chase you nor destroy you
just by a look. *(rep.)*

Come on, come on, to the top we'll go! *(rep.)*
Funiculi, *etc.*
To the top we'll go, funiculi, funicula!

Chorus:
Come on, *etc.*

Solo:
It's climbed aloft, see, climbed aloft now,
right to the top.
It went, and turned, and came back down . . .
And now it's stopped!
The top is turning round and round,
around yourself!
My heart sings that on such a day
we should be wed!

Come one, come on, to the top we'll go!
Funiculi, *etc.*
To the top we'll go, funiculi, funicula!

Chorus:
Come on, come on, to the top we'll go!

Solo then All:
Funiculi, funicula funiculi funicula, *etc.*

Now I know that when singing this song, or more likely humming it, that it's about a sad romantic affair and a poor fellow trying to get some lost love out of his system, while traveling up and down in a mountain cable car. This above rendition was sung and was a favorite of the great Italian tenor Luciano Pavarotti. There are many other versions of the song in Italian and English. The more popular American version, "A Merry Life," which most school children learn, goes something like this:

Some think the world is made for fun and frolic, and so do I! And so do I!
Some think it well to be all melancholic, to pine and sigh; to pine and sigh;
But I, I love to spend my time in singing, some joyous song, some joyous song,
To set the air with music bravely ringing is far from wrong! Is far from wrong!
Listen, listen, echoes sound afar! Listen, listen, echoes sound afar!
Funiculi, funicula, funiculi, funicula! Echoes sound afar, funiculi, funicula!
Ah me! 'Tis strange that some should take to sighing, and like it well! And like it well!
For me, I have not thought it worth the trying, so cannot tell! So cannot tell!
With laughter, with dance and song the day soon passes, full soon is gone, full soon is gone!
For mirth was made for joyous lads and lasses, to call their own! To call their own!
Listen, listen, hark the soft guitar! Listen, listen, hark the soft guitar!
Funiculi, funicula, funiculi, funicula! Hark the soft guitar, funiculi, funicula.

Most people prefer the upbeat American version, and so do I! And so do I!

Our beautiful evening ended on a wonderful musical note, which we hummed as we hopped and skipped back to our hotel for a well-deserved night's sleep.

Our bus ride to the ferry docks from Sorrento was brief, but gave me an opportunity to read the literature that Fran had distributed the day before about "The Island in the Sun." She suggested that we pronounce the Island the Italian way "CAH-pree," instead of the American "Capri." If we did, she said, the natives wouldn't suspect that we were tourists. As we reached the docks, an unexpected downpour stranded us on our bus for about an hour, giving me time to catch up on my reading of the history of the Golden Island. It seems, but no one will swear by it, that the island was first inhabited by the ancient Greek people of Teleboi, of the Ionian Islands (no dates available). The etymology of the name is disputed between the Greeks and Italians. The Greeks insist it was named *Kapros,* after the wild boars that inhabited the island, and the Italians claim its name was derived from the Latin *Capreae,* after the goats that resided there. The tour members discussed the differences in the source of the name for about a minute and a half, and decided to relax and enjoy the bus ride rather than exhaust the topic.

When the rain stopped, we quickly exited the bus and went to the departure gate for our ferry crossing to the magnificent island, which took about 40 minutes across the beautiful blue-green water of the Bay of Naples. Fran took the opportunity to review some history of the island and our scheduled day's activities. We settled into our comfortable seats and enjoyed some hot drinks, which helped to get the chill of the day's dampness out of our bones, while Fran gave us a brief history lesson about our destination. There isn't too much documented history of the Greek period, but the Roman era is filled with historically fascinating information, both actual and fanciful:

> Caesar Octavius Augustus, the Roman Emperor, fell in love with his vacation island around 29 CE and, in short order, purchased it from the City of Naples, probably at a very reasonable price. His successor, Caesar Tiberius, moved his seat of power from Rome to the island, and spent ten years ruling the Roman Empire from the remote location. His claim to fame on the island is a cliff named for him called *Tiberius's Fall,* from which he and his successor, Caligula, deposited people that displeased them off the cliff from that high point, onto the rocks and into the water. It's believed that Tiberius built twelve villas on the island, but only remnants of three remain.

The most elaborate and his main residence, Villa Jovis, was one of our scheduled visits, time permitting.

Crossing the Bay of Naples was delightful and comfortable. The sun's beams reflecting and dancing off of the blue-green water were dazzling, and the smell of clean, fresh, saltwater air made my nostrils experience the same wonderful sensation as inhaling the fresh aroma of the first roses of springtime. One of the main features of Capri is the splendid geological formations of the three Faraglioni Rocks along her jagged coast. In ancient Greek and Roman times, fires were maintained on the top of the rocks to assist boats in navigating safely through the treacherous reefs surrounding Capri, which jut out of the water like pyramids. The largest, over 300 feet, is named *Stella,* or Star, and is attached to the island. The second, *de Mezzo,* or middle, is over 240 feet high and has a natural tunnel, roughly 180 feet in length that passes through its center. Many boat tours sail through this large opening to the delight of their passengers. The third is named *Faraglioni di Fuori,* or *Lo Scopolo* (home of the blue-lizard), and is also well over 300 feet high. This rock is one of the few places in the world that has the blue-tinted lizard (*Lacerta Viriden Faraglionesis*) as a tenant, hence the name of the formation, *Faraglioni.* A fourth is found away from the formation by itself, in front of the Port of Tragara, and is called *Monacone,* named after the sea lions that occupied the site many years ago.

We disembarked at the port of Marina Grande. Looking back in the direction that we had travelled, the mainland of Italy loomed in splendid contrast to the small idyllic island of Capri and its integral Faraglioni Rocks, blue-hued foliage, and surrounding reefs. Small white boats were zigzagging around the harbor, while hydrofoils and ferries created white lines in the blue-green water as they transported passengers to and from the mainland to the isolated island. In the background was the ever-present monster, Mt. Vesuvius, overseeing and monopolizing the panoramic view. We were quickly escorted to a nearby funicular, a cable car that would carry us upward to Capri Town, which is one of the two towns on the island. It's here where the views of the island and surrounding waters are proudly boasted to transcend one's imagination of beauty. In short order, we were in the town square, window shopping and taking pictures of the decorative outdoor cafés, shops, people, and assorted colorful Italian flags, fluttering with the breeze, which were positioned around the square to capture the attention and smiles from viewers. We decided to do some shopping and then have lunch at one of the cafés, hopefully before spending our day's budgeted allowance in the inviting boutiques. Fran suggested that those of us who decided to have lunch in the square should try the renowned Capri Salad (*Insalata Caprese*), which is made of sliced tomatoes and buffalo mozzarella and is sprinkled with olive oil, basil, and capers. It sounded good to us, so after shopping and almost staying within our spending allowance, we sat down at a beautiful outdoor café and ordered some local wine. It was white table wine for me and Barbara and red valley wine for Shirley and Dallas, accompanied by delicious Italian bread and plates of *Insalata Caprese.* My, oh my, how could we move from this imaginary place in paradise? Our stomachs made the decision for us, full beyond our expectations from a planned small lunch that seemed to never end; we had to drag ourselves away to get a better view of the surrounding water from our high vantage point.

We found a location that was truly a "Kodak moment" spot. Our cameras went wild, absorbing the surrounding hypnotic, spectacular scenery: turquoise-blue, crystal-clear water, which seemed green-blue up close, but lightened from a distance. There were huge rocky cliffs with gardens interwoven and spreading their colorful beauty in every direction, alongside little white houses accenting the hills that seemed to be intruding on the flow of the natural beauty that abounds in that extraordinary, panoramic and dream-like setting. Of course, in the distance were Naples and the awakening sight of the monster, Mt. Vesuvius, which contrasted dramatically with the natural beauty in our sights, but made for a great backdrop to our photographs. After we calmed down from our divine experience, we had several choices of how to spend the rest of the day. Some in our group opted to visit Anacapri, the only other town on the island. There are two ways of getting there, walking up some 800 steps, which are believed to date back to Grecian times, or by motorized transportation. Considering the small winding size of the precarious road, which was built in the 20th century as an alternative to the steps, and looking at the endless steps, we decided to forego either choice and return to Marina Grande for a boat ride to the famous *Blue Grotto* (cave).

Our return trip down on the funicular was much more fun than our first experience, when we were unsure of the safety of the cable cars. The passengers started singing some Neapolitan songs, prompted by the cable car attendant, which invariably ended the ride with our singing the American version of the song, "Funiculi, Funicula." We soon discovered that the *Blue Grotto* boat rides were best taken in the morning when the water is calm. Due to rough water conditions, all the boats were staying in port for the afternoon. So, what should we do next? The four of us decided to find a scenic perch, get some drinks, and just enjoy the rest of the day by goofing off. We had no trouble finding a table at a nearby outdoor café and settled in for the remainder of the afternoon with drinks in hand, smiles on our faces, and good conversation. We agreed that we would save the *Blue Grotto* experience for another time on a more extended vacation to the magical Island of Capri.

Our boat ride back, at about 5:00 P.M., was more exciting than our original experience earlier that morning. We boarded a hydrofoil, which got us back to our home port in half the time of our first crossing by a conventional ferry—20 minutes versus 40 minutes. We decided to get seats on the upper deck so we could enjoy the magnificent scenery; being an old salt, the wind in my face would be a welcome treat and heaven on earth to me. The hydrofoil moved forward and then up and out of the water as it increased its speed; we hadn't had time to settle in before we were disembarking. The calming affect that fresh saltwater air has on people is amazing; our short bus ride back was filled with yawns, and more yawns, with most of the passengers pleasantly napping. What a wonderful way to end our excursion to one of the most beautiful places on earth. We all promised that we would return, but for a much longer visit—like forever.

On our brief bus ride back to our home base, Fran reminded us that dinner at the hotel was included in the tour price, followed by an orientation of the next day's activities. After refreshing, we met Shirley and Dallas for cocktails in the lounge, which had spectacular views of the Bay of Naples and its tenants. We were joined by some of our tour members and enjoyed socializing and reminiscing about the past few days. We all agreed that the trip was as exciting as we had expected, and more. It's human nature to be concerned about the next phase of a trip being as fulfilling, but invariably the new adventures are always just as exciting; so we toasted to tomorrow and all of the days to follow on our Amalfi Coast Tour. We pried ourselves away from the camaraderie and strolled to dinner in the main dining hall, stopping to admire the magnificent view of the green-blue water scene and its varied occupants, from the oversized viewing windows. We were reluctant to pick up our menus as our clothes were starting to get a bit tight, and there was a look of panic in the girls' eyes. Barbara and Shirley decided to have salads with no bread and absolutely no desserts for dinner, but Dallas and I couldn't resist the veal scaloppini with a side order of pasta in marinara sauce that our neighbors at the next table were having; it looked so good we decided that the aromatic cuisine would be our night's delight. The taste complemented the aroma and, if the girls had not been with us, I'm sure that we would have devoured a second portion.

At orientation, Fran told us that we would be visiting The National Archaeological Museum of Naples the next day and handed out extensive literature explaining some of the more important exhibits that resided at the museum. The venue is considered one of the most important and leading archaeological museums in the world, containing extensive collections of Roman-Greco antiquities from the surrounding areas, including Pompeii, Stabiae, and Herculaneum. The most famous and exotic exhibit is the *Gabinetto Segreto* (Secret Cabinet), containing artifacts of erotic or sexually explicit finds from Pompeii, which were deemed by the Italian authorities to be too obscene for public view. Therefore, they were collected and put in this mysterious chamber, under lock and key, and only viewed under certain strict conditions. We would find out what those restrictions were when we visited the Cabinet the next day, as they seemed to change daily. Of course, the information made everyone chomp at the bit to get the morning activities underway. We were told that our group would have a private docent who would guide us through the various exhibits and explain their significance and history. We were also informed that we would be spending the morning at the museum and, after the guided tour, had a choice of staying on unescorted for the remaining part of the day, or we could explore the city of Naples on our own. In any event, our bus would be ready for departure from the museum at 5:00 P.M. sharp, and it was strongly suggested that we leave promptly, as the city is not considered a safe place for tourists after dark.

The four of us decided to spend the day at the museum, and to only briefly break for lunch at one of the outside cafés that we noticed on our bus ride through the city. We met our beautiful, dark-haired, olive-skinned, Neapolitan, thirtyish docent, Angelina, at the main entrance on the ground floor. She briefed us on the exhibits we would be visiting, which included the world-renowned *Farnese Collection,* the Egyptian section, and, of course, the *Gabinetto Segreto.* She asked if there were any particular places of interest that we would like to see first? Most of the girls replied in unison: "*The Farnese's Gem Collection.*" What a surprise; most of the guys were ecstatic at the prospect of their wives getting in the mood to buy jewelry, ugh!

We learned that the building we were in was built during the latter portion of the 16th century. It was originally the Royal Riding Academy, but, due to water shortages, it was transformed into the Palace of Royal Studies and the headquarters of the University of Naples. In the 18th century, when Naples was under the rule of the Bourbons, Ferdinand IV vacated the premises and established the Bourbon Museum and Royal Library. The Bourbons donated and are responsible for many of the collections at the museum today. When Italy became unified, the new regime took possession of the building, moved the library and art gallery to a new location, and gave the museum its current name. The most outstanding compilation was the *Farnese Collection.* It was developed by Alessandro Farnese, who became Pope Paul III in 1534. He started a new trend during his tenure: collecting antiquity and works of art for his private enjoyment. His predecessors' collections were primarily added to the holdings of the Vatican Museums in Rome. The ground floor of the museum displayed many of his collections, including sculptures of the *Colossal Statue of Hercules* and the *Farnese Bull,* both uncovered from the excavation of the Baths of Caracalla in Rome. Both are Roman copies of ancient Greek antiquities, dating back to the 2nd century BCE. Of special interest was the spectacular *Farnese Bull* ensemble, which is a huge sculpture depicting the torment of Dirce, condemned to be tied to the horns of the Bull for eternity for her indiscretions and cruelty. The Pope's inscription and cameo gem collection were extremely impressive, but the center of the attraction was the *Farnese Cup*, which was made in Alexandria, Egypt, and dates back to 150 BCE. It's made from sardonyx agate and is one of the largest cameos in existence. The girls were a little disappointed at the collection, as they expected to see diamonds, rubies, and other precious gems on display, such as those residing at the Museum of Natural History's gem collection in Washington, D.C., which includes the Hope Diamond. The *Farnese Collection* consists mainly of artistically engraved intaglio and cameo antique jewelry, originally collected by such illustrious men as Cosmo and Lorenzo de' Medici, Pope Paul III, and Fulvio Orsini. It includes the aforementioned *Cup*, a C*ornelian of Apollo, Marsyas and Olympus, Artemis Holding a Torch,* and an unending number of creative and beautiful works of art.

The Egyptian section illustrated the relationship of the ancient world and Egypt, beginning in the 4th century BCE. The main collection, begun by Cardinal Stefano Borgia in the 18th century, is the nucleus of the Egyptian sections. He was able to establish connections with Catholic missions around the world and was responsible for accumulating vast amounts of rare Egyptian antiquities from returning missionaries, resulting in one of the finest collections in the world. The second main Egyptian collection was accumulated by Giuseppe Picchianti, a 19th century traveler from Venice. He visited Giza, Saqqara, and Thebes in his quest for Egyptian antiquity. He collected many objects, but was mostly fascinated by funerary furnishings. Upon completing his journey, he sold part of his valuable collection to the British Museum and, after he died, the remainder was acquired by the Royal Bourbon Museum. Some of the fascinating collections are an embalmed crocodile; the funerary stele of the *Royal Scribe Hui* holding an ape; the statue of *Anubis* with a jackal's head; a statue of the *God Serapis* seated on his throne; and many mummies. We all rushed from these fascinating exhibits to explore the *Gabinetto Sergreto.* The Secret Rooms should have been our first visit, as some people in our group were preoccupied with seeing its contents, and became annoying in their anxiety and curiosity as they rushed Angelina through her well-planned dissertations of what we were viewing.

We expected to see a guard at the door of the Secret Rooms, but there was none. As a matter of fact, the door was open, and most of our group walked in past a sign stating that the rooms were a "**Restricted area** for mature guests only and a special entrance fee is required to enter." Many of the ladies chose to remain outside of the chambers for obvious reasons, but one by one they eventually succumbed to the magnetism of the anticipated mysteries that awaited them. Before we entered, Angelina gave us a history lesson on Roman morality and some background on the convoluted circumstances of the venue throughout the ages. Although she did not join us in the Secret Rooms, she was well versed in its contents. Ancient Roman culture did not have the same standards that we have today in regards to sexuality; it was a normal part of their life and they chose to regard and display it with impunity. Different cultures viewed its openness in various ways, but in the 18th century, strict standards for obscenity developed into our modern-day concept of pornography. When the Enlightenment Project for the excavation of Pompeii began in the 19th century, new methods of identification had been developed, enabling the experts to distinguish what was obscene and unsuitable for viewing by the general public; hence, a definition of pornography was established in regards to the items uncovered. These precious relics were locked away in a Secret Museum, and the only people allowed to visit the stronghold were those with impeccable moral character. This excluded all women, and included mostly scholars and, of course, religious men. The nude statue of *Venus Kallipygos,* erotic to 18th and 19th century eyes, was included in the Holy Sanctuary due to her partially nude body and the exposure of her "beautiful buttocks." To further the religious cause of morality, the doorway to the collection was bricked close in 1849. The stronghold was opened, closed, and reopened many times before its present-day location at the museum became a tourist attraction. With this knowledge, we entered and began gazing and admiring the remnants of Pompeii's artwork, which were varied indeed, and included frescoes depicting sexual activity and sexually explicit symbols. There also were depictions of the God

Priapus doing his godly things; even everyday household items, such as phallic oil lamps and kitchen utensils were strewed throughout the room. The main male anatomy part was displayed in every imaginable way, doing the most unimaginable things. There was a lot of giggling going on from the females in the group and a lot of "no ways" coming from the male members. After seeing the contents of the rooms, I could understand why Angelina decided to remain in the outside corridor. After satisfying our curiosity, we left the popular area just in time for a late lunch. Before exiting, Angelina directed us to a large cork, wood, and paper model (scale 1:100) of the city of Pompeii, in its excavation stage in the mid-19th century. It is outstanding for its minute attention to detail, including an urban layout, monuments, and accurate watercolor reproductions inside the roofless, replicated buildings. Thanks to this relief, there still exist today, reproductions of frescos and mosaics that have since been lost or destroyed. On exiting, I thought how incredible it is that relics, some dating back 2,000 years and more, have survived. Frescoes, sculptures, scrolls, pottery, gems, and other antiquities have outlived not only the anger of the monster, Mt. Vesuvius, but the ravages of time, and are extant for civilization's perusal and enjoyment.

We said our goodbyes to Angelina with hugs and kisses, as if we were old friends or relatives. She strongly reminded us that the city of Naples was not safe and that we should be on guard for unusual happenings, and most of all to "travel in groups," as personal property was fair game for thieves in the populated, busy city. The four of us felt pretty safe as we lived in large cities; Shirley and Dallas were from the Washington, D.C. area, which is not only the capital of the U.S. but probably the crime capital as well. Barbara and I are from New York City, which is also known for its "misbehaved residents"; so away we went on our fearless journey to find a pleasant sidewalk café overlooking the center square of the city. We had our choice of several restaurants and chose one with a balcony view of the autos and bustling pedestrian traffic. It's shocking to walk the streets of a cultured metropolis and see an enormous amount of litter scattered throughout; beggars were all over the place and approached people with impunity, hoping to either get a hand-out or to get their "hands-in" your pockets.

We had to ward off several beggars and women carrying infants, who tried to get close to us to gain access to our valuables. Sitting in a restaurant was a lot safer than wandering around the noisy, crowded city, and was a wonderful respite from our unpleasant experience on the streets of Naples. Watching cars moving around the traffic circle from our balcony seats in the restaurant at a snail's pace with inches in the back, sides, and front of cars seemed unreal. Surprisingly though, the traffic did move, but ever so slowly, with no noticeable incidents, but lots of Italian insults exchanged by the frustrated drivers.

We decided that, being in the city that boasts of the invention of pizza, we might as well enjoy one of the various types available, at somewhat reasonable prices. Their bragging that they made the "best pizza in the world" is well deserved; the aroma coming from the kitchen alone was worth the price of the pies. We shared two large pizzas with pepperoni, sausage, mozzarella cheese, and mushrooms. Italian Peroni beer was in order, so we ordered a few bottles and enjoyed the cool refreshing complementary flavor as we devoured our pizzas. We made a habit of ordering espresso after our meals; the coffee aroma was inviting, so we quickly ordered a pot of the brew for our table. There should be another proud boast of Naples; their delicious coffee, without a doubt, is one of the best I have ever enjoyed. It's strange, but back in the States, Barbara and I avoid drinking regular coffee due to the hyper effect it has on us. But in Italy, their regular espresso, which is somewhat stronger than what we are used to, gave us no concern, as we had no adverse reaction from its caffeine. After our leisurely lunch, we decided not to return to the museum, as it was getting close to our departure time. Instead, we strolled through the crowded, busy streets, window shopping, and being ever so cautious of our surroundings. While walking, another danger occurred: boys riding bicycles; they would come close to us and reach for the girls' bags, but being that we were from cities that have similar problems with street thieves, we stayed close to each other and away from the curbs, with the girls' bags tucked under their arms, away from the traffic flow. We were relieved to board the bus and return to our familiar and comfortable place of rest. We were reminded that dinner was included in our tour price and that there would be an orientation session covering the next day's relocation to the town of Amalfi.

The four of us met for cocktails in the relaxing, beautiful lounge facing the Bay of Naples, and were joined by several other group members anxious to share their day's experience with us. One of the girls told us that her pocketbook was stolen right off her shoulder by someone on a motor scooter, while she was walking and window shopping downtown with a group of friends. Fortunately, the only things in the bag were comfort items, such as lipstick, wipes, etc. She made sure that her valuables remained in the hotel's room safe, and her cash was in her pants pockets. After a couple of very necessary drinks to calm us down from the stressful day in Naples, we went into the amazingly picturesque dining room, always smiling and enjoying the view from the large bay windows of the serene waters surrounding the boats and the islands on the distant horizon. Aside from the items listed on the menu, one of the main course specials for the evening was *pesce de mare,* consisting of shrimp, scallops, clams, and other tiny shrimp-like fish, over linguine, in a red sauce. The second special was steak pizzaiola served with roasted potatoes. The girls decided to stick with the salad plates, while Dallas and I ordered both specials and shared them—what a delight. Of course, the girls managed to take samples from each of our plates, satisfied that they were not betraying their diets by nibbling small portions from us. After dinner, we joined our group in one of the conference rooms for our orientation session.

The review of our next day's journey was exciting. We would travel north to the town of Caserta, to visit the Bourbon's answer to the Versailles Castle in France, and then on to the town of Capua, to visit the scene of the great Roman rebellion by the famous gladiator, Spartacus. Fran handed out material that gave us some insight into both towns and their historical significance in their respective time periods.

An early morning start got us on our way to the town of Caserta. The bus ride wasn't long enough for us to get some much-needed shut eye, as we were awakened several times by the loudspeaker announcements from our constant companion and advisor, Fran. Her usual explicit dissertation informed us of what to expect at the Palace of Caserta, while the passengers' questions kept us awake and unwilling participants in their dialogue. But I did manage to snooze, as many of our comrades did, in between the sounds of chatter and loudspeaker announcements.

The monumental complex at Caserta was created for King Charles VII of Naples in the mid-18th century to rival the complex of Versailles in France and the Palacio Real in Madrid, where Charles was raised as a child. Its primary purpose was to move the royal court's location from Naples, which was situated by the sea and exposed to the dangers of foreign invaders, to a more secluded and more readily defensible stronghold, with its own military barracks. The king was also determined to escape the tumultuous activity and filth of Naples, which was one of the largest cities in Italy, for the quiet and peaceful environment of the out-of-the-way inland location that was bordered by protective mountains. The *Palazzo* was designed to bring together an extravagant palace, park, and gardens, surrounded by woodlands, hunting lodges, and a disguised industrial pavilion for the production of silk. The original plans called for approximately a half-million-square-foot fortress, with 1,200 rooms, two dozen state apartments, 1,742 windows, a national theatre, a 10,000-volume royal library, and a university, all insulated from the disorder, noise, and squalor of Naples. The plans were designed to emphasize the financial strength of the Bourbons' monarchy, but the king never spent a moment in his dream palace. He resigned his throne to become the King of Spain. It wasn't until the mid-19th century that the palace was completed and occupied by Ferdinand II. It was used as the royal residence and government administration offices, hosting countless balls, receptions, and hunting parties.

Several historical events occurred in the Province of Caserta. In 1860, the famous "Handshake" between Victor Emmanuel and Giuseppe Garibaldi took place. After spending most of his adult life fighting for the unification of Italy, including living in exile on Staten Island, New York, for many years, Garibaldi turned over his Army and authority to King Victor Emmanuel on October 26, resulting finally in the unification of Italy under the House of Savoy. During World War II, the U.S. Fifth Army used the Palace as its headquarters and a rest and rehabilitation center for its troops. On April 29, 1945, the surrender of German forces to the Allies took place at this location. In the 1999 film, *Star Wars Episode I: The Phantom Menace,* and, again in the 2002 film, *Star Wars Episode II: Attack of the Clones,* the palace was used as Queen Amidala's and Queen Jamillia's residence, respectively. The location was also used in *Mission Impossible III*, in 2006, as a holy room in Vatican City. The action scene where a Lamborghini is blown up was in the square inside the Palace.

I was unable to see the entire outside walls of the half-million-square-foot complex from the window of our bus. But walking along the compound, we easily determined that it was vast in its size and incomprehensible in the synergy required to produce such a magnificent structure. The palace is a crown jewel in the midst of a 300-acre paradise, surrounded by protective esplanades, formal gardens, ornate fountains, a large fish livery, a miniature castle, an English garden, an open-air theatre, and a magnificent waterfall that is enriched with many sculptures. The park starts from the back facade of the palace, and is flanked by a long alley with fountains and cascades fed by the Carolina Aqueduct of the incredible architect, Luigi Vanvitelli, and extends to the nearby mountains for about one and a half miles. When looking at the pools and alleyway extending to the horizon, my field of vision was engulfed with just that view; there was no room for anything else. Fran allotted an hour for us to visit the park and then return to the entrance of the fortress, where we had been dropped off, to continue our visit into the Palace with its antiquated exhibits.

We didn't have much time, so we hired a covered horse-drawn carriage to carry us through the immense scenic park. We let our horseman, Antonio, decide which of the many beautiful places we should visit, while we sat back and enjoyed the ride. We were not surprised that Antonio spoke perfect English, as many Italians do, but he had a very pronounced Brooklyn accent. He explained that he spent most of his teenage years growing up in the Italian East New York section of that borough, which is where I was born and bred. It was precious to hear a mixed Italian and Brooklyn accent again; it reminded me of my relatives who came from Italy and spoke with the same inflection. His voice put a happy smile on my face all day, especially when he narrated the sights we were visiting. Closing my eyes, I was almost able to visit with my long-departed father, Luciano, and my grandparents. They all came from Italy and had the same-sounding voice as Antonio. He decided that due to our time limitation, the best approach would be to begin at one of the furthest sculptured fountains and work our way back to the entrance of the palace. The *Fountain of Diana and Actaeon* was our first stop. The ensemble is in a basin supplied by a water cascade with large rocks as a backdrop, and is fed by an impressive waterfall from above, which boasts 14 statues of huntsmen and huntswomen supported by balustrades. The group sculpture of Actaeon depicts hunting dogs attacking their master who had turned into a stag. According to our narrator, one of the most prevalent myths surviving is as follows:

> Actaeon, a famous Theban hero, trained by the centaur Cheiron (Master of Arts and science), suffered the fatal wrath of Artemis (Diana) when he stumbled across Diana bathing, thus seeing her naked. He stopped and stared, gazing at her beautiful body, which left him speechless. As punishment, she forbade him speech; if he tried to speak, he would be turned into a stag. What retribution, all because he saw her sacred body, or, because, upon seeing her, he didn't take any manly action toward her. Subsequently, upon hearing his hunting dogs, he called to them and instantly turned into a stag. The dogs immediately attacked him and tore him to pieces.

Truly a Greek tragedy! We stared at the marbled presentation of the popular myth, which defies description. How such a depressing story could turn into a beautiful sculpture, depicting a pack of hunting dogs tearing a man-stag into pieces, is beyond my comprehension. The silvery pond surrounding the group, the rocks and cascade background, turn a horrific sight into one of mystery and beauty, so common in the works of Italian artisans. To balance the sculpture with a more pleasant beauty was a magnificent group of ladies: *Diana Surrounded by Nymphs,* as she prepares to bathe. You could almost hear them singing while attending to Diana, quite an impressive sight and a more enjoyable vision than its neighbor. Antonio decided to restrict the remainder of the tour to some of the other fountains situated along the road back to our starting point.

We were frustrated, realizing that it would probably take more than a whole day to begin to appreciate what the park had to offer, not the mere hour we were allotted. While briefly passing the incredibly luxurious formal English Gardens, which we had no time to explore; Antonio described some of its exotic flora, glasshouses, a beautiful little lake with a statue of *Venus* bathing, a chalet, and groups of ruins, including a miniature Roman temple and a botanical garden. What a perfect place to bring a picnic basket, a blanket, and music, to pass the time of day sipping on a bottle of local Italian wine. When we hopefully visit the site again, we will certainly devote more time at the incredible locale, which combines nature's beauty with the creativity of Italian artisans, resulting in a world-class place to visit. Again, the threatening Mt. Vesuvius was evident in the background; its majestic appearance put our cameras in action, as the film absorbed the beautiful scenery with the monster and the sky as wallpaper.

Our last stop was the sculpture of the *Fountain of the Dolphins.* Again, I was looking at my watch and wishing we had more time to appreciate the beautiful sights we passed on our return trip. I would certainly make a point of mentioning to Fran, that spending only a half a day in Caserta exploring the park and palace is not conducive to a well-planned study-sightseeing tour. Antonio was full of information about the spectacular sculpture. It was a monumental aquatic fountain with three enormous dolphins protruding from rocks, spouting water from their mouths into a huge fishpond. The large curious fish inhabitants followed our shadows on the water in whatever direction we were walking. In the days when royalty reigned, the pond supplied fresh fish for the tables of the elite and their guests. I could just envision an elongated dinner table, dressed with the finest accoutrements, being used by these privileged people, enjoying their delicious fresh fish, prepared by the finest Italian chefs. I could smell the aroma of the most gourmet food in the world and almost taste the cuisine. Unfortunately, we still had a couple of hours before our scheduled lunch stop on the way to the town of Capua. It wasn't easy pacifying my whetted appetite, but a packet of peanuts in my carrying bag took the edge off of my hunger. We hugged and kissed Antonio, thanked him for his friendly and informative guidance through the gardens, wished him lots of luck, and joined our tour group for the next phase of our journey.

We were allotted an hour and a half on our own to explore the Palace. Electronic docents were at our disposal to explain the various places of interest we were visiting. Describing the appearance after entering the facility is beyond my capability, but the handout pamphlet summed up what I saw precisely:

> The entire complex suggests the idea of order and symmetry, but it also conveys strong integrations between central power, state administration, and between the court and its subjects. This relationship between the building and the park, created by means of the gallery-telescope and constituting an integral part of the fabrication, appears clear and rigorous against the emerald background of the lawns, which makes the white avenues stand out. The mass of trees, open in the middle, show the expanse of water in the distance, modeling itself to the contours of the land. In this sober austere picture, the spirited architecture of the Palace appears in all its monumental worth, in which space, colors, shapes and surfaces unite in unmatched unity of expression.

Thanks to the creativity of the architect, Vanvitelli, and his benefactor's generosity, their plan to build one of the most magnificent palaces in the world was accomplished. The pamphlet continues:

> One of the most delightful Vanvitellian innovations is the use of galleries and vestibules, which are aligned to the axis of the building, and the aesthetic and practical purpose given to them, intrinsically connected to the development of the main design. The internal circulatory system is perfectly achieved with radial passages, which connect the vestibules to the courtyards

> and entrance halls, which, in turn, link the courtyards with each other and the exterior. A balanced network of passages and squares facilitate the performance of parades, balls, processions, and banquets, without confusion, blockage, or conflicts. The vestibules are peristyle octagonal, capped by column-supported vaults. The central one is very wide and bright. On the right is the royal stairway; on the left is the statue of *Hercules* balanced on a podium. Opposite, against the green background of the hills, a waterfall glints in the sunlight. The courtyards are as wide as squares and are seen through the arches of the gallery. They all have a function in accordance with the standards of Vanvitellian architecture. In the Royal Palace, the place of the courtyard is taken by an axial gallery, offering a deepened perspective. The four courtyards are sources of light, places of transit or for lingering; factors necessary in the playing out of the life at court.

The dissertation must have been written by a poet. Not only did it describe the visual aspect of the setting, but it also captured the feeling and excitement of the moment.

The right side of the central entrance hall is the Stairway of Honor, which leads to an upper encircling line of columns, opening into a chapel and the royal apartments. A brightly lighted stairway, made from a single piece of marble, leads to dual staircases guarded by two symbolic lion statues. The lions are there to greet all visitors and to remind them that they are in the midst of a powerful presence. Viewing the two parallel stairways on opposite sides of the hall, each guarded by a male feline, we proceeded with caution, ever aware that we were being watched by the two authoritarian cats. Barbara and Shirley took the right staircase and Dallas and I the left. The magnificent colors reflected from the various shades of marble throughout the hall leading to three arches at the top of the flights are picture-frame perfect. I felt as if the view at the top of the steps was an enormously large painting, instead of the reality I was witnessing. At the top of the stairways, elegant vaults were gathered together in a cupola, arches, and cornices and three archways linked to the stairways, which gave testimony to the prolific genius of Italian artisans, which is truly unmatched, and was without a doubt, a one-of-a-kind architectural delight.

We chose to continue on to the Hall of Nativity, where a three-dimensional manger scene representing infant Christ and his entourage are replicated in human size. The more important pieces were done in clay, while other statues had heads and limbs of clay, and bodies of wire and oakum. The statues and ornaments were on a bed of cork, in accordance with religious canon respecting scenes like the Nativity. The display of the *Presepio* (feeding through), signifying the Christ Child's initial resting place, is a widespread custom throughout the Christian, and particularly the Catholic, world. This tradition can be traced back to the 13th century, when St. Francis of Assisi celebrated mass before a sculptured group of the *Holy Family*, flanked by a living ox and ass (sometimes described as a "Living Presepe," consisting of costumed people as well as animals) in a small village setting. An industry has developed in the Naples area that produces statues and figures that are displayed in manger scenes throughout the world at Christmas time, continuing a tradition established by the Bourbon Kings in the 18th century. Every year, the royalty, princes, and even ladies in waiting, would participate in a joint venture, creating different presentations of the *Nativity* scenes, and proudly displaying their new creations for the Christmas season. The tradition is still carried out today. I remember as a youth, my grandfather, Peter, who was from the Naples area, building a *Nativity* scene from clay and a variety of stones, which were painted to present hair, eyes, and other appropriate bodily parts. Clothes were handmade to dress the entourage and decorate the manger. There was the Christ Child watched by Mother Mary and Father Joseph and the three wise men and several animals breathing on the Child to keep him warm from winter's cold air. Then, I didn't realize the traditional significance of that scene and the love, patience, and skill required to produce such a beautiful display for our Christmas seasons, but I do now.

A view of the *Presepio* with hundreds of terracotta figures created in the 18th and 19th centuries is magnetic and overwhelming in its complexity. The figures are extremely realistic, inviting the viewer's imagination to enter and become part of the diorama. The manger scene was exquisite in its life-like presentation. A feeling of warmth ran through my body as I was drawn into the barn scene with which I was so familiar, recalling my religious lessons and the family stories told over and over throughout my life about that spiritual event. Another interesting scene was that of the *Journey of the Three Kings*, which was detailed with a black woman suckling atop a camel followed by their entourage consisting of small black children, a small camel, and a hand-traveling carriage decorated in the finest cloths. After glancing at my watch, I gathered my friends so we could visit some other places of interest before our time ran out.

From the literature that Fran distributed, we decided to visit the rooms of the controversial Queen Maria Carolina and her Palatine Library, which is home to over 14,000 books and documents. She was the daughter of Queen Maria Theresa of Austria and Francis I, Emperor of the Holy Roman Empire. Maria Carolina was one of 16 children; her younger sister was the extravagant and unfortunate Maria Antoinette, Queen of France, whose famous words after hearing of her subject's plight of starvation, supposedly were "If there is no bread, then let them eat cake." Of course, she and her husband, Louis XVI, were beheaded for their reckless administration and wasteful spending by revolutionary partisans. Her oldest sister, Maria Louise, became the second wife of Napoleon I, Emperor of France. Queen Maria Carolina was betrothed to Ferdinand I and married at the young age of 16; her husband's age exceeded hers by one year. The new Queen was able to dominate her marriage and the running of the monarchy as her mother did with Emperor Francis I. Her mother made sure that all her offspring were educated and prepared for the rigors of royal life. Her father was an enlightened Freemason member (who believed in the Brotherhood of Man under the Fatherhood of a Supreme Being), and was very liberal in his actions and thinking toward his subjects and children. The young Queen Carolina immediately took charge of the administration and running of the Bourbon Kingdom. Over the years, she replaced French and Spanish influences in the court and country with that of the English, going as far as appointing Sir John Action, an Englishman, as Minister of the Navy, Minister of Finance, and, finally,

Prime Minister. Sir John seemed to have dual roles as Minister, that of keeping the kingdom in England's sphere of influence and the more important role of administering to Maria Carolina's personal needs. Considering that her husband's father was King of Spain and abdicated his dominions in Italy to his third son Ferdinand I, and that her sister, Maria Antoinette was Queen of France, it was a neat maneuver that she could accomplish a change in political influence without going to the guillotine herself.

Being her mother's daughter, although ruling her domain was a full-time endeavor, she still had time to do one better than her mom; she had 17 children. Most of the work on the Royal Palace was accomplished under the supervision of the two monarchs, including much of the landscaping and, in particular, the English Carolina Gardens. The garden designers were imported from England to create a beautiful formal setting that contrasted with the surrounding rural area, and was in keeping with her attachment to England, especially after the execution of her sister Maria Antoinette by French revolutionaries. The relationship worked to the monarch's benefit, as England's military came to their rescue on more than one occasion while they occupied their dual thrones. The queen was also her father's daughter in her belief in Freemasonry, although she was often criticized for not practicing her beliefs, as she was dictatorial and quite often cruel—particularly after the assassination of her sister, Maria Antoinette. Many of her accomplishments were due to her conviction in human progress and enlightenment during the New Golden Bourbon Age.

We briefly visited her apartments, which consisted of four rooms decorated in typical rococo taste. The first room (Work Room) was striking in its yellow satin walls and framed mirrors; a Stucco Private Room led to a bathroom and private toilet, with Venetian mirrors and white marble baths. Passing her sealed Boudoir, which was closed for cleaning, etc., we came to the Company Room and Room of the Ladies in Waiting, decorated in bright friendly colors. Finally, we arrived at the rooms we were interested in and which were also part of the queen's apartment. Two reading rooms led into the three rooms of the Palatine Library, which was considered her true "Kingdom." She again chose to import foreign artists to do extensive paintings and frescos; the German painter Friedrich Fugger chose classical images for the rooms assigned to him. The themes celebrated the new Bourbon "Era of Gold." He created a fresco, the *School of Athens,* which emphasized the banishment of ignorance and the protection of the arts, in accordance with her beliefs in Freemasonry. His other paintings continued with the same theme. Outstanding was a rotating small mahogany and rosewood library case created according to her wishes, which was freshly stocked with books to facilitate what she was interested in reading, whether for royal business or pleasure. A display of an ancient telescope and an antique earth globe rounded out the impressive 14,000-volume library. An unusual painting done by the Italian artist Forgola, *The Inauguration of the Naples Railway,* in 1840, which was out of the queen's time period, was proudly displayed in the Reading Room and captured the essence of what she was trying to accomplish; she often said, "Enlightened people do remarkable things." We found ourselves again racing against the clock as our scheduled time was running out. We had just about enough time to visit The Court Theatre before joining our tour group, so we walked at a quick pace and entered the astonishing mini-replica of the San Carlo Theatre in Naples.

The Bourbons established themselves in Naples in 1734 in an age when the French court influenced most of European culture with its levity, love for luxury, comfort, love for music, poetry, literature, and even a love for the sciences. It was at this time that King Charles had the 3,000-plus-seat San Carlos Theatre built to reflect the power of the Bourbons and to show off his prize city of Naples, which at that time was considered the largest city, by population, in Europe. Till this day, the theatre is considered one of the most beautiful opera houses in the world, drawing performers of the highest caliber, such as Luciano Pavarotti and Placido Domingo. When he decided to build the inland Royal Palace at Caserta, to escape the hazards of invasion by sea and the eruptions from Mt. Vesuvius, he subsequently added a small version of the San Carlos Theatre to his plans for the palace. The Court Theatre was not in the original plans by the architect Vanvitelli, but was the only project that the king saw completed during his lifetime; most of the remainder of the construction was completed by his son, Carlo, and Charles's third son, Ferdinand, and his wife, Maria Carolina. The

San Carlo 3,000-plus-seat theatre was built in eight months, while its younger sister's 400-plus-seat Court Theatre took over ten years. The smaller theatre is an exact reproduction of the San Carlo Theatre and was completed in time for the inauguration of the wedding between Ferdinand and Maria Carolina. There are three staircase entrances into the theatre, of which two were closed, the royal entrance in the middle and the second public entrance. We walked up the marble staircase to the opened entrance and were startled by the ambiance: the layout of the theatre was horseshoe in shape, with forty-two private boxes, finished in imitation marble placed in five rows, all decorated with cupids and floral festoons of various types. The royal box was the size of three regular boxes, with rich drapery in Bourbon blue with golden lilies. Looking directly ahead at the stage, we could see the back curtains were open, giving us a surprising view of the park through the oversized windows. We were lucky, as there was a rehearsal going on for a flute concert, so we rested for a few minutes and enjoyed the music and the opulence of the venue. My mind drifted back to an earlier time, when the music hall would have been occupied by privileged Italians and guests attending a concert, opera, or play, and taking pride in seeing their king and queen displayed in the royal box while enjoying the performance. The Bourbons certainly had the feeling of that period: luxury and comfort for us now, and worry about tomorrow later. Unfortunately, tomorrow would come sooner than expected, and the period of royalty in Europe would quickly fade away. It was time to catch up with our tour members, so we departed quickly to meet our bus and were shortly on our way to the town of Capua, which fortunately was only a few miles north of Caserta.

On the way, we stopped at a quaint Italian restaurant that was decorated in bright Neapolitan colors: red, blue-gold, and pink. There were many paintings on the walls showing off the seashore scenes along the Amalfi Coast, with emphasis on the blue-green water, small boats, and the Isle of Capri in the background. There was also an attractive display that seems to be found throughout Southern Italy, especially Sicily, of colorfully painted wagons referred to as Sicilian wine carts (*carretti*), ranging in size from six inches to two feet. Traditionally, these carts were used to transport wine and food to small villages. The scenes painted on the sides reflected the history of a particular village or location. Especially colorful were the carts depicting legends and historical events of their country or locale. It immediately transported me back to my youth. My ancestors displayed similar carts, usually in a prominent place on a special pedestal; the artwork probably depicted the history of their towns or favorite legends. Unfortunately, I didn't know the significance of the objects or I would have somehow made a point of inheriting one or all of them. Some of the carts we saw that were drawn by small painted donkeys, were done in colors representing the corresponding towns of origin. The restaurant's atmosphere will forever be etched in my mind, especially the likeness of the carts to those proudly displayed by my relatives. We were the only patrons in the restaurant, as Italians don't eat their lunch at one o'clock; they prefer a 3:00 P.M. extended lunch and a very late dinner. We were expecting a light lunch, but a buffet of fish, veal, mozzarella, tomatoes, and antipasto was laid out and was too beautiful to pass up. We indulged ourselves as if it were our last meal on earth. Of course, we complemented the food with local Italian red and white wines. It was easy to forget that we had another stop before our trip to the Town of Amalfi, where we would be spending the rest of our trip. Fortunately, Capua was a short distance away, so after what seemed to be a never-ending feast, we reluctantly exited the hospitable restaurant, and bid farewell to the owners and staff in a manner that would suggest a long-standing relationship with them, instead of the two hours we spent enjoying the wonderful cuisine. I wondered if the bus could accommodate the extra weight we were bringing with us from all the delicious food we had consumed.

I took the opportunity to read the literature Fran distributed the night before to familiarize myself with the ancient town we were visiting. Two historical events propelled Capua into prominence: its defection to Hannibal in 216 BCE, followed by its subsequent recapture and harsh punishment by Rome in 211 BCE, and the fact that it was the birthplace of the gladiators' revolt led by Spartacus in 73 BCE. The original city (*Casillinum*) was evacuated during an invasion in the 2nd century CE. The modern city of Capua was established a few miles north, while the ancient city was rebuilt and is now the modern city of

Santa Maria Capua Vetere. Our destination was the former ancient city to investigate the Coliseum-amphitheatre, which is one of the largest structures in Italy, second only to the one in Rome. Some experts believe that it predates its brother in Rome, while others claim that it was built 100 years after the more popular one in the Roman capital. Whatever the case may be, it did not exist when the Spartacus revolt took place in 73 BCE. Cicero wrote, "The amphitheatre seated up to 100,000 people," but this has been disputed by modern archeologists who claim that it could hold no more than 50,000 spectators. In either case, both numbers are a respectable representation of the size and complexity of the site. The structure is colossal in size and no better for the wear and tear that has occurred over the centuries. It is in worse condition than its bigger brother in Rome, but it does have enough remaining so that with a little imagination it comes to life easily. With an overlay booklet that I purchased at the entrance center, the coliseum was resurrected on paper and in my mind, with many extinct decorations and smaller buildings shown in all their glory, and glory it was. The site was an architectural marvel; it had high columns with arches surrounding the structure, which was created with sweat, blood, and whip lashes, and was all handmade, and certainly a testament to Roman ingenuity and their effective use of slave labor. The difficulty of running a sports arena of that size without the modern technology we have today, is, to say the least, amazing! Throughout the structure, there are stairways and ramps; animal and man-drawn elevators were strategically located to bring the gladiators, scenery, and beasts to the arena's surface from the underground vaults, for their scheduled performances. Crowd control was accomplished much as it is today: numbered tickets were given to the spectators directing them to the gates, stairs, and levels where their seats were located. Most of the construction lies naked of its once-beautiful marble and decorations, leaving the underlying brick exposed to the elements. The site could use some serious major renovating, and if done, would most likely bring enough additional revenue from tourists, who would spend more time at the location, to cover the costs of a restoration. For instance, the grounds were covered with litter, and there are probably hundreds of friendly, well-fed stray cats and dogs wandering around, unattended, their droppings covering a good part of the walking paths. To compound the problem, it was difficult walking around due to the many unsafe areas because of the holes that were scattered throughout the grounds. Although the main structure and surrounding area were worthy of further investigation, most of our group couldn't wait to leave the unsightly complex and get on with our journey.

On our bus trip to the town of Amalfi, I read extensively about the gladiator, Spartacus, and his true story, versus the popular movie version. Spartacus was born in Thrace, which was probably, but not absolutely, a part of Greece. Today, many countries, such as Greece, Turkey, Bulgaria, and Macedonia, claim it was a part of their territories. It's likely that he served as an auxiliary in the Roman Army and became a slave as punishment for deserting. The instigating reason for the revolt of the first 78 gladiators was probably their harsh treatment at the school of Lentulus Batiatus, near Capua. Upon scaling the walls of the training center, they were fortunate to come across an unguarded wagon loaded with weapons. This gave them the opportunity to begin supplying themselves and new recruits with sophisticated weaponry and, thus, started what was to become an enormous slave army that would threaten the Roman Empire's existence. Initially, their objective was to flee Italy and the oppressive conditions that they were subjected to, but they became so successful at raising an army, estimated at its peak to be upward to 125,000 soldiers, that they began systematically pillaging for profit and power, overcoming any opposition from Roman legions. During their peak, they made their headquarters at the base of the Monster, Mt. Vesuvius, winning all of their battles against Roman legions at and around that area. In the two years that they were plundering and roving around most of Southern Italy, they defeated the Roman forces in at least eight battles, inflicting great losses of Roman soldiers, treasury, and pride. Needless to say, the loss of pride at being defeated by a slave army was too much for the proud Romans to bear. Fear spread through Rome in anticipation of the rebels attacking the defenseless capital and enlisting the large slave population of the city to their cause. Rome was vulnerable to attack by such a formidable force, as most of its seasoned armies were on foreign soil protecting and expanding their empire. After many defeats, the Senate recalled the armies of Pompey and Lucullus from their foreign campaigns to put an end to Spartacus's victories, but they arrived too late to participate in the final battle. The Roman praetor, Marcus Crassus, was the only commander in Rome brave enough to volunteer for the task of facing and defeating Spartacus's army, but it was not an easy task. So cautious was he that, having cornered the slave army in Southern Italy with its back to the sea, instead of attacking, he decided to build a 32-mile trench across the peninsula. It was 15 feet wide by 15 feet deep and included a fence to keep the rebels isolated, with hopes of starving them into submission. However, the rebels broke through and headed in the direction of Rome.

Upon hearing that the armies of Pompey and Lucullus were on their way and would arrive shortly, Spartacus decided to make a stand against Crassus's forces and, then, after winning, his troops would turn on the other two armies. Spartacus had his horse brought to him and killed it with a sword, announcing "Victory or death; there will be no retreat." And so the rebels, who outnumbered the Roman legions, attacked in human waves hoping that their sheer number and passion would overwhelm and defeat the Romans, but it was not to be. Spartacus and most of his men were killed by the well-trained soldiers in the battle; some slaves escaped but were not pursued by Crassus, as his legions were decimated and had to return to Rome for rest and rehabilitation. It was left to Pompey to hunt down and slaughter the remnants of the brave army. The bodies of over 6,000 slaves were crucified and hung along the road from Capua to Rome as a testament to the strength of the Empire and the severe consequences of rebellion. Rome never forgot the anxiety and fear that this uprising caused throughout Italy, and went to great lengths to ensure that gladiators never again had the opportunity to gather and form another rebellion. It took an additional 400 years of cruelty and bondage to gladiators and slaves before the sport of pitting man against man and beast would finally come to an end.

Of course, the spectacular 1960 movie *Spartacus* told quite a different story. The extravagant movie follows the slave revolt of Pre-Imperial Rome in 73–71 BCE. The fantastic story (told with quite a bit of literary license), set in ancient times, had some outstanding acting from such renowned actors as Kirk Douglas (Spartacus), Laurence Olivier (Crassus, as the general), Jean Simmons (Varinia, Spartacus's wife), Charles Laughton (Gracchus, as a senator), Peter Ustinov (Lentulus Batiatus, as a slave trader who purchases Spartacus), John Gavin (Julius Caesar, as Commander of Rome's Garrison), John Ireland (Crixus, as Spartacus's loyal lieutenant) and last, but not least, Tony Curtis (Antoninus, as Crassus's young slave and later Spartacus's comrade). The story traces the escape and then the rise and fall of its leader and the end of the rebellion. It begins when he is rescued from a brutally run Libyan mine by Lentulus Batiatus to be trained as a gladiator. He learns his trade quickly and is allowed visitation rights with Varinia, whom he treats with respect by refusing to take the opportunity to sexually perform with her for the benefit of their overseers' viewing pleasure. So a relationship develops between them out of respect and admiration, and after his escape, they eventually marry. But before that blessed event, Crassus takes a liking to Varinia, purchases her, and then takes her to his mansion for his amusement and pleasure, which of course, never happened. When Spartacus finds out, he is enraged and the beginning of the uprising is set in motion. He and some of his trusted friends overwhelm the guards and escape from their place of bondage.

As the rebels march through Southern Italy, looting and freeing slaves, Spartacus is chosen to lead the new army and to turn them into a fighting force, so they could fight their way out of Italy and return to their homes. Rome is upset about the slave army but not overly concerned, as they consider it only a minor uprising. They send a small military party to uproot the upstarts and bring them to Roman justice. Of course, Spartacus's small army annihilates the unprepared Romans, which, in short order, gets the undivided attention of the powers in Rome. As the growing slave army moves through the southern part of Italy, there is much debate in the Senate about letting them escape from Italy. The consensus became, "It is bad business to allow an escape to go unpunished, especially of slaves." So they send 19,000 troops to put an end to the rabble force; the soldiers march into a trap and are defeated in short order. During all the confusion, Spartacus and Varinia get together and consummate their marriage and quickly have a child to make the story more interesting. In the meantime, Crassus makes some overtures to his slave Antonius while getting a sponge bath, and is rejected; shortly after, the slave decides to escape and join Spartacus and his forces. This scene perpetuates the belief that many of the Roman elite were bisexual, in spite of their heroic manly conduct in battle.

The end of an era is in the making when Crassus raises an army and begins to hunt down the now fearless rebel forces. Only after being pursued and then cornered, does Spartacus give the order: "Meet the enemy head on in a fight to the end." The rebels are defeated and many captured in one of the most spectacular battle scenes in film history; the heroic Spartacus and Antonius are spared the fate of their comrades and survive. Crassus promises the defeated troops that if they surrender their leader, their lives will be spared. When he asks, "Who is Spartacus?" first Spartacus raises his hand and then, one by one, the slaves raise their hands and proclaim, "I am Spartacus." As a punishment, Crassus has them crucified along the Appian Way, from the battlefield to the gates of Rome, all except Spartacus and Antonius. Crassus, still not sure if Spartacus is dead or alive, has the two men fight to the death, the winner having the honor of being crucified with the rest of the rebels. Spartacus reluctantly fights, but only to prevent his friend, Antonius, from being nailed to a cross, so he now becomes his friend's savior. Well, Spartacus wins the duel and is quickly crucified alongside his men. Varinia and her newborn are taken captive by Crassus and she is sent to his home as a love slave. She soon finds a friend in Gracchus, an influential senator, and escapes the grip of her new master. And that is the End.

There are considerable historical inaccuracies in the film, such as:

- The "I am Spartacus" scene never happened, as he was killed in the final battle and, therefore, the duel between him and Antonius never occurred.
- There are fewer battles in the movies than actually happened, including Spartacus's army escaping through the 32-mile ditch across the peninsula that Crassus built to contain them.

- It was not Crassus who crucified the remnants of the rebel army, but Pompey; Crassus's army was decimated in the final battle and was forced to return to Rome for rest and rehabilitation.
- In the film, Spartacus is born into slavery when, in reality, he was an auxiliary Roman soldier and was imprisoned for deserting.
- Antonius and Varinia (with a British accent) were totally fictional. Antonius played to the rumors that many Romans were bisexual and Varinia's British accent predated Rome's contact with that barbarian island by many years.

But, all in all, the movie was one of the most exciting and technologically advanced shows I have been fortunate to see. I graduated from college in 1960, the same year the movie premiered, and a friend of mine treated me to see the movie as a graduation present. It was certainly a surprise and a greatly appreciated treat.

We arrived at the Hotel Luna Convento, which is situated on a mountain cliff a short walking distance from the Town of Amalfi, where we would spend the next couple of days. It was dark, so we didn't get a chance at a daylight view of the area, but what we saw from the cliffside was a remarkable view of the Gulf of Salerno and the lights of boats in the distance, bobbing to the rhythm of the waves. I couldn't wait to get a better view in the morning. We were assigned our rooms, and I was sure that we would have preference over the other guests as to a choice of rooms, being that I had an Italian last name and the owner of the hotel had a similar name. Additionally, my grandparents came from the Naples region, which I informed them of upon our arrival. But, great ideas come and go, and mine went when I saw an exceptionally small room with a twin bed. Fortunately, it was clean and the toilet was adequate. After refreshing ourselves, we went down to the dining hall for dinner. The restaurant was magnificent, with seascape paintings decorating the walls and colorful furniture highlighting the contours of the rooms, some with arches, others rectangular, and others square. The dining room was decorated simply but, as is so common along the Amalfi Coast, the water view from the oversized window was breathtaking. Shirley and Dallas Peck joined us for dinner and immediately raved about the wonderful first-floor suite that they were assigned, with an additional alcove room and a courtyard garden area—all their own. Well, my theory of having preferred treatment because I was Italian went right down the tubes—no such thing in Italy. We ordered some local Italian wine and decided to eat family style. Each of us ordered main courses that we shared: pasta puttanesca for Barbara, baked ziti for Shirley, eggplant parmesan for Dallas, and veal scaloppini for me. We shared fried calamari for an appetizer and the last plate, as is usual in Italy, was a wonderful salad that no one could finish. I could never understand why Italians eat their salads last. As a youth, eating something I didn't like last was never a pleasant experience, but, if I didn't eat the traditional dish after a full course meal, "I wouldn't be able to digest my food," so I was told by relatives who knew better than the young boy. After marrying Barbara, who is from a Russian-Jewish background, I was introduced to eating salads before the main course. What a positive difference it made to the enjoyment of a meal. We decided that after the orientation, we would walk to the Town of Amalfi, which was a short distance from the hotel, to enjoy some espresso and dessert.

Fran handed out material for the following day's trip to the Royal Palace and the Museum of Capodimonte, which are located in a park bearing the Capodimonte name. She also reminded us that the next day was the end of our tour, and that a farewell dinner and dance would take place at the Bersagliera Restaurant. We leisurely strolled down to the Town of Amalfi, enjoying the night's stillness and the tranquility of the sea. We were led on our walk by the aroma of coffee, which we followed to a small street side café that was crowded with patrons enjoying their after-dinner espresso and sweets. We gladly joined the happy faces, and nodded recognition to some of the guests that we knew from our tour. We passed a pleasant hour drinking our *caffe*, munching on anisette cookies, and enjoyed watching people walking around the busy street. We were all exhausted from the day's activities and decided to return to the hotel and get some R&R. We joined several of our tour members that were "expressorizing" at the café, and headed back to the hotel quite happy with the day's experiences and how smoothly the trip was going—so far.

We woke up in the middle of the night scratching ourselves intensely; I switched on the lights to find small black ants crawling all over our pillows and sheets. Barbara screamed as we pounded the pillows against the bed. I immediately called the front desk, and, of course, no one answered. I left my room and went directly to the owner's room and knocked on her door. She opened the door quite annoyed that we interrupted her sleep, even after I told her of our dilemma. All of a sudden, she didn't understand English, even though when she greeted us upon our arrival, she spoke the language very well. Her son appeared and assured us that we really didn't have a problem; I suggested that if that were the case, he wouldn't mind exchanging rooms with us. He came with us to our room with fresh bed sheets and pillows, reassuring us that changing them would solve our problem. He also brought along a can of insect spray for good measure. We didn't sleep well that evening and were happy to see the sun come up so we could shower, dress, and get the hell out of the room to escape the little critters; exacerbating our problem was the noise developing outside our window from the traffic below: tires squealing, engines revving, and horns honking. When we left for breakfast, there were still ants in the room but not many on the bed.

When we saw the innkeeper at breakfast, I strongly suggested that she change our room to one without unwanted visitors and a lot less noise from the outside traffic. She said there were no vacant rooms at the hotel and being that we were only staying one more night, she would have our room fumigated while we were away touring, and that would certainly solve our minor problem. She also assured us that by the time we returned later in the day, the traffic noise would be less. The only redemption we had was the magnificent view of the Bay of Salerno from our seat at the terrace's dining table. The sparkling blue-green water, with boats passing by and the magnificent Island of Capri painted into the background, was just the calming influence I needed to get my blood pressure back to somewhere near normal. The view; smell of sea air; aroma of *caffe*, bacon, eggs and slightly burnt toast, was all that was needed as a turning point to begin our day anew and bring smiles back to our faces. This was especially so when we were served blood orange juice, which is, without a doubt, Barbara's favorite breakfast drink, and is in abundance in Southern Italy. It's amazing how in such a short period of time, she went from screaming and pounding ants to purring as she drank her juice of choice. What a wonderful turn of events, going from a horrific beginning, to welcoming a new day with anticipation and excitement of what was yet to come.

After breakfast, we had some time before our bus left for the Naples area to explore the former convent that we were staying at. The hotel is located in the Commune of Amalfi in the province of Salerno, which is a part of the region of Campania, Italy. The town lies in a deep ravine at the foot of Mt. Cerreto (4,300 feet), surrounded by cliffs and beautiful coastal scenery. It's just over 20 miles from Naples, but is low keyed, clean, and a beautiful seaside resort location that many people from the overcrowded city of Naples escape to for fresh air and relaxation. The town is a main stopping place for tourists along the *Costiera Amalfitana*, which includes other hillside towns, such as Positano and Ravello. A huge cathedral is in the center of town, which we noticed the night before while searching for a café. It was lit up with an abundance of lights that gave it a silhouette image. So large and spectacular was the church that it made the surrounding area disappear from sight, and all that could be seen was the electrified cathedral. It is dedicated to St. Andrew (as is the town) and is probably the town's largest manmade tourist attraction, both in size and attendance. St. Andrew's relics are preserved in the enormous church, punctuated with the largest steps in width and elevation that I have ever seen, leading up to the large doors of the cathedral. The steps reminded me of the Aztec pyramids' stairway in Mexico City and those of the Mayan ruins in Chichen Itza, only there is no provision in Amalfi for human sacrifices. The Saint's remains were brought to the area in 1210 from Constantinople by Cardinal Pietro, and placed in the cathedral for safekeeping and religious worship. The former convent that we were residing at was founded in 1222 by St. Francis of Assisi and converted into the first hotel on the Amalfi Coast in 1821. Wow, what history! I wondered how long the ants were occupants of our room and if their ancestors knew any of the people of Assisi's famous order. The hotel itself is perched on a cliff directly above the sea, with the most spectacular views of the coast, to be enjoyed from almost every window and terrace in the resort-like hotel. At sea level, there is a spectacular infinity pool with comfortable lounge chairs and equipment that is easily accessible for snorkeling in the pristine blue-green waters containing an abundance of small sea life. Oops, we forgot, it was bus time again, so off we went for our short trip to the Capodimonte area.

Although Naples was only a little over 20 miles from our hotel, it took more than an hour to get to our destination due to the heavy traffic around and in the city. I put the time to good use and read the material Fran so wisely distributed the night before, on the history of Palazzo Capodimonte and the plethora of sights surrounding the palace. The monarch Charles VII kept himself pretty busy; in addition to having the Royal Palace of Caserta built, he decided at about the same time to have a summer residence built by another renowned Italian architect, Giovanni Antonio Medrano, who also built the beautiful Teatro San Carlo Opera House in Naples. One of his primary objectives was to house the fabulous Farnese art collection that he inherited from his mother, Elizabetta Farnese, who was the last descendant of her majestic family to carry that name. He had his enormous collection, which consisted of paintings, drawings, statues, medals, coins, gems, cameos, and other archeological antiquities, transferred to Naples. The king didn't remain in Italy to see the palace completed, as his father, the King of Spain, had died and he inherited that superior, more prestigious, royal crown, passing the Kingdom of Naples and Sicily to his third son, Ferdinand. His son, who became one of the longest-reigning monarchs in Europe, had the distinct honor of overseeing, with the assistance of his capable wife, Queen Maria Carolina, the completion of both monumental projects. The palace is located on top of a hill (*Capodimonte*) and is the largest open area park in Naples. It shares the park grounds with the former Capodimonte Factory (currently the School of Ceramics), the Church of San Gennaro (built to provide religious services for the numerous colony of workers who lived in the park at that time), the *Casina dei Pincipi* (Prince's House), the *Casina della Regina* (Queen's House), many beautiful statues, and a maze of gardens with topiaries of every size and shape, mostly favoring arches.

There was so much to see and so little time to see it in. Fran's plans for the day were for us to spend one hour at the Palace Museum, one half hour at the former Capodimonte Factory, a leisurely hour exploring the Park, lunch, and then returning to our hotel for an afternoon on our own. Again, we would have to prioritize which of the sights to see; it seemed that each, individually, could probably consume all of our day's allotted time. We decided to stick with Fran and follow her lead. We followed her into the park, exiting the hustle and bustle of the crowded city streets of Naples. The lush foliage that we saw upon entering was unexpected, due to the contrast between the serenity and silence of the park and the noise and squalor of the streets we left behind. It reminded me of the feeling I always get when entering Central Park in New York City, except the streets there are a lot cleaner and the foot traffic less dense. We quickly located the palace, which dominated the park and attracts people like a magnet, due to its large rectangular size and its pinkish appearance in the sunlight, sharply contrasting with the greenery of the surrounding flora. Seeing the structure and recalling the Palace of Caserta and the Teatro San Carlo, one becomes cognizant of the complexity of King Charles VII and his passion for architectural beauty, appreciation of art and, eventually, his love for Capodimonte porcelain, which he developed in Italy.

The palace gained museum status after the unification of Italy, and is now the proud repository of Neapolitan and the general Italian cultural heritage of the city. The ground floor was the showcase of the museum, displaying the elaborate Farnese collection of classical, mostly Roman, monumental sculptures. The first and second floors house the National Gallery, with paintings from the 13th to 18th centuries, featuring works of the great masters, such as Michelangelo, Raphael, Titian, Caravaggio, El Greco, and Botticelli. It is one of the few museums in Italy that features classical as well as contemporary art, which is displayed on the third floor and is highlighted by Andy Warhol's *Mt. Vesuvius* (1985). A magnificent staircase led to the royal apartments, where flashy ornate antique furniture and a staggering collection of highly decorated porcelain and majolica from the various royal residences are on display. The state apartments, located on the basement level, had room after room of gilded mermaids, Venetian sedan chairs, ivory carvings, a porcelain Chinoiserie salon, tapestries, the Farnese armory, and a glass and china collection. After a briefing by Fran of what we would expect to see if we had a couple of days to explore the museum, she asked: "Which of the exhibits would you like to visit in the one hour remaining?" What a complicated question; what should we visit next? The four of us decided to use the map of the floor plans that were distributed to us and wander around on our own to locate Michelangelo, Raphael, and El Greco, and, time permitting, to study Andy Warhol's famous painting of *Mt. Vesuvius*. We located Michelangelo among the other incredible masterpieces. His drawing of the *Three Soldiers* is more of a sketch than a drawing. Raphael's *Moses and the Burning Bush* is also a drawing and it was difficult to distinguish the burning bush without the benefit of color. We visited the *Crucifixion of Christ* painting by Masaccio, Botticelli's *Madonna with Angels, the Gypsy* by Correggio, Giambellino's *Transfiguration*, and the outstanding painting depicting the brother of Robert Anjou being crowned King of Naples by the bishop of Toulouse, by Simone Martini. After leisurely gazing at the splendid collection of artwork, we decided we had better hurry along and get to the top floor to see Andy Warhol's *Mt. Vesuvius*. As is usually his style, the coloring and configuration of the mountain were distorted, but surprisingly, I recognized the painting from its exposure in various publications that I had read over the years. Next we rushed to explore the gardens in the magnificent park; if only we had the rest of the day to visit the incredible venue. I made a mental note to return soon to spend more quality time at the one-of-a-kind location.

The park's name, "Head of the Mountain" (*Capodimonte*), is not an Italian exaggeration. The park is on a high plateau overlooking Naples, its fabulous bay, and the city of Sorrento jutting out just across the bay. In the background, the ever-present monster, Mt. Vesuvius, loomed in all its ugly glory, occasionally making sounds as if to remind the inhabitants of the surrounding area that it still has some fire in its belly. Walking through a high gate brought us to the *Porta di Mezzo* (Middle Doorway). Entering the largest expanse of open space one can imagine, which is hidden in a metropolis far removed in its activity and appearance from nature, it was hard to believe that this respite from the city's reality existed. The scene was occupied by Holm-oaks, tall umbrella pines, and eucalyptus trees, and abounds with topiaries with arches enclosing statues in every direction. The great number of people in the park in the middle of the day, escaping from the stress and strain of the concrete jungle outside its green environment, was surprising, but understandable. Teens playing soccer, mothers and nannies pushing and attending to little ones, children chasing butterflies, joggers running in every direction along the wide paths (probably imagining that they were running a great marathon), and what has become a fixture in parks around the world, men, young and old, playing checkers or chess, while discussing and solving the world's problems, and momentarily at peace with one another. We leisurely strolled through the park and consumed the planned hour journey, while enjoying some espresso and cappuccino, which was readily provided by roadside vendors.

We didn't have much time left before our rendezvous with the returning bus, so we thought we should visit the Capodimonte Factory, being that it was such an integral part of the history of the park and palace. Unfortunately, it was closed for renovation but there was a docent on sight who showed us some the rooms being restored and was happy to tell us about the checkered history of the place:

> It was commissioned by the illustrious and prolific King Charles VII in 1743. He married Princess Maria Amelia Christina of Saxony, who was the granddaughter of King Augustus II, who, in addition to being the monarch of Poland, also founded the first European hard paste porcelain factory in Meissen, Germany. Her dowry consisted of extraordinary examples of Meissen porcelain produced in her father's royal workshop, which King Charles immediately fell in love with. His love became a passion and he ordered the greatest of Italian artisans to duplicate the porcelain, which at that time was a royal secret held by Maria Amelia's family. The king set up a school to research and train students in the preparation of porcelain, but it took many years of experimentation to finally develop what is today

known as Capodimonte Porcelain. Their first pieces, which were considered on a par with the collection held by Maria Amelia, were fired in 1759. The king was allergic to flowers, but loved their beauty, so he commanded that the artisans create delicate floral arrangements, each a tribute to his love of nature. His passion became so profound that he built a room to store their porcelain in the summer place in the city of Portici. In addition to the collection, the ceilings, walls, and floors were constructed of porcelain and mirrors. This dazzling display of beauty also inspired his son, Ferdinand, to continue his father's passion for the art, but it didn't come easily. When his father left for Madrid to take his place on the throne of Spain, he dismantled the factory and took all the tools and molds with him, so that no one other than himself would have the pleasure of overseeing the production of such beauty. So the Capodimonte factory was operational for a very short period of time, 1759 to 1780. The king's son couldn't get over his passion for the new art form and upon his father's death arranged to have the molds and paraphernalia returned to Naples. Ferdinand was an outdoorsman, so he made sure that his artisans reflected this in their creations. All was fun and games with him until the turn of the century, when Napoleon invaded Italy and forced Ferdinand and his royal party to flee to Sicily. From that time on, the factory fell into disrepair; the ownership changed hands many times, scattering the production of Capodimonte throughout Italy.

What a fascinating history lesson. Fran's high-pitched whistle sounded loud and clear, announcing that our journey was at an end. Box lunches were waiting for us to enjoy on our tedious journey back to the Town of Amalfi, which consisted mostly of moving in slow traffic, but, at least we had an opportunity to have some food during the boring, never-ending trip.

We arrived at our hotel and quickly went to our room to change into bathing suits so we could enjoy the exquisite swimming pool at the seawater's edge. We spent the rest of the afternoon relaxing in the sun, drinking local limoncello liqueur, snorkeling, and chasing colorful little fish that were in abundance twenty yards out in about four feet of water, in the magnificent blue-green waters of Sorrento Bay. After doing some serious napping under the protection of luscious green trees, we retired to our room to prepare for our farewell party at the family-owned Bersagliera Restaurant in the seaside area of Santa Lucia, Naples. Upon arrival, we were greeted by the current matriarch of the family that has been running the restaurant for three generations. We were led to our tables in a semiprivate room with views of the exquisite bay, especially from the terrace, where the stationary city lights combined with moving automobile headlights gave me the feeling of being inside a giant Christmas tree, looking out. On the way to our table we passed a signed picture showcase room of famous people that have enjoyed the cuisine of the renowned restaurant, such as Sophia Loren and Ingrid Bergman. The house specialties for the evening were clam and mussel soup, *taglierini* (fine ribbon pasta) with baby octopus, black olives, and tomatoes smothered with gorgonzola cheese. The one thing I learned about Italy in my several visits was, if there are house specialties, don't pass them up, because the chef invariably pays special attention to his creations, which have passed the tests of time and taste. So, we all ordered the chef's suggestion and were not displeased with our choice. As usual, the local wines were not only palate pleasing, but quite strong. After a couple of drinks, we were all feeling melancholy; unhappy to be leaving the incredibly historic and beautiful Amalfi area, and especially unhappy about leaving our newfound friends. There was pleasant background music playing, so many of us took the opportunity to visit the terrace, which had a surprisingly large dance floor, and danced under the hypnotic skies of Santa Lucia, inhaling and absorbing the sea air, the stars, the city lights, and the aroma of the moment. Only a dozen couples occupied the floor at any given dance, which left lots of room for us to dance without interruptions or collisions. There was a very sophisticated-looking couple, named Giovanni and Sophia, dancing a waltz that turned the other dancers into spectators. We couldn't keep our eyes off of them; they danced the waltz with great form and confidence. When they finished their dance we applauded and gave our verbal approval. They seemed embarrassed, but recognized our good taste with slight bows and enormous smiles on their faces. Barbara and I approached them and told them, in English, which they understood perfectly, how much we enjoyed their performance, especially a particular routine they did with exceptional style and grace. They were so flattered that they offered to teach us the steps; we accepted their offer without hesitation. They took us aside and showed us in ten minutes how to do the routine. Several other couples joined the class and they too were astonished at how easily we perfected the beautiful interpretation from the delightful couple. Giovanni asked the DJ to play another waltz and we all performed our routines fairly well; in the meantime, other restaurant guests were attracted to our exhibition and rigorously encouraged us with energetic applause and whistles. We danced the night away with additional bottles of wine, which our two new friends gladly shared with us. We couldn't have been more pleased with the dinner, wine, camaraderie, and the addition of a new waltz routine, which were complemented with the delicious sea air that engulfed the entire venue.

On our trip back to our place of rest, we were given mementos of our trip: Smithsonian pins and decorative majolica cups with the name of the restaurant imprinted on them. Neither would ever be able to take the place of the memories etched in our minds of the most incredible experiences in and around the city of the birth of my mother's parents, Naples. We were looking forward to the next leg of our unescorted journey to Rome on our own, for three days of just relaxing and visiting some of the places we enjoyed on our previous trips to the Eternal City.

We asked the hotel manager the best way to get to Rome from Naples and he said without hesitation, "Take the very fast Eurostar train and you will be in *Roma* in just one hour and a half." He secured train tickets for us for eight thirty the next morning. The tickets included reserved seats, which is mandatory when traveling on the busy trains; otherwise there is no guarantee that there will be any seats available. That evening we bid everyone farewell and exchanged addresses and telephone numbers, along with promises of keeping in touch. An unexpected bonus was the friendship that we developed with Shirley and Dallas Peck who would became our life-long friends. We would spend many happy occasions with them when visiting the Washington, D.C. area. They in turn were welcomed to our homes in Florida and New York.

The next morning we took a taxicab to the station and boarded on schedule with our four pieces of luggage, ever so alert of our surroundings, and keeping a close watch on our belongings, as we were told that pickpockets were rampant at railroad stations and on trains. We arrived in Rome's 30-plus-platform train station, on time, with our luggage intact. Now the fun began. On our previous trips to Rome, traveling by train and intersecting at that major station was always confusing. The language was always a big problem, so getting a "red cap" to carry our property to the street was not a pleasant experience. We struggled with our suitcases and finally got to a taxi stand at the entrance, passing thousands of travelers on the way and noticing that a Tourist Station was available that we didn't recall from our previous visits. Unfortunately, it was of little use to us, as the most difficult part of our journey was almost over. But, we both made a mental note of its location just in case we had to use the *Termini* in the future.

Our destination was the hotel Intercontinental *de la Ville* on *Via Sistina*, at the top of the Spanish Steps. We researched staying at the renowned Hotel Hassler right next door, but the rates were more than twice as much, even though both were rated as five-star hotels (European standards). The excitement of approaching our hotel through the busy, noisy, narrow Roman streets felt like a dream come true; we were not used to staying at a fine hotel in the middle of so much activity. On our previous trips to the Eternal City, we were on economy tours and stayed at small hotels in out-of-the-way places, which were surrounded by extremely noisy traffic and without the benefit of air conditioning, even though they were rated as three-star hotels (European standards). We were going to a choice hotel and couldn't wait to be pampered by its advertised luxury and fine service for the next three days. The outside of the hotel was deceiving; it was not decorative and could have been mistaken for a one-star hotel. However, once inside the lobby, the feeling of the hotel's inadequacy was quickly dispelled. The beautifully furnished lobby, featuring oriental rugs and marble table tops, were welcomed sights. An elegantly appointed marbled floored lounge, situated off the lobby, served refreshments and tea, which was more than a welcome sight as it was around lunch time and we were both famished. We had a leisurely lunch and discussed our game plan for our short visit in *Roma*. Foremost on our itinerary was a visit to the Sistine Chapel, which we had visited twice before. The first time, Michelangelo's paintings were dark and covered with centuries of soot, which made much of the famous artwork's colors difficult to distinguish and appreciate. We recalled how upset we were when we saw the condition of the one-time heavenly ceiling, and spoke of it with frustration on many occasions after our first visit. Our second visit was in the midst of the Chapel's restoration and seemed like an epiphany. We saw about half of the ceiling restored to its original bright colors, sparkling in contrast to the untouched dull parts of the ceiling. The refreshed views hypnotized us, as Michelangelo originally intended. The incredible fete of painting religious stories on ceilings not only required his astonishing artistic talents, but his patience and stamina, which seems to be reserved for gifted artisans of his caliber. The restored artwork couldn't be appreciated before the restoration process, but scenes that were not noticed, seemed like a revelation; radiant colors burst into life, decorating the holy scenes and enriching each story's message. What a contrast between the "before and after." Trying to get any meaning from the soon-to-be renovated remaining ceiling was an eye strain, as their true colors were mostly a dull gray, with many areas blurred. We were anxious to see the ceiling completely renovated so we could appreciate the artistic talents of the many artisans who were responsible for adding beauty to the glorious chapel.

Second on our list, or on Barbara's list, was to leisurely stroll to visit the shops on the Via Condotti at the bottom of the Spanish Steps, which was right below our hotel. Her fondest memories of *Roma* were visiting Gucci and Valentino, plus every designer-named clothing and jewelry store listed in her "wish book." We finished our lunch and immediately went to our mini-suite on the seventh floor facing a courtyard, which we chose so that the local traffic noise wouldn't keep us awake at night. The rooms with outside terraces facing the street had better views of the Eternal City, but we decided that forgoing the views for better sleeping conditions was worth the sacrifice. Views of the city from the terraces throughout the hotel were almost mystical. In the distance was St. Peter's Basilica, the almost 2,000-year-old Pantheon, a monument honoring the first king of unified Italy, Victor Emmanuel, and the uneven tops of building, most predating the discovery of America in 1492, by the Italian explorer, Christopher Columbus. In the opposite direction were views of the "Borghese Gardens" and the hotel's beautiful central courtyard with gracious flower displays and a unique intermittent dancing water fountain. The most thrilling view to me was the Spanish Steps when the azaleas lining both sides of the stairs are in bloom. Having seen many picture postcards of the colorful steps and its surroundings is just a tease to actually seeing them first hand; you feel as if you are drawn into the picture as one of the figures in the beautiful magical scenic view. Our room was what we had hoped for; quiet with a terrace view of the colorful courtyard, displaying an abundance of assorted rainbow-colored flowers.

After unpacking, we decided to stroll to the nearby shops that Barbara had dreamed of revisiting since our last vacation in the Eternal City. Walking down the Spanish Steps was a treat; people were moving about with no purpose, or just "hanging" with their friends, chattering away and enjoying the sort of leisurely camaraderie that most people in *Roma* seem to take pleasure in. It was surprising to see the number of young backpackers that were hanging around the bottom of the steps, just rapping and singing to their guitar music. It was a pleasant sight to see young people who were probably from all over the world getting along so well, while sharing their music with each other. Maybe all of the countries in the world should have young people in power who sing to each other when communicating; it might solve some of our major international challenges. From the bottom of the stairs looking back is probably what the "stairway to heaven" looks like, so inviting and surreal in its colorful flowered splendor. Overwhelming in size, a rose-colored church, *Trinita dei Monti*, sits at the top of the steps; a protruding large obelisk in front of the cathedral is dwarfed by two large bell towers that seem to be guarding the steps and the *Piazza de Spagna* below, where we were standing. The Cathedral's huge size and beauty beckons those who believe, to journey up the 12 flights, consisting of 137 steps, to join the religious congregation worshiping within.

On our way to Gucci, we stopped to admire the statue of *Fontana della Baraccia* (a small boat being filled with water). Usually renderings of boats have them floating on water, but not this one; it commemorated the flooding of the Tevere River in 1598, resulting in a small boat beings stranded at the location after the water had returned to its home base in the River. I tried to kill some time admiring the artwork, but Barbara wouldn't let me get away with wasting precious moments, when she could be putting the time to better use shopping. After two hours of browsing and shopping, Barbara was satisfied with her new conquests, which meant we couldn't carry any more packages, so we gave up and looked for our favorite restaurant, *Re degli Amici* (Royal Friends), to see if it was still in business. This little restaurant, which is almost hidden from sight among the fashionable designer stores, is rumored to have attracted many young artists in the '50s and '60s. Some of these artists paid for their meals with paintings, which are festooned on the walls throughout the establishment. It was just where we remembered, so we anxiously made reservations for that evening. It was worth seeking out the trattoria; their buffet bar boasts 32 different antipastos, worthy of many helpings. Unfortunately, after indulging several times at the antipasto bar, ordering second, third, or fourth courses, which is common in Italy, is usually out of the question. But after visiting the antipasto bar that evening, I did find room for some *orrechiette* (ear pasta), smothered with eggplant, Sicilian style, and Barbara did force herself to enjoy her favorite pasta puttanesca. Sharing a bottle of local wine complemented the cuisine, and our waiter, Vito, who we asked for by name, was *par excellence* in charm, politeness, and service, as he was in years past. He continued, to our delight, an Italian tradition, which rewards customers that waiters are fond of with a free pre-dinner drink and a complimentary, after-dinner refreshing limoncello drink. After almost eating ourselves into oblivion, we bid Vito good night and very slowly walked back to our hotel enjoying the cool fresh air and the aromatic aftertaste of the delicious food.

After a great night's sleep, we enjoyed a sit-down breakfast at the hotel, which was part of the package rate for our visit. What is worth mentioning is that they served pancakes, which is very unusual in Italy, and their coffee Americana was pretty good, not the usual watered-down version. We exited the hotel and hailed a taxi for our journey to the smallest sovereign state in the world, The Holy Vatican City. Its official name is State of the Vatican City, or, in Italian, *Stato della Citta' del Vaticano.* It's a sovereign city-state whose territory consists of a walled enclave within the city of *Roma,* spread out over 109 acres, with a population of 800 people. It's an elected monarchy that is ruled by the Bishop of Rome, the Pope, who resides in his Apostolic Palace within the sacred walls. The Sistine Chapel is also located in the Apostolic Palace. It's primarily used for papal religious and functionary meetings, including the Papal Conclave (election of new popes).

The restoration of the chapel was to be done in two stages, the walls first and then the ceiling. If the first phase was successful, then the ceiling's restoration would be tested as a precautionary measure and, if all went well, the whole ceiling would be restored to its almost original renderings. Oddly, the restoration was not paid for by the Catholic Church but by Nippon Television Network and took approximately ten-plus painstaking years to complete. Having researched the history of the Chapel and its restoration made our visit all the more exciting, and we couldn't wait to see the completed accomplishments of so many talented artisans who worked on the chapel inch by inch, for over ten years, to reestablish its artistic splendor. We had a lucky day; there weren't many people in the Vatican courtyard and very few in the chapel. Entering the holy place was like waking in the morning in a dark room and raising a window shade. The burst of sunlight not only wakes your senses but almost blinds you with its intrusion. The colors in the chapel were bright and the backgrounds pristine; what a difference from our two previous visits, where darkness was prevalent in most of the venue, where walls and ceilings were dim, and the atmosphere of the chapel was dusty and smoky. Since the restoration, an air purification system had been installed to filter the enormous unwanted pollution that is imported by the million-plus annual visitors that enter and admire the sacred place. With the use of electronic docents, we began our new adventure of exploring the incredibly creative endeavors of so many amazing artists, such as Pietro Perugino, Sandro Botticelli, Luca Signorelli, and Michelangelo Buonarroti. The original wall frescos took less than a year to complete, and are divided into three epochs: before the Ten Commandments were given to Moses; between Moses and Christ's birth; and the Christian era. Some of the more profound frescos in artistic presentation and historical biblical meanings were Perugino's *Christ Giving the Keys to St. Peter.* The scene references the biblical story in which the "keys of the kingdom of heaven are given to St. Peter." The keys represent the power to forgive and to share the word of God with all people, regardless of race or creed, giving everyone access to the "Kingdom of Heaven." Botticelli's three scenes of *The Life of Moses, the Temptation of Christ,* and *the Punishment of Korah,* who was the leader of a rebellion against Moses, were also descriptive presentations of those historic events. We were fascinated by all the renderings, but absorbed by *the Temptation of Christ* painting. This is a story that all Christians are taught at the beginning of their religious training, and frequently reminded of for the rest of their lives. In this scene, Christ's three temptations by Satan, as described in the Bible, are in the background of the painting, with Satan disguised as a hermit. At the top left, residing on the top of a mountain, he is challenging Christ to turn stones into bread; in the center we see them standing on a temple, with Satan attempting to persuade Christ to cast himself down; on the right side, he is showing Christ the splendor of the world's riches, which he is offering to Christ for his capitulation. Christ finally drives away the Devil, who ultimately reveals his true form. In the middle ground on the left, Christ is explaining to three angels the activity that is taking place in the center of the fresco, which is a Jewish sacrifice signifying the crucifixion of Christ, who through His death offered mankind salvation. Christ's sacrifice is reconstructed in the celebration of the Eucharist, referred to by a gift table prepared by God's messengers, in the upper right side of the painting. The enjoyment I received in viewing these clear and easy-to-read paintings, right down to the minutest detail, can only be described as pure ecstasy. I was fortunate to have had a very religious upbringing, reinforced by detailed readings of the Bible. Seeing the stories of the Bible, which have been vividly imbedded in my mind for so many years, come to life with such clarity in these renderings, were extremely fulfilling, both intellectually and emotionally.

Behind the sacred Sistine Chapel altar wall was one of the most startling, in size and content, mural displays in the world of *The Last Judgment,* painted by Michelangelo, more than 30 years after he and his contemporaries finished painting the magnificent ceiling and wall frescos. His creation was done under duress, as he considered himself a sculptor, not a painter, and his last experience with the masters of the domain turned out to be anything but pleasant. He spent years painting the ceiling with papal interference and without proper compensation, and didn't want to repeat the experience. But Pope Paul III, Farnese, forced him to undertake that enormous project and, to placate Michelangelo, allowed him the freedom to paint the wall without supervision. It took him from 1535 to 1541 to complete *The Last Judgment,* which from a distance is heart shaped, as if engulfing the Biblical stories with divine love. When viewed by the papal entourage, their opinions were mixed and heated; some said the nude figures showing man in all his glory were the work of a genius, others said they were the work of a pervert and should be redone. Whatever, the work is enormous and spans the entire wall behind the altar. It's a depiction of the second coming of Christ and Judgment Day. At the center is the figure of Christ signaling people at the left side of the painting with his right hand, who are trying to rise to Heaven, that they are traveling in the wrong direction. His left hand is welcoming the chosen few to rise to their promised place in Heaven, including descriptive figures of those rising from their graves. The fresco rises from behind the altar in a threatening manner, instilling fear, piety, and respect for the almighty, especially when considering his muscular presence. Even the Virgin Mary at the center seems to be trembling before God. The other figures in the various scenes are also muscular, very much as a sculptor would produce in a statue, and very much how Michelangelo saw humanity. Influential servants of the church began what was called the "Fig-Leaf Campaign," to have the genitalia in the fresco covered with paintings of fig leafs. This was eventually done by the artist Daniele da Volterra, whom history remembers by the descriptive nickname of "The breeches-painter." It's believed that Michelangelo used some of his friends as models for his figures; for sure he painted himself into the mural twice. The first is St. Bartholomew's displaying of his flayed skin; in his left hand is the face of Michelangelo (self-portrait of Michelangelo). He also appears in a figure in the lower left hand corner, looking encouragingly at those rising from their graves and ascending to Heaven. A second known figure is that of that the Pope's Master of Ceremonies, Biagio da Cesena, who complained to the Pope that the mural should be covered over because the obscene renderings had no place in a holy sanctuary. For his complaining, Michelangelo gave him immortality by painting da Cesena's face on Minos, judge of the underworld. Over the years, many more figures were altered for what was considered "justifiable sacred reasoning," and it's miraculous that the restoration, to a great extent, restored much of the original content.

Michelangelo was first commissioned by Pope Julius II to repaint the vault of the chapel, which at the time was a plain rendering of a blue sky with golden stars and not to the Pope's liking. It took him from 1508 to 1512 to complete the enormous undertaking, which originally was for painting the 12 apostles, and ended with over 300 bodies and head figures. The massive scenes included *The Creation, Adam and Eve in the Garden of Eden,* and *The Great Flood.* To successfully produce his stories on the ceiling, he made a flat wooden platform on brackets extending out from holes in the wall, high up and near the top of the windows, instead of from the bottom up, which would have required a monumental structure. The scaffold didn't extend the length of the room and had to be repositioned, as needed. He stood, kneeled, and laid on the platform to execute his creations, which resulted in the painting of 32 monumental figures, sibyls, prophets, and figures of Atlas, all in frames with decorative accessories. In all, he executed approximately 370 figures in ever-changing situations and positions from his memory and deep religious beliefs. To complicate his task, the paintings were done on wet plaster to create a permanent color bond, which was mold resistant, and hopefully more enduring than painting on dry surfaces. This reminded me of the *Last Supper* mural in the back dining halls at *Santa Maria delle Grazie,* in Milan, Italy, painted by Leonardo da Vinci in 1495, which was commissioned by his patrons Duke Ludovico Sforza and his duchess, Beatrice d'Este. Leonardo did not use Michelangelo's wet surface method, instead he painted the Last Supper on dry surfaces, which resulted in the deterioration of the colors and surface within a few years. When we saw the mural, prior to its "repainting," the scene was almost unrecognizable from the many pictures and mini-sculptures we had seen of the famous painting. Leonardo knew of his nemesis' technique, but chose to experiment with his own method, probably to show up Michelangelo, which turned out to be disastrous.

Michelangelo was able to maintain some sense of humor during the creation of the ceiling, and wrote a humorous sonnet and a sketch of his condition. The verse went:

> Here like a cat in a Lombardy sewer! I Swelter and toil!
> With my neck puffed out like a pigeon,
> belly hanging like an empty sack.
> Beard pointing at the ceiling, and my brain,
> fallen backwards in my head!
> Breastbone bulging like a harpy's
> and my face, from drips and droplets,
> patterned like a marble pavement.
> Ribs are poking in my guts; the only way
> to counterweight my shoulder is to stick
> my butt out. Don't know where my feet are—
> they're just dancing by themselves!
> In front I've sagged and stretched; behind,
> my back is tauter than an archer's bow!

The sonnet was accompanied by a sketch of his outstretched body reaching up to the ceiling continuing his painting and suffering.

The essence of Michelangelo's creations illustrates that God made the world a perfect garden and put Adam and Eve in charge to walk with him and flourish. But humanity fell in disgrace and was punished by death. God sent prophets and sibyls to tell humanity that the Savior, Jesus Christ, would bring them redemption, if they behaved themselves and followed his rules. Michelangelo used bright colors and clear formats to describe these stories, which, thanks to the restorations, are still easily visible from below. On the lowest part of the ceiling over the windows, the ancestors of Christ are depicted by name. Above this, he displays male and female prophets, including Jonah, who resides over the holy altar. On what seems to be the highest part of the ceiling, he painted nine stories from the *Book of Genesis,* the first book of the Bible. Trying to comprehend the vast undertaking without specific religious knowledge, and my friend the electronic docent, would have been an impossible task. Just looking up at the ceiling for long periods of time was a major physical effort making it difficult to focus on many of the scenes. These paintings fall into three main categories: *God Creating the Heavens and the Earth, God Creating Adam and Eve,* and thirdly, *The Plight of Humanity,* in particular the family of Noah, the renowned Biblical navigator. Of all the outstanding scenes, God creating light and separating it from darkness was fascinating to me for its contrast in colors and meaning. In the central section of the ceiling is probably the most widely recognized scene in the world, that of God reaching out to touch Adam. It actually comes to life as if you are witnessing the actual creation of Adam. While viewing this scene I couldn't help but remember the movie *E.T.*, where the alien reaches out to touch the boy's finger in the same manner as the portrayal in the ceiling's rendering. The story of Noah in the final panels is outstanding in its rendering of the *Great Flood*, in which Noah, his family, and entourage escapes in the Ark while the rest of humanity tries to find safety from the devastating flooding waters. When viewing the Sistine Chapel in all its glory, it is difficult to comprehend the intellectual complexity and depth of emotion that went into this astonishing achievement. It was best said by Goethe: "Without having seen the Sistine Chapel, one can form no appreciable idea of what one man is capable of doing."

When exiting the chapel, I felt euphorically dizzy; the overwhelming intellectual, artistic, and spiritual journey enriched my heart and soul. The experience is one that will stay etched in my mind and soul forever. We didn't realize how much time we had spent at the chapel, as it was well past lunch time. So we decided to have some treats at our favorite outside café, "Doney's," on the *Via Veneto*, and enjoy some great Italian salads, wine, and to just goof off for the rest of the day. Walking along the *Via* is a treat in itself and just what I needed to clear my head from all the excitement of the day's enriching and mind-boggling experience. There are many sites that are within walking distance from the café that we were privileged to have seen on our former visits to the Eternal City: the ancient Aurelian Wall that surrounds the city of Rome and is still pretty much intact (two-thirds remaining); *Villa Borghese; Trevi Fountain; Pincio Gardens;* and one of our favorites, the Spanish Steps. We found a great viewing seat at Doney's, as it was late in the afternoon but prior to the late afternoon onslaught of people watchers. We ordered salads and cakes with local Italian white wine while relaxing and watching the beautiful locals parading along the avenue, just as in Federico Fellini's 1960 movie *La Dolce Vita* (*The Sweet Life*), starring Marcello Mastroianni playing a newspaper paparazzo. After a couple of hours of relaxation, we strolled back to our hotel, as Barbara peeked into some of the better shops along the avenue. After such a grueling day, we decided to take a nap and have dinner at the hotel's restaurant, *La Piazetta,* which had a reputation of fine dining in a casual atmosphere. We enjoyed a small leisurely meal, which, of course, included some pasta, and spent the rest of the evening hanging around the Spanish Steps, listening to soothing guitar music that filled the air, and the songs from young backpackers gathered at the bottom the steps. I pictured my daughter, Laurie, and her friends in the group of young travelers, expressing themselves in song and music, in their quest to find themselves, which eventually most do.

The next day's schedule included the famous Rome Flea Market. After an apple pancake breakfast, we walked to the Porta Portese Outdoor Flea Market. Who can resist a flea market? This one put all the markets that I've ever seen to shame in its size: over 4,000 merchants with every type of merchandise imaginable for sale. I visited the Tokyo Ginza Outdoor Flea Market, which is now enclosed, when I was stationed in Japan, while serving in the U.S. Air Force in the early 1950s. It was considered, at that time, one of the largest in the world, but was quite small compared to this never-ending Italian merchant's and shoppers' marketplace. It's open on Sundays from 7:00 A.M. to 1:00 P.M., with peddlers from the surrounding area setting up temporary booths and selling every imaginable type of merchandise, including antiques, secondhand clothes, books, magazines, termite-eaten WWII wooden medallions, Etruscan hairpins, bushels of rosaries, and food products. It was located at the gateway to the Roman wall, which was built in the 17th century by Pope Urban VII in response to the horrific sacking of Rome by German mercenaries. The present gateway replaced the original 3rd century ACE one that was built by Emperor Aurelianus, who decided to reinforce the existing Roman wall and include the strategic areas of Trastevere and Janiculum Hill within the wall's protection. It was a treat watching Barbara bargain with the Italian merchants; up and down they would go with their pricing, each trying to outsmart the other, knowing full well, that when the transaction was complete, the vendor would still be ahead of the game, and maybe Barbara would walk away with a bargain or at least with an item she convinced herself she couldn't find anywhere else at such a low price. As far as I was concerned, shopping that takes more than five minutes is not my cup of tea, unless it's for golf clubs, cars, or boats. I think most men would agree with me; shopping and *hondeling* are for girls, who have a lot more staying power than we do. So, when I saw the vendors' temporary booths extended for as far as the eye can see, I had to find a way out of the maze that had turned into a trap for me. The area was quite crowded and seemed safe, so I told Barbara that I was going back to the hotel to work out at the gym. She didn't mind, and seemed quite relieved to get me out of her hair so she could continue her favorite pastime, which is shopping and bargaining endlessly with merchants.

Barbara knocked on the door to our room and woke me from a heavenly nap. Much to my surprise, she was only carrying two shopping bags, one with a small oriental multicolored reddish vase, and the other with leather lipstick holders for herself, my daughter Laurie, and daughter-in-law Donna. The hotel concierge told us about a place on the outskirts of Rome, The Alpheus Club, that was the "in" place for dancing. What better way to spend our last night in the Eternal City than to mingle with the locals and dance the night away? So we decided to have a light salad for dinner, and were off to the club.

We got to Alpheus early, and were surprised to see the crowds already building up. The venue is unique in that it's a multi-club building, with three main halls hosting every type of dance, from Argentine tango to hip hop. The favorite dance seemed to be salsa. The room with the Latin rhythm was already crowded with young people dancing and showing off their sexy salsa routines and totally enjoying themselves. One of the dancers told us, in perfect English, that the salsa craze reaches its crescendo when the annual World Salsa Festival is held in Rome, usually from the first week in July until the first week in September, attracting over a million and a half people from around the world, all coming to Rome to dance salsa. Similar festivals are also conducted in many other major cities around the world. Rome also hosts the World Salsa Championship in the spring, which lasts a few days and includes dance lessons, showcase dancing, salsa performances by world-famous dancers, and championship competitions on every level. Many are an open contest, which means anyone can enter regardless of their credentials or level of dance experience. We joined the dancers and felt right at home doing our mambo-salsa routines, which we've developed over the years, mixing our steps from salsa, mambo, and cha-cha. After exhausting ourselves with salsa dancing, we moved over to the room that was featuring Argentine tango dancing, which is a lot less energetic, and were able to comfortably dance the remainder of the night away in a less crowded, more romantic atmosphere, making new friends as we changed partners during the course of the evening. Changing partners is customary when dancing the Argentine tango, which makes the romantic dance all the more exciting, and enhances meeting new people with the same love of the Latin dance. If we had time, we probably would have stayed, danced, and made merry into the wee hours of the morning with our new Italian friends, but time was short and our drinking capacity even shorter, so we bid farewell to the tango dancers and attempted to pay our check with a 50,000-lira bill. Well, the waiter said the money was "No good." In a state of shock, I attempted to pay the bill with my American Express Card, which also got a "No good" response from the waiter. One of our new friends explained that the bill was a counterfeit and that the club didn't accept credit cards, only cash. Fortunately, I had traveler's checks to cover the bill, offered my apologies, and left the place as fast as possible. While waiting for a taxi, we noticed that the club had an active gay bar with people dancing and socializing without any friction between the various people in attendance at the other dance halls. When we got back to the hotel, I went directly to the manager's office and told him that when I converted my travelers' checks that morning, the attendant at the desk gave me a counterfeit 50,000-lira bill in the exchange. He asked who the attendant was. I tried to describe him as well as I could. The manager apologized profusely, and gave me a new bill to replace the counterfeit one. We learned later that counterfeiting is a major problem in the country and that we should try to only use credit cards where possible to pay for any purchases. It seems that the counterfeiters target tourists, as we are not as familiar with that country's currency as we are with our own.

We ended our last day in Rome a lot wiser and totally satisfied with the entire trip, and reminisced about the good times and the many friends we made on our three-week journey. We made arrangements to fly from Rome to JFK on Alitalia Airlines, with a special business-class program that allowed us to use Alitalia's first-class lounge. As fate would have it, our flight was delayed over an hour due to the baggage handling personnel threatening to strike. We put the first-class lounge to good use again: newspapers, coffee, finger food, televisions placed in convenient areas, comfortable seats, and private toilets. Three hours passed rather quickly, and it was with regret that we boarded our plane and headed home to New York, humming: "Arrivederci Roma, it's time for us to part, city of a million moon-lit faces, City of a million warm embraces; la-la-la-la . . ."

Chapter Six – Traveling Around Upstate New York

When referring to Upstate or Downstate New York, it is difficult to determine the boundaries that separate them. Upstate commonly refers to the topography north of New York City and its suburbs, while Downstate, to the south, is usually considered to be New York City and Long Island. New York City relies on upstate for many of its services, such as its main drinking water supply from the Delaware and Catskill Aqueducts. Much of the city's electric power comes from the state-owned hydroelectric plants in Niagara Falls and the St. Lawrence River. Upstate is also the proud location of New York State's capital in the City of Albany.

Of the many exciting places that we traveled through Upstate, I'll discuss three of the most popular destinations for many vacationers; the Catskill Mountains, Niagara Falls and the West Point Academy.

The Catskill Mountains

When Barbara and I had been married for a couple of years, she decided that it was time to introduce me to her childhood summer playgrounds, the Catskill Mountains and the Borscht Belt, which are in Upstate New York. Borscht Belt is a term for the summer resorts, cottages, and cabins in the Catskill Mountains in Sullivan and Ulster counties. Borscht is a beet soup, popular with people of Eastern European descent, more specifically, of Jewish heritage, hence the name Borscht Belt. Due to the predominately Jewish population in the summer months, the area was referred to as the Jewish Alps, and Sullivan County was referred to as Solomon County. It was primarily a vacation place enjoyed by New York's Jews, who escaped the city's hot summers by traveling, usually by car, in an inordinate amount of traffic, to the cooler Catskills. Well-known resorts in the heydays of the 1940s, 1950s, and 1960s included Brown's, The Concord, Grossinger's, Kutsher, Nevele, Friar Tuck Inn, The Pines, Raleigh, Shawangha Lodge, and the abundance of cottages and summer camps that are spread throughout the region. The upscale places would host famous entertainers, such as Joey Adams, Woody Allen, Milton Berle, Mel Brooks, George Burns, Red Buttons, Sid Caesar, Danny Kaye, Jackie Mason, and Don Rickles. They are only the beginning of a long list of celebrities performing for the ever-gracious crowds. The area's popularity began to decline as a vacation haven with the availability of air conditioning and jet planes, which allowed people to fly to faraway places in comfort in the same amount of time as it would take them to drive on the crowded highways to the Catskills. In addition, the decline of discrimination or "restrictions" in the hotel and travel industries in the 1960s allowed Jews access to other resorts and playgrounds around the world, so they joined the "Jet Set" and gradually abandoned the Borscht Belt. A recent brochure from the Nevele resort described the summer escape perfectly:

"Imagine a place, just a short distance from home, where the natural beauty and clean country air transports you to a state of serene exhilaration. Nestled in a valley bordered by the tranquil Shawangunk Mountain range, there are 1,000 panoramic acres called the Nevele Grande Resort and Country Club. Our 432-room resort offers an intimate estate of guest accommodations, conference facilities, and recreational amenities. Whether you wish to exercise on our 18 holes of championship golf course, 8 outdoor or 5 indoor tennis courts, indoor and outdoor pools, or our state-of-the-art fitness center, or play basketball, volleyball, softball, bocce, or shuffleboard, the Nevele Grande offers an extensive array of family and children's activities. A stay at the Nevele Grande includes comfortable accommodations, bountiful meals, exciting activities and nightly entertainment."

In the winter, after reading the brochure, we booked five days and four nights at the resort and got an early Thursday morning start, hoping to beat the horrific automobile traffic that is so common when traveling from Long Island to Upstate New York. We arrived in time for lunch, checked into our room, and spent the better part of the afternoon enjoying the gym and indoor swimming pool. After a nice late afternoon nap, we went to dinner and ordered from their extensive menu. Unfortunately, none of the food was exceptional and the service was mediocre, but we did pick and choose until we were satisfied and quite full. There was a show that evening in their large, opulent theater, featuring none other than Jackie Mason, one of our favorite comedians. It was rare to see him since his dispute on the Ed Sullivan Show in 1964, when he allegedly gave Ed the **finger** and was fired from the show, becoming persona non grata at the more upscale entertainment centers. His humor 20 years after his TV event was still spontaneous and belly-laughing funny; his ability to poke fun at his Jewish heritage without being offensive was ingenious. After the show, we followed the direction of the music that was coming from the bar area, had a drink, danced a little, and headed for the elevator to our room for some well-deserved rest after a full day of playing and relaxing. On our way, someone called out, "Hey meester, vate a minute." It was Jackie Mason taking a midnight stroll. He asked what our names were. "Mike and Bobby, nice names," he said. "What business are you in? You're an accountant? Do I have a tax shelter for you? Do you like horses? You do? I have a stable that can make us a fortune . . ." He went on for half an hour with his routine, serious as can be, plugging away at his unique tax shelter. Wouldn't you know, the next evening his show had a whole skit about accountants and their tax shelters, specifically for horses and cows.

For dinner that evening, we sat at a table for eight, introduced ourselves, and stated our hometowns. Six degrees of separation came into play again in our lives when one of the couples, Dee and Curt Anderson, said they were from Reston, Virginia. We told them that we had dear friends in that town by the name of Dallas and Shirley Peck; they were shocked, as they are their dearest friends and neighbors and spend every New Year's Eve with them. We exchanged stories and were delighted when they asked us to share the upcoming New Year's Eve with them so we could surprise Dallas and Shirley. Unfortunately, we couldn't accept their offer, as we had already made plans for the holidays, but decided to do the next best thing. We took pictures, individually and together. They planned on videoing Dallas and Shirley's reactions to seeing the photos and promised to send us a copy of the tape, along with the pictures they took of our weekend retreat. We usually plan our annual visit to Reston, Virginia, on our way from New York to Florida during the first week of January. We decided that it would be a great time to get together and again view the video of Dallas and Shirley's reactions to seeing the precious memorable photos. We marked our calendars and made plans with them for the encounter, which turned out to be one of the most cherished experiences of our lives.

That evening, in the large cocktail lounge, which had a nice-size dance floor, we were introduced to the live sounds of the Latin Conjunto Imagen Band, which was one of the hottest new and upcoming Latin bands on the East Coast. Everyone was familiar with their music and thrilled to meet and hear them in person. The bandleaders were Ernie Acevedo and Junior Rivera, who, with their *compadres*, compelled everyone to dance to their great Latin sounds in mambo, meringue, rumba, and cha-cha, until we were exhausted. Considering that many of the people present took complimentary dance lessons that afternoon, it was surprising that there was energy left in any of us to continue into the late evening, but when you're having fun, energy always seems to be limitless.

The short weekend came to a close after lunch on Sunday for most vacationers; we exchanged names, addresses, and telephone numbers with our new friends that we planned on seeing, God willing, at some time in the future. Barbara and I stayed on for another day and after lunch decided to do some toboggan riding down the manmade slopes that were prepared for that purpose. We were a little leery about sitting in a small, closely-fitted sled and zigzagging down the icy manmade hill, until we saw children of every age and size having a great time with their newfound toys. Down we went, excited as excitement can be. The long ride down left us so breathless that we decided not to do a repeat performance. At the end of the run, we spotted snowmobiles that were for the use of the hotel's guests; so, feeling our oats after our non-eventful but scary toboggan run, we rushed to the snowmobiles for another new adventure. There were only a few riders on the large acreage dedicated to snowmobiling; the thrill of flying on the snow was exhilarating and having Barbara holding me tight from behind and screaming in my ears because of my reckless driving and excessive speed (about 20 miles per hour) made the half-an-hour ride all the more fun. I remember hoping that our drive back to Long Island would have the same uninhabited clear roads, with as few obstacles as the snow field.

Niagara Falls

After Barbara and I had been married for about a month, we were able to get a break for a few days from our relatively new jobs, so we decided that a great place to celebrate the "once-in-a-lifetime" marital event would be the spectacular falls in Upstate New York and Ontario, Canada. So we packed our bags, hailed a taxi cab in Brooklyn, where we lived, to the Pennsylvania Station in Manhattan, and boarded the *Honeymoon Express* to the "Honeymoon Capital" of the world. Our destination was a bed and breakfast on the U.S. side of the falls, which was over 400 miles due north from our home. It was a long, tedious ten-hour ride, but being that we were still newlyweds, sitting together in close proximity for such an extended period of time actually made the journey a romantic one.

Niagara Falls straddles the international borders of the Canadian province of Ontario and the U.S. State of New York. *Cayuga* is the collective name of the three waterfalls, which are the Horseshoe Falls, the American Falls, and the smaller Bridal Veil Falls. The Horseshoe Falls is on the Canadian side while the other two reside on the American side. They are located on the Niagara River, which drains Lake Erie into Lake Ontario, then to the St. Lawrence Seaway, and finally to the Atlantic Ocean. Together, they form the highest flow rate of any waterfall in the world, with a drop of more than 170 feet and width of 2,600 feet for the Horseshoe Falls, 70 feet high, and 1,060 feet wide for the American Falls, and 181 feet high and 55 feet wide for the Bridal Veil Falls. The Horseshoe Falls is the most powerful waterfall in North America, as measured by vertical height and water flow rate. When I visited the falls previously, I remembered that from both sides the views were the most dynamic and breathtaking sights that I had ever seen. I recalled that the roar on the Canadian side of the powerful falls was deafening, as the abundance of water poured over its crest and down to the lake below. I also remembered that at various times of the day, rainbows were seen decorating the falls and spanning both countries, resembling colorful bridges shimmering in the sun. I couldn't wait to revisit one of nature's remarkable gifts to the universe and mankind.

Our temporary home was probably made from the cuttings of the gigantic local trees that are in abundance throughout the area. The structure resembled an oversized two-story log cabin. It was hidden in a forest with deer, rabbits, and squirrels wandering around at will. The setting was a flashback to one of the Davey Crocket movie scenes that I had seen of his hunting in the woods for small animals and hoping to catch a raccoon to make into a hat, which was one of his trademarks. The only thing missing from the view were wild Indians shooting arrows at us. The decoration throughout the common areas in the enormous cabin was Colonial, with bearskin rugs in several strategically located places and moose heads hanging over the fireplaces, in addition to muskets and bows and arrows displayed on the walls throughout the building. Our room was decorated simply, with a comfortable double bed and an exceptionally clean bathroom. Unfortunately, we didn't have a view of the falls, but the forest scene from our window was serene and relaxing.

We were fortunate that the daily nighttime rainbow-colored-floodlight illumination of the falls was in progress, in addition to the weekly Friday night fireworks display. So we rushed to the Rainbow Bridge, which was a short distance from our cabin, and walked halfway across to get a ringside view of the multicolored falls and the spectacular fireworks display that lit both sides of the natural bounty of both countries. Another fun part to the bridge was that it connected Canada and the U.S. and we were able to straddle both countries, as there is a line in the middle of the bridge where I was able to put my left foot in Canada and my right foot in the U.S. Barbara did just the opposite; her right foot was placed in Canada and her left foot in dear old U.S.A. We were amused that we could kiss in two countries at the same time.

We marveled at the views from up and down the river of the surreal multicolored falls and the spectacular fireworks that seemed to explode in harmony with the sounds coming from the three falls.

In addition to the 20 million annual recreation visitors to the exciting attractions, the falls also have a commercial value in that they supply hydroelectric power to the surrounding area. We decided that the next morning we would get the feel of all that power by taking a ride on a *Maid of the Mist* boat (there are several) and venture along the Niagara River and up close to the three falls. We had a choice of taking a boat from the Canadian or the American sides; we chose a U.S. departure, as our cabin manager told us that the foreign docks were usually crowded and that there were long waiting lines. It was a good choice, as there were no lines at the dock on our side the following morning. So we boarded the craft and were able to choose a choice viewing spot at the front of the boat. Before boarding, we spent time on the Prospect Point Park Observation Tower viewing the Niagara River and the magnificent falls from a high vantage point. It was a clear day and the sky, river, and falls painted an everlasting picture in my memory that I would pleasantly visit many times in the future.

We were given ponchos to wear to protect us from the mist, and, thanks to our cabin manager's advice, we wore shorts and flip-flops to avoid getting our clothing drenched. Well, there was no mist from the American Falls; it was more of a deluge than a mist, so we began our voyage soaked from head to toe despite the precautionary measures we took. The most exciting part of the trip was approaching the Rainbow Falls; the energy and thunderous roar from the cascade of water not only soaked us again but the sound of the waterfall flowing over the crest and slamming the river was so loud I thought I lost my hearing. At the end of the ride, we disembarked and actually were able to walk under the falls where we received a further shower-bath. Although we were drenched after the experience, it was one of the most exciting and enjoyable journeys of our lives. It may seem strange, but after we returned to our room in the giant log cabin, we undressed and took hot showers to get the chill out of our waterlogged bodies.

We asked our cabin manager if he knew of a nice restaurant for us to have dinner. He said to cross over the Rainbow Bridge and walk around the Canadian side and check the menus that are posted outside the bistros; we did and chose a sidewalk café where we could view the rainbow-colored illuminated falls. We both chose the same French cuisine, trout almandine with steamed vegetables, roasted potatoes, and lots of French wine. Espresso coffee with Sambuca and a couple of biscotti were the finishing touches to a perfect meal and experience. We were so impressed with the day's activity, the spectacular view of the colorful falls, and the incredible French meal, that we daydreamed about moving to Niagara Falls and playing there for the rest of our lives. Our walk back to our cabin over the bridge was another unforgettable event; the cool night air, the sight of the rainbow-colored falls, the roar of the majestic waterfalls, the panoramic clear star-studded sky, and the warmth of my wife Barbara's hand in mine, concluded what was, without a doubt, one of the most perfect days at the beginning of our married life.

In the few days we spent at Niagara Falls, we also visited the Cave of the Winds, which was another wet experience under the Bridal Veil Falls, the Prospect Point Park on the American side and the Queen Victoria Park on the Canadian side. There is no doubt that we could have spent a couple of weeks in the area, but we had both just started new jobs and didn't have enough vacation time accumulated or the finances available to take such a dream vacation. We dreamed that in the future we would return to continue our love affair with the magnificent falls and countryside on both sides of the Rainbow Bridge.

West Point

Although Barbara and I spent our whole lives in New York, we never had an opportunity to visit West Point until we received a wedding invitation from a friend; she was having her wedding ceremony and reception at the Thayer Hotel on the grounds of the world-renowned military academy. We immediately looked up the hotel on the Internet and found that it had 149 guest rooms, was 7 stories high, was a Gothic Revival-style facility made of brownish granite, and is listed as one of the "Historic Hotels of America." It was built in 1829 and named the West Point Hotel. It has served the academy for over a century, hosting a long list of dignitaries such as Robert E. Lee, Ulysses S.

Grant, Stonewall Jackson, Washington Irving, Edgar Allan Poe, and James Whistler. It is associated mostly with one of West Point's famous cadets, General Douglas MacArthur, who became the Superintendent of the Academy after WWI and started a major expansion program of the buildings on the campus that included the Thayer Hotel. A rejuvenated hotel officially opened on May 27, 1926 with 225 rooms, but over the years, the guest rooms have been diminished due to renovations. He returned to the hotel for the last time in 1962 when he gave his famous speech, "Duty, Honor, Country," to the cadets and received the Sylvanus Thayer Award, which was named after Colonel Sylvanus Thayer, the "Father of the Military Academy" and a hero of the War of 1812. The award is presented annually to an outstanding citizen whose service and accomplishments in the national interest exemplify the Military Academy's motto, "Duty, Honor, Country." Thayer was the fifth Superintendent of the Academy and to honor his achievements, which included transforming West Point into one of the foremost engineering schools in the world, the award was created. Active-duty and retired American military servicemen are eligible for this award, but many civilians who have contributed in a positive way to the military, such as Walter Cronkite and Bob Hope, have also received the honor. Currently, West Point graduates are not eligible to receive the award. In the past, some of the famous recipients were Dwight D. Eisenhower, Neil Armstrong, James H. Doolittle, Ronald Reagan, and Henry A. Kissinger.

We were so excited to finally be going to the Point that we made reservations immediately on the Internet to arrive a day early to do some sightseeing. We also asked to have a room, if possible, with a view of the Hudson River.

The hotel and campus are situated halfway up a rocky ledge in the Hudson River Valley with an eagle's eye view of the waterway below. It's approximately 50 miles north of New York City, which made us extremely happy, as we could drive there from Long Island in a couple of hours, traffic permitting.

Well, traffic was not permitting; it took over three hours due to cars backing up on the Cross Bronx Expressway to get to Yankee Stadium to watch a New York Yankees' game. After we inched through the logjam, it was clear sailing. The view from that point on relaxed me, as it seemed as if Nature chose the Taconic Parkway and the roads leading to the Point to show off her ability to transform what's seen from the road when passing the Bronx's decrepit blacktop jungle. The landscape changes to a picture-perfect woodland, with trees and bushes of every color, size, and shape on display. A scene to behold is in the early fall when the foliage sheds its green colors and magically turns them orange, gold, red, burgundy, and a variety of shaded greens. We try to make it a point to visit the autumn wonderland whenever we can in the early fall, when many of the local towns are celebrating Oktoberfest, so we can join them in their festivities for the miraculous changing of the seasons.

We arrived at the hotel famished and just in time for lunch. We checked in and had our luggage brought to our room, while we made a mad dash to the Thomas Jefferson Patio for an al fresco treat. The Patio is situated so you can get a spectacular view of the Hudson River and the surrounding Bear Mountains. The mountains, it is said, resemble the profile of a bear from certain angles; on our short stay in the area, I couldn't capture that view, although I tried several different locations from the high vantage point of the Academy.

We were seated at the far end of the café where we could enjoy the magnificent view of the waterway and mountainside, which are certainly another example of Mother Nature's artistic talents. From our strategically located seats, the river seemed to be impossibly running upstream into the mountains as if the view was placed in that exact spot for the enjoyment and discussions of the diners on the patio.

The panoramic view stimulated our appetites, so we ordered a bottle of New York chardonnay wine and nursed it while examining the afternoon menu. Barbara ordered crab cakes with steamed vegetables; my choice was an "American Caesar Salad with Grilled Shrimp." The leisurely lunch lasted for over two hours, as we just couldn't stop absorbing the beauty of the Hudson Valley and the crisp clean air that engulfed our senses. We finally forced ourselves to leave and headed for our room on the sixth floor. The room was surprisingly small, with just enough walking space around the king-sized bed, but it did have a great view of the Hudson Valley, so we unpacked, tested the mattress, and immediately went to sleep. When we awoke from our short, well-needed nap, we went directly to the concierge and asked her how we could spend the rest of the day sightseeing. She advised us to go directly to the Visitor's Center and, if we had enough time, we should visit the West Point Museum, which is adjacent to the Center. It's worth mentioning that when we were there, before 9-11, the security on the campus and the surrounding area was practically nonexistent; today, the area is secured by up-to-date policing methods and sightseeing is strictly supervised.

We arrived at the center just in time to see a movie about the history of the Academy and its significance in producing many of our leaders and war heroes. West Point was an important stronghold during the Revolutionary War and considered by George Washington to be the most important strategic position in America. It had a bird's eye view of the activity on the Hudson River; so important was the position that a 150-ton chain was run from the Point across to Constitution Island to block any unwelcomed enemy traffic. Oddly, General Benedict Arnold was the commandant of the fortress, which was named Fort Arnold because of his heroic actions at the beginning of the war, in particular his winning of the Battle of Saratoga. After his desertion, the name was changed to Fort Clinton after the Mayor of New York City, DeWitt Clinton. The film also emphasized the importance of the Academy's engineering program that produced the talent that our young country needed to become independent of England and to satisfy our rapid economic growth. United States Military Academy (USMA) graduates were responsible for the construction of our nation's infrastructure, specifically building many of our initial railways, bridges, harbors, and roads.

Especially noteworthy were the exhibitions of full-scale rooms of the cadets' living conditions at the Academy. Throughout the facility, there are reminders of some of the great military leaders that wore the grey uniforms of the USMA, such as Generals Lee, Grant, Eisenhower, MacArthur, Bradley, Patton, Wainwright and astronauts Frank Borman and Buzz Aldrin.

We had to cut our visit short as it was nearing closing time, but we returned the next morning to continue our exploration at the West Point Museum, which was located just behind the Center. We found that its collections included nearly all aspects of U.S. military history, from the evolution of warfare to the development of the current American Armed Forces. Only a portion of the collection was on display, but the balance is available for the training of cadets on an ongoing basis. The artifacts collection began with the capture of British materials, which were brought to the Point after the capture of Saratoga in 1777 by Gen. Benedict Arnold. When the Academy opened in 1802, many of the Revolutionary War trophies were used in training young cadets in modern military warfare. After the Mexican War (1846–1848), West Point was designated, by Executive Order, as the permanent depository of war trophies. Today its artifacts represent a culmination of more than two centuries of preserved military history for the benefit of the cadets, the public, and posterity.

The museum had three levels and a sub-basement and was divided into six sections with galleries that included "Large Weapons," "Small Weapons," "The History of Warfare," "The History of West Point," "The History of American Wars," and "The History of the U.S. Army."

The sub-basement housed "The Large Weapons Gallery." It had over-sized displays ranging from large artillery pieces to a WWI tank. Very impressive were two murals by a veteran depicting the Allied Invasion of Europe in 1944. An atomic bomb housing of the type dropped on Nagasaki, Japan was an eerie sight, also, the WWI cannon that fired the first American shot of the war was displayed in an honorary spot.

The basement balcony displayed "The Small Weapons Gallery." It traced weapons from the Stone Age to modern times, such as axes, clubs, swords, shoulder arms, light machine guns, and pistols.

The first floor accommodated "The West Point Gallery" from the beginning of the Revolutionary War to modern times. It had artifacts from the Polish patriot Thaddeus Kosciusko, who engineered some of the Point's early fortifications, to a splendid exhibit of modern-day cadet uniforms, both male and female. Also featured were some items from famous cadets that graduated, such as Robert E. Lee, Ulysses S. Grant, John J. Pershing, Dwight D. Eisenhower, and Omar Bradley. Also on this floor was "The History of Warfare Gallery," which included dioramas of significant battles, as well as Napoleon's sword and pistols and many trophies of war from Nazi Germany. There was also almost every type of weapon, large and small, displayed with descriptions of their purpose and period of use.

The second floor was home to "The History of U.S. Army Gallery" and "The American War Gallery." The history gallery is dedicated to the U.S. Army's contribution to the growth of the United States. It featured exhibits on the opening of our Frontier, the Buffalo Soldiers, the construction of the Panama Canal, the secret Manhattan Project that built the atomic bomb, and Army aviation from balloons to space explorations. The War Gallery's theme was how our national freedom had been accomplished by the sacrifices of our fighting men and women. Displays exhibited the armor of colonial militiamen and the muddy jungle fatigues of the "Vietnam grunt." Fascinating were a British drum surrendered at Saratoga, George Washington's pistols, and the last message sent by George A. Custer at the Battle of the Little Bighorn. Impressive was the Medal of Honor Wall listing 74 USMA graduates who received our Nation's highest award including General Douglas MacArthur. Also showcased was the fact that two graduates, Generals Grant and Eisenhower, became presidents of the United States and that eighteen graduates were astronauts.

Barbara and I have always been fascinated by historical monuments of famous people, so we decided to take advantage of the pleasant weather to walk around the campus and visit as many as possible. We stopped at the *Eisenhower Monument.* The larger-than-life-sized statue of the General of the Army and the 34th President of the United States sits atop a pedestal of red granite and looks out over the "Plain to the North" as if he was overseeing the activity and safety of the USMA.

The *MacArthur Monument,* which is also larger than life sized, commemorates the former cadet and Medal of Honor winner (his father Arthur MacArthur also won that prestigious military honor) and is located on the western corner of the Plain next to the entrance of the MacArthur Barracks. Surrounding the statue are angled granite walls that bear inscription excerpts from his 1962 Thayer Award address to the Corps of Cadets.

We found our way to the *Kosciuszko Monument* because the Kosciuszko Bridge, which connects the New York City Boroughs of Brooklyn and Queens, is traveled by us frequently and we were curious to find out what the Polish hero did to make him so famous. His monument was dedicated in 1828 only as a base and column. A statue of him was added in 1913 and is neck-breaking high. He is probably one of the most fascinating of our Revolutionary War heroes. He came to the U.S. from Poland to join the fight for freedom and was instrumental in winning the Battle of Saratoga under the command of Gen. Benedict Arnold. His expertise in fortification was one of the reasons the British lost the battle. Because of his success, George Washington recruited him to fortify West Point, as it was considered the most important strategic location during that war. He was promoted to Brigadier General for his heroism and skill at fortifying some of our forts. He returned to Poland after the war and became Supreme Commander of the Polish National Forces in their battle against Imperial Russia and Prussia. He was wounded many times in that conflict and was unfortunately captured. After the war, he was released and exiled, so he returned to America, collected his back pay of over $15,000, and began his recuperation period from his war wounds. While resting, he enjoyed his recognition as an American hero and spent much of his time entertaining dignitaries and the local ladies.

The *Thayer Monument,* which is also another larger-than-life-sized structure, was built to commemorate the "Father of the Military Academy." It's located on the "South Plain" overlooking the central cadet area. The memorial is the sight of numerous gatherings throughout the year as classes return for their reunions. Tradition has it that the oldest living graduate of a returning class rests a wreath at the foot of the monument before the alumni perform their review for the weekend.

Time was running out, but we both wanted to see where George A. Custer and his wife Elizabeth were buried. We had just seen the television presentation of the 1941 movie *They Died With Their Boots On,* starring Errol Flynn and Olivia de Havilland and were infatuated with the romanticized film's version of the Civil War hero and the disastrous 1876 "Battle of the Little Bighorn" in Montana, which he lost to Indian chiefs Sitting Bull, Crazy Horse, and Chief Gall of the combined forces of the Lakota, Northern Cheyenne, and Arapaho tribes. When reading the history of Custer's life, we were puzzled that he was buried at West Point as a hero. When he attended the Academy, he was almost court-martialed for leaving his post. Although the records indicate he graduated at the bottom of his class, he didn't finish his full term at the Academy, due to the beginning of hostilities in the Civil War when many of the cadets were inducted into the military before they finished their time at the Point. He certainly was a Civil War hero, receiving field commissions from lieutenant to general in a short period of time for his heroism, but historically, it seems that his blunders at the "Battle of the Little Bighorn" certainly overshadowed his acts of heroism. He led the 700 men of the 7th Calvary against Indians that outnumbered him six to one without taking his three automatic machine guns (Gatling guns) into battle, which would have probably changed the outcome had they been available for use by his men. He split his regiment into four separate units, which weakened his position, as it removed some of them from the battle area. In the battle, he lost two brothers, Thomas (a two-time Medal of Honor recipient) and Boston, in addition to a brother-in-law and nephew. The total body count, including scouts, was 268 dead and 55 wounded.

Standing next to his 12-foot-high monument, which consisted of a large base and obelisk, was exciting to say the least. Originally, a statue of him in a swashbuckling moment on horseback was exhibited on the base, but his wife was unhappy with the image and had the statue removed. Although his wife is buried next to him, I would have thought that his brother Thomas Ward, who was the first soldier in the armed forces to receive two Medals of Honor, would have shared some space near his famous brother.

We rushed back to the hotel to get dressed for the cocktail hour, which was a couple of hours prior to the wedding ceremony. We passed the MacArthur Restaurant on the way to our room. The hotel has several cafes and lounges, the Thomas Jefferson Patio where we had lunch on our first day, the Zulu Time Rooftop Lounge, and the General Patton Tavern. We had dinner at the MacArthur Restaurant the night before, which has a five-star logo surrounding its name hanging on the wall at the entrance, which is in reference to the stars the general wore on his epaulet; it was also a five-star restaurant for food and service. I had ordered grilled filet mignon with mashed potatoes that was as tender and tasty as any I have ever had. Barbara ordered grilled shrimp with a baked potato and couldn't stop moaning under her breath at the crispiness and flavor of the cuisine. After dinner, we went up to the Zulu Room for after-dinner drinks and exotic DJ music. The food, after dinner-drinks, music, and the spectacular view from the large windows of the lights flickering while in motion on the Hudson River was not only the ending of a spectacular first day, but a memory that repeats itself in my mind every time I come across the words, "West Point."

The hotel has three banquet halls that are named after USMA generals. The smallest is the "General Dwight Eisenhower and General Hap Arnold Room," which accommodates from 50 to 100 guests. The largest is the "George Washington and General John Pershing Room," which holds from 150 to 220 guests, and the midsized venue, which is where our friend's wedding was held, is the "General Ulysses Grant and General Omar Bradley Room," which can accommodate from 100 to 230 guests.

There were over 100 guests at the cocktail lounge. The trays included many delicious hors d'oeuvres of grilled shrimp, small lamb chops, salmon cones, and many vegetable tidbits. Open bars rounded out the enjoyable social event. At dinner, we were seated with friends and relatives. What made the wedding unusual was that the husband was Christian and the wife Jewish, so a priest and a female rabbi conducted the ceremony. It was sort of surreal hearing Jewish-English words from the female rabbi followed by Latin-English words from the priest. But all in all, the experience, though strange sounding, was a pleasant and memorable one.

The dinner menu featured steak or fish with side dishes of potatoes and vegetables. The DJ music was contemporary except for a Jewish Hora dance to "Hava Nagilah," which is done in a circle with skipping and hopping around dancers in the middle of the ring. Not to be outdone, the husband's Italian relatives did a tarantella dance, which was done the same as the Hora, except it's done to Italian music with minor variations.

The next morning we left the hotel. Being that it was a Sunday and traffic was light, we were able to return to Long Island in two hours, relishing the experience of the USMA, the Thayer Hotel, and a unique dual-religious wedding experience.

The places of interest to visit in Upstate New York are endless, so I'll only briefly mention a few that we have visited on our many trips to the area.

The Thousand Islands has close to 2,000 islands in a region that stretches from Lake Ontario along the St. Lawrence River and up to Lake Champlain. Driving on the Great Lakes Seaway Trail, which is more than 500 miles long, takes you through many beautiful parks and has such beautiful views of the water that it's difficult to concentrate on driving safely. On route, a great stop is at Alexandria Bay for a taste of the area's history and a trip on Uncle Sam's Boat Tours to Heart Island where you can explore the 6-story, 120-room Boldt Castle. The name of the island reflects the intention of Mr. Boldt who built the castle in the early 1900s for his wife Louise. Unfortunately, she died very young and so distraught was he that he abandoned the citadel after her death, never to return again. Subsequently, the Thousand Island Bridge Authority purchased and refurbished the castle to its original condition.

An exciting day on the river is renting a runabout boat and exploring as many islands as possible; I did just that in my younger days and visited ten islands before sundown. It was an exhilarating and exhausting experience, not soon to be forgotten.

Other places we have visited are **Lake George, The Finger Lakes, St. Regis Canoe Wilderness, and Howe Caverns;** it would take several lifetimes to visit all of the exciting and unique places in New York, so I'll sign off now and will discuss in a later chapter our visits to Downstate New York.

Chapter Seven – Sailing on the Mississippi Queen Riverboat and on to Mardi Gras

~*~

AROUND THE FLOOR: JULY/OCTOBER 2000
TRAVELING AROUND by Barbara Bivona

As a young girl, I remember being fascinated with the adventures of Tom Sawyer and his friend, Huck Finn. So much so, that I would daydream about the Mississippi River and spending days on a paddleboat. Mike, on the other hand, told me he would daydream about the Mardi Gras in New Orleans, so both became items on our "Wish List" of things to do before we "kicked the bucket." One magical day, we received a brochure in the mail from the Delta Steamboat Company advertising a cruise on the *Mississippi Queen Paddlewheel* boat; the theme was big band dancing and Mardi Gras. The first and last stop would be New Orleans; in between, she would cruise the Mighty Mississippi, stopping at many local towns and cities along the way. The cream on the cake was being guests at a Grand Mardi Gras Ball. We couldn't ask for more; this was everything we both wanted in one great package.

If you've never been paddle wheeling, it's like no other cruise experience. It is strictly Americana; the food is authentic Southern cooking, complete with great barbecues and with all-you-can-eat chicken, fried catfish, cornbread, biscuits, and lots of other delicious regional specialties from the heart of the Deep South.

When we settled in on the *Queen*, we were given all the raw materials to create our own Mardi Gras costumes to dress up for an onboard celebration to the music of the great Guy Lombardo Band on the last night of the cruise. We were delighted by their dance music. Not just the playing of hits that made Lombardo famous, but for their good and very danceable arrangements for Swing and Latin. Earlier in the week, we were treated to the music of the Les Elgart Band; we danced the evenings away to his music that has held its own with the passing of time. He enjoyed sharing stories about his big band days with anyone who cared to chat with him. It was his music that we danced to the night of the dance competition. Most of the contestants were not really experienced dancers, but that didn't stop them from having a great time while getting into the spirit of Mardi Gras. Trophies were awarded to all the participants, which put a smile on everyone's face after the contest.

Following the cruise, we spent six days in the French Quarter of New Orleans, attending the parades and festivities, culminating with a Grand Mardi Gras Ball at the Fairmont Hotel, hosted by a Krewe from the Mardi Gras parade. The Krewes are organizations that put on the parades, which includes many floats, all with their own variation of the main theme. The year was 1992, which was the 500th Centennial celebration of the discovery of America. The theme of Mardi Gras and our Krewe was "The Discovery." The Grand Ball commenced with Queen Isabella, King Ferdinand, and their court being presented to the guests. In addition, Christopher Columbus, Amerigo Vespucci, and their shipmates circulated among the guests and introduced themselves, one by one, with chivalry and flair. I was shocked and delighted when Columbus came over and asked me to do the first dance of the evening with him, a spellbinding Waltz.

END OF ARTICLE

~*~

While sorting through our mail, a colorful brochure stood out from among the other documents. It was a vacation invitation from the Delta Steamboat Company requesting our presence on one of their Mississippi River cruises. The one that caught my eye was a theme cruise featuring big bands, such as Guy Lombardo and his Royal Canadians and Les Elgart and his Manhattan Swing Orchestra. The cruise coincided with the annual New Orleans Mardi Gras and the 500th anniversary of the discovery of America by Christopher Columbus, which was the main theme of the festival. Well, there it was: Barbara's childhood dream of traveling down the Mississippi River with Tom Sawyer and Huck Finn on a paddlewheel boat and my dream of going to a Mardi Gras festival in New Orleans. Both of our dreams of sailing on a showboat (like the one in the great musical of that name), and my passion and infatuation with collecting books on the Age of Discovery, especially concerning the great navigator, Christopher Columbus, were all in one package. Barbara and I couldn't believe that so many of the items on our "Wish List" could be satisfied in one vacation. We figured that we could take a riverboat trip on the Mississippi Queen Paddlewheel, for seven days, which began and ended in New Orleans, and then extend our trip to include six days in a centrally located hotel around Bourbon Street, so we could really get into the Mardi Gras spirit. We spent a previous vacation in New Orleans many years ago, but not at festival time—although it does seem that every day in New Orleans is a festival. We were familiar with the layout of the area and what would be the most advantageous location for our stay. On our prior visit to the city, we stayed at the Royal Sonesta Hotel, which was in the Bourbon Street area, but the people and traffic noise made the stay less desirable than we had hoped for. We did have occasion to enjoy a great dinner in an upscale restaurant at the 17-floor Hotel Monteleone, also in the French Quarter off of Bourbon Street, but was located in a less noisy area than the Sonesta Hotel. It also boasted a rooftop swimming pool with spectacular views of the French Quarter and the historical city. We called our travel agent, Barbara, at Liberty Travel, and told her what our plans were and asked her to put together a travel package for us. Considering that the trip would be quite extensive and somewhat complicated, we decided to leave all the arrangements and details in her experienced hands. Our decision turned out to be wise; within a week, she laid out our itinerary, including all the sightseeing that we had planned, plus some extra goodies.

We flew American Airlines to New Orleans, and that's when the fun began. Our luggage didn't appear on the arrival carousel; the sinking feeling in my stomach got worse when we were the only passengers left waiting for our baggage to appear. After wasting a couple of hours with representatives of the Steamship Company and American Airlines, and filling out numerous forms describing our missing property, we left the airport and took a taxicab to the New Orleans Port where our ship, the *Mississippi Queen*, was docked. Our cab driver got lost in a downpour that restricted his visibility. I brought to his attention that what seemed to be the buildings of the city were behind us; he said, "Sorry, my mistake" and then turned his cab around in the right direction. We finally got to the embarkation point just as the rain stopped. There was a crowd of people on the dock in a covered area enjoying a small combo band's music, while they imbibed drinks provided by several waitresses from the ship. I immediately had a scotch and water, which was my drink of choice in those days, and before I knew it, down went several more, but to no avail. I was so hyper from the loss of our luggage and the prospect of going on a two-week vacation with little or no clothes, which was exacerbated by our getting lost on the way to the ship, that I was convinced that the whole journey was going to turn out to be a disaster. Barbara, although upset, tried to calm me down. She wasn't overly concerned, as the prospect of buying a new wardrobe for the trip wouldn't be an unhappy event for her. My mind formed prayers, hoping that the representative of the steamship company, who remained behind at the airline terminal, would locate our baggage. Until then, we just had to make the best of things. We boarded the paddlewheel boat and checked with the ship's coordinator, who informed us that due to our misfortune, they were upgrading our room, at no charge, to a full suite. Well, maybe things were starting to turn around; in time, my drinks did their job, and I calmed down quite a bit, returning to my optimistic, fun-loving self.

We went to dinner and felt the boat moving away from the dock, which brought back that helpless feeling that one gets when things happen that are out of their control; where was our luggage and what's next? How will we replace all of our personal belongings? The delicious French cuisine being served tempered my feelings of anxiety, somewhat, but sharing a bottle of wine with Barbara was more effective. We hurried back to our cabin, opened the door, and miracles of all miracles, our baggage was staring at us. I lifted a piece and panic returned; the luggage was weightless. Now we had our bags, but there was nothing in them. Unbeknownst to us, our cabin steward had unpacked our bags and put our belongings in the dressers and closet. After locating our precious possessions, we both collapsed on the queen size bed and just remained silent and motionless for about 15 minutes. We regained our composure, freshened up, and journeyed to the lounge meeting area for the tour orientation and to meet fellow passengers. When retiring for the evening, we both agreed that we should put the day behind us and erase the mishaps from our minds. Hopefully, we would continue with our wonderful journey with no further unhappy incidences. Mark Twain aptly said, "The face of the river, in time, becomes a wonderful book . . . not one to be read once and thrown aside, for it has a new story to tell every day." Well, we were hoping for a new story when we awoke the following morning.

And a new story it was. The sun peeked through our partially opened drapes; fresh Mississippi River air forced its way into our senses, while a whiff of bacon and eggs floating by got our attention, so we quickly dressed and hastened to the place creating the aroma. I would have been content just to sit on one of the outside chaise lounges and breathe in the fresh air and intoxicating smells from the food being prepared for our morning meal. What a wonderful beginning to a new day. After breakfast, the first mate took some of us on a guided tour of the *Mississippi Queen*. His dissertation was robotic, but precise as to the history and specifications of the paddlewheeler:

> The boat was built in 1976 in celebration of the bicentennial of the independence of the United States, and, when built, was the largest steamboat in existence. It's 382 feet long, 68 feet wide, weighing 3,364 tons, has 208 staterooms accommodating 422 passengers and a complement of over 100 crew members and staff. Its red circular paddlewheel at the stern of the boat weighs 70 tons; located forward of it, is the largest steam-driven calliope on the river, boasting 44 pipes, resulting in music that is magical and can be heard for five miles, announcing the majestic ship's presence on the river. The décor of the boat is Americana, with floral wallpaper and matching fabric, beveled mirrors, crystal chandeliers, and polished brass railings. The staircases are red carpeted with ornate wooden handrails, chairs,

> and the accessories are in the Victorian style. The Grand Salon is the center of activity and is used as a showroom and gathering place; its dance floor is large enough and will accommodate the swinging dancers on the ship.

Being a member of the U.S. Power Squadron and a boat owner, I had the privilege to spend time in my favorite place on the boat, the wheelhouse, which was on the forward part of the vessel. What a thrill it was to steer the ship—with the captain's permission of course, and under his watchful eyes. He let me navigate an easy part of the river for about five minutes. "The steamboats were finer than anything on shore – they are like palaces." Mark Twain was right when he wrote those words in his book, *Life on the Mississippi.* I was navigating a palace down the waterway, with images of the great river flowing through my mind from the Broadway musical *Showboat.* I was humming the river's song, "Ol' Man River" and, for a few minutes, I became a riverboat captain transporting my passengers and cargo to the faraway towns along the majestic river during the heyday of paddlewheel boats.

We spent a relaxing and friendly day traveling the river, making friends, and just enjoying the homey feeling that is prevalent on river boats. A big difference with cruising on a riverboat is that the staff is usually American, not what we had experienced when traveling on larger vessels, where most of the crew members are foreigners with difficult names to remember. It didn't take long to get use to the odiferous surroundings in the air of deep Southern fried cooking, and the comforting feeling of the sun resting on my body as I enjoyed reading some of Mark Twain's adventures, while spreading out on a chaise lounge in the open air at the stern of the boat, lulled by the rhythm of the bright red paddlewheel and dozing into dreamland between paragraphs. The ship's small combo band of six, which included two piano players, played music on and off all day. Their lively sounds floating through the air, mixed with the aroma of our next meal, gave me the feeling of being at a carnival. Dinner was a cholesterol nightmare. Barbara and I ordered the same food: Southern fried chicken, tons of biscuits, candied beans, and, for dessert, Shoo Fly Pie. It took many turns around the boat to try to alleviate the guilt of overeating before we came to terms with the fact that we were on vacation and an occasional "pig out" wasn't going to kill us, at least not right away.

That evening we followed the sound of music to the Grand Salon, where Les Elgart's Manhattan Swing Orchestra had guests busy on the dance floor doing a cha-cha. It was surprising how many single ladies were in attendance, but the cruise operators evidently anticipated this and provided some male hosts to dance and talk with the girls throughout the evening. Between sessions, the ship's smaller band entertained us with light jazz and singing from their female vocalist. We danced until the wee hours and returned to our upgraded suite, content that the forgettable mishaps we experienced were being replaced by "happy times." We were welcomed in our cabin by a complimentary bottle of champagne and chocolate heart kisses strewn on our bed. We decided to save the beverage for another time, but the temptation of the chocolates was too much to resist, so we munched while listening to the smooth and lazy, soft piped-in music, and concluded a relaxing, pleasant day on the Mississippi River, as we entered from the beginning of a dream vacation into our evening's dreamland.

We were awakened the next morning by the ship's deafening steam whistle: toot-toot-toot, which announced to the town of Natchez and everyone else within its listening range, that we were coming to town to explore its beauty and meet the local folks. One of the pianists joined in on the calliope and began harmonizing with the whistle's tooting. We followed the scent of bacon and eggs and, after indulging in a hearty breakfast, which included Southern biscuits, which I was becoming addicted to, we followed passengers to the stern of the boat to watch the ship maneuver alongside the town dock. Longshoremen were waiting, large lines in hand, and quickly secured the ropes to the cleats on the Queen. The crew magically extended a platform from the bow of the boat to the levee, which allowed for easy exiting from the boat. A committee of the town's people and a small brass band greeted us to their historic antebellum town. We planned on spending time exploring and visiting at least one of the plantations that were located in and around the quaint settlement. The area of the town dates back to the 8th century, when the Natchez Indians were masters of that part of the country. Built on the sight of an ancient Indian village, it takes its name from that tribe. Around 1730, after several wars, the French defeated the inhabitants and disbursed the Native Americans, keeping many as slaves. Today most of the remaining Natchez tribe has integrated with the Chickasaw, Creek, and Cherokee Indians, and are mainly in Oklahoma within the Cherokee and Creek nations, quite a distance from their ancestral lands. The town boasts a population of about 18,000 people including some native Indians, who are probably the descendants of slaves. It is probably one of the oldest cities in North America; elegant, well preserved, and a showcase for antebellum homes and magnificent plantations. Walking through the town was a throwback to pre-civil war times, especially when viewing areas where town folks were dressed in period costumes for the benefit of tourists. Like many Southern towns, the fragrance of flowers, particularly magnolias, freely occupied the air to the enjoyment of its recipients. We couldn't avoid walking into the Stanton Hall Plantation, which was an entire full block in the town. It was built in 1851–1857 for Frederick Stanton, a cotton broker, who went to great lengths to import building materials from Europe, such as moldings, marble fireplace mantles, wrought ironworks, and a great deal of the furnishings, some of which are still intact and displayed throughout the mansion. The entrance immediately impressed us and the other visitors with its 17-foot-high ceiling and 72-foot-long hallway. The parlor displayed gilded French mirrors and the fireplaces and mantles throughout were stunning in color and glaze. While exploring the mansion, the smell of biscuits caught our attention, we were pleased to learn that the mansion, which became a National Historic Landmark in 1974, had its own restaurant, The Carriage House. The stately gardens were inviting and spending a few minutes enjoying the colorful flowers and topiary, while sitting on a bench, was refreshing and tranquil. The compelling "call of the biscuits" finally overcame us and we went with haste to the place where the aroma was being created. We had our favorite foods: biscuits with gravy, fried chicken legs, toasty fries, berry ice tea, and more biscuits. The steamboat's whistle, toot-toot-toot, announced that it was time for us to return. The picture below was taken when we disembarked the *Queen* to explore the quaint town.

When we returned to our cabin, there were written instructions and competition rules for the dance contest that was to be held that evening. There was also fabric laid out on the bed for us to make costumes for a Mardi Gras party, which was to be held on the last day of the cruise while heading back to our last stop, in time for the live New Orleans festival. Much to do and so little time to do it in! The competition rules included trophies for first, second, and third place in cha-cha, rumba, foxtrot, waltz, and swing, and the same prizes for best overall dancers. No professionals, dance hosts, or crew members were allowed to enter the contest. We only knew the basics to all the dances except swing, which we took some lessons in over the last year. So we reluctantly entered the swing contest just to get into the spirit of things.

The music of Les Elgart's Band could be heard throughout the boat. We followed his sound to the Grand Salon, where many of the passengers were warming up their dance routines for the competition. We were both intimidated by the better dancers showing their stuff on the dance floor and were inclined to withdraw from the competition, but we gathered our courage and picked up our numbers 25, which we pinned to the back of our clothing. It wasn't long before we realized that we made the right decision in entering the competition, which resulted in our meeting new friends at a very rapid pace. Before the main event, everyone on the dance floor was having a great time moving and jumping around to the sounds of the band and changing partners on cue from the boat's dance master, which, again, enhanced meeting many of the passengers. The various dance competitions had from 15 to 20 couples in each category: cha-cha, rumba, foxtrot, waltz, and swing, ranging from beginners to somewhat good dancers, but absolutely no top-notch competitors, which made the atmosphere a lot less tense. The judges included some dance hosts and different ranks of crew members; all in all, they did a commendable job in judging the contestants. It seemed that everyone won a prize, including us for coming in third place in swing. The evening felt more like a jamboree than a dance competition; the atmosphere was relaxed and jovial without the stress that usually accompanies competitions. We ended the evening as champions (as previously mentioned, we won third place in swing) and retired to our cabin, wishing our many new friends a "fond farewell until the morrow."

We awoke again to the toot-toot-toot of the steam whistle, reminding us that today we had a mock race with the *Mississippi Queen's* older sister, *Delta Queen*, the undisputed current champion paddlewheel boat on the river. The *Delta Queen* was born in 1927, weighed 1,650 tons, is 285 feet long and 60 feet wide, and carries 200 passengers and 80 crew members. Quite a small ship compared to her younger sister, which is 3,364 tons, 382 feet in length, 68 feet in width, and carries 422 passengers and over 100 crew members. But the *Delta* was a feisty ship and has won the symbolic "Golden Antlers," which she proudly displayed outside and below her pilot house, attesting to the fact that she was the fastest steamboat on the Mississippi River (based on her pilot's expertise and having won its last annual encounter). The history of the Golden Antlers dates back to 1963 when the steamships, *Belle of Louisville* and the *Cincinnati's Delta Queen*, ran their first race. It was a 14-mile battle up and down the Ohio River, on the first Wednesday in May before the Kentucky Derby. Over the years, the race has been drawing as much attention from the locals as the Derby race. Since the first race, boats race against each other every year for the bragging rights as "The fastest boat on the river" and the coveted Golden Antlers. The antlers are from an elk and are sprayed gold, signifying the sleekness and speed of the animal and the purity of gold. Our race with the champion was to begin at "Dead Man's Bend" and to end at "Washout Bayou." These names conjured up all kinds of images; stories have come down through the years and have been repeated so often that they are accepted as fact. According to Jeffery, our ship's historian:

> Over 150 years ago, during the heyday of the rootin' tootin' steamboat era, the river landings were lawless and violent places to live. The most popular of these roughhouse places was the 'Natchez-Under-the-Hill-Landing,' located just below the bluffs overlooking the river at Natchez, Mississippi. There were brawls and knife fights daily, so violent that the local police would not venture down Silver Street, which stretched from the top of the bluffs down to the river's edge. It was a busy stop for the steamboats and a hangout for cutthroats, thieves, mustached gamblers, and ladies of the night. With all that violence, there were always dead bodies that had to be disposed of, and the river was a convenient repository. The bodies would float down to a bend in the river and accumulate there. Many of the bodies that were retrieved still had knives protruding from their decaying bodies, hence the name Dead Man's Bend.

The crew members spent the morning decorating our boat with banners, and placed noise makers throughout for our use to add to the festivities. The male members dressed in period costumes; many were mustached gamblers, gentlemen of the day, or unsavory-looking characters. The girls wore riverboat attire from that era, which included frills on their beautiful dresses, fancy hats, and pom-poms for the cheerleaders. The calliope played continuous music, including some songs of Stephen Foster, such as "Oh' Susanna," "Nelly was a Lady," "Nelly Bly," "Old Folks at Home," "My Old Kentucky Home," and, of course, "De Camp Town Races." The *Delta Queen* pulled alongside us and blew its challenging whistle loud and clear, "toot-toot-toot." Our response was a spontaneous, "toot-toot-toot"; back and forth they went with their whistles blowing, playing music from their calliopes, and battling each other for supremacy of the air and waterway. In addition to the *Delta's* jazz band playing on her bow, the passengers on board seemed to be having a post-victory celebration, a little premature for our taste, so we also started singing, howling, and making all sorts of loud sounds with our noise makers to balance the disturbance coming from *Delta*.

The anticipated long whistle blast from the champion signaled the start of the race; being the smaller and lighter of the two vessels, she was off and running ahead of us with ease. We struggled for what seemed to be an eternity to get our heavier craft ahead, but to no avail, even though our boat had more powerful engines. The little mistress moved ahead; its pilot evidently had more experience than ours, and found more of the slow water (slack water), which allows a boat to move with less resistance, and, therefore, more speed. Near the end of the race, our boat's engines began to show their strength and started pulling up to her older sister; inch by inch we finally caught up, but it was too late. The *Delta* seemed to become jet propelled as she approached and crossed the finish line ahead of us by several boat lengths. She would retain her title as "Queen of the Mississippi" and hold onto her "Golden Antlers" until challenged by a faster boat. The celebration noise raised a few decibels from her majesty as she sped away, whistle blowing and calliope singing, while the passengers swayed to the jazz band's rhythmic sounds and waved goodbye to our losing vessel. Her bright red paddlewheel churned and splashed water far and high as the boat picked up steam and disappeared around the bend and out of sight.

We retreated to the cheerful Golden Antlers Bar, which had floor-to-ceiling windows and a beautifully decorated table laden with coffee, tea, hot chocolate, and freshly baked cookies, which were available around the clock for the passenger's delight. We enjoyed our snacks as we listened to Jeffery, the "Riverlorian's" voice, coming gently from the loudspeaker system, explaining the sights and history of the various places we were viewing through the large windows. He was our river historian throughout the voyage, his pleasant manner and knowledge of the Mississippi River greeted us every morning explaining the history of various places of interest on our scheduled stops. He was a young Southern nobleman that relayed fascinating historical information to us in a very gentlemanly manner.

Our dinner was another unique Deep Southern treat, with biscuits. We both had side orders of steaks to complement the many biscuits we stuffed our faces with. We finished our meal with key lime pie, downed with a wonderful secret blended coffee with a light taste of hazelnut, which totally did us in, as getting off our chairs became a strenuous event. We headed to the Grand Salon to exercise and stretch our legs by dancing, hopefully enough to lose some of the weight that we were rapidly gaining. There weren't too many people on the dance floor; our new friends all seemed to be sitting around complaining that they were eating too much and having a hard time moving, even if only to perform simple dance steps. We shuffled around the floor for about an hour, and noticed that many of our friends were no longer in attendance. It didn't take long for us to come to the same conclusion, so we retired for the evening, dragging ourselves away from the dance floor and slowly moseying along to our cabin with light hearts and heavy stomachs.

The next day we were scheduled to visit the historic city of Vicksburg, Mississippi. The Confederate and Union armies fought for this strategic location during the Civil War; it was thought to be impregnable and was known as the "Gibraltar of the Confederacy." The battle resulted in the loss of many lives on both sides. Strategically, it was considered the key to controlling the Mississippi River and, therefore, the outcome of the Civil War. It was imperative that General Grant capture the fortress city so he could divide the South and bring the war closer to a conclusion. After several battles lasting 47 days, the city surrendered to the union forces on July 4, 1863, giving control of the river to the Northern Forces. Vicksburg National Military Park was established to memorialize that battle and the brave men who fought and sacrificed their young lives for what they believed to be a just cause. The brochure I read stated: "Today, the battlefield at Vicksburg is in an excellent state of preservation. It includes 1,325 historic monuments and markers, 20 miles of reconstructed trenches and earthworks, a 16-mile tour road, an antebellum home, 144 emplacement cannons, the restored Union gunboat-*USS Cairo*, and the Vicksburg National Cemetery." The town is another antebellum Southern-hospitable place to visit and welcomes tourist to explore its antique shops and plantations or just to walk around and enjoy the friendly surroundings. It has a population of about 25,000 people and is quite a bustling place. We decided to visit the ship's library the next day and find a couple of interesting books to read, skip the sightseeing of the famous historic town, and just enjoy the boat's facilities.

The toot-toot-toot of the steam whistle and the striking music coming from the calliope announced to all within listening range that the *Queen* was arriving at Vicksburg. Before reaching the town, Jeffery brought to our attention that we were passing the very place that the Union gunboat, *USS Cairo*, was sunk by confederate artillery. As the story goes:

> The *USS Cairo* was one of the seven ironclad gunboats named in honor of the towns along the upper Mississippi and Ohio rivers. The powerful ironclads were formidable vessels; each carried 13 big deadly cannons. The North had hoped that these ships would help in gaining control of the Mississippi River and split the Confederacy in two. The *Cairo* saw limited action before meeting its destiny. Its captain, Lt. Commander Thomas O. Selfridge, Jr., was a daring and ambitious leader who decided, on December 12, 1862, to lead a small flotilla up the Yazoo River, north of Vicksburg, to destroy the Confederate's gun placements and clear the way for General Grant to mount his attack on the city. Although the gunboat had iron around its superstructure, which offered protection from enemy artillery, its hull was made of wood, and that is where fate decided to place two direct hits, from electronically detonated torpedoes. It sank in 36 feet of water in just 12 minutes and was to remain in its

> burial ground until 1965, when it was excavated and brought to local shipyards to be restored. In 1972, Congress gave its permission for the gunboat to be placed in the Vicksburg National Military Park, where it still remains as a reminder, that the victors in wars still have losses.

The town's welcoming committee was there to greet us, band and all; its music along with our calliope's contribution reminded me of the sounds coming from the merry-go-round I rode as a child in Coney Island Amusement Park, in Brooklyn, N.Y. The horses and buggies on the landing brought to mind the many horses I rode on the carousel at my favorite childhood playground. It brought back the same warm feelings of my childhood that came with being with loved ones and enjoying the fresh sea air and the aroma of a carnival. Many of the passengers disembarked, while Barbara and I went to the library to fetch some reading material. I spotted *The Songs of Hiawatha,* by Henry Wadsworth Longfellow, which I read many, many years ago and couldn't remember anything from the book other than "from the shores of . . ." I chose it as my companion for the day while Barbara thumbed through many books before finding *It* by her favorite author, Stephen King. We found our way to the Paddlewheel Lounge, which had only a couple of guests relaxing and enjoying the view from its large floor-to-ceiling windows. We found two comfortable chairs and, caressing cups of coffee in one hand and our books in the other, we began what was to become a very quiet and relaxing reading experience, with a great view of the river and town to boot. While enjoying our "alone time," an announcement came over the public address system that the surviving Guy Lombardo Band (he died in 1977), was expected to board our boat within the hour. Although we enjoyed the music of the Les Elgart Band, we were thrilled that the Lombardo orchestra was going to join us for the remainder of the trip. His was the premier orchestra throughout my youth and into adulthood; New Year's Eve seemed meaningless without the sound of his music being played on the radio from the Roosevelt Hotel, and later on television from the Waldorf Astoria Hotel in New York City. He and his sweet saxophones would bid the old year farewell and welcomed the birth of the New Year with smooth sounds from his orchestra playing "Auld Lang Syne." As with the Les Elgart Band, the Lombardo Band was a smaller version of the original, which was appropriate, as the boat didn't have adequate room to accommodate a full orchestra. The name "Guy Lombardo" brought to mind when I was on a two-week furlough while serving in the U.S. Air Force. My buddies and I decided to be at Times Square, in New York City, for the "dropping of the ball" to celebrate the turn of the year. The four of us chipped in and rented one room at an off-beat hotel that we could afford, just blocks away from Times Square. On that eventful evening, we waited with upward of a million jubilant people, who were crowding the streets in every direction. Revelers, stretching out from windows of the surrounding buildings in Times Square, seemed to be directing the people below with the waving of their arms, throwing paper trailers, blasting noisemakers, and howling strange noises from above. At 11:59 P.M., the 1,070-pound, 6-foot-diameter Waterford crystal ball located at the top of a 77-foot flagpole, high above One Times Square was lowered; it reached the bottom at exactly 12:00 Midnight. The revelers became a vast, well-rehearsed choir, singing in unison, on cue, to Guy Lombardo's rendition of "Auld Lang Syne." The performance was broadcast every hour throughout the world in each time zone, to the music of Guy Lombardo and his Royal Canadians; beginning from the International Time Zone in the South Pacific and ending in Western Samoa. So much a part of our lives was Guy Lombardo that, in our early years as owners of a 28-foot Chris Craft cabin cruiser, we would go out of our way to drive down Guy Lombardo Boulevard in Freeport, Long Island, and pass his home on our way to our boat, hoping to get a glimpse of the great impresario. On many occasions we would see him on his boat and get a "sailor's wave" from him and his mates. We spent many a pleasant evening at the 15,000-seat amphitheater in Jones Beach State Park, which was built on a landfill surrounded by a moat, enjoying concerts and Broadway musicals that were orchestrated by Guy Lombardo. His band played there often and, on other occasions, during a performance's intermission, he would sail by on his large yacht with some members of his band and entertain the audience with his special style of music. His passing was felt deeply throughout the locale and, surely, the world.

While sailing down the busy Mississippi, I distinctly remember seeing a barge breaking through the light fog, carrying an enormous red derrick. As it approached our vessel, its large size dwarfed us and everything else within sight. It must have been over 50 feet in height and was propped on a floating barge that seemed too small to carry such a large structure. It reminded me of the uneasy feeling of watching a human pyramid, a small person on the bottom supporting layers of people above, and swaying as if preparing to collapse. All the viewers ran to the opposite side of our boat in anticipation of the crane falling and crushing our craft, along with its passengers. As it passed, the little red towing tugboat's pilot smiled and waved; he seemed to sense that we were in awe of his cargo and that his smile and wave would reassure us that all was well. An announcement over the public address system was welcomed and broke the anxiety that many experienced while passing the fearful cargo:

> The kite-flying contest will begin in one hour from the deck at the stern of the boat, by the paddlewheel. The material for making the kites is in the Grand Salon. Whoever keeps their kite in the air for the longest time, will become the 'Kite Master' of the cruise and have the honor and privilege of wearing the boat's 'Kite Hat,' which is a large white hat with a small colorful kite sitting on top, it entitles the wearer to a salute of respect from fellow passengers and members of the crew. We consider the event almost as prestigious as winning the Golden Antlers.

Barbara and I hustled to the Salon and picked up our kite kits and began assembling them. She was a lot more successful than I, as putting together the child's kit was beyond my comprehension. One of the crewmembers had to assist me with the job, but we finally did get the four-foot beauty assembled. Many of the passengers gave up trying to put their kites together and decided instead to watch the contestants vie for the title of "Kite Master." My kite, although there was sufficient wind to get it afloat, went straight down into the Mississippi River. Barbara was more proficient than me and got hers in the air with ease, being helped along by a nice stiff breeze. Everyone, sooner or later, lost their kites, which kept the boat's small skiff that followed busy retrieving the remnants. An 80-year-old grandmother, Louise by name, took first place by having her kite stay airborne for three minutes, which was quite an accomplishment, considering most of the kites went straight down like lead balls. In addition to being named "Mistress of the Kite," Louise was given an enormous complementary mint julep drink for her bravery and skill, in addition to the coveted "Kite Hat."

After dinner that evening, we meandered over to the Grand Salon and joined four of our friends at a ringside table; we had the wine steward pop open our complimentary bottle of champagne and pour everyone at the table a glass, which we drank slowly while waiting in anticipation of hearing some great dancing music from the famous band. We were not disappointed. They played great romantic music, like "Harbor Lights," "Red Roses for a Blue Lady," "The Anniversary Song," and "My Old Flame." They also played swing: "The Music Goes Round and Round," "Hot Time in the Old Town Tonight," and the great "Beer Barrel Polka" (Roll out the Barrel). We danced ourselves into oblivion doing foxtrots, waltzes, polkas, and swing. While dancing and reminiscing, I visualized the great Lombardo leading a much larger full orchestra at the Jones Beach Amphitheater and on his large yacht, floating around the moat surrounding the theater, making his special sound of music to the applause of his beloved audience. We returned to our cabin exhausted with euphoria. I quickly went into a deep sleep with the sweet sounds of his big band music echoing in my mind.

One of the advantages of traveling on a small boat, rather than a large cruise ship, is that whatever is cooking in the kitchen fills the air throughout the vessel. The next morning was no exception; a whiff of breakfast's fragrance sped our dressing, hastening us to our next feast. While enjoying our buffet, Jeffery informed us of the day's activities on board: "Bingo games in the morning and cha-cha dance lessons in the afternoon in the Salon. Also a reminder that it is the last day of the cruise and everyone is invited to the Mardi Gras Ball and don't forget your costumes. After lunch, we will be arriving in Louisiana's capital, Baton Rouge, and spending a couple of hours ashore."

We took advantage of the free cha-cha lesson given by a sweet Southern Belle named Lulu. About ten couples attended the class; the men and girls were told to line up facing each other on opposite sides of the room, leaving enough room for Lulu to demonstrate the steps she planned on teaching us. She asked if everyone knew the basic steps of the dance and, fortunately, the response was a hearty "Yes," which meant we didn't have to start with the basics. She demonstrated an underarm turn followed by an open break, which most of us caught onto quickly. After a few moments of dancing with our partners, everyone was asked to rotate to the next person on their left and repeat the steps again. After doing this several times, with the help of Lulu for those of us having some difficulty with the pattern, we were all able to perfect the routines to the satisfaction of our instructor and to our own amazement. I couldn't wait to dance the new routines to live band music that evening.

The boat's whistle sounded its alarming toot-toot-toot accompanied by the calliope blurting out, "On a Clear Day," as the *Queen* announced to "The City of Seven Flags," Baton Rouge, that she was preparing to pay it a visit. The colorful history of "The City of Seven Flags" got its name from the seven nations that occupied it over the centuries: France, England, Spain, the Florida Republic, the sovereign State of Louisiana, the Confederate States, and the United States. Of course, when you think about it, history invariably discounts the original inhabitants when compiling information of this sort. Considering that the area, according to archaeologists, dates back to BCE, there must have been many other flags and teepees of Native Americans that also inhabited this region that were not considered when the nickname was developed. The city is quite different from the small towns we passed or visited on our voyage. It's a metropolis of the first order, having as its occupants the tallest Capitol Building in the U.S., which is also the tallest building in the South; one of the largest Neo-Gothic castles in the U.S. (old Capitol Building); two universities, the Louisiana State University, home of the Tigers football team, and Southern University, home of the Jaguars football team; several museums, a major zoo; and the state's two largest shopping malls: the Mall of Cortana and the Louisiana Mall. These are just some of the inviting venues that the great city has for its populace and guests to visit and enjoy. The city boasts a population of over 800,000 people, which is the second-largest city by population in Louisiana, second only to New Orleans. We decided that, due to the limited amount of time we were allotted in this historic place, we should visit the *USS Kidd*, a WWII Fletcher-class-destroyer that was docked close to our berth and was currently in the water. At certain times of the year, due to the high tides and inclement weather, the boat museum is in dry dock on land. Time permitting, we wanted to also visit the old Neo-Gothic Capitol Building, which is currently a museum. It was replaced in 1934 under governor Huey Long's administration, by a new 450-foot-high Art Deco Capitol Building. If we got lucky and had enough time remaining, Louisiana State University with its 250 buildings, which were built in the Italian Renaissance style, and its stadium, considered one of the largest in the U.S., would be a nice addition to our touring for the day. We would have to forego seeing the many antebellum buildings and colonial-influenced neighborhoods for another time, maybe on our next Mississippi River cruise, which was already being formulated in our minds. We were so thrilled with our experience that we signed up for another cruise down the Mississippi and then on to the Kentucky Derby. That adventure is told in Part II of my next travel book.

With the assistance of electronic docents, Barbara and I began our tour of the famous ship and learned that "The *USS Kidd* is one of 175 Fletcher-class destroyers and was commissioned on February 28, 1943, in Kearny New Jersey. It is 376 feet long, 40 feet wide, had a complement of 330 officers and crew, with a top speed of 37 knots." I thought it was named after the infamous buccaneer Captain Kidd, who strangely was raised from age five in New York City, since it flies a Jolly Roger from its foremast. But, its name isn't that romantic:

> It was named after Rear Admiral Isaac Campbell Kidd, Sr., who was killed aboard his flagship, the *USS Arizona*, on December 7, 1941, during the surprise aerial attack by the Japanese on Pearl Harbor. The Admiral's nickname was Capt'n Kidd, referring to the pirate, so his wife petitioned the powers that be to have a Jolly Roger displayed from the ship's mast. No other

> American naval vessel has ever flown a pirate's flag before or since, but due to the high regard that she and her husband were held in by officials in Washington, permission was granted to fly the infamous cross-skull flag. On her maiden voyage into New York harbor, the first American naval vessel ever to fly a Jolly Roger entered the harbor, giving honor to the Admiral and to a native New Yorker, Capt'n Kidd.

The ship earned 12 battle stars while in service in the Pacific during WWII and the Korean Conflict. During WWII, she was part of Destroyer Squadron 48, which was composed of nine Fletcher-class destroyers. These ships were small, fast fighting ships, and were used to screen task forces, escort convoys, bombard shore positions, and deliver torpedo attacks. No aircraft carrier or battleship ventured into enemy waters without escorting destroyers leading the way. On April 11, 1945, during the battle of Okinawa, the ship suffered a kamikaze attack when a Japanese pilot targeted and crashed into her, killing 38 crewmen and causing major damage. After the Korean Conflict, all surviving destroyers were modernized, except for the *Kidd*, due to the poor condition of the vessel. Modernization consisted of replacement of the rear island of the ship with a helicopter platform, the addition of side launch torpedo tubes, and the installation of hedgehog depth charge launchers. Some of her officers, crew, and friends were granted permission to save the ship as a war memorial and had it towed from Philadelphia to her new home in Baton Rouge in 1982 for restoration, to bring the ship back to her original condition. The crew's quarters on these naval vessels always amazed me, as the area they occupy is quite small and in a double-bunk formation, one on top of the other. Not much room to spread out, but evidently adequate enough to get a decent night's sleep. The toilet facilities were also primitive, made of trenches with saltwater entering one side and flushing out the other end, very much like the ancient Roman's public latrines. One of the saving graces of being on naval vessels is their food, which I experienced many years ago when I was in the U.S. Air Force traveling from Oakland, California, to Yokohama, Japan, and then returning two years later. I was fortunate to have a piece of plain vanilla sheet cake with chocolate frosting. The same delicious cake was being served to guests on our tour of the *Kidd*; the quality and taste hadn't changed one iota from my earlier experience. I was delighted that they let me have a second piece of the tasty cake, which brought back many youthful memories of my days in the military. We moved quickly around the ship so we would have time to visit the Old Capitol Building, which was just up the street.

The sight of the Old Capitol Building, known as the Castle, looked strange in its setting. The Castle is a 15th century neo-Gothic building, set on a hill overlooking the majestic Mississippi River, with turrets, parapets, exterior stained-glass windows, and gables; the only things missing were a moat and drawbridge, to make it an authentic castle, as seen in many movies showing its European counterparts. A strange scene to find in the Deep South, but one that Baton Rouge is proud of, as it probably is the only castle of its size in North America. We entered the grounds through an iron gate, and were overwhelmed with the beauty and size of the building. The stained-glass dome and spiral staircase leading to the upper level was equivalent in beauty and artistic design to any I've seen in cathedrals throughout Europe. We both inserted electronic docents into our ears and began our journey through history. We learned:

> In 1846, the Louisiana state legislature in New Orleans decided to move the capital from that city of 102,000 people to Baton Rouge, which only had a population of slightly over 2,000 residents. New Orleans at the time was the fourth-largest city in the U.S. and many thought that it was getting too powerful, so they decided to move the capital to another location to spread the wealth and power around. So, Baton Rouge donated land high on a bluff, believed to be the location of the 'Red Pole,' or 'le baton rouge,' where Native Americans gathered to have their council meetings for many centuries. A New York architect, James Dakin, designed the building, but not in keeping with current trends, which copied the Federal Capitol Building in Washington, D.C. Instead, he decided to copy the

> styles of Neo-Gothic castles in Europe and make the new (old) Capitol Building a one-of-a-kind in North America, which it probably still is today. The great paddlewheel captain and writer Mark Twain said when he saw the structure: 'It is pathetic that a whitewashed castle, with turrets and things . . . should ever have been built in this otherwise honorable place.' Of course, many people didn't agree with his assessment of the Castle. In 1862, a short time after its completion, it was occupied by Union soldiers, when the city's leaders abandoned it for a safer and more defendable location in the city of Shreveport. In 1880, Baton Rouge was again the capital; the building had to be resurrected, as it was the victim of two fires during the war and in need of major reconstruction. It was restored beyond its former splendor in 1882, by architect and engineer William A. Freret, by adding a magnificent spiral staircase and a stained-glass dome, which has become the center of attraction in the castle.

The staircase and stained glass dome captivates the viewer with its dark polished curved wooden design and a kaleidoscope of colorful glass panes, which seemed to be moving with the sunbeams reflecting through them and bouncing off the hallway and staircase. In the distance, the toot-toot-toot and music of the calliope beckoned us to return to *Queen*; any other touring would have to wait for our return, hopefully in the near future.

We were soon sailing on our way to New Orleans at what seemed to be a very slow pace, as the paddlewheel's churning of the water was quiet and not its usually loud, splashing, hypnotic self. The late afternoon event was a passenger calliope contest to determine who could play the mysterious steam instrument with some degree of skill. Barbara, who is proficient in playing the piano and guitar, couldn't wait to sit down and give it a try. About 15 passengers decided to master the instrument. They lined up in alphabetical order, Barbara Bivona being the first. She played Dixie and did a pretty good job stretching her small fingers over the large keys. After rising from her seat, she received loud applause from the audience and some hoorays from me. She finished with a bright smile on her face and very pleased with her accomplishment. The next lady was annoyed that Barbara played "HER" song and said so. She also played Dixie, to the amusement of the spectators, and received loud applause from the audience as well, but her playing in my opinion, didn't measure up to my wife's. All the contestants were surprised that they were able to get recognizable tunes out of the beautiful and melodic steam instrument. For everyone's effort, they all won first prize and were awarded a *Vox Calliopus* certificate, which made them members of the exclusive club of calliope players.

We finished making our costumes for the Mardi Gras Ball. Barbara created an outfit that looked like a large salmon: pinkish sequins, with drawings that resembled fish scales. The strange thing about it was her head sticking out from the fish's mouth and her little feet protruding from the fish's tail, but overall her walking fish was quite effective. I took the easy road and made a toga from a white sheet and wore a Roman laurel wreath painted gold on my head, which I put together with some of the material supplied by the crew. The ball was surreal; there were a variety of people dressed as fish, many men and women dressed in togas, (but none as good as mine), mustached gamblers all over the place, and lots of girls dressed as ladies-of-the-night. We danced and sang the night away, which wasn't an easy task, especially if your costume was bulky like Barbara's. Her fish's stomach kept getting in the way of our dancing close, and my toga had the habit of sliding off my shoulder and showing my hairy chest. But, all and all, the evening was delightful, especially the laughs at seeing such strange creatures jumping around trying to dance without tripping on themselves and their partners. We raised our champagne glasses to the music of Guy Lombardo and the Royal Canadians, and ended the evening singing "Auld Lang Syne." To help us with the words, we were given an envelope marked "Don't Open till Midnight." An American version was written in clear large letters, so we could all enjoy singing the whole song. The words are somewhat bastardized from a poem written by Robert Burns in 1788; here is the rendition we sang:

Should old acquaintance be forgot, and never brought
to mind?
Should old acquaintance be forgot, and old lang syne?
For auld lang syne, my dear, for auld lang syne,
We'll take a cup o' kindness yet, for auld lang syne.
And surely you'll buy your pint cup! And I'll buy mine!
And we'll take a cup o' kindness yet, for auld lang syne.
We two have run about the slopes, and picked the
daisies fine.
But we've wandered many a weary foot, since auld lang
syne.
We two have paddled in the stream, from morning sun
till dine.
But seas between us broad have roared since auld lang
syne.
And here's a hand my trusty friend! And give us a hand
o' thine!
And we'll take a right good-will draught, for auld lang
syne.
For auld lang syne, my dear, for auld lang syne.
We'll take a cup o' kindness yet, for
Auld land syne.

And thus, on that note, we ended our final night and voyage on the majestic *Mississippi Queen Paddlewheel.*

Chapter Eight – New Orleans and Mardi Gras

We awoke the next morning to a very quiet and new environmental aroma. The paddlewheeler's relentless churning resonance was gone and the motion of the boat was still. Peeping out of our porthole explained the reason for the changes: we had arrived and were docked in the *Laissez les bons temps rouler* (Let the good times roll) City of New Orleans. We dressed, packed our luggage, and spent extra time filling out the destination tags to make sure that our baggage would be sent to the right location, the Monteleone Hotel, in the heart of the French Quarter. Check-in time was 1:00 P.M., and considering our previous experience, we were very apprehensive about being separated from our suitcases. I was tempted to buy homing devices and place them in our luggage to ensure that they wouldn't get lost or misplaced, but I couldn't locate any homing devices on the ship, or anywhere else for that matter. I made a mental note to invent a device that could be used for that purpose. We hypnotically followed the scent of breakfast, which seemed to be extending an invitation to all the guests to join in a farewell feast, which we obligingly did. Once again, I devoured more biscuits and gravy than my stomach could bear, but, what the hell, it was vacation time so why not let the good times roll. I assured myself that any discomfort would be quickly remedied by the ever-present "Tums" anti-acids that I carried in my pocket.

We had a few hours to kill before check-in time at the hotel, so we decided to explore the incredibly complex and beautiful New Orleans

Riverwalk. It was developed to accommodate the 1984 World's Fair, and transformed a run-down industrial area consisting of railroad tracks, warehouses, and waterfront activity, to a world-class pedestrian promenade, marketplace, aquarium, and a host of other interesting tourist attractions. On our previous visit to the sleepless city, Barbara had made a mental note to spend some time at the Riverwalk Marketplace. I made some mind etchings that included the Audubon Aquarium of the Americas and the New Orleans Zoo, which I thought would be good places to spend some quality educational time. As usual, I followed the leader and we headed to the mall. In 1986, the Riverwalk Marketplace opened for business, featuring in excess of 200 merchants selling creative artworks and keepsakes in national and international stores, such as Brookstone, Nine West, Foot Locker, and The Body Shop. The great food options housed in the magnificent air-conditioned mall included The Café du Monde, serving their world-famous beignets (hot French doughnuts), sushi stands, Italian bistros, Mexican delights, and French and Cajun cuisine. The indoor Marketplace is located at the foot of Canal, Poydras, and Julia streets, and is across the street from Harrah's Casino and adjacent to the spectacular, glimmering Hilton Hotel. We spent over an hour browsing through the women's clothing stores and, much to my surprise; Barbara didn't find anything to buy. "Why?" I asked, "Didn't you like anything you touched and investigated? After all, you left your DNA on all those garments and shoes and have nothing to show for it?" She whispered in my ear: "Wow, these prices are high." With a delighted grin on my face, we exited the marketplace and headed for the aquarium. The New Orleans Zoo was now out of the question, as the outside temperature was beginning to get uncomfortably warm and spending time outdoors was no longer an option. We would have to save that adventure for our next journey to New Orleans.

Walking along the river walk was an absolutely pleasant experience. It is very visitor friendly; benches are conveniently situated, and the shade trees displayed beautiful designs of various colors of green, while the scent of magnolia tickled and pleased our senses. We viewed the ever-present, magnificent sparkling Mississippi River giving life to riverboats, cruise ships, and people actually sitting on the riverbank and paddling their feet in its murky water. Street musicians performed along the walk, adding to the ambiance, with sweet music from their trumpets, saxophones, and tambourines. An interesting sight caught our attention as we moseyed along: a rather large barge was docked and had about 20 house trailers on its deck. Some of their awnings were open, sheltering the owners from the sun, while they enjoyed breakfast and drinks on their portable patios. We were fascinated, and, knowing that boaters are friendly and ever ready to converse with anyone passing by, we struck up a conversation with Louise and Tom. They asked us to join them on their nautical patio, which we did without hesitation. Tom asked if we would like breakfast; as I was still trying to digest the morning's biscuits, I only accepted a cup of coffee. Barbara, although she shops in the children's or women's petite sections of most stores, accepted the breakfast offer knowing that no matter how much food she consumes, not one ounce will stick to her ribs. Tom and Louise, who resided in Michigan, told us of their barge trip on the Mississippi. They towed their house trailer from Michigan to Memphis, Tennessee, making their first vacation stop at Elvis Presley's Graceland and then on to the pier where the barge was waiting for them to board, which was done in a similar manner as boarding a large ferry. After securing their car and trailer, the house trailer was connected to electricity, fresh water, and a sanitation system. Their power was provided by onboard generators, the fresh water tanks were filled at predetermined stops, and the holding tanks disposed of frequently, as needed. All of these annoying tasks were done by polite and pleasant crew members without inconveniencing the passengers. They travelled down the Mississippi River stopping at many of the same places we visited; the big difference was that when they docked at various cities, they had the option of taking their cars to go sightseeing and exploring, usually doubling up with other travelers from the barge to save fuel. Well, talk about a unique way of travelling; being on a boat, taking your vacation house and your car with you, and not worrying about driving long distances or finding a first-rate trailer camp accommodation, which, to say the least, is not an easy task. We wished them a continued happy "barge-house trailer-car" vacation and decided that we would, hopefully in the near future, try the same type of adventure and maybe talk some of our boating friends into joining us.

The New Orleans Audubon Aquarium of the Americas is rated as one of the top five aquariums in the U.S. When entering, there was an astonishing exhibit of a Caribbean coral reef that required walking through a transparent plastic tube, which put us in the midst of a large number of stingrays, hammerhead sharks, turtles, and an assortment of sea life, all located above, in front of, and around us. Their *Adventure Island Exhibit* offered an action-packed interactive play zone designed for persons of all ages. The main attraction was a 2,600-gallon pool, where people were invited to pet the cow nose stingrays. Guests are also encouraged to purchase feed to help fill the rays' stomachs at feeding time. There was an unusual penguin colony that featured two species of warm water penguins, the African black-footed penguin, and the rock hopper penguin. I was expecting to see snow among the little birds, but there are only two species that live in the Antarctic, and the aquarium did not have adequate facilities to accommodate either of them. It is always fascinating to watch these birds meandering around; they seem to be busy talking to each other and are constantly in motion. But what is it that they are accomplishing? I wouldn't be surprised if they scrutinized the onlookers and made comments about their appearances, such as, "Wow, look at the size of that fat guy's nose," or "Did you see the terrible face lift on that blonde? HE HE HE!!" We learned that the African black-footed penguins were the most numerous in the colony and that the majority of them were born in captivity. The rock hopper penguins are distinguished by their orange feet and bright yellow tufts of feathers above their eyes. Our next stop was a white alligator's habitat in the *Mississippi River Gallery.* The big guy's name is Spots and was one of 18 rare white alligators found in the Louisiana swamps in 1987 during a preservation safari to save the near-extinct animals. Although Spots is white, he is not an albino, he is Leucistic (a gene mutation), which gives him his white color and steely blue eyes. Spots and his all-male siblings probably wouldn't have lived long in the wild since their white color wouldn't camouflage them from predators anxious to dine on them. Spots and his brothers are considered goodwill ambassadors for Louisiana and are celebrities around the world, having appeared on entertainment programs such as *The Tonight Show*, *CNN*, *The Today Show*, *Nashville Network*, and *CBS Morning News*. Although their history was fascinating and their appearance rare, watching several alligators lying around doing absolutely nothing left much to be desired. So we moved on to the *Seahorse Gallery.* The exhibit had an unusual assortment of seahorses and sea dragons, both becoming rare, and unless the governments of their native homes become more proactive in protecting their habitats, many of the species will become extinct in the near future. There are only 32 known species of seahorses and, unfortunately, they live in some of the world's most threatened habitats, which is why aquariums, in conjunction with the international organization called Project Seahorse, are working to ensure their survival by breeding them in captivity. The exhibit was one of the most beautiful in the aquarium. Watching them floating through the water, reflecting and then becoming part of the multicolored lights, was absolutely beautiful to behold. Another unusual attraction was the sea dragons with their flowing appendages resembling yellow and orange leafy plants. Their seahorse heads were in startling contrast to their leafy bodies. Only two species of these Australian dragons are known to exist, the weedy and the leafy, and both were represented in the amazing display. These little creatures conjure up thoughts of mystical sea monsters, which in their original size are quite beautiful, but on a larger scale, like 100 feet long, would be quite scary. We only had time to visit one more exhibit, although we probably could have spent the rest of the day exploring the rain forest, sea otters, the *Gulf of Mexico Exhibit* (which is supposed to be the centerpiece of this venue), the *Jellyfish Exhibit*, and the many other nautical displays. We chose to visit the *Jellyfish Exhibit*, as it was close by and we were in a hurry to get to our hotel to see if our luggage arrived without incident. This exhibit always fascinates me when visiting seaquariums. Observing jellyfish hovering and dancing around a tank with the backlights reflecting through their various sizes, shapes, and colors, is similar to watching a ballet while listening to a symphony orchestra playing smooth, floating music. Watching the performers' harmony in the water stage was reminiscent of the tranquil feeling I get when attending ballets and concerts, which is always relaxing and gratifying to me.

We exited the seaquarium post haste and headed to the Monteleone Hotel, which is off Canal Street and only a short distance from where we were. But, what can happen in a few blocks in New Orleans is absolutely bizarre. The streets were busy with revelers celebrating Mardi Gras, with drinks in hand, and partying to beat the band. The city allows drinking on the streets as long as the cups are plastic. There were many plastic cups being chug-a-lugged by two-fisted male and female partiers. As we walked at a quick pace to avoid some of the rowdy activity, I got ahead of Barbara, as she decided to peek in one of the girly storefront windows. While her nose was pasted to the shop's window, a young, rather handsome, inebriated man approached her and asked, "Would you like some beads?" Barbara said, "How nice, I'd love them." He then said, "Then show me your tits." She screamed and ran over to me and said, "That man wants to see my breasts." I looked back at the smiling procurer and started to head in his direction, when a policeman appeared from a doorway on my right and said, "Don't be concerned, it is customary for men to offer girls beads to show their breasts at Mardi Gras time." At that moment, I saw several young ladies flashing their cannons and accepting gifts from their happy admirers. Barbara calmed down while I began daydreaming about our week's adventure in the city of *Laissez les bons temps rouler* (Let the good times roll). We reached our hotel at check-in time and went straight to the reception desk, got our key for a "no smoking" room on the 7th floor facing the courtyard, and ran to the elevator, opened the door to our room and behold, our luggage was sitting in the center of our mini-suite. Two major surprises awaited us: our luggage was intact, and the steamboat company had arranged for a room upgrade, at no charge, to further apologize for the problem we had with our misplaced baggage.

We chose the right hotel for location; it was within a few blocks of Jackson Square, the Canal Street shops, the Riverwalk, Harrah's Casino, an abundance of renowned restaurants, and lively Bourbon Street. The 17-story, family-owned hotel dates back to 1886 and boasts a striking *Beaux Arts* style (French for fine arts, which was popular in the late 19th century). Two wonderful, exaggerated examples are found in New York City: the New York Public Library, which stands out in all its splendor on 42nd Street and Fifth Avenue as a testimonial to creative architectural excellence and lasting artistic beauty, and the Grand Central Terminal, located on 42nd Street and Park Avenue, which I consider to be one of the most imaginative and complicated architectural events of the 20th century. It was built to coordinate the multitude of trains coming into and leaving New York City and is light years ahead of any railroad station in the world that I have seen, when considering its imaginative ceiling mural of a Mediterranean Sky, featuring 2,500 stars, its trendy shops, restaurants of every ethnicity, and a multitude of places to relax and enjoy people traffic.

It's said that the "French Quarter starts at the lobby of the Hotel Monteleone," which happens to be just one block from renowned Bourbon Street. The 100-plus years of continuous ownership by the Monteleone family has resulted in a host of hard-earned awards for its restaurants, rooftop swimming pool, and unique Carousel Piano Bar with a wild circus design that revolves slowly, completing a circle every 15 minutes and taking its riders on a childlike journey while viewing the dancing night lights of Crescent City (another name for New Orleans). American authors, such as William Faulkner, Tennessee Williams, Truman Capote, and Ernest Hemingway, who immortalized the hotel in his story "Night Before Battle," were all repeat residents of this illustrious venue when they visited fun city. For those of us who are "gymaholics," there is a modern state-of-the-art, 24/7 fitness center and spa.

It was time for a well-deserved nap, but before dozing off, I picked up a booklet that was in the pile of paraphernalia on my night table about the festive event. It read:

> The Mardi Gras Carnival begins on the 12th night of Christmas, January 6th, which is the day the three Magi presented Christ with gifts, and ends on Fat Tuesday, the day before Ash Wednesday. *Mardi Gras* is French for Fat Tuesday and is the day that fasting stops and glutinous eating is allowed. Ash Wednesday is 47 days before Easter, and therefore, varies from year to year. Carnival in New Orleans is a season of parades (up to 28), balls, and continuous festivities. *Carnival*, which is Latin for 'kiss your flesh goodbye' (loosely translated), builds slowly from January 6th until Fat Tuesday; the intervening weeks are filled with all the popular activities that make the season attractive to the four million-plus visitors that attend the events each year. Although Mardi Gras applies only to the day before Ash Wednesday, it has become interchangeable with Carnival, and locals refer to the long party as Mardi Gras-Carnival. Contrary to the impression that people get from mass media coverage, it doesn't take place primarily on Bourbon Street, nor does it consist mostly of drunken revelry and indecent

> exposure in exchange for cheap beads. Although many of the traditional celebrations are centered on the popular street, the majority of the historic parades don't even include Bourbon Street in their routes. Entire extended families stake out prime spots hours in advance, often the same location every year for generations, in order to have close-up views of the passing themed floats and to collect as many throws as possible from the passengers on the passing extravaganzas. Mardi Gras is a great time for families to celebrate and spend quality time together. Thousands of King Cakes are baked and decorated in the official Mardi Gras colors of purple, green, and gold, representing justice, faith, and power, and are consumed each year by families and friends as a testament to their continued love and commitment to each other.

Parades are planned as much as a year or more in advance by Mardi Gras Krewes, who sponsor elaborate balls and parties to honor their organizations. Some balls are stylized and formal, complete with tableaux performances and royal marches, while others more closely resemble large dinner-dance parties. One party is even held in the New Orleans Superdome with tens of thousands of revelers in attendance. The balls have become so popular that New Orleans is now one of the country's largest markets for formal wear, including tuxedos and floor-length evening gowns, which are required attire at many of the more exclusive balls. Thanks to popular singer-actor Harry Connick, Jr., and his many native New Orleans friends, all the Krewes' organizations now are required to allow members from all walks of life to join their clubs, regardless of race, color, or gender. This was not the case prior to Harry's heroic efforts, which made the festivities in the past rather un-American, to say the least. The majority of parades are held the last five days of the carnival, Friday through Fat Tuesday, at which time all the streets in the area are cordoned off to accommodate the many enormous floats and the thousands of participants celebrating the festivities.

A brochure in our hotel room gave us some very useful information about maneuvering the congested streets when parades are in motion: "It's advisable that folks stake out a spot on the street where the parade of their choice will be reviewing, or get a prepaid balcony available at many of the hotels that overlook the parade, or find restaurants that have views of the activities and will allow diners to hang around and visit awhile; this should be arranged prior to the frenzy that occurs during the parades. A map of the parade routes and time schedules are at the end of this brochure to assist people in choosing the parades they wish to view and those areas they should avoid."

We awoke the next morning refreshed and ready to face the new challenges of the day. Having at our disposal a clearly defined walking map of the French Quarter and the surrounding area that would help us safely navigate the places we wished to see and those congested areas we wished to bypass, gave us confidence to explore the unknown without any hesitation. We decided to walk around and see what we would discover before the hectic activity started the following day, which was the beginning of the five days leading up to Fat Tuesday, and the start of major parades showing off their creations and occupying the streets in and around the French Quarter. Walking through the French Quarter is like visiting a foreign country. While strolling on Royal Street, there was a mix of French and Spanish architecture garnishing the beautiful buildings dating back to the 18th century. Throughout the 6x13 block area of the French Quarter, which was laid out in 1722, the same feeling prevails. First, you're traveling through some of the quaint towns in France, where small buildings are lined up in symmetrical rows boasting their ornately decorative facades, and then you're visiting a small town in Spain where buildings are more irregularly shaped, decorated with wrought iron balconies and gates, and beautifully adorned with flower arrangements of every imaginable color. This is the atmosphere of the last remaining French Colonial and Spanish settlements in the U.S. Our hotel was at the head of Royal Street, which is an antique shopper's paradise. I'm not a shopper and usually try to avoid visiting stores with Barbara; my usual position is at the outside of stores striking up conversations with other distraught husbands. But I must say that the quaint shops drew my attention. The intriguing shops possessed wares ranging from museum-quality continental antiques, to Art Deco statues, to weapons used during the Civil War, to furniture from almost every period—all in like-new condition. We spent over an hour browsing the shops and questioning salespeople about the origin, history, and cost of many pieces of furniture and memorabilia. One of Barbara's favorite pastimes is her love of music; she plays the piano, synthesizer, and classical guitar. When she practices her instrument of choice at home, I often hear the hollow **click**, **click**, **click** sound of her electronic metronome resounding throughout our home, which is annoying to no end. In one of the shops specializing in French antique furniture, I spotted the most beautiful, highly polished, wood-grained antique metronome, which was made in Paris, France, dating back to the 19th century that supposedly once belonged to a Miss New Orleans beauty contest winner. I wound it and heard the same **click**, **click**, **click**, but this time it was different; instead of the plastic tinny sound of the one at home, it made a soft, solid, vibrating sound, tick, tick, tick, which was pleasant to my ears. What a great Christmas present for her. I knew she would love it, and if not, at least I would enjoy listening to the more pleasant cadence of the mellower tick, tick, ticks, instead of the hollow **click**, **click**, **clicks**. After some serious browsing, we decided to return to the hotel to see if our concierge, Jean Paul, could get us reservations at the renowned Fairmont Hotel's restaurant for dinner, while there was still a chance of beating the crowds. Jean Paul said, "No problem monsieur, I will make sure you are seated tonight." We dressed and confirmed with Jean Paul that our reservations were in order. He said, "But of course, I have a friend . . ."

The world-famous Fairmont Hotel was only a ten-minute walk from our home base. A Carnival atmosphere surrounded us as the revelers were on the streets celebrating their good fortune at being in such a festive place. The smell of food mixed with the strong odor of liquor was pleasantly shocking to my nostrils. It was surprising to see that people were already drinking on the streets at around seven o'clock. They all seemed to be sucking on straws protruding from their oversized plastic cups, while talking, smiling, and even eating, all at the same time. We were offered a drink called an "N'awlins Hurricane" by one of the store-street vendors. It was a tall, plastic, tulip-shaped pinkish drink consisting of (this is the vendor's recipe) the following ingredients:

½ cup of ice
2 fluid ounces of light rum
2 fluid ounces of passion fruit-flavored syrup

1 cup of lemon and lime-flavored carbonated beverage
1 ounce of lime juice, and
1 fluid ounce of 151-proof rum;

Put everything into a shaker, except the 151-proof rum, and shake it well. Pour the mix into a Hurricane glass and then gently top it off with an ounce of 151-proof rum.

It is important that the drink is consumed with a straw, the result being, that as you get closer to the top of the concoction and near the end of the brew, the drink becomes more potent.

Well, what the hell, we were in "merry-land" so why not try one. We continued our walk, becoming two of the merry-makers. We became part of the party scene, with drinks in hand, smiles on our faces, and walking in a zigzagging pattern while attempting to walk a straight line to the Fairmont. We got there a little lightheaded, but it complemented the mood we were in as we entered the astonishing lobby of the famous hotel. It was like entering a mansion-museum-castle, all rolled up into one. We wanted to explore the venue, but decided to save the visit for our final Mardi Gras Ball, which was being held in their elaborate ballroom.

Jean Paul made reservations for us at Bailey's Restaurant, which is usually quiet and laid back, as opposed to the other "hang-out" eateries in the hotel, such as the Sazerac Room, which is named after a renowned Southern potent drink, and is quite busy, with a large bar with layers of patrons vying for the bartender's attention. Our dining room's atmosphere was perfectly subdued, with soft piano music, which immediately took us out of a hyper-festive mood and into a more relaxed dining one. We were expecting a very pricey food menu, but were surprised that the prices were just slightly above average. For appetizers, Barbara ordered New Orleans crabmeat and I went for the crawfish cakes, which we happily shared. Instead of ordering a bottle of wine, we thought we would go easy, especially after the hurricane drinks experience, so we both ordered a glass of the white house wine.

The special soup of the day was "hearts of palm, with asparagus & endive," which we both ordered and consumed very slowly to savor its taste, which complemented the white wine we were nursing. The wine seemed to be made for the food we were enjoying, so much so, that we decided to have a second glass. For the main course, Barbara ordered *breast of duck Andreas,* while I opted for the *veal escalope Acadian.* The food was divine, complementing the piano music and the soft, delicious white wine. We found our glasses empty and couldn't resist having them filled once more, which was really way beyond our limit, but we were on vacation and decided "what the heck." After finishing a perfect supper, in an exquisite restaurant, with beautiful soft piano music, I asked for the bill. The price of the meal was what I expected, but I never asked how much the wine cost. Well, it cost as much as the dinner. Shame on me! We swore never again to order anything in a restaurant without first finding out the price beforehand. But then, if we would have known the price in advance, we certainly wouldn't have ordered the divine nectar and would have missed out on an exceptional dining experience. When faced with this kind of a situation, where we spend more than expected for something we enjoy, we have learned to pacify ourselves by saying: "It didn't cost us anything; we paid for it with our kids' inheritance." Uttering those words magically makes us feel better.

Walking back to our hotel through the Halloween neighborhoods was like being in an *Alice in Wonderland* fantasy. It seemed that everyone was insane; people's behavior was out of the ordinary, to say the least. Girls were showing off their bare breasts, and then some, for trinkets; most men were in some sort of frenzy and groping everything in sight with impunity. We actually had to push our way back to our place of rest, UGH! All of this was going on while policemen were in sight, patrolling the area and ignoring the unusual behavior of the revelers.

We decided to spend the next morning walking around the French Quarter and the afternoon trying to get a good spot to view the Columbus 500 Centennial float, which was named King (Rex) of the Mardi Gras. We again asked our friend, Jean Paul, where he suggested was a good place to have breakfast, and where a good starting point for a walking tour through the French Quarter would be. He said, "Mon Ami, you must have breakfast at the Court of Two Sisters; the food is the best. If you would like to walk and see some of our great sites, start at Jackson Square, which is just down the street, and then just walk and enjoy yourselves." So away we went to the Court of Two Sisters; a courtyard is exactly what it was, the largest in New Orleans, with a turn-of-the-century look (19th century). It was beautifully landscaped with flowers and plantings surrounding the outdoor dining area. A jazz combo's music filled the air and seemed to carry the flavor of the food with it into my nostrils. It was brunch time and we were famished, so I ordered eggs Benedict while Barbara chose oysters Bienville. While waiting for our delights, I read a brief history about the café that occupied the back page of my menu. "The restaurant was named for two sisters, Emma and Bertha Camors, born in 1858 and 1860, respectively; they belonged to a proud and aristocratic Creole family. Their successful *rabais* or notions shop, outfitted many of the city's finest women with formal gowns, lace and perfumes imported from Paris. But, their dream was to open a common people's restaurant with the finest food in New Orleans. Although they both died within two months of each other in 1944, their dream restaurant, fortunately, still survives." The brunch more than lived up to its reputation, and the strong French coffee and jazz combo made for a great start to a promising day.

Thanks to a walking map that Jean Paul provided, we had no trouble finding Jackson Square, which was a short distance from the restaurant. When approaching the square, the scene filling the lens of my eyes and overwhelming my brain was that of the statue of Andrew Jackson on Horseback, the three enormous steeples of St. Louis Cathedral, the Cabildo (Council) Museum on its left, and its twin, the Presbytere (Priests' House) Museum on its right. After taking pictures of President Andrew Jackson in all his military glory, we headed straight for the three steeples accentuating St. Louis Cathedral. The walking map had a brief description of the three buildings. "The Cathedral was first established in 1718 and is the oldest continuous operating church in the U.S. It stretches one block between St. Peter Street and St. Ann Street. It's not considered the largest or grandest of the city's Catholic churches, but it's the seat of the Roman Catholic Archdioceses of New Orleans." Its three cone-shaped steeples, a large one in the center flanked by two smaller ones, sparkled in the sun, which at certain angles look like halos. The Cathedral has survived fires, bombings, and hurricanes, and each time was restored more magnificently than prior to each tragic event. We entered and were immediately taken in by the beauty of the stained-glass windows, murals, and altar. I'm always surprised and proud when finding medieval beauty in the U.S. that favorably compares to its European ancestors.

To the left of the Cathedral is the Cabildo Museum, built in the early 18th century by the new Spanish rulers. It is a three-story-high building designed in old Spanish colonial architecture, featuring arched columns on the first and second levels and tulip-shaped windows on the top floor. In the center is a "widow's walk" overlooking the city and its waterways. The walk was an excellent perch as a lookout for hostile activity in the area and a great spot for photos and viewing some of the parades. The first exhibit we visited was the *Native American Section*, which concentrated on the history of Louisiana's Indians prior to the European invasion. The artifacts and a mini-village were good representations of what life was like back in that more peaceful era. Next, we visited the *Colonial Exhibit*, which outlined the first French settlement and how the intruders lived. A highlight was the *Iberville Stone*, which marked the founding of the first settlement in Louisiana by the French. There was a special place exhibiting the original plans for the building of the city of New Orleans. An especially interesting room was a reproduction of the place where the signing of the Louisiana Purchase occurred. It was complete with paintings of those present and copies of the colonial wooden furniture used on that historic occasion. A painting showing how the town square looked on the day of the signing was highlighted with spotlights and was amusing to behold, considering what the sophisticated city has developed into today.

Another room displayed many artifacts from the Battle of New Orleans, which took place in 1815, when Americans under the leadership of General Andrew Jackson defeated the supposedly invincible British forces in the War of 1812. An especially interesting artifact was a lock of Andrew Jackson's hair, enclosed in a well-guarded case. Not to be outdone by Americans, the French somehow managed to send us the death mask of Napoleon Bonaparte (it is said that it was donated by the doctor who serviced Napoleon on his deathbed). I could have sworn that I had seen the mask in other museums around the world, so I guess someone made a nice profit in reproducing that sacred artifact, or maybe there was more than one Napoleon! The museum certainly gave a respectful historical picture of pre-colonial times and the development of the great state of Louisiana. We could have spent all morning at the museum, but were anxious to visit the Presbytere Museum before lunch.

The Presbytere Museum, on the right of the Cathedral, was built in the late 18th century to house the Capuchin monks, but was never used for that purpose. It was designed to match the Cabildo, which is on the other side of St. Louis Cathedral. It was used for commercial purposes and finally housed the Louisiana Supreme Court. Currently, it is the foremost Mardi Gras museum in the state. It has five major carnival themes: History, Masking, Parades, Balls, and Mardi Gras. The exhibits trace the festival from its ancient origins to the 19th century emergence of the parades and balls of New Orleans, and to the present statewide celebration that attracts millions of visitors each year. There were three galleries filled with dazzling Mardi Gras memorabilia, including handmade gowns worn by kings and queens of some of the city's Krewes; magnificent crowns and scepters adorned by royalty; and costumes made by local Indian tribes with hundreds of masks worn by various Krewes, parade participants, and street people. There was an area set aside for watching a parade from an imitation float, which includes parade watchers on a movie screen in front of the float, allowing the viewers to pretend that they are throwing beads at the people below. It was exciting imagining that we were on a float, and almost as interesting as the amusing restrooms in the museum that masquerade as Fat Tuesday port-a-potties and were decorated with Mardi Gras costumes.

We were attracted to their unique gift shop and couldn't resist buying exotic Mardi Gras masks for our kids. They were a respectable representation of the skills of the local craftsmen that have come down through the centuries from their ancestors, two of which were being held in my hands to bring home as playthings for our children. We exited the incredible museum and headed for a spot a few blocks away that would allow us to see the "Columbus and the Age of Discovery" floats as they passed in their entire historical splendor.

On the way to our spot, we noticed that many restaurants had street side bars selling oysters on the half shell, grilled shrimp, crab cakes, and other kebab foods. It was surprising how many people were eating at these places while downing their hurricane drinks, dancing, making all sorts of loud noises, and the most startling scene, women willingly showing their breasts for trinkets. The scene was probably similar to the one that shut down Sodom and Gomorra in biblical times. We headed for a less busy bar and ordered oysters on the half shell and grilled shrimp. We totally enjoyed the treat that was so readily available from street vendors throughout the area. We devoured our food and rushed to find a spot where we could view the Columbus floats that were scheduled to pass around 1:00 P.M. The three floats arrived on time; the first one was a replica of Columbus's main ship, the Santa Maria. The original ship was built in Spain and was approximately 77 feet long, by 26 feet wide, with a complement of about 40 men. At the float's head was a costumed Columbus waving to the crowd and throwing beads and fake doubloons to lucky recipients. Seated behind him were King Ferdinand and Queen Isabella in all their glory, waving, and also showering gifts to the peasants. The second float was a reproduction of the Nina, which was originally 67 feet long and 27 feet wide, had a complement of 20 men, and was captained by the youngest of the three Pinzon brothers that sailed with Columbus, Captain Vincente Yanes Pinzon. The brothers were from the small seaside town of Palo, Spain. Vincente and his shipmates duplicated the actions of Columbus and showered trinkets at the onlookers. The third replica was the Pinta, originally 70 feet long and 22 feet wide, with a complement of 26 seamen. It was owned and captained by the eldest brother, Captain Martin Alonzo Pinzon. His brother, Francisco Pinzon, went on his voyage of discovery as Martin's pilot. It was befitting the Pinzon brothers were represented in the parade, Columbus and the Age of Discovery, as it was their combined efforts that enabled Columbus to secure the ships and men required to begin his journey. As a matter of fact, Columbus was required by the realm to put up one-eighth of the cost of the expedition, but he did not have the funds. Martin Alonzo Pinzon put up the required funds, again becoming instrumental in helping the expedition on its way. Unfortunately, the flagship, Santa Maria, went aground while anchored off one of the Caribbean islands. Columbus used the smaller and faster Nina to continue on his journey and finally to return to Spain, overcoming unimaginable hardships, including what was considered to be one of the most severe hurricanes in recorded history at that time.

I couldn't stop taking pictures and videos of the ships and the other floats in the parade, and continued to do so up until Fat Tuesday. The leader of the main parade on Fat Tuesday was the trumpeter Al Hirt, a son of New Orleans, as Grand Marshal of the Festival. This enormous man at the head of his float blasting his high, sweet notes from his trumpet caused the crowds to become ecstatic as they howled and screamed as his float passed by. His harmonizing partner, Pete Fountain, played a smooth, high-pitched clarinet, and made the event a perfect ending to the parade celebrations. I wasn't sure if I could get many of the pictures that I took of people misbehaving developed at our local camera store, but I was sure that the videos, which were more revealing than the photos, wouldn't be a problem. Exhausted, we returned to our place of refuge, and searched for Jean Paul to get directions to Preservation Hall and reservations to a fine restaurant. Directions to the famous hall were easy as it was just a couple of blocks away, but reservations at a fine restaurant during Mardi Gras were out of the question. He suggested that we just walk along the French Quarter and try whatever restaurant had vacant seats. We decided not to hassle with the crowds outside and went to the hotel's bistro, which had a table available. I ordered a soufflé stuffed with crabmeat and Barbara ordered blintzes filled with apples. We washed our meals down with strong French coffee, and again were surprised at the rich deep flavor of the brew. We were anxious to get to Preservation Hall before the crowds gathered. We had visited the world-renowned venue many years ago, when "Sweet Emma Barrett" was still performing there. She was in her 80s and had to be pushed in her wheel chair to her piano in order to perform. She was the personification of Jazz, and carried her title as "the Bell Gal of Jazz" for over 50 years. I remembered so well her singing "Somebody Else is Taking My Place" and "Just a Closer Walk with Thee." She was so weak from her advanced age and her many other ailments that she could barely finish either song. But, her weak voice singing "Just a Closer Walk with Thee," had people in the audience pulling out handkerchiefs and wiping tears from their faces, including me and Barbara. The words of the song, by an unknown author, went something like this:

> I am weak, but Thou art strong
> Jesus, keep me from all wrong
> I'll be satisfied as long as I walk, let me walk close to Thee
> Just a closer walk with Thee

Grant it, Jesus, is my plea
Daily walking close to Thee
Let it be, dear Lord, let it be
Through this world of toil and snares
If I falter, Lord, who cares?
None but Thee, dear Lord, none but Thee
When my feeble life is o'er, Time for me will be no more
Guide me gently, safely o'er
To Thy kingdom shore, to Thy shore

What a memorable evening so many years ago, when we were not only fortunate to hear her sing, but also to speak to her and tell her how much we loved her singing. Barbara reminded me that at that time the small, decrepit room was packed with people and that the heat was oppressive, causing her to become faint, so we had to leave, but we did get to see the most cherished of Jazz singers, "Sweet Emma." We had promised each other that we would return, hopefully on a cooler night, and enjoy the rest of the Preservation Hall Jazz Band's music. So here we were many years later, fulfilling our promise to return to the same small, dilapidated room, which hadn't changed since its opening in 1961. We again were sitting on uncomfortable wood benches and it was "hot to beat the band." The charisma was still there: the smoky air, moldy smell, light jazz music, and humming patrons clapping and tapping their hands and feet to the beat of the blues music perfected the feeling of the place. None of this had changed one iota from our last visit, except "Sweet Emma" was no longer a part of the New Orleans Jazz scene, as she made her last walk in 1983. The music coming from the 70-and 80-year-old musicians was still sweet and kept the audience humming along to "Hindustan," "Tishomingo Blues," "Put on Your Old Grey Bonnet," "Savoy Blues," and finally, "When the Saints Go Marching In." The last song was played just in time, as Barbara was again feeling the effects of the oppressive heat, which was compounded by the number of people and volume of smoke present in the small room. So away we went, satisfied that we had fulfilled a promise to ourselves and "Sweet Emma" to return to Preservation Hall. As we were leaving, they performed my all-time favorite song, "House of the Rising Sun," as if to reward us for returning. One of the versions that has come down over the many years of this mysterious blues song that was first recorded in the 1920s comes from a popular story about a house of ill repute in New Orleans around the mid-19th century called the Rising Sun, named after its owner Madam Marianne LeSoleil Levant, whose name translates from French to "The rising sun." That story helps to give meaning to the words of the song, which I have loved hearing over the years by singing groups, such as the Weavers and the Animals.

Following are the words that I prefer to this fascinating song:

> There is a house in New Orleans
> They call the Rising Sun
> And it's been the ruin of many a poor boy
> And God I know I'm one . . .
> My mother was a tailor, sewed my new blue jeans
> My father was a gamblin' man, down in New Orleans
> Now the only thing a gambler needs
> Is a suitcase and trunk
> And the only time he's satisfied
> Is when he's all drunk
> Oh mother, tell your children
> Not to do what I have done
> Spend your lives in sin and misery
> In the House of the Rising Sun
> Well, I've got one foot on the platform
> The other on the train
> I'm going back to New Orleans
> To wear that ball and chain they call the Rising Sun
> And it's been the ruin of many a poor boy
> And God I know I'm one . . .

We walked back to our hotel via Bourbon Street, which is lined with bars, jazz clubs, hotels, restaurants, "gentlemen's clubs," and boutiques. I'm sure if we had looked long enough, we would also find a "lady's club," but we didn't have the time or inclination. Somehow we were again holding hurricane drinks and enjoying the great music coming from the clubs. Jazz, blues, and rock 'n' roll flowed from the joints, mixing in the air, as the sounds became part of the street scenery, accompanying people dancing as they drank their night away. We pushed our way through the crowd and finally arrived at our sanctuary, where we could get some relief from the street noise and heat. We decided to spend the next morning sightseeing and the afternoon viewing parades. Again, we would try to have Jean Paul reserve a table for us at one of the local restaurants.

In the morning, we immediately approached Jean Paul and asked, "What is the best way to get around the area and avoid the parade traffic?" He said, "Walk to Jackson Square, hire a buggy, and tell the driver where you would like to go; he will know how to avoid the busy parts of town." I responded with, "Great, now can you get us a reservation at a local restaurant?" "I will try, *Mon Ami*, come see me after breakfast." We had a light meal at the hotel's Le Café bistro and hurried back to Jean Paul. He still wasn't able to get us a table, but was sure that he could find us a suitable place to have dinner by the time we returned from our excursion. We walked to Jackson Square, which was busy with street musicians, fortune tellers, artists, jugglers, and many tourists. We were intrigued by an artist painting portraits at a street side setting; his work was quite good, so we decided to have a pastel painting of our heads put on paper. The rendering still hangs in our home in New York; unfortunately, the painting has little resemblance to us today as time has altered our appearances somewhat. While sitting for our portrait, we heard music and singing coming from around the corner and asked our painter what was happening. He said, "There is a funeral procession in progress." We asked if it was alright if we interrupted his painting while we took a quick peek, and he said "Okay." What an amazing sight! A coffin was being carried by six pall bearers, followed by a four-piece band playing "Just a Closer Walk with Thee," followed by a line of family and friends all singing that oh, so very touching song.

We hired a mule and buggy and asked the driver, Manuel, to take us around the area and point out places of interest. He suggested that the least crowded area would be around the waterfront, which was only a few streets away; we agreed and he headed for the river area and Woldenberg Park. Manuel told us that

> The Park replaced the run-down areas along the river in the 1970s and 1980s, and is now a five-acre grassy open

space with landscaped walkways, river views, fountains, a sculptured garden, and stages for live music. The park was named after a local philanthropist named Malcolm Woldenberg, and its Moonwalk was named after a popular New Orleans mayor, Maurice 'Moon' Landrieu.

A bronze statue of Malcolm was at the center of an informal sculpture garden along the riverfront. Near his statue was a stainless steel sculpture called *Ocean Song,* which was created by a local artist, John Scott, which depicts the motion of water in eight narrow pyramids, polished to a reflective gleam that emphasized the water flows. Further downriver we saw an elegant *Monument to the Immigrant* statue, crafted in white Carrara marble by sculptor Franco Allesandrini. The structure faces the riverfront with a ship's prow topped by a female figure reminiscent of our *Lady Liberty.* Behind her is a turn-of-the-20th-century immigrant family statue looking toward the French Quarter. Further downriver was a sculpture of Robert Schoen's *Old Man River,* which was also made from beautiful white Carrara marble, and standing approximately 18 feet tall. The statue reflected the river's power and majesty in its muscular body presentation. Street musicians could be seen along our path playing their saxophones, trumpets, and banjos in time with our mules clippity-clopping; their soft harmony and the increasing heat almost put me to sleep several times. The area also included the Audubon Aquarium of the Americas, which we previously visited, and the Entergy IMAX Theater. Further upriver was the Spanish Plaza, dedicated in 1976 during the U.S. bicentennial. It was a gift from Spain as a gesture of friendship to its one-time colony. It featured a beautiful fountain inlaid with Spanish mosaic coat-of-arms tiles representing that country's provinces. Fortunately, there were vendors in the plaza serving food and drinks; we took the opportunity to stop and have some tacos and beer for lunch, picnic style, while sitting on the lush and inviting green lawn. Exiting the mule-drawn carriage brought us a welcomed bit of fresh air and much-needed shade from a beautiful tree that helped cool us off from the rising temperature. While eating, we relaxed and just enjoyed the view of the river's activity. Watercrafts of every size and shape traversed the mighty river. Small sunfish boats and sail kites were everywhere, zigzagging between the larger vessels.

Returning to our carriage, we noticed the indoor Riverwalk Marketplace Mall that we visited on our first day, and were tempted to visit again just to get some relief from the ever-increasing heat, but instead told our driver it was time to end our excursion and head back to Jackson Square. He said we couldn't end the trip unless we saw the golden bronze statue of *Joan of Arc,* which was a short distance away, residing in front of the French Market Place. The sculpture was remarkable; it was an exact copy of the famous 1880 equestrian statue of *Joan* by Emmanuel Fremiet, located at the *Place des Pyramides* in Paris, France, that we saw on our visit to that magnificent city. The statue was a gift from the people of France and President Charles de Gaulle, during his state visit to the United States in 1959, and was certainly one of the main centerpieces on the Riverwalk. If not for the rising temperature and the abundance of tourists, we would have continued exploring the riverside walk, as there was so much more to see, but it was getting hot and we hadn't seen the grandest parade of the Festival. We found a spot and synchronized our watches, right to the minute that the Bacchus Parade would pass our location. Bacchus was the Greek God of wine. While the floats passed, artificial wine grape throws seemed to be coming from every direction. There were over 25 floats in the parade, including super floats with descriptive names such as *Bacchagator*, *Bacchassaurus*, and *Bacca-Whoppa*. Some of the illustrious celebrities portraying the Greek God have been William Shatner (Captain Kirk), Bob Hope, Dick Clark, Dom DeLuise, Charlton Heston, and Raymond Burr. The Krewes' large signature floats had mixed themes of grapes and its importance during the "Age of Discovery." It seemed as if all the floats' participants that were dressed as Native Americans were squeezing, throwing, or imbibing the fruits of the grapes. The parade was endless, with music coming from every direction, while the organizations' members marched in front of, in between, in back, and on the sides of the various floats. I think all of its 1,000-plus members were participating in the parade, marching, singing, acting, juggling, hula hooping, performing acrobatic stunts, and throwing beads plus other ornaments to the roaring crowd. When the last float passed, we were exhausted from jumping around, catching trinkets, and yelling at the top of our voices. And then again, there was the heat, which was quickly overwhelming us, so we headed back to our cool hotel and went directly to the revolving Carousel

Bar on the roof. Barbara ordered a tall Mud Slide and I ordered a tall, cool, frosty glass of Corona beer with a piece of lime. We decided it was a perfect time to change into our bathing suits and enjoy the refreshing rooftop pool. With cold drinks in hand, and our bodies in the cool pool, we were able to enjoy Mardi Gras from a distance with some degree of privacy, as most of the hotel guests were on the streets enjoying the festivities or in their rooms getting over their excessive celebrating.

After a well-needed nap, which almost turned out to be an around-the-clock marathon sleep-in, we were awakened by our telephone ringing—it was Jean Paul. He said we had better hurry if we wanted to keep our 9:30 reservation at the Broussard's Restaurant. It was just nine o'clock, so we quickly dressed and ran down to meet him and get directions to the restaurant. As usual, the place was a short walking distance from our hotel. Again, Barbara's advice saved the day. She had said, "I think you should wear a dinner jacket," which I reluctantly carried over my arm to the restaurant. Who knew that Broussard's Restaurant was one of the most celebrated places in New Orleans to dine? Our reservations got us past the line that was forming outside and we were surprised that we were seated immediately. The grand entrance was similar to a Parisian promenade; we were surrounded by beautifully hand painted Italian tiles of cherubs and Napoleonic insignias on the walls. Our table was in a picturesque cobblestone courtyard; it seemed that soft French music was coming from the soothing water flow of the fountain in the middle of the room, and from the lush tropical foliage. I was happy to be wearing my dinner jacket, as the place certainly deserved customers that dressed well. Barbara ordered another Mud Slide while I was content with a refreshing tall glass of very cold tap beer. The smell of jasmine and magnolia in the courtyard turned our drinks into ambrosia. The menu was extensive, but we decided to stay simple and just order salads and main courses. We both ordered Valencia orange, fennel, and *jicama* salads, with blood orange vinaigrette and seasonal greens. For her main course, Barbara ordered Parasol of Shrimp Marcus, with jumbo gulf shrimp in basil lemon and sherry butter with a zesty seafood risotto cake. Not to be outdone, I ordered a simple Louisiana Bouillabaisse with plump oysters, gulf shrimp, and fish in a savory tomato broth, flavored with saffron and topped with crabmeat and rouille croutons. Well, our simple meals were consumed in short order; French cuisine is without a doubt one of the most delicious delights on earth, if prepared properly. I must say, the food was prepared to perfection by their chef, Gunter Preuss, whom we personally complimented for our exquisite meal. He in turn supplied us with a complimentary after-dinner cognac drink. Totally satisfied with our dining experience, we left the superb establishment and fought our way through the crowds back to the Monteleone for a well-deserved night's sleep.

When on vacation, we often take a trolley or bus ride through the city to see the different neighborhoods and to get a feel of the place. So we had a quick breakfast and headed for the St. Charles Avenue streetcars. The conductor was very pleasant and gave us a brief description of some of the places of interest on his route. The trolley took us along the river past Audubon Park, which includes the Audubon Zoo, and Tulane University, which dates back to 1834 and is the largest employer in New Orleans. Loyola University, which was founded in 1849 by Jesuit priests, was also on the scenic route and boasts a six-level recreational sports complex. The RecPlex includes two floors of racquetball, tennis, basketball and volleyball courts, in addition to a natatorium with a diving pool, whirlpool, sauna, steam room, an elevated jogging track, and an elaborate weight-lifting room. The complex also houses a four-story parking garage. On the route there was an outstanding Confederate Museum that devotes itself to the Civil War and the outstanding efforts of the Confederate Army in that conflict.

While we were taking in the views, a young couple came on board, dressed in country western outfits. He was dressed in fancy cowboy clothes that included boots and a high hat. She was dressed in beautiful cowgirl clothes, also with boots and a high girly hat. I asked them why they were dressed that way. They said they were on their way to the annual "Country Western Festival Dance." After speaking with them for a few minutes, they asked us to join them at the dance, which we accepted without any hesitation. The dance hall was about 3,000 square feet and was filled to capacity. It's probably one of the most festive dance sights that I have ever witnessed. The dancers' outfits were dazzling. The boots that the girls wore would stop a fashion show.

They were high heeled and in every imaginable color: red, white, blue, green, two-toned, and striped. Their outfits were just as spectacular; some wore short skirts, while others wore long skirts or slacks, with matching boots. There was an incredible variety of sequined colors in a variety of shapes on their clothes. What was interesting was that none of them were dressed exactly alike. On the other hand, the men all looked alike, although they wore different-styled clothes; their boots were primarily black, their dungarees blue, and their hats either black or white. Everyone danced in a counterclockwise circle, repeating steps in strict patterns. There was an instructor tutoring two gents on the sideline in the western two-step. He was repeating: quick-quick, slow-slow, as they repeated their steps, with much difficulty. We immediately copied the pattern: one, close, three and four, which is what we saw the fellows doing. Barbara and I joined the dancers in the first two-step that was played and had a great time. After our dance, the instructor, Jimmy, came over to us and introduced himself. He said we were doing the dance wrong; there is no close on the second step, to which I replied, "But I'm doing the exact pattern that your students did." He said, "I've been trying for weeks to get them to stop closing on the two, but they just don't seem to get it." Well, the next two-step dance, Barbara and I fell in with the crowd and did quick-quick, slow-slow, just like everyone else, except the two gentlemen, who evidently had four left feet. The price of admission included a buffet lunch, which we helped ourselves to, and were introduced to "jambalaya soup and gumbo." Hot, hot, hot—but, oh, so delicious! We spent a couple of hours dancing and socializing with the most pleasant, well dressed, and synchronized dancers that we have ever met. We didn't want to leave, but we wanted to catch the Zulu Parade that passed our spot late in the afternoon. We hopped on a red trolley that took us back to the French Quarter, just in time to occupy our place and witness the Zulu floats. The music was what I expected, African jungle, and lots of great jazz, with very tall natives dancing and singing, while throwing gifts to the admirers that were lined up along the way, begging for trinkets. The Zulus appeared incredibly tall on the floats and almost gave the impression of being on stilts. They were dressed in various native costumes. The tall, lean men wore colorful headgear and rattled deadly looking spears. The women showed off their shapely figures and danced to their respective native rhythms. It was one of the most colorful parades that we were fortunate to see; not only was the music and their dancing spectacular, but the size of the natives on the floats made them look like fearful giants waving deadly spears and making grimacing faces at the crowd.

We were at a point where avoiding parades was more appealing than witnessing another one. The festive attitude and noise were fine for the first few days, but when combined with the heat and poor manners of the crowds, avoidance seemed to be in order. The days rushed by and before we realized it, we were preparing for our "Columbus and the Age of Discovery Ball," which was at the Fairmont Hotel's Grand Ballroom.

My dream of dreams became a reality in 1992. I was at Mardi Gras in New Orleans with a "Columbus and the Age of Discovery" theme. The reason we were both excited was that we had plans for a trip to Spain later that year to join in the "500 Centennial" at the "1992 World Expo," celebration of the landing of Columbus and his three ships on our continent. I had been collecting "Columbus and The Age of Discovery" books and memorabilia for over 20 years, and that night I was going to meet not only Cristobal, but Amerigo, Queen Isabella, King Ferdinand, and many of the illustrious members of Columbus's first voyage. I couldn't wait to get to the Fairmont to meet all my historical heroes. For the first time on our trip, I didn't mind getting dressed in my Sunday best so I would make a good impression. A short walk found us in front of one of the most magnificent hotels that I have ever seen. The outside was lined with flags over the entrance and a red carpet lining the outside steps leading to what seemed to be a mile-long hallway-lobby; it gave me the feeling that I was royalty entering an imperial palace. The enormous hallway was lined with flowers and large vases, filled with plants of every color and description. On the right was the famous Sazerac Bar and Grill, filled to capacity, on the left the Court Bar, also filled to the hilt.

It was time for us to make our entrance at the ball. We were welcomed out loud by the Court's announcer: "Mr. and Mrs. Michael Bivona from New York." There were two reception lines; I couldn't believe that I was in the line to shake hands with Queen Isabella, King

Ferdinand, Cristobal and Amerigo; what an unexpected surprise. I asked the Queen if she would save a dance for me, and she responded with a big "YES." The reception lines lasted about an hour, and then to the blasts of the Court's trumpets, the Royal Party was announced as they paraded to their seats at a long table at the head of the room, which was on a slightly raised platform. The ball had in excess of 300 people; it was surprising that most of the guests were received by the Royalty and their entourage, who were lined up opposite each other, in such a quick and orderly manner. The music began and Columbus came to our table and asked Barbara if she would like to dance a waltz. She jumped out of her seat and danced with the Genovese around the large ballroom dance floor. He returned her to our table, bowed, and asked me to dance . . . Oh wait, I must have imagined that . . . I've never seen Barbara so happy! She spent the rest of the evening smiling from ear to ear while floating on the dance floor, with me and other honored royalty. I did get a chance to dance a waltz with Queen Isabella, and while circling the dance floor, I had the urge to ask her if she and Cristobal had something going in the old days. I guess the answer to that question will forever remain unanswered.

A minuet dance was announced. We were told to line up on either side of the dance floor facing the royal table, forming lines of boy-girl, boy-girl. A slow waltz was played and the Royal Party and their entourage went to the front of each line. When the music began, they showed us how to perform the dance by entering in the middle and dancing a waltz through the lines; they then took their places at the end of each station. Fortunately, not everyone participated in the line dance, or there would have been utter pandemonium on the dance floor, due to the large crowd of people in attendance. There was much confusion, but everyone did get a chance to dance with some of the court's entourage, and if they were lucky, as I was, they had an opportunity to dance with royalty. By the time the dance ended, I'm proud to say that I danced with Cristobal and Amerigo. What fun! In my wildest dreams, I never thought that I would ever dance with my two heroes, Christopher Columbus and Amerigo Vespucci. The ball ended with the orchestra playing "When the Saints Come Marching In." The song was originally published in 1896 and is probably one of the most recorded songs in existence. My research came up with the following popular lyrics:

> We are trav'ling in the footsteps of those who've gone before
> And we'll all be reunited, on a new and sunlit shore
> Oh, when the saints go marching in, oh, when the saints go marching in
> Lord, how I want to be in that number, when the saints go marching in
> And when the sun begins to shine, and when the sun begins to shine
> Lord, how I want to be in that number, when the sun begins to shine
> Oh, when the saints go marching in, oh when the saints go marching in
> Lord how I want to be in that number, when the saints go marching in
> Oh, when the trumpet sounds its call, oh when the trumpet sounds its call
> Lord, how I want to be in that number, when the trumpet sounds its call
> Oh, when the saints go marching in, oh when the saints go marching in
> Lord, how I want to be in that number, when the saints go marching in.

The song was not only the end of our beautiful Mardi Gras Ball, but also the end of an incredible vacation. Some years later, I was fortunate to donate my Columbus and the Age of Discovery Library to the Columbus Foundation in New York City. They are the sponsors of the annual New York Columbus Day Parade in Manhattan; my books are now a part of that organization, which is dedicated to honoring and keeping the memory of those brave explorers alive. A copy of an article acknowledging my donation follows:

Foundation News

Bivona Collection Donated

The Foundation has received an enormously generous and essential donation, the Michael Bivona Collection: Columbus, The Age of Discovery and Related Books. The collection, which Mr. Bivona acquired over the course of 30 years, contains approximately 300 books and immediately gives us an extensive group of works about the Foundation's namesake. It will reside in the Ambassador Charles A. Gargano Library.

"This remarkable donation, by Michael Bivona, vastly increases and improves the quality of our library's holdings," said President Louis Tallarini. " We are deeply grateful to Mr. Bivona for his donation, and we are proud that our Member Louis Mangone made the introduction that has brought the Michael Bivona Collection to the Foundation."

"The age of discovery was roughly 1400 to 1700, and of course Columbus was central to the period," said Mr. Bivona. "He had the audacity and the courage to venture out into unknown areas. At that time, very few people would venture out on the water beyond the sight of land. He had few navigational instruments to guide him when he became the first European to discover and record this unknown continent. He found his way back to Spain using his knowledge of celestial navigation, ocean currents and prevailing winds. The route he took is still being used today because of the favorable winds and currents. What he did was just amazing."

Mr. Bivona, 72, and his wife Barbara live in Dix Hills, Long Island and have two grown children and two grandchildren. Now retired, he was a CPA and co-owner and CFO of Manchester Technologies. His main hobbies are boating and ballroom dancing. He owns a 42-foot Cris-Craft boat, which they've taken to Block Island, Cape Cod, Nantucket and Plymouth, among other places, but, unlike Columbus, he said, "with very sophisticated electronic navigational devices."

Mr. Bivona and Foundation Member Louis Mangone belong to a dancing group that meets regularly. Several months ago, Mr. Bivona was in discussions with Brown University, in Providence, Rhode Island, about donating the collection to the school. "I mentioned to Lou Mangone that I was talking to Brown, and he told me that the Foundation would be interested in the collection." Mr. Mangone pursued the collection, which is now coming to the Foundation.

Book collector, philanthropist and ballroom dance aficionado Michael Bivona with wife Barbara in a tango

The Michael Bivona Collection has great depth in its holdings of books about Columbus, from his own letters and journals and contemporary accounts of his voyages to the works of later historians who interpret and comment on the lasting changes brought about by his explorations. Mr. Bivona acquired the books from every type of source imaginable, from specialized booksellers to bookstores and flea markets, and the books range in age from recent to over 100 years old.

"It is wonderful to know that my collection will have a meaningful place at the Foundation to honor a great explorer," Mr. Bivona said. ✦

Chapter Nine – Traveling through Florida

~*~

AROUND THE FLOOR: JULY/SEPTEMBER 1999
TRAVELING AROUND by Barbara Bivona

I recently read an article in the USA Dance Magazine, which stated that Florida was the unofficial dance capital of the United States. This certainly is true for South Florida. There are so many places to dance from West Palm Beach to the Miami area that choosing a venue can become challenging. There are dances in the mornings, afternoons and evenings, seven days a week. It is such an active schedule, that meeting people we know from New York unexpectedly at these dance halls is not uncommon and never surprising. A favorite spot of ours is the Goldcoast Ballroom in Coconut Creek, which was built in 1997, specifically for ballroom dancing. Its dance floor is over 3,000 square feet and is constructed of floating oak wood, which is state-of-the-art flooring for dancers' delicate feet. It's owned and operated by Vinny Munno and Jeff Sandler; Vinny provides most of the DJ music, which is always the right rhythm and duration to satisfy customers, while Jeff handles the management of the facility and occasionally fills in as DJ. You can expect to circle the floor several times when doing a Quickstep, Foxtrot or Waltz, as Vinny's music is never too short, but timed just long enough so that dancers can happily perform many of their routines. Vinny has a good ear for Latin arrangements; his selections are authentic and the tempo is good for the various Latin dances. Mike and I especially enjoy dancing to his Mambo-Salsa music. A plus is that he takes requests and will play any dance music that is requested by his followers. On most dance nights the crowd thins out after 10:30 P.M., from over 300 people down to about 100 dancers, which gives us an opportunity to enjoy dancing the smooth dances. With less people occupying the floor, International Ballroom dancers can perform their fast, long-stepped movements without much interference, and fortunately without bumping into anyone, which is a major problem on many dance floors. What makes Vinny's music so popular is his understanding of what dancers require to perform properly, as he is a competitive dancer himself and has won many awards. I have found that the best DJs are those who are proficient dancers and know the kinds of music that allow performers to dance at their best. As a bonus, Tuesday evenings will see dancers enjoying one of two free 45-minute dance lessons in Latin and Smooth dancing.

When we returned to Florida as snow birds this winter and learned that one of our favorite dance spots for the last five years had closed, we were disappointed and asked our dancing friends where they were going on Saturday nights. The latest popular dance hall was "Dazzle Me Twice," located in West Palm Beach. So we joined our friends at the large hall that has a 2,000-square-foot dance floor and were immediately comfortable with the place, and happy at being reacquainted with many of our dancing companions. They have showcase dancing, usually with professional instructors and their students (Pro-Am), and unique theme nights celebrating whatever holiday is current, such as Valentine's Day, where everyone is requested to dress in some form of red, or St. Patrick's Day, where green is the color of choice. Once a month is birthday night, where large cakes are presented and the world's most popular song, "Happy Birthday," is sung loud and clear to those celebrating another year in their lives. Another special event is the movie stars look-a-like contests, where contestants dress and try to imitate such celebrities as Charley Chaplin, Liza Minnelli, Frank Sinatra, and other famous personalities. A large Christmas celebration tree is a permanent fixture; decorations are changed with each holiday, which puts everyone in the spirit of the occasion. Dances are Thursday and Saturday nights with music by DJ Gordon and free lessons by his lovely wife Pat, who is a proficient dance instructor with a following of some of the more advanced students in the area.

END OF ARTICLE

~*~

Barbara covered very well some of the dance venues in South Florida, so I'll skip embellishing on her words and just mention that for those of you who are interested, accessing "South Florida Ballroom Dancing" on the Internet will list many other exciting places to place your feet in the wonderful social experience of dancing.

Over the years, we have travelled extensively through the sunny state of Florida, visiting such places as Orlando-Disney World, LEGOLAND Water Park (formerly Cypress Gardens Water Park) in Winter Haven, the Florida Keys (Key West is the most southerly part of the U.S.), Ft. Lauderdale (the Venice of Florida), Sarasota (home of the Ringling Bros. and the Barnum & Bailey Ringling Circus), St. Augustine (the oldest settlement in the U.S.), the twin-cruise capitals of the world, Port Everglades and Port Miami, and on and on . . . Each location that we visited seemed to be the most amazing place in the world, until we traveled to our next destination where another unique adventure was awaiting us.

Florida is without a doubt a winter wonderland, where instead of snow it has an abundance of sunshine and delightful waterways, which is why we currently leave the cold weather of Long Island, N.Y. behind and head down to the warmer climate of the magical state every November, returning to New York when the warmer temperatures visit that state in mid-May. Of the many places we have visited in the *Sunshine State,* I will write about two places in particular, St. Augustine, in the northeastern part of the state, and Sarasota, which lies on the southwestern part. I chose St. Augustine because it was one of the first attempts at colonization in the United States by Europeans and still retains some active original buildings within a small village. Sarasota was chosen because it probably has one of the most colorful histories due to its famous residents, the Ringling brothers, and was partly responsible for the influx of tourism to Florida at the beginning of the 20th century. Before visiting Sarasota, we spent a couple of days in Ft. Myers with very dear New York friends who had recently relocated to that city. There was one attraction in particular that I thought was historically fascinating, the Thomas Edison and Henry Ford Winter Estates, so before writing about Sarasota, I'll briefly describe how our experience at the Estates led us to visit the City of Sarasota.

To begin our story I'll briefly describe our first stop in Washington, D.C.

Washington, D.C. and St. Augustine

The vicinity of the city was first explored in 1513 by the Spanish explorer Juan Ponce de Leon, who claimed the region for the Spanish crown. He is most remembered not for his explorations but for his search of the illusive *Fountain of Youth*, which he thought was located somewhere in the marshlands of Florida. The magic fountain that he was searching for was reputed to turn the clock back to a youthful time for anyone drinking from the flow of its cascade. Although the fountain was not found, it does seem that the people in the area do have extended lives; maybe the answer wasn't water but the air that people breathe, and of course, its warm weather with lots of sunshine.

The city was founded in 1565 by Pedro Menendez de Aviles whose goal was to build a fortification to protect his people and supplies and to colonize the area for the benefit of Spain. Under Pedro's leadership, the first African slaves were brought to the territory that would eventually become part of the United States—500 slaves in all. As a result, the first African American was born in his settlement. To even things out, the first European American was also born under his reign.

We first discovered St. Augustine on our initial car trip to Florida when we decided to leave January's freezing weather in New York behind us. We left Long Island at 8 A.M. on a Saturday morning and took two-hour shifts driving until we reached Washington D.C. in mid-afternoon, which was our first scheduled stop. It is probably one of the most exciting places to visit in the U.S.; in addition to the many government buildings, the Smithsonian Museum Complex offers visitors an endless number of places to explore, at no charge. We planned on spending three days at the Hyatt Regency Hotel, which was in the heart of the city, and leisurely walking around visiting the Smithsonian's Air and Space Museum, the National History Museum, and then the National Zoo, and, time permitting, some other fascinating sites, such as the *WWII* and *Korean War Monuments*.

As we had a few hours before our scheduled dinner and show at the John F. Kennedy Center of Performing Arts, we decided to take a cab for the short ride to the administrative offices of the Smithsonian Institute (the Castle) and get updates on the current museum's schedules and any other information that we might put to good use while visiting the nation's capital. The Castle is one of D.C.'s treasures; it was built in 1855 from the design of architect James Renwick, Jr., who also designed St. Patrick's Cathedral in New York City and the Smithsonian's Renwick Gallery. It was the first of 19 Smithsonian buildings to be built on the National Mall. It is constructed of Seneca red sandstone from the state of Maryland and looks like a bona fide castle, turrets and all.

The first thing we learned at the information station was that there was an impending snow storm that might hit the D.C. area. Barbara insisted that we cut our trip short and immediately leave for the warmer Southern states. But macho me, I decided that the weather forecast was the usual hyper attention-seeking news media mumbo-jumbo. So we decided to stay and returned to our hotel to dress appropriately for the theater.

We arrived at the JFK Center around 6 P.M. and went directly to their cafeteria-style restaurant for a very nondescript dinner. After our meal, we joined fellow theater goers in the large lounge area and treated ourselves to after-dinner martinis while we enjoyed the music of a four-piece combo band and a female singer whose voice was an echo of Dolly Parton's. A second drink put me in the mood to see the musical *The Who's Tommy*, which wasn't to our liking, as the rock and roll music was too loud and the audience unruly, probably due to the fact that President Bill Clinton, his wife Hillary, and their daughter Chelsea were in the audience. What saved the evening for us was the fact that the first family was sitting in the lower balcony that extended just below from where we were seated on our right. We had a ringside seat of their happy faces for most of the evening, as they left before the show ended. They also probably didn't appreciate the loud music and the audience's noisy response.

We exited the center and found a white surprise waiting for us; the streets were covered with snow. The wind was howling so loud that it sounded like a high-pitched whistle, and the white snowflakes looked like the size of half dollars. Our problem was getting a taxi cab to take us to our hotel. After watching an untold number of cabs pass us by without paying attention to our waving and whistling, one did stop and asked us where we were going; we said the Hyatt Regency. He said, "You're lucky, it's on my way home. Hop in." The usual 15-minute ride took 45 minutes, as there were cars stranded all over and blocking many of the streets to our hotel. When we finally arrived, I was happy to double the meter amount and almost kissed the driver goodnight.

I could feel the fire coming out of Barbara's eyes as she stared at me and said some undistinguishable words into my ears; all I could hear in my mind was, "I told you so; you should have listened to the wise one." But good sport that she is, she never said a word, but the fiery looks were enough to transmit her telepathic message. When the snowfall ended, the D.C. area had two feet of snow, with winds of up to 40 mph causing a fog effect throughout the neighborhood we were in. I knew I had to make peace with Barbara, so I promised her that in the future, regardless of the circumstances, if we were ever faced with a similar situation, without question or discussion, if she thought it was wise to pack our bags and move on, her wish would be my command.

Although we were only a few blocks from the I-95 Interstate Highway, the heavy snowfall would take four days before a path could be cleared to the highway and we could head for warmer southern weather. Fortunately, the Hyatt Regency had four restaurants. They closed three of them and set up buffet-style meals on the main floor restaurant to accommodate the remaining stubborn guests, such as me, who refused to heed the weather forecast. The gym, spa, and swimming pool at the hotel made life quite tolerable, especially when we saw on TV that people were stranded in motels with no food or entertainment facilities. We spent the four days enjoying the facilities, especially the large lounge and bar area, and met people from all over the world, Japan, Germany, Russia and South Korea, while hanging around and trying our best to make time pass as pleasantly as possible, under the circumstances.

On the fifth day, a path was cleared to the highway, so we moved our Lincoln Town Car slowly to I-95 and were surprised that only one lane was somewhat cleared on that roadway. We literally inched our way through Virginia, stopping at every rest stop for refreshments and hoping that the sun would melt some of the snow from the highway. As we traveled through North and then South Carolina, snow was visible on the side of the road, but no longer a risk to our driving. As we crossed into the State of Georgia, our outside car temperature gauge read 60 degrees, a welcome reading from the 20-degree temperature we left behind in D.C. After an overnight stop at a Holiday Inn Express, we headed due south at the high side of the legal speed limit and before we knew it, the car's outside temperature gauge was up to the mid-70s. We arrived at St. Augustine in the late afternoon and were shocked when we got out of our car at the difference in temperature. I think that's when we first fell in love with Florida: no snow, just sunshine and an occasional rainy day to break up the heat.

We headed straight for the recently renovated Casa Monica Hotel, which was in the heart of the historical district of St. Augustine. We chose the hotel because of its location and its illustrious history, which dates back to 1888. It was built with land sold to Boston architect Franklin W. Smith by Henry Flagler, who is considered the father of Miami, Palm Beach, and probably the whole eastern portion of Florida. Flagler, a founder of Standard Oil, loved the city so much that he built what are now the Flagler College and the Lightner Museum, which were across from our hotel. He also developed the East Coast Railway that serviced the area and extends down to the southernmost part of the state into the Florida Keys. His investments and foresight were certainly instrumental in accelerating the development of Florida. He eventually purchased the Casa Monica Hotel from Smith and turned it into one of the showcase hotels in the state. The hotel had a checkered history over the years; it went from a glamorous 138-room venue, to a county court house. In 1999 the hotel was renovated and its original name and grandeur restored, operating once more as a luxurious hotel. How could we pass up an opportunity to stay at one of the oldest hotels in America (it's a member of the *Historic Hotels of America*) that was located right in the middle of the oldest settlement in the United States?

Approaching the hotel was breathtaking. It appeared to be a Moorish castle rather than a place of rest in an American city. It is several stories high and exudes old Spanish style, with small reddish balconies and small turrets at the corners of the building. We drove to the palatial entrance and were greeted by pleasant valets that removed our auto burden in short order. We were pleasantly surprised at the large lobby's décor, which transported us to our visit to Spain, oh so many years ago. There was beautifully carved dark furniture, dark red accessories, mosaics strategically located, and bronze trim all over the area, just what one would expect in a Spanish castle. Our check-in was brief and our luggage handled professionally. Our fourth-floor room was small but had a great view of the old city, the Lightner Museum, and Flagler College. I had ordered the "Love St. Augustine" package, so there was an aroma of roses in our room, which came from a beautiful bouquet of red roses displayed on the table near the spectacular view of the city. A few moments after our arrival, there was a knock on the door and a delectable plate of chocolate-covered strawberries and a bottle of champagne on ice was presented to us on a silver tray; the package was certainly money well spent as the goodies put us in a romantic mood that would last throughout our stay in the mystical city. Hopefully, my thoughtfulness would erase some of the memory from Barbara's mind of my foolish and stubborn decision to stay in Washington, D.C. to greet the storm.

We decided that after such a long drive a nap was in order, and away we went into dreamland. When we awoke to the fragrance of roses, it was after 9 P.M., but the view from our window was anything but dark. The strange thing was that although it was evening, the city's view resembled a bright Xmas tree, as the entire city seemed to be ablaze with lights, mostly white, with brilliant reds, blues, and greens mixed in to perfect the view.

We asked the concierge Jonathan what the brightness was all about; he said that it was the "Nights of Lights" that is celebrated every year during the Xmas holidays. He gave us a pamphlet that explained the festive occasion. It read:

"St. Augustine, Florida's annual 'Nights of Lights' provides one of the Southeast's most memorable holiday events. It begins on November 18th and continues through January 31st.

"In a manner befitting the Nation's Oldest City, this inspiring display of lights is based on the tradition of the town's original Spanish colonists who placed a white candle in their windows to brighten the nights during Christmas holidays. The festival features more than two million tiny white lights adorning the palm trees and buildings of the city's historic district. Reflected in the waters on Matanzas Bay, outlining the colonial city, and including nearby beaches and lighthouse, the display creates a holiday wonderland in a place with American history on every street corner.

"In the gentle glow of the lights, a dazzling array of special events and activities await visitors. Nighttime tours of ancient building and inns led by storytellers in period clothing, rollicking train and trolley tours through the narrow brick streets, festive shopping, art walks featuring more than 20 galleries serving free holiday refreshments on the First Friday in December and January, luminaries in the town plaza, holiday concerts – even a Christmas parade – are among the special events to be added to the memory books of visitors and residents alike.

"This is also a special time to celebrate the brief 20 years when the town was occupied by the British (1763-1784). 'British Nightwatch' is fun, and is a re-creation of holiday frivolity with a torch-lit parade through town by hundreds of authentically clad re-enactors, house tours, wine, caroling and volleys of musketry."

Well, the pleasant surprise became more pronounced as we walked to the Raintree Restaurant & Steakhouse on San Marco Avenue. Looking at the sparkling bright scene from our hotel window was similar to viewing a picture from a distance, but while walking among the lights we actually became part of the view, a small part with only an internal glow, but still an integral part of the scene. The restaurant was in a two-story Victorian house on the main street across from the Matanzas River and the Bridge of Lions that leads to Anastasia Island, a barrier island that is right across the river from the historic city. The view of the "Bridge of Lights"—that's what it's called during the festival—is a sight to behold. White lights were strung across the 1,500-foot, two-lane bridge on the upper and lower parts, complemented by lights running up and down the bridge's stanchions. What is considered a small bridge seemed to stretch out of sight at night as the lights magically prolonged its length as they combined with the lights of the structures on Anastasia Island.

Jonathan recommended the bistro and said that our visit to the historic city would not be complete unless we tried the food of one of the city's finest eating places. How right he was. The restaurant was decorated in keeping with the holiday spirit; lights outlined the building and surrounded the terrace and patio eating areas. A koi pond welcomed us and a blazing fireplace and soft background music set the stage for a romantic evening of fine dining and drinking. We sat on the open-air terrace with a view of the busy street and the "Bridge of Lights." Barbara ordered Seafood Au Gratin and my choice for the evening was their Beef Wellington. We complemented the meal with a bottle of Moscato wine. I couldn't brag enough to our friends about the quality of the food we had that evening, and the perfect choice of wine that rounded out the meal perfectly. The restaurant has become one of our favorite topics when we speak about St. Augustine. We so enjoyed our experience that in subsequent winter drives to the sunny state, we made it a point to stop at the city just to have dinner at the one-of-a-kind bistro.

After a buffet breakfast at the hotel the next morning, we decided to take a horse and carriage ride around the historic district to really get the feel of the renowned settlement. We were fortunate to get a driver, Pedro, who was an amateur historian. He had a bit of a Spanish accent, which made his oratory all the more interesting and somewhat mystical. Our first stop was Flagler College; we sat back and relaxed as Pedro began his narrative about the world-class university:

> The most beautiful and central part of the college was once Henry Flagler's hotel, the Ponce de Leon, that he built in 1888 as part of his Gilded Age experience. There are Tiffany stained glass windows, lamps, and furniture, complemented by golden chandeliers throughout the building, with murals that lend authenticity to the Spanish charm of the outside façade that is dominated by two large watch towers. It not only looks like a Spanish-style castle, but its huge size indicates that a village was attached to the main venue. The 19-acre college began its journey in 1968 and today is considered a world-class university with a student body of approximately 3,000 undergraduates.

We could see the large watch towers and the incredible architecture from our coach and would have joined the tour that was gathering to explore the palace if we had enough time, but our time was limited, so we made mental notes to return and visit the beautiful sight on our next trip.

Our second stop was the Lightner Museum, which was also commissioned by Henry Flagler as the Alcazar Hotel in 1887, a year before the Ponce de Leon Hotel. Pedro enlightened us with:

"The architects Carrere and Hastings designed the Alcazar Hotel as well as the Ponce de Leon Hotel, which are located across the street from each other. They were both built in the Spanish Renaissance Revival style and if you look closely you would think that the Ponce de Leon was an extension of the Alcazar, or vice versa. Both buildings are among the earliest successful experiments with poured concrete, so much so, that the architects were subsequently commissioned to design and build the New York Public Library in Manhattan, N.Y., and the U.S. Senate office building in Washington, D.C. Flagler built the Alcazar to attract wealthy tourists who had the privilege of also traveling on his new, extended railroad. The hotel boasted a steam room, massage parlor, gym, and sulfur baths, as well as the world's largest indoor swimming pool, 120 × 50 feet, which at that time was considered huge. An unusual feature of the building was its three-story ballroom where large social events took place with such illustrious guests as Thomas Edison and John D. Rockefeller. After being an elegant winter resort for wealthy patrons, the hotel closed in 1932. In 1946, Chicago publisher Otto C. Lightner purchased the building to house his extensive collection of Victoriana. He opened the museum two years later, and subsequently donated it to the city of St. Augustine. The museum now occupies three floors of the former hotel with primarily American Victorian antiquities."

We made mental notes, again, to explore the beautiful open courtyard, palm-treed site on our next visit to the historic city.

Our most exciting stop for the day was the 15-acre waterfront Fountain of Youth Archaeological Park. Pedro told us that we had a 30-minute stop to explore and, if we liked, we should drink some of the water from the *Fountain of Youth.* Before we began our brief journey, he gave a brief dissertation of what the area was all about:

"The location is the Birthplace of our Nation as Pedro Menendez de Aviles established the first European settlement in 1565 on the very spot we are visiting. Although Florida was first explored by Ponce de Leon in 1513, it wasn't until De Aviles arrived that a successful lasting European presence was established. You might want to visit one of the many attractions of the park such as the Planetarium, the Native Timucua Indian Village, the 600-foot-long Observation Tower, or walk among the many peacocks along the waterfront; whatever you decide to do, make sure you don't miss the wonderful gift shop for a souvenir of the historical site."

We left the carriage and went directly to the mythical *Fountain of Youth* that Ponce de Leon spent so many years searching for. The fountain was a little strange looking, more like a drinking well, but we both had a cup of the magical (we hoped) water and were satisfied that it would add some years to our lives, hopefully in good health. We didn't have much time so we decided to walk around the waterfront and just enjoy a pleasant stroll on the comfortable, breezy, 75-degree day. The choice was a wise one; not only did we see and hear the firing of an old Spanish cannon; we also saw the most beautiful and amazing peacocks. The multicolored iridescent large birds, which were without a doubt spectacular in their colorful dresses, weren't as unusual as their white relatives. We had never seen white peacocks and couldn't stop following them around and gasping in amazement at their extended plumage that seemed to sparkle in the sunlight. We just had enough time to visit the gift shop, where I purchased a beautiful Xmas tree peacock ornament to remind us of the beauty in the pure white fowl's simplicity that attracted the sunlight and magnified its splendid place in the world of wild life.

We boarded our carriage for our last stop at the *Castillo de San Marcos National Monument*. Pedro again gave us a brief history of the enormous fort:

"Building the 320-acre complex was begun by the Spanish in 1672 and took 23 years to complete. It was constructed from almost indestructible limestone comprised of broken local sea shells and coral, and has passed the test of time, as its walls have never been breached by the many enemy forces that tried to penetrate its impregnable 33-feet-high walls. It is the oldest masonry fort in the Continental U.S. and was successful in protecting its citizens and the city from hostile naval intruders who tried to destroy its huge walls with cannon fire from ships on Matanzas Bay and from cannon fire from Anastasia Island across the bay."

His narrative ended our horse and coach ride, which prompted Barbara and me to again make mental notes to return to the humongous structure on our next visit to St. Augustine. It was lunchtime, so we decided to dine in the historic village and walk around the single block visiting structures that dated back to the 17th and 18th centuries. The small old village was a picture of when Spain was the dominant tenant in Florida. There were several original homes dating back to the 1790s, an old school house, and even a jail. Stores selling ice cream and T-shirts were scattered throughout the old village, which diminished the feeling of our being in an 18th century town. There was no lack of places to have lunch, so we chose the quaint Bunnery Bakery & Café because of the cinnamon aroma coming from the bistro. We were served hot coffee as soon as we sat down, which was delicious and put us in the mood for a hearty lunch. Barbara ordered Panini Pollo and I chose a Panini Veggie; both were absolutely perfectly made, with a bit of a hot spicy flavor. We were haunted by the aroma of cinnamon from the moment we entered the café, so for dessert we ordered a sticky cinnamon bun that we shared. Splitting the out-of-this-world bun justified, in our minds, the calories that we added to our meal. We spent the rest of the afternoon just walking around the village and surrounding area enjoying the sights, the beautiful nautical scenery from the bay, and the perfect weather.

We took well-needed naps when we returned to the Casa Monaco Hotel. In the evening, we had a light salad dinner at their Cobalt Lounge before returning to the decorated outdoor light extravaganza for another stroll through the "City of Lights." This time we had full stomachs, so our walk was strictly to enjoy the bright lights throughout the city and the pleasant refreshing breeze coming from the ocean and passing over the bay to our location. We also noticed that the Bridge of Lions boasted large sculptured lions on either side of the entrance; they were glowing from the lights that decorated their manes and muscular bodies. The lions are supposed to be exact replicas of the *de Medici Lions* in Florence, Italy. We sat in front of them for quite some time just chatting and planning our next trip to the oldest city in the Continental U.S.

The next morning we woke up early as we had a long ride to our next location in Boca Raton. It's funny but we both had a hankering for cinnamon buns. So away we went and had breakfast at the Bunnery, but this time we had no guilt feelings about eating the sticky buns, as they were the only delights we had for breakfast, instead of our usual large unhealthy breakfasts of bacon and eggs, grits, bagels, and lots of coffee. We left the city regretting that we didn't have enough time to explore and enjoy the hotel's facilities, such as their cabana-style swimming and whirl pools, the complimentary beach facilities at the Serenata Beach Club, and the many golf courses that were available for the hotel's guests. Also, exploring Anastasia Island and its beautiful beaches went to the top of our list; as a matter of fact, on our subsequent visits to St. Augustine, we would stay at the Hampton Inn, which is located on the island and has one of the most beautiful beaches in Florida.

Sarasota

Our romance with the southwestern city of Sarasota, Florida began with a trip across the four-lane super-highway Alligator Alley, also known as Everglades Parkway and I-75, to our friend's home in Ft. Myers on the West Coast of Florida. The Alley runs from the City of Weston on the lower southeastern part of the state to Naples on the lower southwestern part. The trip is approximately 85 miles straight across the state, and was probably one of the most boring driving events that we ever experienced, as the foliage was dismal and colorless. There was only one place to stop for gas and refreshments, and that was a Seminole Indian Reservation gas stop about half way across the parkway. The station, rest rooms, and food court were seedy and didn't smell clean, so we topped off our gas tank and exited the rest stop as soon as we could, leaving behind us a memory that till this day makes me cringe. By the way, fortunately, we didn't see any alligators on the long dull trip across Florida.

We exited the Alley near Naples and drove due north for about 35 miles to Ft. Myers, while admiring the beautiful seascape of the Gulf of Mexico on our left. The sight of the turquoise-blue water of the Gulf and the smell of fresh sea air quickly erased the foul odor of the rest stop from my senses. We arrived at our friend Maureen and her son Steven's home and were thrilled to see our old friends after being apart for several years. They were our next-door neighbors for over 20 years in Melville, Long Island, and were considered as part of our family, as we experienced the growth of our children, Maureen's three and our two, from infancy to adulthood.

After many hugs and kisses, we enjoyed a delicious fruit and frozen chocolate and vanilla yogurt lunch, with lots of lemonade, while we reminisced about the good old days. After our delightful and healthy meal, Maureen said she wanted to take us sightseeing. She seemed to have her dissertation memorized; while she drove us downtown, her story began:

"The City of Palms (Ft. Myers) is located on the banks of the Caloosahatchee River. The city is named after the fort that was built there in 1850 during the Seminole Indian War. Most people come to the seaside city to enjoy its beaches, play golf, and go deep sea fishing or to drive over the bridges to explore the two most beautiful islands in Florida, Sanibel and Captiva, which are just west of Ft. Myers. An interesting point is that there are no buildings higher than the tallest trees on both the islands. If we had time, I would take you on a sightseeing tour of the islands, but we'll leave that trip for the next time you visit. Today I'm taking you to the Thomas Edison and Henry Ford Winter Estates."

We were excited to visit Edison's laboratory because when we first were married, our first apartment was in Menlo Park, New Jersey, the home of his first lab. We visited the Edison Menlo Park Laboratory often and were curious to see what his winter lab was like. Thomas Edison (1847–1931) first visited Ft. Myers in the early 1880s and fell in love with the mild winters and the active fishing in the area. He completed building his vacation home in 1887 and named it "Seminole Lodge" after the local Indians that dominated the area before the European intrusion. He was so in love with the lifestyle that he persuaded his friend, Henry Ford (1863–1947), to build a winter retreat on vacant property adjacent to his in 1911. Ford called his winter home "The

Mangoes" because of the abundance of wild mango trees growing on the site. Both properties were built beside the Caloosahatchee River, which runs for over 70 miles from Lake Okeechobee to the Gulf of Mexico, and was named after the Calusa Indians that occupied the area. They enjoyed the same outdoor activities as Edison and Ford, boating, fishing, and exploring the Everglades. The main difference was that the Native Americans needed the river for survival; the two industrialists used the river for relaxation and pleasure.

At the entrance of the 20-acre estate we were welcomed by a life-size statue of Thomas Edison that seemed almost alive and ready to join us on our journey of his and Ford's winter homes. We spent the afternoon exploring Edison's two identical main houses that had spacious wrap-around porches, the guest house, caretaker's house, and a swimming pool area that also had a tea and bath house. Ford's home was somewhat smaller but had a spectacular riverfront view of the Caloosahatchee River. It is claimed that on its large porch, Henry Ford developed the popular Ford eight-cylinder engine. Both homes were furnished in period furniture of that era.

The highlights of the visit were the Estate's Museum and elaborate Research Gardens. The 15,000-square-feet, air-conditioned museum boasts, "It encourages intellectual exploration and stimulates the senses with galleries featuring an impressive collection of inventions, artifacts and special exhibits." A walking tour brochure covered what we saw very well:

"*Main Gallery* – On display are exhibits of Edison's work as an inventor including the telegraph, telephone, x-ray machine and his original custom-made Model T that was a gift from Henry Ford.

"*Edison After Forty*—Which is on loan from the Smithsonian Institution, exhibits images of Edison's life after the age of forty as well as Edison artifacts from the Estate's collection.

"*Into the Wild: Edison, Ford & Friends*—The exhibit chronicles the camping adventures of Thomas Edison, Henry Ford, and friends Harvey Firestone and John Burroughs. The 'Vagabonds' as they referred to themselves, camped outdoors throughout Florida and the U.S. The exhibit includes Henry Ford's original 1918 Model T Camper that they used on their camping expeditions.

"*Movies, Music and Dance of Edison & Ford*—On exhibit are selected artifacts of movie projectors, phonographs, nickelodeons and other entertainment devices that they personally used.

"*Family, Friends and Fun*—This exhibit showcases photographs of Edison and Ford, their families and friends enjoying Southwest Florida. The majority of the photos came from their personal albums and is a part of the Estate's archival collection.

"*The Wizard Invents*—For people of all ages, this exhibit presents a timeline of Edison's inventions beginning with his first commercially sold invention, the stock ticker, as well as the progression of the electric light bulb.

"*Hall of Inventions*—This gallery includes phonographs, early movie equipment, Edison Cement Company artifacts, and business machines. The gallery also has a performance stage for regular science shows.

"*Edison Electric Light & Power*—This display includes a variety of generators and information panels about Edison's power system, and leads into the *New Solar Power Exhibit.*

"*Edison's Green Energy Solar Power*—In collaboration with Florida Power & Light Company, the installation includes a *Solar Education Station, a Learning Center* and *a Real Time Station Exhibit.* The 'Real Time Station' of solar energy is where visitors can see how much solar energy it captures throughout the day, while providing energy for the Estate's Museum.

"*Edison Botanic Research Corporation (EBRC)*—This exhibit includes original artifacts and information about EBRC, a visible storage vault containing a variety of Edison's artifacts from his lab including chemical storage bottles, soxhlet extractions, cylinders, and a prototype of a leaf stripping machine. Also shown are some of his documents, images, and examples of his research and analysis."

After visiting the unique museum and enjoying the surrounding pristine grounds, we headed for Edison & Ford's Gardens. Again, a readily available pamphlet described the intricate landscaping and laboratory facilities, as follows:

"Thomas Edison's original design for his winter estate included areas for a research laboratory and family gardens. His garden designs were geometric, dominated by wide alleys and avenues. His plan was a practical one, not as much a design for a formal botanical garden as it was for an evolving family and research garden plan oriented to their changing interests. The landscape today is still dominated by huge Ficus trees planted by Thomas Edison, Henry Ford and Harvey Firestone during the time of their quest to find a viable domestic source of rubber (latex) to grow in the region. It also includes varieties of palms, citrus, bamboo and orchids. The small Heritage Garden represents the original truck garden of fruits and vegetables used by the families for food. Today, the Estates houses more than 1,700 plants and trees, including royal palm, bamboo, mango, papaya, lychee, and the most extensive collection of banyan trees in the state of Florida, in addition to having one of the largest banyan trees (400 feet) in the continental United States."

We spent the better part of the afternoon exploring the one-of-a-kind facility and on the way out through their gift shop, I noticed a brochure that had a clown's face on the front page; it was an invitation to visit the "Ringling Museum of the American Circus" in the city of Sarasota, which was just about one and one-half hours north of where we were. Barbara and I have always been circus fans and decided, on the spot, to extend our visit to the west coast and travel north to where the circus action was. We ended our stay with Maureen and Steven with a nice surprise dinner at her home of oven-baked trout, roasted potatoes, burnt broccoli, and homemade apple pie a la mode. We spent a pleasant evening in their quiet guest room. We awoke the next morning after a peaceful night's rest to a bright sunny day and the aroma of bacon, eggs, and hazelnut coffee. "How sweet it was." After a delightful breakfast and sweet reflections of our youthful days when we were next-door neighbors in New York, we bid them farewell and headed straight away to the seaside Circus City of Sarasota.

There are two ways to cross the wilderness from east to west in South Florida. There is the four-lane super-highway known as Alligator Alley that boasts of 21,000 cars a day crossing at its speed limit of 70 miles an hour, and there is the two-lane scenic highway, Tamiami Trail, that has speed limits that range from 35 to 60 mph. The Trail averages about 3,000 vehicles a day and cuts through the most beautiful section of the Big Cypress, which gets its name from the size of the trees in its million-acre forest. Along the Trail on a normal day, alligators, black panthers, hogs, and deer can be seen wandering along the roadside. Tamiami Trail got its name because it originates in the Miami area on the East Coast and initially ended on the West Coast in Tampa as an extension of US 41, a distance of about 265 miles. The road has such beautiful sights that it has been designated a "National Scenic Byway." Over time, it was extended south on the West Coast for about 165 miles from Tampa to Naples. As we took the non-scenic speedway across Alligator Alley to get to the West Coast, we decided that the 75-mile trip from Ft. Myers to Sarasota would be more picturesque and enjoyable on the slow-paced Tamiami Trial. We weren't disappointed; we never exceeded 50 mph and even stopped twice at rest stops to admire alligators and large turtles, at a safe distance, along the roadside. Again, the view of the Gulf of Mexico was spectacular as the turquoise-blue water and the mild surf tempted us to stop and spend the day at one of the pristine beaches along the way.

"Sarasota has been described by Money Magazine as the 'Best small city in American,' and by Fortune as the 'Most romantic city for well-off older singles.' It has become a magnet that brings countless newcomers to the area for its sandy beaches, water sports in Sarasota Bay and the Gulf of Mexico, its exceptional golf courses and an arts scene that includes the respected Sarasota Opera, the Asolo Theater and the Sarasota Ballet of Florida. It's also considered a small community where you know your neighbors, yet has the attributes of a much larger city." That is what the brochure about the city stated; we couldn't wait to visit and explore all the wonderful places, including the circus venues, that we had read so much about.

As with many of the settlements in Florida, Sarasota didn't escape the harsh European intrusion by Spanish conquistadors, such as Ponce de Leon, Panfilo Narvaez, and Hernando De Soto in the early 1500s. Two of the men had interesting and somewhat illustrious backgrounds: Ponce de Leon sailed with Columbus on his second voyage of discovery and is remembered in history as the person searching for the Fountain of Youth in Florida. De Soto, believe it or not, was designing automobiles in the 16th century, but exploration and the quest for wealth distracted him from his first passion. To honor the genius, an American car was named after him . . . the Chrysler De Soto. Amusingly, the hood ornament on the popular car was a bust of the conquistador. Narvaez in his quest for riches made his mark in history infamously; he is associated with the harsh treatment of Native Americans, resorting to genocide when it suited his purpose. He also is purported to have carried smallpox to Mexico on one of his warships when he went to that country to do battle with Hernando Cortes for control of New Spain. He was defeated and held prisoner for two years before embarking on his Florida expedition with five ships and 600 anxious conquistadors. Most of his men died in the wilderness or from battling hostile Indians; of the original men, only four survived to tell their tales of woe; Narvaez was not one of them.

One of the most prominent and influential people in the history of Sarasota was John Ringling, of the Ringling Brothers and Barnum & Bailey Circus fame. In the 1920s he and his wife, Mable, built a magnificent Venetian-style estate on Sarasota Bay and called it *Ca d'Zan*, which means "House of John" in the Venetian dialect. They also built an art museum for their collection of works by Peter Paul Rubens and other 17th-century Italian and Flemish artists. In addition, he used his circus elephants to help build the first bridge from the mainland to St. Armands Key, which he developed into a commercial and residential center. His crowning achievement for the area was moving his circus winter quarters to Sarasota, forever changing the city from a quiet seaside residential town to the "Circus Capital of the World." The city became home to many circuses, resulting in the establishment of a gymnastic program at Sarasota High School that included circus acts. The county has the only public school system in the U.S. that sponsors an after-school youth circus program known as the "Sailor Circus"; it is also home to Ringling's Clown College. In 1997, "Circus Sarasota" was founded; its goals are to enhance, produce, and propel the "Circus Arts" with innovative programs of the highest level.

When we arrived at the 66-acre site, we had two surprises; there was an actual tented circus in progress and it was a Monday, so the Ringling Museum was free, but there was an admission charge for the Circus Museums and the *Ca d'Zan M*ansion. We have enjoyed many circuses in our travels, so we skipped the big tent and went directly to the John M. McKay Visitors Pavilion, which was named after a popular senator from Sarasota, for some orientation information. The pavilion had a grand lobby with state-of-the-art admission stations, a Museum Store, the Treviso Restaurant, an orientation video theater, a children's gathering area, and the restored Historic Asolo Theatre. We learned from a video presentation that the complex consisted of the John & Mable Ringling Museum of Arts, the Ringling's Mansion, the Circus Museums and Learning Center, and the Historic Asolo Theatre, which was actually located inside the visitor's center. In addition, the grounds had a world-renowned rose garden, many banyan trees, and extensive walking paths leading to the beautiful waters of Sarasota Bay. Our problem was where to start; as the Asolo Theatre was in the visitor's center, we decided to try that venue first.

Although John and Mable were frequent travelers to Italy, it wasn't until the 1950s that the museum's board agreed to purchase the 18th-century Venetian theatre from Asolo, Italy, for $10,000. The small theatre had been dismantled in the 1930s by the Fascist Regime and placed in storage until it was purchased and reassembled on the grounds of the Ringling Estate, at which time it became the only state theatre in Florida. From that time till the 1990s, the Historic Asolo Theatre Repertory Company presented live performances of popular plays. The theatre was once again dismantled for restoration and installation in the new Visitor's Pavilion, fully refurbished.

The 265-seat horseshoe-shaped interior of the theatre is a work of art in its own right. It was created in Asolo, Italy in 1798 to honor the 15th century exiled Queen Catherine Cornaro of Cypress. As the theatre is small, the stage can be seen clearly from the main floor and the three balconies. The gold trim around the balconies with various paintings, including that of the Queen's face, is a reminder of the luxury that was once so prevalent among Italy's nobility. We felt like spending the day at the beautiful historic theatre and hopefully experiencing a play, but the compound was huge and we didn't have lots of time to spare, so the best we could do was take many pictures of the beautiful royal decorations and architecture, and move to our next destination, the Ringling Museum of Arts.

John and his wife Mable were lovers of fine arts and avid collectors. When they had the museum built in the late 1920s they had already accumulated 600 paintings, numerous sculptures, and 25 tapestries from the works of major baroque artists from the 16th through 18th centuries, such as Rubens, Hals, Van Dyck, El Greco, and many other renowned artists from that period. At the time, John was ranked as the fifth-richest person in America, so it was natural that he would spend part of his vast fortune, which came not only from his cash-rich circus business, but from his oil and real estate holdings, on the finer things in life. So to preserve and display his impressive fine art collections, he summoned architect John H. Phillips of New York City to design and build a 30,000-sq.-ft. museum on his property in the Italian Renaissance style with a large interior courtyard surrounded on three sides by terraces, just as they had seen on their visits to Italy. The courtyard actually has a towering bronze cast life-size replica of Michelangelo's David overlooking it, complemented by two Italian-style water fountains that were also replicas of what they had seen on their visits to Italy. Continuing their love affair with Italian art, they lined the top of the courtyard with statues that resembled those in the Vatican City. The museum was subsequently extended 30,000-plus square feet by Florida State University, the current owners, in their expansion program that brought the entire estate's buildings to over 168,000 square feet. There is no doubt that the museum and its gardens are a world-class facility, and have been designated the "State of Florida's Official Art Museum." In addition to the Roman architecture, which has to be seen to be believed, the 21 art galleries inside the palace were also built with Italian decorative influences, with tapestries and religious painting throughout the facility. What fascinated us the most, were the wall-to-ceiling religious paintings by Rubens. It is inconceivable to me that a human being could create such beauty in large paintings; not only is there great talent in his work, but the patience required to complete so many enormous works of art is beyond my comprehension. We spent a couple of hours admiring the paintings of El Greco, Van Dyck, and other amazing artists of that era, and could have spent the whole day in the museum, but there were other places that we were anxious to visit.

We exited the Italian-Style architectural pinkish masterpiece building and were drawn to the fragrance coming from the rose garden. How do you put into words the artistic beauty created by someone who had a love and passion for natural floral creations and Italian artistic designs? Mable Ringling started her plantings in 1913 before any of the buildings of the estate were completed. She patterned her masterpiece after a traditional Italian circular garden design. The entrance to the garden was lined with statues of beautiful, varied-sized ancient ladies and 14 scattered Roman posts. A pamphlet that we picked up at the museum explained the design of the gardens much better than I could:

"Mable's Garden is organized as a combination of four concentric circles within two enclosing rectangles, and is divided by four linear paths which run through the center of the garden. At the center of the circle is a pergola. The four paths that lead to different parts of the estate run North, South, East and West. The garden is 27,225 square feet and is the proud possessor of Tree Roses, Hybrid Teas, Floribundas, Grand-floras, miniature roses, shrubs, and Old Garden Roses, among other magnificent flora, which includes a variety of over 1,200 rose specimens. The garden was named 'The most Outstanding All-American Selections Public Rose Garden in the United States.' Also on the estate is Mable's Private Garden where she planted many of the floral gifts that she received over her lifetime. In this garden there are varieties of Bromeliads, Philippine Violets and many Variegated Bougainvilleas, in addition to other flowers and plants."

What else can one say after seeing the magnificent results of the partnership between man (in this case a woman) and nature. We couldn't drag ourselves away from the beautiful variety of roses, the masterful Italian style statues, and the surrounding, enormously multifaceted Banyan trees.

We exited from the East path through a forest of Banyan trees and headed for the *Ca d'Zan* mansion. What a sight. It's probably one of the most beautiful structures that you could find in the U.S.; it certainly matches the mansion of the 19th century "Captains of Industry" that are in such abundance in Newport, Rhode Island. The main difference between the Ringling's winter home and those of the Astor's and Vanderbilt's in Newport, is that Ringling not only built a mansion that matched the other Captains, but he also built a complex that included a museum and massive gardens. His home is purported to be the last of the "Gilded Age" mansions built in this country.

Another available pamphlet describes its history and architecture as follows:

"Construction on the 'House of John' (*Ca d'Zan*) began in 1924 during the height of the successful Ringling Bros. Circus. It took over a year to build the Venetian Gothic masterpiece at a cost of $1.5 million. The Ringling couple loved everything about Italy, especially Venice, and wanted their winter home to resemble the structures they admired on their trips to that country. One of the reasons they chose the Sarasota Bay location was because the waters resembled those of the Grand Canal in Venice. A good deal of the elements in their home were modeled after some of the great buildings of Venice, such as the Doge's Palace and the *Ca d'Ora* (Golden House), which is a splendid 15th century Venetian palace that remains in impeccable condition. It is said that Mable possessed a portfolio full of postcards, photos, drawings, and other items from Venice that aided the architects in the design of *Ca d'Zan*.

"The mansion is 200 feet long and includes approximately 36,000 sq. ft. of interior space. It boasts 41 rooms and 15 bathrooms, and stands five stories tall with a full basement. The highest point of the mansion is a watchtower that stretches 81 feet high and includes an open-air overlook.

"Materials used for the exterior of the mansion include terracotta T-blocks, concrete, and bricks covered with stucco and ornamented with shiny glazed tiles. The terrace that fronts Sarasota Bay is made of both imported and domestic marble; the tiled roof is constructed with recycled 16th century tiles imported from Spain.

"Inside, deep reds and gold dominate the décor. Reproductions of Louis XV furnishings bought from major auction houses in New York are resplendent and indicative of the opulence of the Gilded Age.

"Artwork is everywhere inside the home as the Ringling's were major collectors of art. Pieces included not only paintings and sculptures, but also tapestries that span several centuries. Even the insides of closets were hand-painted with bucolic scenes of the Venetian countryside.

"Today, visitors can enjoy docent-led tours of the mansion, narrated by museum aficionados who can share colorful anecdotal stories about the circus mogul and his wife. The mansion remains one of Florida's most visited tourist attractions."

When approaching the mansion, I got the feeling that it didn't belong in Florida. The large stained glass archways that surrounded the building on the lower and upper floors are like something out of a fairytale. Looking at the stucco building and its 81-foot watchtower that was surrounded by various irregular-sized posts was awesome in its unique Medieval European design and color. An interesting set of nude terracotta statues that are supposed to resemble John and Mable was also outstanding, although the couple purportedly denied that the images were theirs. Walking through the large stained glass arch-shaped door into the foyer, one is overwhelmed with the black and white checkerboard marble floors that run throughout the mansion. In the great hall (court), there was a two-and-a-half-story galleried space with a hooded fireplace and oversized windows looking west to Sarasota Bay. The gem of the mansion was a two-story Aeolian organ that houses 2,289 organ pipes that were concealed behind two 17th-century Flemish tapestries on the mezzanine level of the court. The organ was installed in January 1925 with a custom-made console having gothic detailing to match the flavor of the mansion. The unique organ included a Duo-Art mechanism that could play recorded music from paper rolls. As organs became less fashionable and costly to maintain, many were removed from the old mansions and given to churches, theaters, or used as scrap metal during WWII. The organ in Ringling's mansion was maintained to perfection and is still used for concerts, parties, and wedding receptions. It is probably one of the only remaining functional Aeolian organs in Florida. Of note was an

Otis elevator that was probably the first one installed in a residence in the state.

Walking through the court and onto the 200-foot-long terrace, there was a Venetian-style dock with a colorful gondola bobbing in the water. The only non-Venetian thing was the zigzag floor pattern of the paved marble deck that extended throughout the terrace and almost made me dizzy.

Back into the mansion and through the foyer is a reception room, with a solarium beyond. The reception room seemed like a staging area, preparing one for the entrance to a large ballroom that featured a rosewood Steinway piano, walls covered with yellow brocade, and a coffered ceiling painted with colorful figures; certainly the hosts must have had many a crowded dance floor in the large room. Walking south across the great hall, one comes to the breakfast room, which had green leather dining chairs with pillows under each chair that kept people's feet from getting cold on the marble floor. Further south was the dining room, with walnut paneling, a colorful coffered ceiling and Italian Renaissance furnishing. Beyond the dining room was a passageway that led to the service wing and large bar area; the paneled room was purchased and moved intact from a restaurant in St. Louis.

We were running out of time, as we wanted to see the Circus Museums. There was a tour of the upper floors that included seeing the bedrooms of John, Mable, and his second wife Emily, plus the many guest rooms for their rich and famous friends, but we didn't have enough time to visit the upper floors in the mansion . . . maybe the next time.

It was around lunchtime and we were able to locate the open-air Banyan Café, which was nearby and ordered some hotdogs and French fries for lunch, while admiring the beautiful banyan trees and the forestry atmosphere of the surrounding woods. When we finished, we headed straight for the first Circus Museum.

We picked up a pamphlet about the museum and read it before we entered the building; it told us that:

"The museum was established in 1948 and is the first 'Museum of the American Circus' of its kind to document the rich history of the circus. With so many circus people living in the immediate area, the collection grew quickly. Because of this, the museum has a fine collection including rare handbills and art prints, circus paper, business records, wardrobe, and performing props, as well as all types of circus equipment, including beautifully carved parade wagons, sturdy utility wagons, tent poles, and massive ball rings. There are also 19th and 20th century posters and props used by famous performers. A large collection of circus history and literature includes newspaper clippings dating as far back as 1816.

"The Ringling Circus Museum documents, preserves, and exhibits the history of the circus, which parallels the development of America. Its mission is to present the history of the American circus to visitors and to make circus artifacts accessible to the public. Part of its mission is to present a permanent circus collection in an environment that actively engages the visitor, and helps make a personal connection with the work of artists and performers who made a unique impact on the ever-changing face of the American circus.

"The Ringling Circus Empire was founded by five of the seven sons of August and Marie Salome Ringling. In 1884, the brothers premiered their first show and charged a penny for admission. In less than a decade, 'The Ringling Bros. Circus, World's Greatest Show,' developed from a small wagon show to a major railroad show covering most of the United States and Canada. John Ringling attributed the brothers' success to 'Hard work, common honesty, and a close study of what the public wants.' With the acquisition of the Barnum and Bailey Circus, the brothers controlled a major part of the circus business in America. The two circuses were run separately until 1919 when they were combined to form 'The Ringling Bros. and Barnum & Bailey Circus, The Greatest Show on Earth.' It was John Ringling who made Sarasota synonymous with the circus throughout the world when he moved their winter quarters from Bridgeport, Connecticut, to Sarasota in 1927, forever changing the face of the West Coast of Florida."

Ironically, John and Mable never thought of establishing a museum for the history of the American Circus. However, the board of directors of their estate approved construction of a circus museum on the site of Mable's garage. It opened to the public in 1948, giving visitors their first glimpse of memorabilia from the famous Ringling Bros. and Barnum & Bailey Circus. Many famous people earned international acclaim as circus artists, and their personal mementos are on display in the museum, including clowns Lou Jacobs, Otto Griebling, and Emmett Kelly; animal trainers Clyde Beatty and Gunther Gebel; the Zacchini Human Cannonballs; and the famous Wallenda high-wire-walking family.

In 2006, the Tibbals Learning Center opened as part of the Museum of the Circus. Built with money donated by philanthropist and master builder Howard C. Tibbals of Longboat Key, Florida, the 36,000-sq-ft facility houses the Howard Bros. Circus, the world's largest miniature circus, which Tibbals constructed over a 50-year span.

We took a docent tour when we visited the Tibbals Learning Center (new museum). What we saw was amazing, a 3,800-sq.-ft. miniature model of an American tented circus. "The model displays 8 main tents, 152 wagons, 1,300 performers, over 800 animals and a 59 car train. It is the largest miniature circus model in the world." Lights were dimmed to give an evening feeling, with miniature street lights coming on and then brightened to show off its daytime appearance. Tibbals' attention to detail was astonishing. It took him over 50 years to get to the point where you can actually read signs like: "Hippopotamus in captivity" on animal wagons; even some of the faces of the circus artists were distinguishable, such as the famous clown Emmett Kelly. There were horse stables and changing rooms, all with people and animal figures in them. The posters that were at the entrance didn't give justice to what was inside the replicated model. Inside the tent, you could see aerialists twirl, horses speed around the ring, and observe 7,000 folding chairs in various positions. On the second floor there was a viewing platform where we looked down in amazement at the circus town. The scene actually puts you in the circus; I could picture the circus arriving in a town by rail at night and setting up the tents by morning, then mystically disappearing the same evening after the performances, and heading for the next circus assignment in another town. After my visualization, I realized that there were displays built into the walls under glass that continued, almost around the whole perimeter of the floor we were on, of a circus parade that included elephants dressed as clowns, lobsters, and winged horses, and a menagerie of other circus participants. The entire display was accompanied by real circus sounds—lions roaring, elephants trumpeting, music playing, and a crowd cheering. The only thing missing as I could remember on my visits to a live event were the circus smells of popcorn, cotton candy, and, of course, animals.

We left the building and were dizzy from the amount of work that the sculptor Howard Tibbals put into the project for over 50 years. A funny aside is that although it was a replica of the Ringling Bros. Barnum & Bailey Circus, he couldn't get permission to call it by that name . . . so he called it the Howard Bros. Circus. Next we visited the old original Ringling Bros. Circus Museum.

One of the newest exhibitions was the *Wisconsin Train* that was the private Pullman railroad car that John and Mable used when they traveled with the circus or were on vacation touring the country. Looking inside the finely decorated car brought images to my mind of the meetings, dinners, and sleeping accommodations that they experienced in their wonderful life as important players during the Gilded Age. We admired actual circus cage cars and the Bruno *Zacchini Super Repeating Cannon Exhibit* that was mounted on a silver truck from which human cannonballs would be shot and fly across an arena. It is claimed that the actual operating mechanism was removed and "remains a guarded family secret as to how it operated." We stopped and admired a beautifully red-and-gold-decorated *Animal Parade Bandwagon* that was certainly inspired by their trips to Venice. A separate show room was set aside as a movie theater; extracts from the movie that won the Academy Award for Best Film and Best Story, *The Greatest Show on Earth* (1952), starring Betty Hutton and Charleston Heston was being shown. I remember as a young man seeing the movie that featured the Ringling Bros. Circus and instantly fell in love with how the carefree spirited people of the circus lived, and imagined that one day I would join them on their fascinating journeys.

It was nearing night time when we finished viewing the main attractions of the estate, and again made mental notes that another visit in the near future would be a must. As it was getting late, we headed south to Alligator Alley for our return to the reality of our winter home in Delray Beach.

Chapter Ten – Sailing the Caribbean – On the Good Ship Costa Fortuna

This chapter is not a continuation of one of our articles, but some of our experiences when vacationing in the Caribbean. Over the last few years, theme cruises have become very popular. We have traveled on ships with themes of the New Orleans Mardi Gras, Kentucky Derby, and big bands. Recognizing the latest trend, Stardust Dance Productions of Woodbourne, New York (www.Stardustdancecruises.com) extended their successful land dance get-away adventures to the ocean. Under the auspices of Vinny Munno and Jeff Sandler of Goldcoast Ballroom, Coconut Creek, Florida, a dance cruise was organized from March 9 to March 16, 2008. Vinny and Jeff helped organize the cruise, which started in Fort Lauderdale and sailed to many of the islands in the Eastern Caribbean. Vinny was also one of the great DJs that provided music on the ship, while Jeff co-hosted the sea venture. Over 300 guests signed on for the sea adventure, from as far away as Russia, Hawaii, California, Texas, and, of course, New York and New Jersey, just to name some of the many ports of call that were represented on the cruise. The night before sailing on the Italian liner, *Costa Fortuna*, dancers were transported by bus from Ft. Lauderdale, about a 30-minute ride, where many of the travelers stayed at hotels in preparation for leaving the next morning for their new dancing journey from Port Everglades, to Goldcoast Ballroom for a BON VOYAGE PARTY. Over 150 guests arrived at the ballroom dressed in nautical attire. The girls wore mini, maxi, and every other type of white nautical outfits that one can imagine. Even the guys looked like real sailors; some wore bellbottom trousers and navy caps, others dressed as officers, all spit and polished. When they entered the hall, the place turned white from the color of their outfits; it seemed as if snowflakes blew in with the wind and engulfed the sunny Florida venue. The white outfits mingled with the colors worn by the other 200-plus dancers, making the dance floor look like a checkerboard of black and white. We danced the night away to Vinny's music: foxtrots, waltzes, cha-chas and mambos-salsas, all the wonderful dance tunes that helped create a pre-cruise camaraderie that was to last throughout our Caribbean voyage.

We boarded the Italian cruise ship, *Costa Fortuna*, (not to be confused with her sister ship the Italian liner *Costa Concordia* that ran aground on a reef, January 13, 2012, off the coast of *Isola del Giglio,* Tuscany, Italy and of this writing, is still capsized where it sank). The *Fortuna's* brochure stated that, "It's the largest ship ever built for an Italian company, 890-feet long with a 124-foot beam. Built in late 2003, it boasts, an elegant three-level Rex Theatre, four swimming pools, a spa and gym, tennis courts, 11 bars and a state of the art gambling casino. The four dining rooms are smoke free, as are most of the common areas of the ship. It accommodates 2,720 guests in 1,358 rooms and has a complement of 1,027 crew members. Its 18 elevators carry passengers to their destinations, from deck 1 to 13." I would say that it was a pretty impressive ship, even by today's standards.

Stardust personnel had an orientation booth set up for our group and distributed programs for the dancing and planned activities, which included information, on a daily basis, of dance classes and social events for the coming week. Everyone was required to choose their dance classes in advance, and after confirming the availability of the classes, were given information as to the time, place, and dance instructors teaching the lessons. The dance classes were broken down into A, B, and C, signifying the level of proficiency required by the students participating in each lesson: (A) for beginners, (B) for intermediate, and (C) for advanced dancers. The levels of proficiency were strictly monitored, as a beginner in an intermediate or advanced class can slow down the progress of the other students and can be embarrassing and annoying for everyone. There were eight dance instructors conducting over eighty classes during the eight-day trip. Seven dance hosts were provided for the ladies, in addition to the dance instructors. Music for general dancing was provided by five DJs, all with their own style of music, so the dancers had a choice of where to enjoy their favorite dances after classes. All dance lessons were restricted to our group and were closely monitored so strangers could not interfere with the private sessions.

Barbara and I decided that we would take classes with Donna DeSimone and George (Jorge) Maderski who we knew from our New York dancing community. Donna was the Stardust dance director and is a renowned dancer and choreographer, with her own dance studios. She also won the 1986 "USBC American Rhythm Championship" in Florida. We had taken group lessons with her at various dances that we attended and were happy to have the opportunity to learn from her again. Most of her classes were on the advanced level and were usually attended by ten to twenty students. We signed up with her for two West Coast swing lessons, two mambo-salsa lessons and one Lindy and hustle lesson. She lived up to our expectations, as her teaching method gets to the core of a dance routine and with some practice is easily learned. A bonus was that I had the opportunity to dance with her in the evenings at the general dances, performing many of the steps that I learned in her classes.

We knew Jorge from the many dance halls we attended since we began dancing many, many years ago. He and his partner were dance champions at the 1986 and 1987 American Star Ball Theater Arts competitions and the 1987 Harvest Moon Ball Professional Cabaret Championship. He gave lessons at many of the dance venues in New York that we attended. Although he is proficient in many of the popular dances, he is considered an aficionado of Argentine tango, which he teaches with passion and a unique styling. Many years ago, we attended a dance in Westhampton, Long Island, at Alfonso's Touch Dance Studio. We were all just learning and loving Argentine tango, which was the featured dance of the evening. We were glad to see Jorge there and happy to share our steps and stories about the popular up and coming Argentine tango. Alfonso and his partner, Agnes, have been promoting the dance for many years and did an exhibition that thrilled everyone. After their performance, Jorge asked him to play another Argentine tango and then asked Alfonso to dance. Well, it is common in Argentina for men to dance with each other, but that sight here in the U.S. was a bit unexpected. Jorge's leads were amazing, while Alfonso followed as if they were long-time partners. Then Alfonso played another tango and took the lead away from Jorge as a challenge. Their performance and improvisation of the dance was a once-in-a-lifetime experience, with both dancing fast, slow, and moderate steps to the uneven tempos and sways of the Argentine tango. The attendees were ecstatic and couldn't stop applauding and howling in admiration of these two very talented dancers who seemed to be at war with each other on the dance floor. Alfonso can be seen on New York television channels 56, 17, and 20 at various times of the week, teaching a variety of dances at different levels. More information can be obtained at his website, www.mnn.org, or at www.touchdancing.com. We decided to take two Argentine tango lessons, two American tango lessons, and two rumba lessons with Jorge. His teaching lived up to his reputation, as we left his classes feeling that we had a pretty good understanding of what we were taught; all we had to do was get on the dance floor and allow his teaching to come through in our performances.

After departing Ft. Lauderdale, our ports of call included San Juan, Puerto Rico; St. Thomas and St. John in the Virgin Islands; Catalina and La Romana Islands, in the Dominica Republic; and Nassau Island in the Bahamas. Included in our package with Stardust Cruise were:

- Seven night's accommodations in an outside room with a balcony
- Five Theme Nights: Mediterranean, Tropical Calypso, Italian Festival, Captain's Reception and Roman Toga Dress Competition
- Two formal dress nights
- Fabulous meals, gourmet midnight buffets, and 24/7 room service

- A separate dining area for our Stardust dancers in the Restaurant Raffaello
- Three complimentary themed cocktail parties:
- A Jack n' Jill Dance Contest
- Stellar Broadway shows in the Rex Theatre
- A Stardust hospitality desk set up during the entire cruise
- Dance classes every day for all dance levels in private areas
- Over 30 practice workshops

Our primary concern was our luggage, which arrived intact to our small cabin somewhat worn by the Red Cap handlers. There was just about enough space in the room to hang our clothes and hide our suitcases. Our balcony was outstanding, it was small but had enough room for us to sit and enjoy the view; especially exciting was the departure from the pier at Ft. Lauderdale, which was on our side of the ship, which gave us an opportunity to wave to our imaginary friends on shore as the ship sailed off into the horizon. The ship line has a unique infrastructure; it has many small rooms, approximately 180 square feet, and few suites, thereby increasing its passenger capacity accordingly. Its common areas are also downsized compared to other ships we've sailed on, but overall the accommodations were adequate and the overall feel of the ship was new and pristine. Its best feature was that it was an Italian ship, and pasta was served 24/7. I didn't waste any time going straight to the pasta bar for lunch on our first day and ordered "little ears" pasta in a marinara sauce, with lots of parmesan cheese, cooked to order right in front of me. I would have gone for seconds and thirds, but Barbara's watchful eyes always seems to know where I am and what I'm up to, so salad was her more sensible choice to round out my lunch. Exiting the lunch area, I dreamed of capturing the palliative aroma of the various Italian sauces being brewed and spreading them on a piece of semolina-seeded warm Italian bread; what an interesting sandwich that would make. "Dream on."

We spent most of the afternoon exploring the magnificent ship and enjoying its "adults only" swimming pool, which was on the upper deck and quite secluded from the hustle and bustle of the rest of the ship. There were no lessons scheduled for the first day, but we had general dancing for our group from 6:30 P.M. to 8:30 P.M., on the Colombo Pool deck on the 9th level. Vinny was our DJ and his excellent music put us all in a dancing mood that would last for our entire voyage. Our group had the late dinner seating at the main dining room, Restaurant Raffaello. We were seated with Joan and Alice from New Jersey, who were traveling together and hoping to improve their dancing skills beyond beginner's level. Also, my dear friend, Louis Mangone, who was instrumental in placing my Columbus Book Collection with the Columbus Citizen's Foundation, rounded out our table. The surrounding tables were occupied by many people we knew from Goldcoast Ballroom, which made for a very relaxed and chatty dining environment. The menu was extensive and favored Italian food. I was determined not to gain any weight on that trip, so keeping it simple was the way for me to go. I ordered an appetizer of sliced tomatoes with olives, covered with balsamic vinegar and olive oil. Although simple, it has always been my favorite salad, so I chose to have it as an appetizer every evening for our trip. Needless to say, I was delighted to order different pasta every evening, to the chagrin of my fellow diners who were enjoying a variety of fish, pork, beef, and enormous salads and desserts.

After dinner, we moseyed along to the three-level Rex Theatre, which accommodated over 1,300 people and was full to the brim. The theatre is decorated in Art Deco, which gives the impression that you're surrounded by metallic polished, glittering mirrors. It's built like an amphitheater, giving all the patrons good views of the stage from their comfortable cushioned seats, with armrests and small tables to accommodate drinks. That night, the ship's staff of about two dozen performers danced and sang many scores from Broadway musicals. The spectacular performance was on a par with the original shows, but more exciting because we didn't know which songs were coming next, plus they had their own spin to the music, costumes, and settings. A major advantage was that the stadium-style seats were the same as those in a private stadium room, so no one's head or hat became an obstruction, which is something I'm plagued with when attending a theatre. The one-hour show was timed perfectly for us to attend Stardust's "Welcome Tropical Cocktail Reception," which was held at the Colombo Pool area on Deck 9 and was reserved for our group.

The dress for the occasion was colorful tropical clothing, the louder the colors the better. Some outfits were so imaginative in their color combinations and brightness that they were traumatic to my eyes and kept me alert the whole evening, allowing me to do some pretty serious dancing. Again, Vinny was our DJ and played lots of music from the Tropics; we even did a limbo dance that turned out to be hilarious as the movement of the ship made getting under the rod somewhat difficult and many participants ended up on their backsides. We struck up an acquaintance with a couple that we saw around the Long Island dance scene but never really had any conversations with. Christine and Peter were from our hometown and are serious dancers. When we saw them at various dance halls, we always admired their smooth and technical dance routines, which in many ways were similar to ours. So we became friendly and exchanged many dance steps with them that evening and for the remainder of the cruise. The Tropical Night theme was complemented with piña coladas and a mysterious red-colored rum concoction that had a slow sneaky side-kick. The evening flowed by while we danced cha-chas, mambos-salsas, meringues, foxtrots, waltzes, and tangos. Fortunately, the seas were relatively calm so we didn't have too much trouble keeping our balance while maneuvering around the deck; keeping our balance from the potent tropical drinks was an entirely different matter. We met many new dance companions and reacquainted ourselves with our New York and Florida friends. What made the evening especially pleasant was that the male and female dance hosts and instructors mingled and danced with many of our group. The music stopped around 1:00 A.M., while the camaraderie was at its height, so many of the dancers retired to the 24/7 coffee shop or went to the other dance venues that were provided by the *Costa Fortuna*.

We awoke around ten the next morning after a delightful night's sleep, which was enhanced by the fresh Caribbean Sea air in our room that came from our open balcony door and filled our nostrils and minds with clarity and serenity. What a delightful way to start our first full day at sea. We checked our dance schedule and were disappointed that we had already missed some classes that began at 9:00 A.M., but there were other classes every hour on the hour until 6:00 P.M. So we quickly organized ourselves and chose to eat at the elaborate breakfast buffet, instead of the time-consuming sit-down breakfast at the more formal restaurants. Our rumba class with Jorge was at 11:00 A.M. There were only a dozen people attending the class, which made it easy to understand and follow his instructions. As this was an advanced class, he spent most of the lesson working on the proper look and posture for the dance, which Barbara and I were delighted with, as we always seem to lose our postures in the excitement of following beautiful rumba rhythms. Our next class was West Coast Swing at 12 noon with Donna DeSimone. The class was quite crowded, about 20-plus students, but thinned out after the first lesson when it was determined that there were many beginner dancers attending the advanced class; they were asked to step outside of the dance area to make room for the qualified dancers. They were allowed to stay and watch the lesson, but couldn't participate as they were colliding with everyone and disrupting the class. This dance is particularly confusing due to the speed and technical acumen required to perform the routines. It must be performed with couples facing in the same direction as if on "railroad tracks"; the girls travel the tracks back and forth while the men step aside and let them pass. All of this is done to a quick "country western/lindy" timing and can become dangerous if dancers are not proficient in this type of dancing, which was the case with the beginners that were asked to leave the dance floor. Donna always comes through with her special type of teaching; we left very pleased that we learned some nice underarm turns, which we subsequently put to good use. Finishing the lesson unscathed was a very pleasant experience and was due to Donna's strict monitoring of the dance participants' skill levels.

We chose the buffet lunch to save time, as we wanted to attend one or both of the two general dance sessions that ran between 2:00 P.M. to 6:00 P.M. One of our favorite New York DJs, George Morse (Cody), was playing ballroom music at the Grand Bar *di Savoia* on Deck 6, and DJ Johnny Ortiz was playing salsa, hustle, swing and Argentine tango at the *Vulcania* Disco on Deck 4. We walked quickly to the dining area, passing the magnificent swimming pools where passengers were enjoying the blue-green water and sunbathing. Following the aroma of the various sauces being brewed by the Italian chefs, I visited the pasta bar and had the chef make two plates filled with my favorite pasta, ears and ziti, with marinara sauce for the pasta ears and meat sausage sauce for the ziti. I was able to accomplish this quickly, while Barbara chose the long lines at the buffet and didn't have an opportunity to scale down my meal. By the time she found me among the many tables scattered throughout the restaurant, one plate of pasta was already devoured and removed from my table by one of the ever-present bus persons, so I was safe eating the second delicious plate of Italian cuisine without being lectured. What Barbara brought back from the buffet was astonishing: sausage, pizza, pepperoni, orzo with veggies, and a variety of desserts. I said, "Honey, what happened to your diet?" She said, "Honey I'm only sampling a little of each." End of story.

We went to the *Vulcania* Disco to sample some of the music by DJ Otiz. Many of our friends were floating between his hall and DJ Cody's. We spent over an hour dancing Latin, switching partners and practicing the new routines we learned that day. We then visited the Grand Bar *di Savoia* hall to dance and continue practicing some of the steps we learned to DJ Cody's music. We always enjoyed dancing and listening to his great selection of dance music. Barbara especially enjoys when he spins her around the floor a few times; he is an exceptional Latin dancer and she cherishes dancing routines with him. Barbara surprised me some years ago with a birthday party in which he was the source of our music, much to the pleasure of our guests. The hosts and instructors were busy at both locations dancing with the girls and making them very, very happy. Many of the single ladies looked forward to this as their favorite part of the day because they got to dance with very polite, young proficient dancers, and learned a great deal about dancing from them. We stayed till the music ended at 6:00 P.M., and then joined some of our friends in the Pizza Parlor for a pre-dinner snack and some juicy gossip. The topic of the week, or maybe month or even year, was the romantic escapades of New York's Governor Spitzer. No one could fathom why such a well-renowned crime fighter and governor of one of our most important states could conduct himself so recklessly and in such a stupid manner, embarrassing himself, his wife, and children in the process. The consensus was that he certainly isn't the only fool that has gone astray in the past or present, but he certainly was the fool that got caught due to his arrogance and blatant disregard of the secrecy that extramarital affairs require. Stupid man!

That night was the Captain's Formal Night, which required that I wear my black double-breasted and uncomfortable tuxedo. As a lark, I wore my famous bright red nautical suspenders, which were hidden under my jacket. I always get a rise out of people when I take my very formal jacket off and the bright red suspenders appear, capturing everyone's attention, resulting in lots of laughing and joking around. The passengers met in the Rex Theatre for a Gala Cocktail Party where everyone toasted Captain Claudio De Fenza and his officers as they were presented, one by one, on the theatre's stage. After the ceremony, the Captain was available for photo taking with the guests, which has become a very popular event on cruise ships. Being that we have so many photos from prior voyages, we decided to go straight to the dining room and order some lovely Italian wine before the festivities began.

The highlight of the Captain's Formal Night was a procession by the kitchen staff marching through the dining room, dressed in kitchen garb, carrying large Baked Alaska Cakes (ice cream lined with sponge cake and topped with meringue), with sparkling fiery candles aglow while singing "What a Lovely Way to Spend an Evening." What a great way to begin an evening's dining experience. At that time, many of our group was table hopping and even changing seats for the evening with other willing guests. We had a visit from a beautiful blonde from the Russian Ukraine who couldn't stop raving about the wonderful time she and several of her friends were having on the cruise, dancing and meeting new people and hopefully making lifetime contacts. The dinner and camaraderie was so pleasant that we didn't want to break away to see the late show at the Rex Theatre, but we reluctantly said our goodbyes and headed for the theatre to see the extravaganza of the evening.

The show's theme was acrobatic; the feats were performed by the cast, whose muscles seemed to be bulging from their bodies as they carried out their intricate movements that defied description. They built an inverted human pyramid, one person at a time, starting with one individual at the bottom and growing to several layers, rising upward until it was unbearable to watch for fear of their crumbling down on each other and the astonishing anchorman at the bottom. However, they didn't crumble and received an overwhelming reaction from the audience as they completed their unbelievable act.

After the show, we had a choice of two dancing venues. One was the Colombo Pool on Deck 9 with DJ Chris Marcelle, who was originally from Long Island, New York, and now resides with her husband, Larry (one of the dance instructors), in Vero Beach, Florida. We have become good dancing friends of theirs over the years and make it a point to dance at many of their events whenever they are the hosts. Tonight she was playing salsa/hustle/swing and Argentine tango music. The second late dance session was in the Grand Bar *Conti di Savoia* on Deck 5 with DJ Michelle Friedman playing general ballroom dance music. Both sessions were from 11:00 P.M. to 1:00 A.M. We decided to join Chris for the evening, and, as usual, enjoyed dancing to her music. She too is a proficient dancer, which made her choice of dancing music easy to follow and right on the beat. There were many dance hosts and instructors dancing with our guests, while the moonlight shining off the water of the swimming pool created a romantic atmosphere as we danced around its water's edge. I removed my tuxedo jacket to expose my bright red suspenders and not only got some chuckles from the dancers, but was outmaneuvered by some of the other guys who also exposed their suspenders, some of which were more outrageous than mine. Some were pink, purple, and orange, while some boasted scenic decorations, such as Christmas, Halloween, and Thanksgiving. We decided that on the next cruise we should have a suspender contest and give awards for the most outrageous ones. Another delightful, exhausting night passed on the magnificent ship. We finished our tropical drinks and then slowly strolled back to our place of rest to enjoy another calm night's sleep, with fresh warm Caribbean air filling the room from our open terrace door.

Our destination on the third day was the Island of San Juan, Puerto Rico; estimated time of arrival 5:00 P.M., and departing at midnight, which didn't give passengers much time to explore the island. Many decided to see a flamenco dance show in town; we had visited the beautiful island many times, so decided to stay on board and enjoy more general dancing. I'm always thrilled when we approach one of the major islands in the Caribbean; all the books that I collected on the age of discovery over the years and many of their stories pleasantly passed through my mind, reminding me of the courage and audacity of the many brave men who dared to venture out into the unknown, not quite sure of their destinations, or if they would ever return to their homes and loved ones. The first European to visit the islands was Christopher Columbus on his second voyage in 1493. The island was inhabited by friendly Arawak Indians, known as Tainos, who thought that the sailors were Gods and treated them accordingly. After many years of abuse by the Spaniards, the Indians rebelled, but to no avail. They were disbursed throughout the Caribbean or enslaved by their taskmasters, almost to the point of extinction. One of Columbus's crew, Ponce de Leon, returned many years later to govern the island of Puerto Rico and was primarily responsible for the unfortunate fate of the indigenous people. He later left the island in search of the Fountain of Youth, which he thought was in Florida; however, he is responsible instead for what is now known as the Fountain of the Aged, because many senior citizens visit the fountain and drink what will hopefully prolong their lives. Anyway, if Columbus was a little off course on his second voyage, he would have missed this island and hit the mainland, and what is known today as America would probably be called Columbia. Puerto Rico became a Spanish stronghold for their conquered lands throughout the Indies, Central, and South America. They built a formidable fort at the entrance of Old San Juan to sustain their supremacy over their new conquests; the fort still remains pretty much intact today.

We decided to limit our dance lessons to no more than two a day, as we also wanted to enjoy the ship's facilities and didn't want to make our days onboard stressful by taking too many dance classes. Some of our friends took several dance lessons every day and totally enjoyed the chance to learn new steps and routines from the accomplished dance instructors provided by Stardust. In the morning, before arriving at our destination, we took a 10:00 A.M. advanced American tango lesson with Jorge. The class was very private; only about ten people were in attendance, which made it easy to understand and learn the new steps and routines he taught us. One step, in particular, was fun and sexy. It's called a *Gaucho,* where a basic tango step is done and continues into a left-hand turn in place, with lead hands lowered, for two complete counts of eight, a sexy maneuver and real eye catcher. There were two afternoon workshops: ballroom dancing with DJ Vinny Munno and salsa/hustle/swing and Argentine tango with DJ Cody. We wanted to take our second lesson and then do some general dancing to the music of these two great dance music aficionados and practice the steps we had learned.

After lunch, we took our second lesson with Donna DeSimone in Advanced West Coast Swing. Her classes always draw large numbers of dancers because she is such a proficient and easy-to-follow instructor and the dances she teaches are very popular. Again, she had to weed out dancers that didn't qualify for the advanced lesson; it seems that many people think that because they buy a pair of dance shoes, that they suddenly have the ability to dance like Fred Astaire and Ginger Rogers. So, after the weeding out, the class had about 20 students, which made the lesson much more manageable and enjoyable. We learned a couple of underarms variations and the importance of dancing this very quick-paced dance in the same direction as everyone else, on an imaginary railroad track to avoid collisions or what we call "train wrecks." We hurried to Vinny's and then Cody's dance workshops and practiced the steps we learned; some came easily, others took quite a bit of practice, but when the sessions ended, we had the patterns under control. At least, that is, until the next time we tried the steps.

We arrived at the beautiful harbor of San Juan at exactly 5:00 P.M., tied up to the pier, and dropped the ship's boarding steps, which allowed those passengers who wanted to visit the area a speedy exit from the ship. We joined our fellow dancers for general dancing with DJ Johnny Ortiz at the Leonardo Da Vinci Lounge on Deck 5. Many of our group disembarked to go sightseeing or attend a Flamenco Dance Show, so the dance floor at the workshop was not crowded, and we were able to do some smooth dances (foxtrots and waltzes) easily, without the usual interference from other dancers. After the session, a poolside nap was in order, so we moseyed over to the pool, had the attendant set up chaise lounges, quickly settled in, and, in short order, we were napping. A post-nap dip in the pool rounded out our perfectly relaxing day before we returned to our cabin to dress for another exciting evening with our friends aboard the wonderful Italian liner.

After dinner, it was back to the Rex Theatre for an Amateur Hour Contest between passengers. The bold volunteers performed to the best of their abilities: some very good and others not as accomplished. The fun of amateur contests is that contestants always give it their all, but many come up short. One participant in particular was outstanding. He sang "On a Clear Day," but got the words of another song mixed in, which made the performance belly-laughing funny. After the show, we hurried to the Colombo Pool area on Deck 9 where our group was having a Calypso night theme party.

Our friends were already partying and were one up on us, drinking red concoctions with floating mini-umbrellas stuck in pieces of pineapple. The umbrellas didn't taste good . . . but the drinks were excellent. We spent the evening dancing to mostly Caribbean Calypso music, and then went to the late-night session at the Grand Bar *Conte di Savoia* on Deck 5 where DJ Michelle Friedman was playing general ballroom dance music till 1:30 A.M. The calm waters that we were having on the first days were starting to act up, making it a little difficult to hold our balance while dancing. But we adjusted as best we could and danced the rest of the evening away to great music and lots of laughing and exchanging of dance partners, which is always fun and one of the nice features of dancing with a friendly group. When the music ended, some of our group decided to continue the camaraderie at the Pizza Palace. Our day had been quite full, so we opted instead for a good night's sleep, and looked forward to opening our terrace door, filling the cabin with fresh Caribbean air, and being lulled to sleep by the sound of the waves gently transporting the ship to its next destination, Charlotte Amalia in St. Thomas, Virgin Islands.

We arrived at St. Thomas at 8:00 A.M., with a scheduled departure of 5:00 P.M., which gave our group a full day at the beautiful island to water ski, snorkel at the beaches, parasail, scuba dive for treasure, catamaran sail around the island, sail to the neighboring islands of St. John or St. Croix, swim and sunbath at one of the many beaches, visit duty free shops, or just stay onboard and enjoy the scheduled activities that were planned for the day. The onboard activities included a lesson in Italian, group exercise classes, a miniature golf tournament, tennis on a respectable-sized court, dance lessons, or just relaxing at the poolside reading one of the many books available in the ship's library. Of course, the gym and spa were also always available for our use and relaxation. We decided to take a dance lesson with Jorge in Argentine tango, and after lunch visit the many duty-free shops in Charlotte Amalia. Barbara carried a map with her of all the jewelry stores in the town and which ones had the best discounts; she kept notes from our previous visits to St. Thomas tucked away in her traveling bag, and was determined to put them to good use.

There are over 65 islands that make up the Virgin Islands. The U.S. Virgin Islands (USVI) consists of St. Thomas, which is 32 square miles, St. John, which is 28 square miles, and the larger island of St. Croix, which is 84 square miles. Columbus visited these islands on his second voyage in 1493 and named them after St. Ursula and her 11,000 beautiful virgins. The first residents of the islands were the Ciboneys, Caribs, and Arawaks, who Columbus called "Indians" as he was searching for a shorter route to India and thought he had found the elusive land; consequently, his misunderstanding forever labeled Native Americans, "Indians." Being that the Carib Indians were hostile and cannibalistic, the islands were considered unfriendly and remained outside of Spain's dominance and sphere of influence for some time. In the early 1600s, the Dutch, French, and English conquered these lands and found that the indigenous Indians had all but perished from European disease, Spanish abuse, and slavery. The United States purchased the islands in 1917 for $25 million from the Dutch. Subsequently, St. Croix, St. Thomas, and St. John became the U.S. Virgin Islands, which gave the residents the opportunity to become U.S. citizens. However, not all thought that the option was a good one, so many remained on as guests.

After breakfast, most of the ship's passengers disembarked to take advantage of the many attractions of the Caribbean paradise. Christine and Pete went to the one-mile-long heart-shaped Magen's Bay Beach. It's without a doubt one of the most beautiful and well-maintained beaches in the world. The sandy bottom slopes down gently, which encourages snorkeling, swimming, and playing among the many small fish that inhabit its blue-green waters. We were considering spending some time at the magnificent beach, but it would have taken a good part of the day, and as we spent time there on a couple of other vacations, visiting the town for a short period of time seemed to be a better alternative, especially since the temperature was expected to reach into the 90s and my remaining red hair and fair skin has difficulty dealing with the sun or heat. Oh, for the good old days when nothing seemed to bother me and I could spend days outdoors enjoying the warmth of the sun. I recalled the last time we visited Magen's Beach and swam for hours among the local inhabitants living in the water; we were comfortable swimming out into deep water, knowing that we were under the watchful eyes of the lifeguard on duty. A big surprise, however, was when Barbara and I swam a short distance to a nearby beach and discovered that it was a NUDE beach. Barbara was shocked and dragged me away, under protest, as I always felt that people should do whatever their fancy dictates. Unfortunately, my wife didn't agree, so we left all those beautiful people who seemed so at ease with their choice of bathing and returned to the more traditional part of the beach.

The next morning, we took a morning class in Argentine tango with Jorge, which was a pleasure, as we were the only students in the class. The Argentine tango takes some explaining, as it is one of three types of tangos. International and American tangos are competition dances originating from the Argentine tango, which was a street and brothel dance in Argentina in the late 18th century. In time, it was accepted as a social dance and became popular through many movies featuring its passionate movements, especially when performed by the actors Rudolph Valentino and George Raft. Over the years, it was refined into the American and international styles, which are performed in worldwide competitions. But the main differences are that the two competition dances are done in ballroom positions: straight backs, with the male looking to his left and the female leaning back with her eyes directed over the male's right shoulder. There are strict routines and patterns that are followed, and whichever couples perform these the best are chosen winners of the competitions. The dances are done in a counterclockwise direction, with zigzag variations. The Argentine tango, on the other hand, usually begins in a cheek-to-cheek position with partners caressing each other rather than holding. As the dance progresses, certain established routines and steps are performed, but the beauty of the dance is in the improvisations that each does to the changing rhythm and pace of the dance. It is considered one of the most complicated dances to learn and requires, in addition to many dance lessons and practice, a feel for the music, as this turns it from a dance of steps to a harmonious and coordinated work of beauty. In the tango world, this is called dancing with the right *attitude*. Another major difference in this dance is that it can be done in the line of direction (counterclockwise), which is salon style, or in place as an exhibition style, which is the sexier of the two and allows for more improvisation.

Jorge was pleased that we were the only students taking a lesson, as it gave us time to catch up with the events in our lives that brought us to the Goldcoast Cruise. He took the opportunity to dance with Barbara, which was a sight to behold. I didn't realize how beautifully she danced, as I'm always holding her close and don't ever get an opportunity to see her perform. She followed him perfectly and displayed an exemplary attitude for the music. He also danced with me and showed me some attitude steps that were fun, especially the steps where I look at Barbara with a matador stare and challenge, while she throws a couple of kicks between my legs. He concentrated on our styling and polished our routines to a point where he was happy with our performance and then had us do a private show for him before the lesson ended. We headed for lunch and a change of clothing before we left the ship for Charlotte Amalia to visit the stores that Barbara had plotted for us.

The temperature was nearing 90 degrees, so we dressed accordingly. There were several shuttle buses from the ship to the center of town, which was only a few minutes away. Barbara led me to the first of several jewelry stores, looking for what I thought was someone named John Hardy. I couldn't understand why she was bargaining with the salesperson for John Hardy. Then, she let me in on the secret: she was looking for a John Hardy bracelet, which is a silver or gold wrist band with some sort of stones. We went into four different stores before she decided that the first store had the best price. So we went back and she bought the bracelet for herself and one for my daughter, Laurie. I didn't ask her how much it cost, as we have an arrangement: I don't ask what her jewelry costs and she doesn't ask me how much it costs to play golf or buy clubs. I spotted a Christmas shop and headed directly for an ornament that was in the store's window, a beautiful angel with shiny gold sparkles. I bought it without bargaining, which annoyed Barbara, as she is one of the world's consummate *hondlers* and I deprived her of one of her most enjoyable pastimes by not letting her conduct the transaction. The temperature was rising and the heat was beginning to get oppressive, so we grabbed a taxicab back to the ship and then headed for our cabin to put on our bathing suits. We spent the rest of the afternoon in and around the pool, reading, and taking delicious naps. There were no afternoon classes scheduled, as most of our group left the ship and took advantage of the beautiful sightseeing and sea sport activities available in St. Thomas, and of course, the duty-free shopping. The late afternoon workshop was in the Grand Bar *Conte di Savoia* on Deck 5, with Chris Marcelle playing her great ballroom music. We danced for a couple of hours on a pretty empty dance floor, as most of our crew was still exploring and making contributions to the local economy. It gave us an opportunity to practice, without too much embarrassment, many of the new steps we learned at our dance classes. We then returned to our place of rest to refresh and prepare for the ship's *Fiesta Italiana* Night.

After dinner, we headed to the Rex Theatre for the *Fiesta Italiana* Show with international headliner John Ciatta performing the best of Dean Martin, Frank Sinatra, and other popular Italian singers. I closed my eyes and listened to him sing "That's Amore," "My Way," and many other popular songs. I couldn't tell the difference between him and the original artists that recorded those renowned songs. We exited the theatre and went to the ship's *Tarantella Dance Party*, which included a dance lesson by some of the ship's staff. The ship's instructors, who also participated in the dance stage shows, were just as accomplished as the teachers provided by Stardust. Learning the *Tarantella* was a real treat for me. As a young boy, it was a favorite dance of my family and their friends. On many happy occasions, someone would produce a guitar, harmonica, tambourine, and even a kazoo, and get the music going for the girls who loved to dance the *Tarantella*. It is very similar in many ways to the Polish Polka. I remember the girls trying to coax the men to dance, but to no avail, so the girls would enjoy dancing with each other. I danced Barbara around the floor a few times, doing the steps we had just learned and having one heck of a good time, while reminiscing about the fun I had dancing that dance in my youth with my older sisters, Anne and Mae. We then left to join our friends at the Stardust Late Night Dance Session at the Colombo Pool on Deck 9. Dancing under the stars to DJ Chris Marcelle's music was romantic, even though the ship rocked and rolled, and keeping one's footing was a challenge. But, we all somehow managed to balance ourselves and enjoyed the ending of another beautiful day at sea, dancing till the wee hours of the morning. Breathing in the intoxicating sea air seemed to enhance my sleeping senses; when I rested my head on my pillows at the end of the day, sleep was immediately imminent.

We were awakened in the morning to the ratcheting sound of the anchor being dropped off the shore of *Isla Catalina* in the Dominican Republic. The island was baptized by Christopher Columbus in May 1494, on his second voyage while he was still seeking a shorter route to India than the long and dangerous prevailing overland routes. The island is famous for Captain Kidd's sinking of his ship *Quedah Merchant* in the 17th century (which he captured with considerable booty from the Spanish) to avoid being captured as a pirate by several English man-of-wars that were pursuing him. While returning to the safety of his home port in New York City in an inconspicuous sloop, it's said that he buried some of his treasures in Block Island, Massachusetts, and Gardener's Island, New York. The mythology and legend has been kept alive by such literature as Edgar Allan Poe's *The Gold-Bug,* Washington Irving's *The Devil and Tom Walker*, Robert Louis Stevenson's *Treasure Island*, and Nelson DeMille's *Plum Island.* They also gave impetus to the never-ending treasure hunts on Oak Island in Nova Scotia; in Suffolk County, New York; in both the Charles Island in Milford and the Thimble Islands in Connecticut. The most exciting myth or legend is his attacking the island named *Takarajima* (Treasure Island) that belonged to Japan. The pirates landed on the island seeking food and cattle from the inhabitants, which was refused and resulted in the pirates burning the village and killing its natives. Legend has it that he buried his considerable treasure in one of the cave-grave sites where the deceased's cremated natives' ashes were scattered. He never returned to claim his booty, as he was captured and brought to England for prosecution, and, finally, his execution. Ironically, he was once a privateer in the service of "Grand old England," but decided it was more profitable to go into business for himself as a pirate, much to the dismay of his employers. His hanged body remained on display for two years as a warning to anyone else contemplating being a pirate instead of a privateer (for the benefit of the crown). As odd as it may seem, the *Quedah Merchant* shipwreck was discovered on December 13, 2007, off *Isla Catalina* in 10 feet of water just 70 feet off the beach, centuries after its sinking, and a short distance from where we were going to picnic for the day.

The plan for the afternoon was for passengers to be transported in the ship's launch boats to the island for a BBQ, Calypso music, dancing, lounging on beach chairs, swimming in pristine waters, sunbathing, or relaxing among the 1,000-plus passengers that chose to leave the ship for a day on a tropical island. But, before our new adventure, there was an early morning advanced dance class with Donna DeSimone in salsa. As usual, the class was crowded, and, as usual, she had to weed out many students who were not proficient at the level of the lesson being taught or were not a part of our group. It became evident how important maintaining the proper level of dancing is, as was witnessed in one of her West Coast swing classes, where a beginning-level student got into an advanced-level class. He not only caused a major collision with other students, but his carelessness also resulted in his partner falling and injuring her knee. Barbara and I consider mambo-salsa to be one of our better dances, and totally enjoyed the swivel and underarm routines that Donna taught us that we were not familiar with. Mambo-salsa requires a lot of energy to really enjoy the dance; learning to improvise is paramount to really look special while performing. It's amazing to watch good dancers doing completely different steps and routines than other dancers, while looking equally proficient and enjoying their own motions and improvisations. Although it is an energetic dance, it seems that many people prefer dancing only the mambo-salsa all evening long, and go out of their way to attend the Latin workshops that highlight the dance.

We boarded the launch boat with about 100 other passengers, defying the choppy seas and currents to arrive at Catalina Island, which took about ten minutes from the ship to the beach. The island is uninhabited and approximately 1.5 miles from the mainland on the southeast corner of the Dominican Republic, near the islands of *La Altagracia* and *La Romana*. The highest elevation of the island is 60 feet above sea level and is about four square miles in size, with a diverse preservation of eco-systems including sand dunes, mangroves, and reefs. The sea around the island is rich with wildlife and many species of birds. Tropical fish can be observed by walking out into the waters safely due to the many shallow sandbars. It was lots of fun walking out 50 yards, visiting many small fish in their natural habitat, and being accepted by them as part of their scenery. We paired off with Christine and Pete and secured chaise lounges under a large palm tree, which allowed us to relax without getting too much sun exposure. A seven-piece Calypso band's music filled the warm air, as many of the passengers began gyrations that almost resembled dancing, while kicking up powder-like sand with the motion of their feet. Most were just jumping around and having a good time, while others chose to play volleyball and others walked or swam the shallow waters, all in unison with the music of the rhythmic sounds coming from the steel instruments. The BBQ lines were quite long, so we decided to go swimming instead of fighting the procession and heat. Christine, who is blonde and quite fair-skinned, and I, a fair-skinned redhead, poured suntan lotion on to protect us from the very strong tropical sun. The temptation of the blue-green water was too much to resist and we all ran in to enjoy its cooling effect. We had to run out pretty far before the water was deep enough to swim in. The run was worth it, as the water felt like a welcomed cool shower that brought my body temperature down by at least 15 degrees. I could have spent the whole afternoon in the delicious Caribbean water, but previous experience with the sun warned me to get out before it was too late. So out I went, dripping the magical liquid from my body, while taking notice that I was the only one exiting the gifted waters. Barbara is dark skinned and can tolerate the sun better than most, but Christine, who is really fair-skinned, and Sal, who is a little darker, also decided to stay in and enjoy the refreshing experience, hopefully not to their regret. We finally got to the BBQ and took our booty to our secluded, shaded palm tree and devoured all the food in short order. There was an abundance of hot dogs, hamburgers, spareribs, conch fritters, watermelon, and papaya fruit, which we pleasantly washed our portions down with tropical pineapple drinks, some with and some without boosters.

We left the island of paradise by reversing our course and heading for the massive *Costa Fortuna* that was anchored some distance away. Its white superstructure contrasted with the blue-green water and the pale blue sky that featured just the right amount of clouds to create a tropical postcard scene of the first order. Upon boarding, we headed directly to our cabin to get rid of the salt and sand that was imbedded in our suits and hair.

There were two dance workshops at 4:00 P.M. Vinny was playing salsa, hustle, swing, and Argentine tango music, while Chris was playing general ballroom dance music, mostly smooth. We decided to dress comfortably and attend an hour of each session and then enjoy watching the ship pull into our next port, the city of La Romana, which is one of the largest cities in the Dominican Republic with a population exceeding 250,000 people. I'm always fascinated when pulling into a port, either on my own boat or on a large cruising ship. The feeling of accomplishment and the excitement of a new experience are invigorating, and gets my mind imagining all the wonders that will be awaiting us when we go ashore. Kudos must be given to the captain and his crew for their ability to bring the humongous 890-foot vessel into the small harbor and eventually ease it into its berth, all in a matter of minutes.

There is always a reception committee waiting when we dock, and La Romana was no exception. A small Calypso band greeted us with the song "Yellow Bird," which automatically had everyone singing or humming the words to it: "Yellow bird way up in banana tree, yellow bird sitting there just like me . . ." The passengers waved and made all sorts of happy sounds in anticipation of what was to come from visiting that beautiful city. One of the city's famous attractions is the "Teeth of the Dog" golf course, which is one of three championship courses at the *Casa de Campo* Resort. Many of the passengers brought their golf clubs on the trip in anticipation of playing the world-renowned championship course. Unfortunately, I didn't, and had to resign myself to listening to the players tell of their great experiences and wonderful imaginary scores, when they returned from their outing. Maybe the next time I visit the city, I'll be better prepared. We decided not to leave the ship and retired to our cabin for a well-deserved nap, and were again lulled to sleep by the fresh sea air, and soft magical sounds floating into our room from the Calypso band on shore.

We arrived at the Rex Theater early that evening to get good seats for the Grand Variety Circus Show featuring acrobats Duo Markov and Duo Errani. Their skill with ropes, which seemed invisible, was astonishing; they actually extended themselves over the audience as if flying through the air, arms and legs outstretched and balanced on their stomachs, to the delight and fright of the spectators. Two other performers imitated the actions of snakes that wriggled and squirmed and then entered combat with each other. The whole scene was surreal, and gave me goose bumps to watch such large creatures in combat and then kissing and making peace. The ship's dancers performed some exotic routines as circus lions, tigers, elephants, and zebras, and received continuous applause from the audience. Much of their performance reminded me of the Broadway show, *The Lion King,* where the animals ran through the aisles toying with the guests, as the ship's dancers did.

There were two late dance sessions scheduled for the evening, both featuring general dancing: DJ Johnny Ortiz at the Colombo Pool on Deck 9, from 10:00 to 12:00 midnight, and DJ Michelle, playing in the more private Grand Bar *Conti di Savoia* on Deck 5, from 12:00 midnight until 1:30 A.M. We decided to dance at the early session and leave the Grand Bar to the more hearty souls in our group. There was a particular technique that Barbara and I wanted to practice to Argentine tango music, and John willingly accommodated us with a song that had a varied tempo. When we took our lesson with Jorge, he emphasized the importance of the right attitude for the dance, so we decided to experiment with some attitude and see if we could capture the spirit of the dance. At the beginning of the routine, I approached Barbara as she retreated, dodged, and shied away. I followed her and abruptly cut her off and then held her in my arms. We did a balancing move, turning our bodies from left to right with our feet in place. The music intensified; we were wrapped in each other's arms, she reluctantly and me aggressively. Slowly, to the beat of the music, we began to dance as one, enjoying the passion of the moment and then caressing aggressively at the finale. We were told that tango dancing tells a story, and the story must be relayed to those watching. If this can be accomplished, then the right attitude for the dance is captured. We must have gotten the attitude right because our friends applauded and did some hooting; even Jorge came over and complimented us by saying: "You almost got it right." Satisfied that we "almost got it right," we continued dancing till the session ended and then joined our friends at the Grand Bar for a late evening of switching dance partners. We danced and socialized until we were exhausted and then moseyed along to our cabin for another great night's sleep, breathing in the fresh salt air entering through our terrace door, and being lulled to sleep by the hypnotic sound of the waves gently splashing on our ship.

The following day was at sea, as we headed for Nassau Island in the Bahamas' chain before returning to our final port of call in Ft. Lauderdale, Florida. We squeezed in three dance lessons for the day: in the morning, Advanced Lindy with Donna DeSimone and Advanced American Tango with Jorge; in the late afternoon, we had an Advanced Hustle lesson with Donna. Having some spare time in the afternoon, we decided to take an Italian lesson given by one of the pretty crew members. We both decided to skip breakfast, which was becoming our largest meal of the day, and hold off for the famous Midnight Buffet that evening, which featured finger sandwiches, sushi, and every combination of dessert imaginable; we couldn't wait. My Pollyanna attitude figured that by missing breakfast, eating a variety of desserts at midnight would even the calorie score, especially if I ate lots of unsweetened fruit. Further supporting my Pollyanna reasoning, we decided to spend some holistic time at the gym and then get stone massages at the spa, which would certainly enhance our health and probably help us lose some weight.

The dance lessons went according to our plans and we picked up some valuable dance routines to add to our repertoires in Lindy,

American tango, and the hustle. The highlight of the day was the stone massage that we both had in the cruise liner's state-of-the-art spa. I was put in a private room with soft natural music playing the sounds of rain drops and animal calls. Stripped down to my birthday suit, heated basalt stones (black volcanic rock) that retain heat well were placed on top of my vertebrae. The stones were heated in 120 to 150 degrees in boiling water, and, when applied, immediately penetrated my body with heat, causing the most relaxed feeling imaginable. The therapist performed the same traditional Swedish massage strokes that I experienced when getting my regular massages at home, except that she held the heated stones in her hands while plying her trade. When finished, my body not only seemed at peace with itself, but was mysteriously energized. After cooling down and dressing, we headed for our Italian lesson in the *Conte Rosso* Lounge on Deck 5.

Although I'm of Italian descent and my older sisters have told me that I was able to speak Italian very well as a child, the language somehow has left my memory. Learning to speak the language as an adult has become a challenge to me. I've taken lessons with Berlitz instructors, listened to Berlitz tapes, and have written the language until the wee hours of the day, all to no avail. I just don't have foreign language retention. On the other hand, Barbara has a good understanding of Spanish and Yiddish, which gives her great insight into many languages. When we visited Greece many years ago, it only took her several days before she deciphered that difficult alphabet, and when we visited Italy on several occasions, she had no trouble grasping their language. So she coaxed me into taking an Italian lesson on the ship, and as her suggestions are usually my commands, I followed her to the *Conte Rosso* Lounge for another lesson in Italian. The lesson went as follows: *Buon giorno* = Good morning; *Buono sera* = Good afternoon or Good night; *Bene* = Well; *Grazie* = Thank you; *Si*= Yes; *No* = No; Signore = Sir or Mr.; *Signore* = Madam or Mrs.; *Signorina* = Miss; and *Scusi* = Excuse me. Barbara gobbled the information up and I was quite surprised that I mastered these few words as well. Pleased with ourselves, we left the classroom and went to the *Vulcania* Disco Room on Deck 4 to join Michelle for general ballroom dancing. I asked her to play some Argentine tango music, which she did immediately. This gave us a chance to practice some more attitude routines, which were becoming second nature to us as we were really getting into the passion of the dance. Many of our friends were pleased by our improvement with the dance and tried copying our moves. I told them if they wanted to get a passionate feel for the dance, they had to develop the right attitude. As the words left my mouth, I pictured Jorge saying the same thing to us. I guess "imitation **is** the best form of flattery."

After taking a prolonged nap, we dressed for a formal evening, which was directed by the captain, and, again, I was plagued with wearing my tuxedo, which seemed to be shrinking by the minute. But, I remembered so well the pleasure I received from seeing Cary Grant in a movie wearing a tuxedo while smoking a cigarette on the deck of an ocean liner and telling his lucky leading lady how much he loved her; that scene, so indelible in my mind, made wearing my tux a little more tolerable. I felt I was Cary Grant as I looked in the mirror remembering the scene; however, taking a longer look at the mirror quickly dispelled my fantasy.

Our evening show time was prior to the formal dinner and featured *In Concert* to be performed by the crew's singers and dancers. There were lots of sing-along songs and fancy ballroom dancing choreographed by the cruise director, Max. He also did some very serious baritone love songs, such as "On a Clear Day," "Some Enchanted Evening," and "September Song." We exited the show singing and humming some of the songs we had just heard, while moving on to the Raffaello Dining Room for our "Farewell Dinner," which, strangely, was two nights before the end of our journey. I had my usual pasta delight with trimmings, while toasting and congratulating Captain Claudio De Fenza and his crew for the splendid job they had done in transporting us around the Caribbean Islands without incident. As the champagne was gratis, there was lots of toasting going on around the dining room, passengers to crew, crew to passengers, tablemates to tablemates, students to dance instructors and tour leaders, and on and on.

While Chris was entertaining our group with her special music, some of us decided to try DJ Jascin, the ship's music aficionado at the Disco *Vulcania* Lounge on Deck 4. His music equaled our DJ's; the only problem we had was trying to dance among so many non-dancers without colliding with them. Our experiment of mingling with non-dancers was short lived, and we swiftly joined Chris in the larger Colombo Pool area on Deck 9. The buzz from our group that evening was about the midnight *Buffet Magnifico* and the exact time it would begin. Sounds strange, what time will the midnight buffet begin? Well, it was a good question, because it didn't start until 12:30 A.M., in the Raffaello Dining Room.

It's amazing that the staff could put together such a display of ice artwork and food in such a short period of time. The whole dining room was inundated with ice sculptures of swans, female Roman figures, Roman gladiators, and beautiful flowers. Tables were lined with finger sandwiches, sushi, hors d'oeuvres, and every imaginable dessert, presented in artistic surroundings and designs. Fruits were presented in various art forms, such as watermelon fruit baskets, cantaloupe butterflies, and pineapple hats. Tropical flowers were artistically placed throughout the hall, emphasizing birds of paradise and an abundance of lilies. Chocolates and more chocolates were everywhere, and would certainly win first prize for the most consumed treat in the shortest period of time. The feast lasted till after 2:00 A.M., which gave passengers an opportunity to sit with their booty and enjoy cappuccino, espresso, or any other number of drinks, with or without boosters. Most people just sat around till the wee hours of the morning, mingling and just having a great social experience with other guests on the incredible ship.

Our last day at sea included a short visit, from 1:00 P.M. to 5:30 P.M., to Nassau Island in the Bahamas. The Bahamas are an archipelago with almost 2,400 islands consisting of rocks, white sandbanks, and coral reefs, extending from Palm Beach, Florida to the coast of Cuba. Only 40 islands are inhabited. It was on one of these, the Island of San Salvador, that Christopher Columbus made his first landfall. Nassau was one of our favorite vacation spots during the great "Jet Set" era in the 1960s. At that time, I was working as a Certified Public Accountant, and looked forward with a passion for the tax season to end on April 15. Barbara would have our bags packed and our kiddies ready to go on the following day, and off we would fly to the incredible turquoise-blue water paradise. On one of our visits, we witnessed the groundbreaking and the beginning of construction on the barren Paradise Island for the

Paradise Beach Hotel, while we were sunning ourselves on the beach across the channel. So we immediately booked reservations to revisit the now resort island of the Greek philosopher Plato's imaginary city, Atlantis, in the afternoon. We were anxious to see how the pristine white sand island we visited and enjoyed so many years ago looked after being developed and civilized. We invited Christine and Pete to join us for the exciting excursion; they gladly accepted our invitation.

We scheduled three dance classes in the morning: Advanced Salsa and Cha-Cha with Donna and Advanced Argentine Tango with Jorge. All the lessons were well attended and we proudly added more routines to our ever-growing repertoires. Hopefully, we would remember what we learned after leaving the ship. We decided to have a sit-down lunch at the Restaurant *Christoforo Colombo* on Deck 9. We were lucky to get a window table and ordered some of the fish specialties, with pasta, of course. It was really a treat to sit down for lunch in an upscale restaurant with white-gloved waiters serving us. My Pollyanna trait went into gear as I tried to convince Barbara that a hearty lunch would energize us for the exhausting trip we planned to Paradise Island.

We disembarked and were transported by jitney to a waterfront depot in town and got on line to board the *Paradise Island* 50-passenger boat launch, which would take us to the dream island. Approaching the island was shocking; I never expected to see the extent of development that had taken place since we swam at its isolated white-sand beaches, with no large structures in sight. Townhouses were lined up along the shore, as well as a multitude of hotels, which were all dwarfed by the 97-acre Atlantis Paradise Island Resort. Its Royal Towers, which are joined by a bridge section, is one of the most expansive hotel divides in the world. We were deposited on a fairytale entrance to the resort and couldn't figure out where to look first, due to the most unusual marine architecture imaginable. Fortunately, we were able to pick up a guided tour and followed the leader through the maze of water and marine exhibits, each with its own unique attraction. We went directly to Aquaventure, which opened in 2007. The 63-acre, 200-million-gallon seawater display combines water slides, lazy rivers, and rapids into one large waterscape. The centerpiece of the colossal attraction was the 120-foot Power Tower that contained four water slides and a rock climbing wall. The slides included *The Abyss*, *The Drop*, *The Falls*, and *The Surge*. Next to these were the Mayan Temple Slides, consisting of four major slides: *Leap of Faith*, *The Challenger Slides*, *The Serpent Slide*, and *The Jungle Slide*. Of particular interest were the five-story Mayan Temple that has a 60-foot vertical drop and ends in a clear tunnel inside a shark-filled lagoon, and *The Challenger Slide* that accommodated people who wanted to race down the water to the bottom and splash themselves into oblivion. Our next stop was the Dig, which is a series of aquariums located beneath the lobby of the Royal Towers and has the world's largest open-air habitat. Hundreds of different aquatic species (angelfish, sharks, manta rays, and various types of colorful jellyfish) could be seen in various tanks. The floors of the different aquariums have wreckage and debris scattered about representing the remains of the "Lost City of Atlantis." The remnants are supposed to mirror what the legendary lost city looked like after its destruction. In other parts of the Dig were subterranean views of Atlantis-themed chambers that stretch the imagination as to what life was like during the city's "day in the sun." Our guided tour ended abruptly and we found ourselves in a smoke-filled casino. Wouldn't you know, it was another sneaky place to deposit our pocket money—it was just what we needed to add to our memories of the once-beautiful pristine island. We raced out of the area to get some fresh air and to take pictures of the spectacular displays around the resort before our excursion ended.

The waterfalls and slides were a photographer's dreams come true; I took pictures of at least six different falls including the fantastic waterfall at Beach Towers and the two Mayan Waterfalls. We had to rush to catch our launch boat and didn't have an opportunity to explore the rest of the magnificent playground, but we promised to return in the very near future to finish exploring the incredible tropical **civilized** paradise. We learned from our launch guide that the island also has two 18-hole par 72 golf courses and a 9,000-square-foot nightclub. The Paradise Island from days of old no longer existed; what took its place was a "concrete Playland," for better or worse, depending on one's point of view. I enjoyed both the uninhabited unspoiled island of yesteryear and the modern architectural genius that brought us the potpourri of personal 21st century delights that exists today. Originally, I preferred the former, but I must confess, I was impressed with what I saw on our adventure. I think the best of both worlds would be the Atlantis Resort standing alone on the island without any "Disney World" or "Coney Island"—type neighbors, which are in such abundance on the island that they ruin what should be a tropical paradise seascape and escape.

We returned in time for a quick nap and found white sheets in our cabin to be used as togas for the evening Roman Night Festival. We did this once before on a *Mississippi Queen* Cruise, and I was unhappy then and uncomfortable now about wearing a sheet through dinner, a show in the Rex Theater, and then the Stardust Going Away Party. But Barbara suggested that I join in the spirit of the evening, and, as usual, her request became my command. So, I wrapped myself like a mummy and somehow did resemble some sort of Roman citizen. We went to our final dinner and were joined by our traveling companions; to my surprise, some of the group evidently were forewarned about the toga dress and wore some pretty fancy outfits. Christine looked like a Roman Goddess in her white, gold-trimmed gown highlighted by her golden hair supporting a tiara. Her red, sunburned skin contrasted beautifully against her outfit, making her look like a glowing Sun Goddess. Pete, by far, had the best male toga ensemble, also with gold trim and sash, and sporting a golden Roman laurel wreath. Together they looked as if they stepped out of a time warp to join our party. There were many farewell toasts and a farewell speech from Captain Claudio De Fenza, who tried to convince us that we were the best passengers he ever carried on his magnificent vessel. After repeating my dining preference with a couple of plates of pasta, we retreated to the Rex Theatre for Roman Night and the Guest Talent Show.

The show featured Cleopatra, Mark Antony, Caesar, Bacchus, and centurions played by the cruise staff. Somehow, lions appeared for a gladiator exhibition that was quite funny; the lions, which consisted of two people, looked quite disjointed while stumbling all over the stage trying to look threatening. Cleopatra, Mark Antony, and Caesar relived their parts in history, from her meeting the great Caesar to her romantic but disastrous interlude with Mark Antony, and her final meeting with a poisonous asp, which concluded the Greek Ptolemy's lineage of Egypt's royalty. The history of her lineage dates back to 300

BCE when Alexander the Great conquered Egypt and left one of his generals, Ptolemy, behind to rule the country. Subsequently, all the leaders were from his line and spoke Greek as their main language, including Cleopatra and her younger brother. The amateur talent show was pretty entertaining. Somehow, all the contestants won first prize, which they certainly deserved for their courage and good-humored attempt at entertaining the passengers.

We were anxious to attend the Toga Stardust Farewell Cocktail Party for our group in the Leonardo Da Vinci Lounge where DJ Michelle was providing the dance music. Our friends were already in full swing when we arrived. The scene looked like a meeting of the Roman Senate gone wild. Everyone was in good spirits thanks to the free spirits (pun intended) provided by our host, Stardust. There was a lot of showcase dancing throughout the evening, provided by the better dancers, and after a few drinks, the "not so better dancers." We couldn't believe how many new friends we made and how many different people we danced with on the trip. Seeing everyone was having fun at the party emphasized how satisfying the dance cruise was to the participants, who were acting as if they were life-long friends. We said our goodbyes with hugs and kisses and by dancing one last time with some of our newfound friends.

It was after 2:00 A.M. when we returned to our cabin, so we had to rush and pack, as we were scheduled to arrive after our 180-mile voyage from Nassau to Ft. Lauderdale, at 8:00 A.M., and begin disembarking immediately.

Vinny and Jeff subsequently booked another eight-day dance cruise on the Royal Caribbean's *Independence of the Seas,* for January 31, 2010. Needless to say, we made reservations for that journey. A copy of their brochure is presented with the permission of Vinny:

Goldcoast
Dance Cruise
Cha Cha Cha
Rumba
Tango
Salsa
Swing
Hustle

Chapter Eleven – Three Trips to Hawaii

~*~

AROUND THE FLOOR: SEPTEMBER/OCTOBER 1998
TRAVELING AROUND by Barbara Bivona

We were in Hawaii recently, visiting our son and daughter-in-law, who are both officers in the U.S. Army and were stationed at Schofield Barracks, about 20 minutes from Waikiki Beach, in Honolulu. We took the opportunity to go to the Ala Wai Country Club in Waikiki Beach several times for ballroom dancing. The enormous dance floor, which we were told is 12,000 square feet, is utilized to its full potential, as there are no tables crowding the dancing space; chairs are strategically located around the perimeter of the dance area so they do not interfere with the performers. The floor has one of the best surfaces we have ever danced on, which is constructed of eucalyptus, making it soft on dancing feet, which gives performers the feeling that the floor is floating. One of the evenings was hosted by the Hawaiian Ballroom Dance Association (HBDA). The HBDA members did various showcases in competition. All of the performances were done in group formations rather than featuring individuals. It must have taken months of training and practice for each group of up to 20 dancers to perfect their routines. The performances were quite an unexpected treat.

During the week, there are no-charge afternoon dances, where the ballroom is divided by portable walls into three sections, each one 4,000 square feet. The popular style of dancing in Hawaii is

International. With these large dance areas, dancers have an opportunity to zigzag in the line of direction with little interference from others, always aware of the courtesies that are required when dancing the fast-paced, smooth dances. In spite of the large crowds, when the ballroom was at full capacity, which is 700 to 800 people, there was very little bumping by the dancers. On the one occasion where we saw a slight collision, both Japanese couples immediately smiled while bowing, apologized, and then continued dancing as if nothing had happened.

We look forward to our next trip to Hawaii for the big event, which is the birth of our first grandchild; a boy is expected. Of course, in between changing diapers and babysitting, we will be going back to the Ala Wai Golf Club to dance. We'll also check out the Latin dance club at the Hawaiian Regent Hotel, where we stayed many years ago on our first visit to Hawaii, and other venues that we were told are scattered around Honolulu.

AROUND THE FLOOR/MARCH-JUNE 1999
TRAVELING AROUND by Barbara Bivona

Once again, Mike and I returned to Hawaii. This time, it was for the birth of our first grandchild, Ian Charles. Of course, he is the most beautiful baby we have ever seen and he definitely has dancer's feet! Although our days were occupied with this gorgeous child, our nights were free. So we returned to the 12,000-square-foot Palladium Dance Hall at the Ala Wai Golf Club in Waikiki. One evening was sponsored by the HBDA and another evening featured two different dance clubs: the Pan Pacific Dance Association and the Aloha Dance Club. For these two events, the floor was divided in half by a portable wall and I was surprised that the music did not filter from one side to the other. We chose to dance at the Aloha Dance Club because the floor was less crowded; the choice was a good one, as we were able to dance smooth dances (waltz, foxtrot, and quickstep) without any interference from other dancers. We were also able to finally dance a samba, which, although it's a Latin dance, is done in the line of direction and not in place. It's very difficult to find dance floors that have enough space or are large enough to perform the many beautiful steps and routines that are part of this wonderful Brazilian dance.

Latin dancing by the "Salsa Hawaii Band" at the Aqua Club in the Hawaiian Regent Hotel is on Thursdays, Fridays, and Saturdays, starting at 10:00 P.M. Featured the night we attended was the seven-piece band led by "Rolando Sanchez." Rolando has been playing at the Regent for three years and is instrumental in organizing and participating in Latin festivals in Hawaii. He has been featured on TV shows and music videos in Hawaii and Tahiti. Although the dance floor was a small nightclub-sized one, we were able to dance with plenty of space, as Latin dancing doesn't usually require much room. We were able to do some good mambo-salsas, cumbias, and meringues. Half of the fun was just listening to this great band.

Also, "Rumors Nightclub" at the Ala Moana Hotel in Honolulu features ballroom dancing on Tuesday and Sunday nights. Although there is no cover or admission charge on Tuesdays, we were surprised by the complimentary buffet, which included sliced steak, various salads, fruits, and Japanese appetizers, and included some really good sushi. There is a $5.00 admission charge on Sunday evenings, which is well worth the unheard of price, considering that a meal and great dancing are included.

END OF ARTICLES

~*~

We Discover Hawaii: Cruising the Islands

Our love affair with Hawaii began when we celebrated our 25th wedding anniversary and decided to cruise the Hawaiian Islands, with ports of call in Hilo and Kona on the Big Island of Hawaii; Kahului, Maui, Nawiliwili, Kauai, and Honolulu in Oahu. We sailed on the vintage ship *S.S. Independence* (built in 1951) from Honolulu, for a seven-day voyage around the most idyllic ensemble of islands in the world. The ship was the perfect size to sail the short distances between the islands. It was 682 feet in length with a 90-foot beam. She accommodated 1,000 passengers in Henry Dreyfuss-designed cabins (ultimate utilization of space), with large-size suites and penthouses. She featured Fifth Avenue shops, for the ladies on board, handsome turn of the 18th century public rooms, and bars decorated in Hawaiian tattoo design. Most memorable were their collection of miniature cruise ships in bottles, including the doomed Titanic. Picture windows in the observation lounge, spanning 125 feet, gave viewers panoramic scenes of the islands and the surrounding waters. In the evening, it was a safe haven for viewing the bright red steaming lava flowing from the Kilauea Volcano and meeting the sea, from the Big Island of Hawaii. We made a stop on the Big Island to explore Kalapana Black Sand Beach, which is a result of volcanic remnants that resembled a scene from an outer space horror film. Its coarse black sand and strange odor combined with the red hot lava flowing from the volcano nearby was unreal. We knew we were on a beach, but absolutely wouldn't lie on the sand or swim in the water because of its black appearance and pungent odor, although there were people sunbathing and swimming in the turquoise-blue water and enjoying their somewhat unusual adventure. Our most fascinating experience was visiting the Kilauea (spewing) Volcano, which is 4,091 feet above sea level, and is the most active volcano in the world (45 eruptions in the 20th century). It's flanked by the much larger, less active snow-capped Mauna Loa Volcano (13,677 feet). Barbara went berserk; she ran to the cordoned-off area and took pictures of the bubbly stuff with smoke spewing from its crest. Kilauea is considered to be the home of Pele, the volcano goddess of ancient Hawaiian legends. Several special lava formations are named after her, including Pele's Tears (small droplets of lava that cool in the air and retain their teardrop shapes) and Pele's Hair (thin, brittle strands of volcanic glass that often form during the explosions and accompanies the lava flow as it enters the ocean). In Hawaiian mythology, Kilauea is where most of the conflict between Pele and the rain god, Kamapua'a, took place. Since it was the residence of Pele, Kamapua'a, jealous of Pele's ability to make lava spout from the ground at will, covered it with the fronds of the fern. Choking from the smoke that could not escape, Pele emerged, realizing that each could threaten the other with destruction; the gods had to call their fight a draw and divided the island between them: Kamapua'a got the windward northeastern side, and Pele got the drier Kona leeward side. Our dear friend, Dallas Peck, who we wrote about in Chapter Five, must have had the time of his illustrious life when working and doing research at the Hawaiian Volcano Observatory (HVO) in his early years as a geologist, specializing in volcanoes. On the 75th anniversary of HVO in 1987, when he was the Director of the U.S. Geological Survey that manages the HVO, he wrote an article called, "The Celebration on a Volcano," which stated:

> The Kilauea Volcano sure knows how to prepare for a party. During the two months prior to last week's

festivities commemorating the 75th anniversary of the nearby HVO and the opening of its new facilities, the volcano added 18 acres of lava to the Island of Hawaii. And since the eruptions began three years ago, Kilauea has produced a record-breaking 850-million cubic yards of lava. The amount could cover, to a depth of almost 31 feet, four lanes of an interstate highway from New York to San Francisco, approximately 3,000 miles." He writes on, "The new HVO building, perched on Kilauea's rim, is equipped with an elevated tower from which both Kilauea and the neighboring Mauna Loa Volcano can be observed. The HVO, which is the first and oldest volcano observatory in the U.S., has been responsible for the development of most of the volcano monitoring techniques now used worldwide." What an exciting and fulfilling life Dallas had during his 23-year tenure as the presidential nominee of the office of Director of the U.S. Geological Survey, and an additional 18 years as a scientist and researcher at that world-renowned organization. He would say that "Working at a job he was totally infatuated and absorbed with, and being around all the mythical gods of the volcanoes and the Hawaiian Islands, was the world's greatest dream job; being paid for the work was the icing on the cake.

Next, we made a stop at the Captain Cook Monument in Kealakekua Bay to pay homage to the great sea captain who was the first westerner to discover the Hawaiian Islands. The obelisk lies a short distance from where Captain Cook was killed in a battle with hostile local natives. His sailing master was the much-maligned Captain William Bligh of the infamous ship, *Bounty*, whose crew chose to stay with the beautiful women and easy life of the islands rather than return to the hardship of a sailor's life on board the *Bounty*. It was Bligh that Captain Cook sent ashore to fetch fresh water and food for the crew, thereby making Bligh the first European to set foot on Hawaiian soil. Cook's men also enjoyed the readily available sexual favors of the local girls and the easy life of living among such bountiful beauty. He would have probably had the same mutinous results as Bligh had the local natives been friendlier; unfortunately for him, they were war-like and actually provoked fights with the intruders, which eventually resulted in the death of Cook and many of his men.

Back on our ship, we enjoyed evenings of delicious food that included a variety of freshly caught local fish. We indulged ourselves with mahi, swordfish, and lobsters, plus varied meat selections. After dinner, we would withdraw to the nightclub for big band music and dancing. They had a ten-piece band playing Hawaiian music that included lots of ballroom dancing numbers. Lucky for us, very few people were dancers, so we were able to request many numbers and do some pretty good dancing to the live music of the colorfully dressed members of the Hawaiian band. Many an evening we were the floor show, doing Latin and smooth dances to the applause of the people in the club; we were embarrassed at the attention, but were really in heaven performing our hard-learned steps and routines in front of an audience that enjoyed watching us.

One evening we had a ukulele contest that was exciting and lots of fun. The passengers were given ukuleles and had three days to learn how to play songs that were assigned to them. I was one of the winners, playing "We Are Going to a Hukilau" while singing "We Are Going to a Hukilau, a Huki, Huki, Huki, Huki, Hukilau." I did my solo topless, wearing only a hula skirt. When all the men performed together, it turned out to be hilarious; the girls couldn't stop laughing at our hairy chests and legs and the disjointed exotic movement of our hips.

We sighted humpback whale pods while passing between the islands of Maui County. The sight of hundreds of humongous creatures breaking the turquoise-blue seawater in choreographed harmony is certainly one of the most spectacular sea wonders of the world. The whales migrate approximately 3,500 miles from Alaskan waters each autumn to spend the winter months mating and birthing in the beautiful warm waters off of Maui. Unfortunately, these beautiful mammals are facing many dangers due to increased levels of pollution in the ocean, the high speeds of commercial vessels, and military sonar testing. They are now considered an endangered species and are protected by many governments around the world.

We spent a few hours on Maui, swimming and sunbathing on a pristine beach of soft white sand, while devouring conch soup and fritters that were provided by the ever-pleasant native attendants. It was difficult leaving the heavenly beauty of the island to return to our ship; surely, there is no other place on earth to compare with the natural beauty and bountiful resources of the island of Maui. That's what I thought, until we visited the Island of Kauai, which is considered the tropical centerpiece of Hawaii. It's carpeted with lush greenery, covered with flowers of every color, and has visible fresh fruit growing in abundance from its many trees. There is even a comforting cool mist that blankets the island to relax the body and soul on hot days.

Kauai is the oldest of the Hawaiian Islands, and it was here that Captain Cook gave the islands their first western name: Sandwich Islands, which were named after his sponsor the Earl of Sandwich. Oddly enough, the Earl invented the sandwich as we know it today. He was an avid card player, and to keep the players at the card table instead of the food bar, he concocted the sandwich to ensure uninterrupted gambling.

We visited Waimea Canyon, which is the largest canyon in the Pacific. It measures ten miles long, one mile wide, and more than thirty-five hundred feet deep. It was carved thousands of years ago by rivers and floods that flowed from Mt. Waialeale's summit. It's not as large as the Grand Canyon in Arizona, U.S.A., but certainly rivals its beauty and complexity. The lines of the canyon walls depict different volcanic eruptions and lava flows that have occurred over the centuries, and from certain points look like the colors of a rainbow. The canyon is in Koke'e State Park, which encompasses 4,345 acres of land, with 45 miles of trails that run through it and the nearby swamps. The park would certainly be a place to revisit for a week to spend time exploring the trails and campsites while staying at the rustic Hale Koa Cabins in the park.

Our next stop was the Spouting Horn. This natural wonder occurs when water rushes under a lava shelf and bursts through a small opening at the surface. Every wave produces another spray, frequently 50 feet into the air. The phenomenon is especially exciting at sunset when the spray becomes incandescent with the colors of the rainbow. There are signs warning viewers to stay behind the cordon ropes, as injuries and even fatalities have resulted to people that wandered too close to the blowhole. Legend has it that the coast was guarded by a large *mo'o* (lizard) that ate anyone who tried to fish or swim in the area. One day, a man named Liko entered the water; when the *mo'o* attacked him, he swam under the lava shelf and escaped through the hole. The *mo'o* followed him, got stuck, and was unable to free himself. The groaning from the blowhole is his cry from hunger and pain as he remains, still trapped, under the rocks. I just love Hawaiian legends; they seem to be steeped in Pollyanna mystique that captures and stretches the imagination. Many years ago there was a much larger blowhole called Kukuiula Seaplume adjacent to the Spouting Horn. It shot water 200 feet into the air. However, as the salt spray damaged a nearby field of sugar cane, the hole was blasted away in the early part of the 20th century. Imagine trying to destroy such a natural wonder today; every environmentalist in the world would be up in arms. Oddly, the cane field no longer exists. The island has such diverse beauty that over 60 feature films have been shot on it, such as the majestic Manawaiopuna Falls in *Jurassic Park*. The Wailua River was used in the movie *Blue Hawaii,* and the Anahola Mountains were used as the backdrop in *Raiders of the Lost Ark*. Again, we had to drag ourselves away from another island in paradise too soon and return to our ship.

Our last night of the cruise was a formal one. Out came my tuxedo, starched collared shirt, suspenders, and a sash wrapped around my waist, which gave me the feeling of being prepared to be mummified. The dinner was spectacular; I again had freshly caught mahi (dolphin, not the playful ones with long snouts, but the blue finned type). Watching the tuxedoed waiters singing Hawaiian songs while serving food was amusing; the only distinguishing differences between their dress and the tuxedoed guests were that the waiters wore white gloves and were singing. Aside from those two differences, all of us looked alike. After dinner, I had to return to my cabin and take off the uncomfortable tuxedo and put on some clothing that would allow me to dance with ease. We spent the evening dancing to the wonderful music of a live band, which went out of their way to play our requests for ballroom dance music. It was the custom many years ago for many cruise vessels to have a different themed midnight buffet every evening. Barbara's favorite was the chocolate buffet on the last night of the cruise. We were used to seeing ice sculptures at these feasts, but they were replaced that evening with chocolate birds, flowers, tigers, and an assortment of other little brown delicious critters. I found it difficult biting into a chocolate canary, but my wife had no trouble devouring her favorite desserts; I thought she would eat herself into heavenly chocolate oblivion. The cruise ships today wisely do not have these buffets every evening, as they resulted in an unnecessary waste of food and added needlessly to the expense of traveling. Today they usually have just one night of "pigging out" with a buffet-style extravaganza, which alleviates the guilt feeling that I always had when eating a late unnecessary fourth meal.

We docked in Honolulu at the same pier from which we departed the populated island. It's easy to understand why more than half of the people in Hawaii live on this island in paradise; it not only has some of the most beautiful beaches in the world, but is also a metropolis of the first order, with cultural and educational facilities readily available every day of the week. It even boasts the world's largest wind generator (20 stories with 400-foot blades), which is employed to create electricity for the island. We headed straight to the Sheraton Waikiki Hotel, which was located on the main beach avenue with commanding views of Diamond Head Mountain, Honolulu, and Waikiki Beach. We planned on spending a few days exploring the sophisticated clubs and some of the local sites.

We decided to spend the first day walking the main street, Kalakaua Avenue, and exploring Waikiki Beach. As luck would have it, we immediately stumbled onto the Waikiki Town Center. The name is deceiving; I thought it was a visitor's center, but it wasn't. It is a shopping mall with about 50 vendors, restaurants, and lots of tourists. Barbara was ecstatic; it was just what she needed after spending a grueling week aboard a ship cruising the Hawaiian Islands with only a few shops at her disposal. Our first stop was an outside vendor displaying oysters. For a price, you could buy one that might contain a pearl. Barbara got lucky and bought one that had a mini-pearl enclosed, and immediately made plans for mounting it in a ring. During our walk, I noticed that everyone seemed to be as lucky as she; they all won pearls with their purchases. The center was dominated by a gorgeous fountain in an open courtyard with shops surrounding it having local names like Red Dirt Tees, Quicksilver Boardrider's Club, and Chin Lan. For the most part, the shops sold Hawaiian souvenirs and clothing. It didn't take long before we were out of the small shopping center, and wouldn't you know it, right next door was the International Marketplace with 130 carts, shops, and artisan stands. It seemed I wasn't going to have a good day, as shopping isn't one of my favorite pastimes, unless it has something to do with golf or boating. I must say, the local craftspeople were very friendly and volunteered tales of their heritage, especially if they were "real Hawaiians" (unbroken racial lineage), which they are very proud of. We took some nice photos of a small cascading waterfall from under a century-old banyan tree. The large eccentric tree was fascinating; the twists and turns of its branches and the bulges in its trunk were anomalies, as if its creator couldn't make up his mind about which direction the tree should travel; its distortions certainly makes the tree one of nature's special works of art. Another unusual attraction was the Swiss Family Robinson-style tree house, which was the original home of one of the locals, Donn the Beachcomber.

Previously, we had made a mental note to visit the Royal Hawaiian Hotel, known as the Pink Palace, on the beach side of the street. The entire outside facade of the enormous hotel is bright pink, which illuminates the beach and sky when the sun sets in the evening. A pink color scheme prevails throughout the hotel, right down to the linens and plush towels. As guests of its sister, the Sheraton hotel, we had dining and beach privileges, so we brought along our swimsuits and decided to spend the afternoon on its private, gorgeous, immaculate beach. Upon entering the hotel, native girls greeted us with leis and pieces of banana bread. The overwhelming pink vaulted ceilings blended in with the huge Art Deco arched mirrors in the public areas and over the shops, which matched the pink outfits the staff members were wearing. We were escorted to dressing rooms so we could change into our swimsuits and rushed to the beach, where bronze-suntanned boys secured pink chaise lounges, pink-striped umbrellas, and pink towels for our pleasure. This pink Pacific gem hotel, which was built in 1927 on Waikiki Beach, has to be experienced to be believed. A BBQ was being prepared, while music filled the air from a live Polynesian band. We ordered Mai Tai drinks from the open-air Mai Tai Bar, where it is boasted that the drink originated. Small handouts were delivered with the drinks listing their ingredients:

One ounce of dark rum
One ounce of light rum
One ounce of orange Curacao
Two ounces of orange juice
One-half ounce of lime
A dash of orgeat
A dash of simple syrup

"Combine all of the ingredients, in the order listed, into an old-fashioned-style glass and pour over shaved ice. Stir with a swizzle stick. Garnish with a slice of pineapple and a cherry and then drink slowly."

We decided to order the concoction in a pineapple with a small pink umbrella on top, which certainly enhanced the drink and made it a truly Hawaiian experience. It was easy to settle in and enjoy the food from the BBQ. The spread included: spareribs and roasted pork strips with pineapple trimmings. We enjoyed the offerings, while sucking in the fresh sea air and the hypnotic aroma coming from the BBQ pits. Watching the four-to six-foot afternoon waves pounding the sandy shore and then gently returning to the ocean quickly opened my heart to the magic of Hawaii as being one of my favorite places on earth.

We replenished our Mai Tai drinks and relaxed for the rest of the afternoon, enjoying hula exhibitions by gorgeous Hawaiian girls wearing exotic hula skirts, which was matched by handsome, young, colorfully dressed Hawaiian men that serenaded us with ukulele music and local songs. We stayed until sundown, which is an experience not to be missed. The sky turned bright red with rainbows abounding, as the sun inched out of sight into the horizon to the moans and sighs of the delighted spectators. We returned to our hotel exhausted from the pleasures of the day and went directly to our room for a peaceful night's sleep.

We woke late the next morning and decided to enjoy the exotic tropical breakfast buffet at the hotel. It was surprising to see the variety of Japanese food presented: miso soup, rice, and even sushi were scattered throughout the maze of food. Looking around explained the reason; about two-thirds of the guests were Japanese who were enjoying sushi with all of its trimmings. It's difficult, when looking around the city or dining room, to believe that the Japanese lost World War II. It seems that what they couldn't conquer during hostilities they succeeded in conquering during peacetime, as the sushi bars and restaurant menus were mainly in their language and English menus in many eateries were available only upon request. Japanese food has always been one of Barbara's favorite indulgences and that morning was no exception. She couldn't stop raving about how wonderful the food was. I satisfied myself with cereal, eggs, and plenty of sweet pieces of Hawaiian pineapple, which I couldn't seem to get enough of.

After breakfast, we picked up a walking map of the area and decided to walk in the direction of Diamond Head Crater, which was a short distance from our hotel and is part of the Kapiolani Park complex. The 500-acre park was created by King Kalakaua in the late 19th century and is home to the famous Kodak Hula Show, the world-renowned 42-acre Honolulu Zoo, and the Waikiki Shell Amphitheater. It has tennis courts, soccer fields, an archery range, and a three-mile joggers' course, but the most spectacular jewel is its beach with the historic Diamond Head Crater in the background. We brought beach mats with us and the first thing we did was spread them under a shady picnic beach area and spend the better part of an hour sipping our coffee while absorbing the heavenly beauty of nature's gifts to us and the very lucky residents of Hawaii. The respite gave me some time to read about the fascinating history of the Diamond Head Crater:

> It's considered one of the most famous dormant volcanic craters in the world, located on the Southeast coast of Oahu at the end of Waikiki Beach, overlooking the Pacific Ocean. It was originally named *Laeahi* by the ancient Hawaiians. The name meant 'brow of the tuna' and looking at the silhouette of the crater from Waikiki you can see the resemblance. The current name was

> given to the crater by British sailors in the early 19th century. When they first saw the crater from a great distance, the calcite crystals in the lava rock appeared to glimmer in the sunlight. The sailors mistakenly thought there were diamonds in the soil and hence they named it Diamond Head. The crater has been extinct for over 150,000 years. It's 3,520 feet in diameter with a 760-foot summit.

Here is what makes it one of the most unusual craters in the world: "When the United States annexed Hawaii in 1898, its harbor defense became one of the government's main concerns. A major defense facility, Fort Ruger, occupied the crater. A battery of cannons were located within the crater, providing complete concealment and protection from invading enemies. An observation deck was constructed at the summit in 1910 to provide target sighting with a four-level underground complex, built within the walls of the crater as a command post. A 580-foot tunnel was dug through the crater wall to provide easier access to the fort. With the advent of radar, the observation deck and underground complex has been abandoned, but evidence of the command post is still present along the Diamond Head Trail. The trail is paved almost its entire length, but is very steep in spots. There are two sets of stairs, one with 99 steps and the other with 76 steps. There is also a 225-foot unlit tunnel. A hike up the mountain is classified as easy to moderate in exertion, but is certainly worth the breathtaking, unparalleled view of the entire west side of the island, from Waikiki to Koki Head." The history was fascinating to read, and even though walking to the top of the crater was considered "easy," we decided to have a relaxing day and just hang around the lower part of the park.

We followed the sound of island music and arrived at the Kodak Hula Show, where we were greeted by beautifully dressed young girls in hula skirts, with leis around their necks and flowered tiaras sitting on top of their long, black, shiny hair. They greeted us with *alohas* and put leis around our necks while they wriggled their hips and waved their arms to the rhythm of the tropical music. The Kodak Hula Show has been a Hawaiian tradition since 1937. The fabulous outdoor spectacular is an historical look at the island through the beauty of the hula performed by Hawaiian native dancers. The show being performed featured a cast of 40 entertainers from the Royal Hawaiian Glee Club. The dancers were dressed in traditional skirts made of green Ti Leaves, coconut bras, and fragrant flowered leis in their hair. The performance was conducted at the Shell Amphitheater and is probably the most synchronized, harmonious, and beautifully choreographed dances that I have ever seen. The music seemed to be coming from within the dancers as they moved around the stage performing soft, flowing, sensual motions in harmony with one another. I must say that Hawaiian dancing and music are integral parts of why so many people love these beautiful islands and why I am so captivated with the magic of it all.

Another incredible attraction was the world-renowned 42-acre Honolulu Zoo, which is unique in many ways. It has an African Savannah with lions, giraffes, zebras, elephants, and many other animals, as well as an abundance of birds. What makes it an unusual place to visit is that it features moonlight tours so that visitors can enjoy wildlife in their evening environments, especially observing nocturnal animals that normally sleep by day, such as skunks, toads, snow leopards, red foxes, raccoons, possums, hedgehogs, fireflies, and badgers. To make a visit more interesting, they have overnight camping on sites where participants bring their own camping equipment and set up for the evening in designated areas, close to the Savannah. Supervised feeding of the animals is allowed. I heard one young girl that spent an evening with her family in the park talking about how she visited the hippo den and fed an apple to a 4,000-pound animal, from a distance, of course. She saw that I was interested in her adventure and excitedly told me of being escorted by the zookeeper to a hyena's home at feeding time and helping him feed the hungry family. I asked her what her most memorable experience was and she said, "Trying to avoid the toads at night, which seemed to be all over the walking paths and were attracted to everyone's flashlights." Her happiest experience was when Pizza King delivered pizzas, sodas, garlic nuggets, and doughnuts. Not an unpleasant way to spend a night out with the family. If we ever return with our kids, we most certainly will spend some quality time at the zoo with them.

We returned to our hotel for a nap, which was becoming a necessary, every day event due to our excessive walking and the soothing sea air that seemed to relax us and make us sleepy. We visited our concierge, Jackson, and asked if there were any good dancing venues close by. He suggested the Hilton Hawaiian Village Beach Resort and the Pink Palace. We asked him to make reservations at the Hilton for dinner and for whatever entertainment that was available for the evening, and to do the same for the Pink Palace for the following evening. We headed to our room and immediately visited dreamland for a much-needed nap; we were so exhausted that we didn't even whisper our usual pre-slumber niceties.

We arrived at the Hilton Hawaiian Hotel just in time to hear loud horn-like sounds coming from conch shells, announcing the end of daylight and the beginning of the Lighting of Torches Ceremony throughout the tropical area to the beat of island drums, singing, and fireworks. We were again greeted by beautiful girls, who pleasantly placed leis around our necks while gyrating their voluptuous hips to the rhythm of the native drums. It certainly was a great way to put us in the mood for an enjoyable time, especially when their second act was to put Mai Tai drinks in our hands. We were seated facing the manmade enormous Duke Kahanemoku Lagoon, and were startled to see a large canoe with about a dozen Hawaiian fisherman land on the Great Lawn in front of us, which signaled the start of the night's *luau*. The Hawaiian fishermen began to mingle with guests, inviting them to learn and dance the *Hukilau*, a traditional song and dance that tells about fishermen and their catch of the day. It was so spontaneous and exciting; we were actually imitating the men doing the *Hukilau* dance within a few minutes while trying to catch and sing the words to the "*Hukilau* Song." There are many versions of the song; I think the one we sang went something like this:

"What a wonderful day for fishing in the old Hawaiian way, where the *Hukilau* nets are swishing down in Old Laie Bay. Oh, we're going to a *Hukilau*, a huki-huki-huki-huki *Hukilau*. Everybody loves a *Hukilau*, where the *laulau* is the *kaukau* at the big *luau*. We throw our nets out into the sea, and all the *ama-ama* come a-swimming to me. Oh we're going to a *Hukilau*, a huki-huki-huki-huki-huki *Hukilau*."

What a great time we had imitating fishermen casting their nets upon the sea and then retrieving them with their catch of the day. We enacted this to the rhythm of the "*Hukilau* Song" as we swayed our hips and arms, trying to imitate the Hawaiian men's motions. While we were still in motion, we were escorted to the *imu* (underground oven) to see the ceremonial removal of the cooked pig from the *imu* and its preparation for the forthcoming feast. The *luau* menu included kalua pig, poi, iomi-iomi salmon, and cold selections, such as island-style macaroni salad and seasonal fruit. Other hot items included grilled huli-huli chicken, mahi-mahi with macadamia nuts, creamed spinach, rice, taro, and sweet rolls. Desserts included haupia, macadamia nut cream pie, coconut cake, and guava cake. To add insult to injury, where our diets were concerned, Mai Tais were included in the price of the feast. We usually try to be very selective and to limit our food intake, but between the two of us that evening, we couldn't help sampling almost everything on the menu.

We needed the long walk back to our hotel to work off the heavy meal and delicious, potent drinks. We swore that we would never again consume such large quantities of food and beverages, and decided that the next day we would avoid any place that had elaborate or tempting food selections. So we spent the next day hanging around the hotel's swimming pool and working out at the gym, hopefully working off some of the calories we forced into our bodies, so unwillingly, the night before (pun intended). We visited our concierge, Jackson, who reminded us that the dress code at the Pink Palace was not casual and that we had an eight o'clock reservation for dinner and dancing. We dressed accordingly and put on our most comfortable shoes for some serious dancing. Entering the large dining hall was a throwback to the WWII era. A large, 17-piece band, its members dressed in tuxedoes, resembled scenes from some of John Wayne's war movies, especially when seeing the many naval officers dressed in formal white U.S. Navy uniforms throughout the hall. The venue has been a naval hangout since the beginning of WWII and, evidently, continues to be a favorite of the sailors stationed in Hawaii. We danced, danced, and danced around the ballroom and on the enormous outside terrace overlooking the Pacific Ocean, surrounded by the distant flames of torches, which not only kept the mosquitoes away, but provided a very romantic setting for slow dancing. The side views from the terrace of Waikiki Beach's glowing nightlights added to the ambiance and mood of the evening. I was surprised at the number of people, especially sailors that were not only dancing acceptable smooth ballroom dancing and swing, but were also quite good at Latin mambo, cha-cha, and meringue. We had a special treat that evening: Martin Denny was in the audience and was asked to play some of his popular music, which he did without hesitation and with a big smile on his face. He played the piano to perfection, entertaining us with "A Taste of Honey," "The Enchanted Sea," and "Ebb Tide." Unfortunately, he didn't have members of his band with him; if he did, we would have heard some of his exotic Hawaiian music. His writings and performances with unusual percussion instruments brought life back to many old standards, such as "Flamingo" and "Sayonara." We ended the evening with a conga line dance, where the guests lined up in back of each other and moved around the floor to the music of "Locomotion." Somehow, I found myself at the beginning of the line leading 100-plus guests to the beat of the music, while everyone was singing "do the locomotion," and moving their arms back and forth, imitating a locomotive train. The dance ended our evening and our 25th "Anniversary Waltz" with the heavenly Islands of Hawaii.

Our Second Trip to Paradise

When our son and daughter-in-law told us they were leaving Korea and would be relocating to the Army's Schofield Barracks in Hawaii, which is about 20 minutes from Waikiki Beach, Barbara and I immediately began to pack our bags for our second trip to that "heavenly wonderland." It had been over ten years since we promised the Hawaiian gods that we would return, and lo and behold, here we were flying first to Los Angeles for a plane change and then to Honolulu. One of the last memorable times we had with the kids was over four years ago in Washington, D.C. We were celebrating my daughter-in-law, Donna, receiving the "General Douglas MacArthur Leadership Award," which is bestowed on twenty Army officers annually for their leadership qualities. The awards were presented by Secretary of State Alexander Haig and the Chairman of the Joint Chiefs of Staff, General Dennis

Reimer. We had no idea how important and prestigious the award was until we saw the high-profile people that were honoring these young Army officers. The recipients were individually presented with a bust of General MacArthur, a wristwatch, and an inscribed pen and pencil set, in addition to a fancy gold medal. After the ceremony, we attended a cocktail party where Donna introduced us to her commanding officer, a two-star general whose name I don't recall. I asked him what she did to deserve such recognition, and he said: "The best person to ask is your daughter." I asked her, and she said: "I don't know, I only did my job." Not the answers that I was looking for, so I nosed around and asked some more questions. The best information I could get was that she was in Desert Storm, and being that she had a law degree, they thought the best job for her in the Army would be as a bodyguard for a field general; this is very common reasoning in the military. She evidently did an exemplary job in Saudi Arabia and her many years in the military. I was satisfied with whatever little information I gathered and as proud as could be, especially when we were given a private tour of the General Douglas MacArthur Museum in the Pentagon and saw a plaque with award recipients' names listed. There it was, Lt. Donna Bivona, listed on the honor roll. It was truly a seminal moment, seeing our family name "Bivona" in such a prestigious place of honor in one of our Nation's most celebrated buildings.

We were primed for our next trip to the Hawaiian Islands and thrilled to be staying with our children in their home and getting a little taste of what it's like to actually live as a local on the Island of Oahu. I decided to do some research on the customs of Hawaiians so we could be better prepared to live among them on our upcoming journey. *Aloha, Aloha, Aloha,* is a word that is heard every minute of every day when traveling through the islands. What does it really mean? It certainly is one of the most beautiful words in the Hawaiian language and conjures up all sorts of beautiful images, such as hula girls dancing, waves embracing the beaches, palm trees swaying in a soft breeze, colorful dresses and shirts, and flowers of every description in bloom year round, lending their fragrances to receptive breaths of fresh air. The word *Aloha* has come down through the ages and doesn't have one meaning, but a combination of meanings that describe its use:

A – means welcome, what I have you may have, share with me.
L – comes from the Hawaiian word *loko maikai*, which means, what I have said comes from my heart and good intentions.
O – comes from the Hawaiian word *oluolu*, meaning happy, this is part of their heritage – a happy people, happy doing for others.
H – comes from the word *haahaa* meaning humility and meekness; we welcome you; we do things for you because we are happy doing it and are very humble to serve.
A – all of these expressions mean *Aloha* and should only be used when you feel them in your heart.

Well, that certainly explained the pleasant attitudes of the Hawaiians that we met on our previous trip. Knowing its history certainly would give us all the more reason to use the word with a lot more understanding and humility.

Another custom is the *shaka,* which is a hand movement that means "hang loose, everything is cool, bruddah." It is done using the thumb and pinky of your hand and doing a little wriggle. It's a friendly gesture and is done with good intentions, similar to our saying, "have a good day" while tipping your hat. It's believed that the traditional *shaka* originated in ancient times when a great chief lost his three middle fingers in an accident. Thereafter, he would greet his subjects by waving the altered hand at them. They, in turn, not to show any disrespect, would respond in the same manner.

Another tradition that is found throughout the islands is the ceremony of *luau*. It has significance far beyond its being considered a BBQ. A *luau* means: "good food, drink, music, dance, conviviality and fun, usually set against a background of a blazing tropical sunset." To ancient Hawaiians it was all this and more, since it was also an appropriate time to thank the gods for good fortune and to ask for future blessings. Among the ancients, the gods were involved in every earthly activity, ruling over birth, marriage, death, war, seasons, sports, skills, and all daily happenings. Major events in the life of a village were commemorated with a communal feast, which was originally called an *ahaaina* and is now referred to as a *luau.* It was only natural that these celebrations should be dedicated to the particular god, or gods, who held primary influence over the event. For instance, a feast celebrating the gathering of crops would be especially sacred to *Lono*, the harvest god. The gods had their favorite *luau* foods: Kalua pig, baked in an underground oven called an *imu*, and chicken were traditional offerings. No *luau* could be complete without the Hawaiian staff of life, *taro*. It's the tender young leaf of the plant called *luau*, from which the current name of the feast is derived; it is cooked with coconut cream and the roots pounded into poi.

While Hawaiian gods now live mainly in folklore, many ancient *luau* traditions still survive. The pig is still ceremoniously baked in the *imu*, and poi is still a favorite food, eaten by people with their fingers. Hula dancing may have modernized, but many implements used in the dance, such as the *ipu* or gourd, recall olden times. In ancient days, the hula was a sacred ritual performed for the gods. The dancers, who dedicated themselves to the goddess Laka, spent many years learning their art. Accompanied by gourd drums and chants, the dancers celebrated the heroic exploits and wondrous feats of the all-powerful gods. Most importantly, the spirit of *luau* still creates a festive atmosphere of companionship, relaxation, and enjoyment, and still remains the same as in the days of the ancients.

With a better understanding of Hawaiian customs, we were ready to journey part way around the world to visit our children and, hopefully, spend some time enjoying the camaraderie of the friendly natives. The kids' new home was in a town called Waialua on the island of Oahu. I looked the location up on the Internet and found the following information: "Waialua is one of the communities that make up the north shore of Oahu. Recreational activities include snorkeling, fishing, sailing, scuba diving, swimming, surfing, and more. The Turtle Bay Resort, in Kahuku, with 36 holes of some of America's best golf, is nearby. Kaiaka Bay Beach Park and Haleiwa Aii Beach Park are both located in the Waialua area, and each is a great spot for parties, swimming, or just hanging out at the beach. Sightseers can visit rainforests, waterfalls, beaches, and art galleries, or take an amazing helicopter tour around the island. It is situated just 30 miles from downtown Honolulu and 20 minutes from Schofield Barracks." We couldn't wait to get there.

The kids were very mysterious about where they lived and wouldn't tell us anything about their new home. They said: "We want to surprise you." When we arrived at their home, we were certainly surprised. They were living in a three-bedroom, two-level house, with a 200-foot-long back yard, leading to the most gorgeous beach in the world. My heart doubled its pace when I saw the view. After unpacking, I laid out on the hammock hanging from the ceiling of the terrace facing the ocean, nursing a tropical drink, when my son Steve asked me: "Dad, did I do the right thing in renting this house instead of living on the base at Schofield Barracks, which is a lot less expensive?" My answer was spontaneous. I said, "Steve, if I were your age I couldn't think of a more beautiful place on earth that I would rather be than right here, on this hammock, looking at the ocean. I don't know what could possibly make me happier." Then he said, "Dad we have another surprise for you." At that moment, I heard Barbara let out a scream from inside the house where she was hugging Donna, as she yelled: "You're pregnant!" That said it all. We hugged and kissed; our first grandchild was on its way. It was one of the happiest moments in my life.

Steve decided to have a cook-out on the beach and invited some of their Army buddies and neighbors for the feast. Steve has always been a great chef and especially enjoyed doing BBQs. About 12 of their friends arrived to the smell of hot dogs, burgers, and spareribs roasting on their oversized pit. I couldn't believe the whole scene; it was dreamlike. We came to see our kids, who were in the military and had just returned from tours of duty in Korea, and were expecting to see them in the drab surroundings of a military base. But instead, here we were on a beach in their backyard, enjoying the surf, tropical fruit drinks, spareribs, and the camaraderie of their friends; what an exquisite turn of events from what we expected. The food had a special flavor, which was enhanced by the smell of fresh sea air, the pale blue sky with an ensemble of various-shaped clouds, the sound of the waves caressing the beach, pleasant company, and, of course, my pregnant daughter-in-law. After our feast, as if rehearsed, everyone donned their swimsuits and ran pell-mell into the delicious turquoise-blue surf, screaming and howling at the pleasure of the water splashing their bodies. While we were swimming and horsing around, we were joined by a neighbor's two Labrador retrievers who couldn't resist an opportunity to join the excitement and add to the splashing and clamor. The setting of the sun was another spectacular event. It made the sky look as if it were on fire, bright-red and orange colors blending in with the clouds and then, very gently, disappearing out of sight beyond the horizon. Steve lit a camp fire and we started roasting marshmallows as we sang. One of the guys magically produced a guitar and began playing Hawaiian songs, including "Tiny Bubbles (tiny bubbles), in the wine (in the wine), makes me happy (makes me happy) . . ." What a memorable way to end our first day in Hawaii with our family, their jovial friends, and the serendipitous surrounding of nature's landscape beaming with perfection.

Waking to the sounds of waves hitting the beach the next morning, gave me an irresistible urge to rush and take a swim; I ran as quickly as I could and dove, head first, into the surf, with my eyes wide open so I wouldn't miss any marine underwater sights. Exiting the water, eyes burning from the salt and my lungs consuming the fresh sea air, I thought I must have died and gone to heaven, so exhilarating and enjoyable was the experience. Steve, who is one of the best chefs around, whipped up my favorite blueberry pancakes for breakfast, which we quickly devoured to the pleasant sounds of "Wow, more, more." He then asked what we would like to do for the day. Barbara and I agreed that we wouldn't mind hanging around their beach, as we still had jet lag from the long flight, and would need rest for the dancing we had in mind for that evening. We asked Steve and Donna if they would like to join us for an evening of dancing at the Ali Wai Country Club; they said yes. So, after dining on delicious leftover food from the BBQ, my son drove us to Waikiki Beach and the dance hall, which took about 45 minutes.

We couldn't believe the size of the dance floor: 12,000 square feet of open space. What was immediately noticeable was that there were no tables for the patrons to sit at in the hall; just chairs strategically located around the floor, so as not to interfere with the performers or take up valuable dance space. As we are members of the Royal Palm Beach Chapter of the United States Amateur Ballroom Dance Association (USABDA), we were invited in for a discounted $3.00 charge and were seated with some of the officers of the Hawaiian Ballroom Dance

Association (HBDA). We were treated as if we were old friends by many of the members, and were bombarded with questions about dancing on the Mainland (U.S.A.). There were over 400 people in attendance, which we were told is a minimal crowd. The venue has functions that hold between 700 to 800 people, especially when competitions are held at the magnificent hall. The dance music was provided by a DJ, who was located on a small platform outside the perimeter of the dance floor, as not to interfere with the flow of dancing traffic. They have a unique method of communicating the dance that is to be performed; a placard, which is about two feet by four feet wide and located above the DJ's platform, is displayed announcing the current dance. This is the dance that everyone must do or they are chastised. We didn't notice anyone who was not conducting themselves properly or being reprimanded for not adhering to proper dancing etiquette. Their dance style of preference was International Style. It's a pleasure to watch hundreds of people dancing smoothly, in the line of direction, with few collisions and all doing the same dance. There were some people dancing American Style, but they followed the same rules and blended in nicely with the International Style dancers, that is, except for us. A tango was flashed on the board, so Barbara and I decided to do an Argentine tango. We immediately had a circle of people around us watching us do our sways, *ochos*, *ganchos*, *boleos*, and kicks. We received applause as we danced in closed position. I moved slowly away from Barbara, putting her in an outstretched position on one foot, the other foot raised halfway up. When fully extended, I moved her around in a circle going about 180 degrees, and then gently facing her, closed the position with a caress. Most of the people had never seen Argentine tango performed up close and were excited at our sensual presentation. We received many handshakes and polite bows. Steve and Donna couldn't believe the reaction the "old folks" received, and joined in the camaraderie that usually follows a dancing exhibition.

We especially enjoyed doing foxtrots and waltzes, as there was ample room to move around the dance floor and perform many of the steps and routines that we love so much. There is a routine that Barbara and I learned many years ago from our Russian instructor Alec that can be performed in the foxtrot and waltz. However, it requires a lot of space, which is not usually available at most dance halls back home. We were able to do the routines several times on the spacious floating eucalyptus dance floor. It was amusing to observe one mishap on the floor between two couples; they briefly brushed into each other and immediately stopped and apologized, while bowing profusely. Considering that more than half the people in the hall were Japanese, it wasn't surprising to see bowing going on all over the place, while greeting people, apologizing, or just saying good night. I noticed that Steve and Donna were almost enjoying themselves dancing; neither had much experience on the dance floor, but they were good sports about being with us, and didn't complain about hanging out with old timers.

The HBDA had a formation competition that evening. The clubs throughout the Hawaiian Islands came to perform their specialty dances. There were more than a dozen chapters present, each wearing their respective colors while parading their incredibly beautiful costumes. We were told that many of the outfits were handmade and had significant traditions attached to them. Pom-poms were displayed on many of the outfits, as well as frills and sequences in every imaginable color and shape. The dancing began with the Maui Chapter performing their formation dance, which consisted of about a dozen dancers doing a cha-cha. It started very much like a line dance, with dancers lined up in starting positions, and then proceeding into dance steps and routines with lots of partners changing positions with each other. The dance was synchronized to perfection, which, without a doubt, probably takes an inordinate amount of practice and patience to accomplish. We were pleasantly surprised at the different routines each team had for doing a cha-cha. Deciding the winning team could not have been an easy task for the judges, as they were all top-of-the-line dancers and incredibly proficient formation dancers. We ended the evening with refreshments: cake and cookies, and lots of bowing and handshakes from our newfound friends. We promised to return as often as we could and then bid our fellow dancers good night.

We woke up the next morning to the ever-present sound of the waves dancing on the beach, but this morning I noticed another delicious delight. The smell of pineapples seemed to fill the air. I asked Donna if she was preparing breakfast that included pineapples; she responded in the negative, saying that the aroma was coming from the Dole Plantation, which was a few miles from their home. It was another pleasant surprise as I imagined how wonderful it must be to smell the delicious pineapple fragrance year round. Steve had the day planned for us; we were visiting the Polynesian Cultural Center (PCC), which is also located on the northern part of Oahu and a short ride from their house. The Church of Latter-day Saints (Mormons) owns and operates the 42-acre Polynesian living museum. Each of the major Polynesian countries has its own area in the park, centered on a replica of a traditional village. Hawaii, Samoa, Aotearoa (New Zealand), Fiji, Tahiti, Tonga, and the Marquesas all have models of living villages prior to the Western world's intrusion into their somewhat peaceful and uncomplicated existence. Each village is inhabited by native students who received scholarships and represent their respective islands. They attend Hawaii's Brigham Young University, and work 20 hours a week during school days and full time between semesters. Working at the park allows the students to attend the university at no charge and to graduate debt free. Upon entering the PCC, there was an exhibit tracing the immigration of the natives to their respective islands and the history behind their migration. There was lots of zigzagging by the natives from island to island, and following the lineage of some of the tribes got a little confusing. Just beyond the center was the Hawaii Temple of the Church, which was built from volcanic rock and concrete in the form of a Greek cross and was surrounded by beautiful reflecting pools, formal gardens, and royal palm trees. Both the Hawaii Church and Brigham Young University were open to visitors, with guided tours available. The park also boasts a huge IMAX theatre and a lagoon where visitors can take rides from one end of the park to the other, visiting the numerous replicated villages.

Okay, where do we start? We decided to purchase VIP passes, which included preferred seating at the evening *luau*. We were given *kukui* beads, which are black and are made from nuts, to identify us as VIP guests. Due to the size of the place and the limited amount of time that we had, we figured that the best approach would be a narrated canoe ride around the lagoon, visiting as many villages as possible. We also had to coordinate our visits to the scheduled show times of each village, which usually lasted from 30 minutes to one hour. In addition, we wanted to join the festivities of Hawaii's largest *luau* and the spectacular evening show, "Horizons: Where the Sea Meets the Sky."

Samoa was our first stop. We were greeted by the beautiful natives with *talofa,* which is their equivalent to the Hawaiian's affectionate *aloha.* The response to this warm greeting is *talofa lava.* The Island of Samoa is located almost 2,500 miles to the southwest of Hawaii, and is in the middle of the Polynesian Triangle. It is sometimes called the "Heart of Polynesia." Their show consisted of demonstrations that take place on the *malae* (grassy area), surrounded by examples of Samoan *fale* (houses). A large, high-roofed *maota tofa* (high chief's house) had distinctive carved beams and coconut-sennit lashings. The other natives live in smaller houses called *fale nofo* surrounding a community kitchen (*tunoa*). The natives invited us to learn how to make fire by rubbing two sticks together, how to crack open a coconut, and how to distinguish the difference between coconut juice and milk. In their society, the men do all the cooking and coconut picking, which was demonstrated by a race between several men climbing 40-foot-high trees and retrieving as many coconuts as possible. Whoever gathered the most coconuts and cracked and peeled them won the competition. It was amazing watching the men climbing trees and then stripping the coconuts off their shells in a matter of minutes. The men also performed a fire dance, where spinning a fire log up and around their bodies was done with precision and was highlighted by sucking the flames into their mouths. I actually had to close my eyes to avoid seeing any mishaps; fortunately, there were none. Bravo to those brave lads!

The infamous Island of Fiji from days gone by was our next stop. The earliest European explorer to sight the island in 1643 was a Dutch sailor named Abel Tasman, after whom Tasmania would later be named. Due to the war-like greeting received from the locals, he quickly left the area. Captain Cook also reached the same conclusion when he visited the island in 1774. The greatly maligned Captain Bligh came closest to landing on the island, but left pell-mell when the natives' war canoes approached his vessel and chased him off. Although he never explored the island, the bay that he dropped anchor in is called Bligh's Water.

They were all fortunate to have fled, as the natives were cannibals and notorious for dining on neighboring tribes or any ill-fated explorers who crossed their paths. The island is located about 2,500 miles to the west-southwest of Hawaii and is also on the border of the Polynesian Triangle. About half of the population of modern Fiji is of East Indian descent, which gives the island a unique cosmopolitan flavor. Our greeting, fortunately, was from friendly non-cannibalistic natives; *bula* is their greeting for good health, and *bula vinaka* is the appropriate response. The most dominant feature of the village was the *bure kalou* (spirit house). Its high-reaching roof is considered a landmark and one of the most distinctive structures at the PCC. Face-painted Fijian warriors performed a war dance with spears, machetes, lots of leaps and noises, and the most unusual distorted facial expressions, which included extending their tongues out about 12 inches. All of this was intended to terrify their opponents in battle. While it may have worked in their war-like days, it was now very comical to the audience. The more intense their fearsome facial expressions, the louder the we laughed. The warriors didn't seem to mind the opposite effect that their terrifying facial expressions had on the spectators; as a matter of fact, they seemed to rather enjoy our response.

The "Rainbows of Paradise" show was to be performed on the lagoon at two different locations, simultaneously. After leaving the Fiji Village, we decided to remain in the area, which was the wider section of the lagoon. The show started with a young Polynesian girl in an outrigger canoe throwing flowers on the water. It is said that each blossom becomes a memory of a visit to Hawaii, and each blossom that returns to shore will insure that the visitor will return. The sounds of the conch shells signaled the arrival of the Hawaiian *alii nui* (high chief) and his followers. The chief proudly displayed a royal cape, helmet, and sash, which were made from choice red and gold plumage of hundreds of birds, who are set free after a few of their feathers are taken. The chief's wife (*alii*) wore a yellow dress, while her attendant's dresses were red. The first dance aboard the double-hulled canoes was *Hula Kahiko,* which began the ancient sounds of drums and chants. The music then shifted to the more modern island sound of the ukulele and guitar and the more familiar songs of Hawaii.

Soon the Tongans appeared on their double-hulled canoe and greeted everyone with *malo e lelei* (good health) as they performed their traditional island dances; the audience's response was *malo aupito* (thank you). The dancers wore red, representing the beautiful red morning skies of their friendly island Tonga. The hip and hand motions of the natives were spellbinding and communicated their love and friendship to everyone watching. The natives are known for their aggressive drumming and rhythmic beats, which they performed with great energy and chanting, while the spectators followed the beats with clapping and feet stomping.

The call of *Tahiti e imua* was followed by the appearance of a large Tahitian canoe on the lagoon. The dancers were dressed in yellow and orange as a gift of honor to *Mahana,* the Sun God. The beautiful Tahitian women, whose ancestors were, without a doubt, partly responsible for the "Mutiny on the Bounty" saga, hadn't lost their charming glow centuries after the notorious event. It's no wonder that Mr. Christian and his mates chose to stay on the beautiful Island of Tahiti and comingle with its beautiful girls rather than spend additional years on the rat-infested *Bounty.* The magic of "Tahiti's Love Call" could be felt throughout the lagoon as the beautiful maidens danced and welcomed visitors with their hand motions to join in their festive mood.

The Maori warriors of *Aotearoa* (New Zealand) came out howling and chanting war cries, as their canoe zigzagged the lagoon. Twirling poi balls and spears, they shouted their *haka* challenges to any and all who would meet them in combat. They were dressed in green as a tribute to "Tane," the Maori god of the lush ferns and forests; precious *pounamu* (greenstone jade) decorated their necks and wrists. The soldiers were fearsome in appearance as they threatened the audience with their aggressive motions and chanting. I was glad when they left my sight. The women, on the other hand, were peacefully sparkled in their colorful red skirts of reeds and beads and performed intricate maneuvers with balls attached to long strings, while balancing their matching feathered headpieces. I was not happy to see them leave the stage as they brought a breath of fresh air to the area.

A friendly Samoan's canoe was hard pressed to balance itself from the exuberance and energy of the hula dancers. The traditional *lavalava* costumes of the men and the *puletasi* outfits of the women were in shades of magenta and pink to honor the beautiful sunsets of their South Pacific island. The natives sang and danced to the rhythm of their drums and chants, and coaxed the audience to join them in singing and hula dancing. The girls threw flower blossoms at the audience and into the lagoon, which had the effect of a snow-flaked blossom shower from the heavens.

Tomi, tomai, was the call of the chief as he again beckoned the Fiji warriors and their canoe. The fighters appeared, doing a dance ritual to the warrior deity "Dengei." The girls wore bark cloth bearing beautiful traditional patterns of natural tones. The men were fierce in their appearance and expressions. The soldiers' faces were decorated with war paint and their spears and poi balls were displayed with aggressive motions. Many wore tattoos with threatening designs; their war-like facial expressions included extending and distorting their tongues in a frightening manner, which got the attention of everyone in the audience. I was glad when their noisy performance finally ended. Their aggressive act was the finale of the Rainbows of Paradise Show.

After the show, we visited the New Zealand Village and were greeted with *kia ora* (good health). The natives call their homeland *Aitearia* meaning "Land of the Long White Cloud." This island forms the southwestern apex of the Polynesian Triangle and is the only one that experiences four seasons. This is immediately apparent by the different clothing that they wore and the types of buildings in their village, which are quite different from their tropical cousins. The appropriate response to the Maori's greeting is also *kia ora,* which the spectators learned to respond to each time the natives sent a greeting. The Maori put on a demonstration that explained the symbolic significance of their beautiful meeting house, unique carvings, facial tattoos, their ancient origins, and the meaning of sticking out their tongues and twirling poi balls. All revolved around their war-like society and their fierce warriors. We learned how to play *tititoea,* a stick game designed to develop hand-eye coordination, and, with much difficulty, how to swing poi balls. Many of the audience volunteered to receive temporary tattoos. Some tattoos were beautiful, such as those with flowers, but others were not as peacefully artistic, symbolizing dragons and demons in threatening positions. The village was a fortified compound that enclosed a *maraw* (open area) that was surrounded by several key structures, including a carved entrance where traditional fighting challenges are issued. The focal point was the *whare runanga* (meeting house), where most presentations and important events in Maori tribal life occur. The central attraction of the village was the Maori's 40-man war canoe, which was humungous, but evidently quite stable, as we witnessed during their war-like presentation in the Rainbows of Paradise Show.

We were greeted with *malo e lelei* (good health) by the natives when we visited their Tonga village. Our response was also a hearty *malo e lelei.* The Kingdom of Tonga is an archipelago in the South Pacific Ocean consisting of 169 islands, 36 of them inhabited. They lie south of Samoa and are about one-third of the way from New Zealand to Hawaii. It's the only surviving monarchy among the island nations of the Pacific, as well as the only island nation never to have been formally colonized. The Islands are known as the "Friendly Isles" due to their friendly reception of Captain Cook in 1773. They demonstrated their *ta nafa* (drumming presentation) and taught us the simple, yet graceful motions of a *mauluulu* (sitting dance), which we practiced while beating on their drums after the show. We were also invited to play *lafo* (a type of shuffleboard game) and to try our accuracy at *tolo* (spear throwing). We tried both, and I must say we were better at shuffleboard than we were at throwing the long spears. The village consisted of a one-quarter scale model of the late Queen Salote's summer palace, which was originally constructed and supervised by her. Inside the palace were a meeting house, a common family dwelling, a cook house, and a game house that contained a version of a shuffleboard playing surface. The people of the village were so friendly and outstandingly beautiful that I felt like spending the rest of the day just hanging around and talking to them about their beautiful lifestyle and pleasant ways.

We were greeted by our Tahitian hosts with their placing leis around our necks and saying in unison, *laorana* (good health). We responded with *laorana* in return and felt immediately at home. I got lost in the dark brown, soft eyes of the Tahitian girls, which was becoming a habit. The softness of their dark eyes and the inviting nature of Polynesian women gave me the feeling that I belonged among these special people. Who could resist joining the mood of the happy, warm, and inviting natives? Tahiti consists of 100-plus French Polynesian islands. It is located about 2,400 miles southeast of Hawaii and is renowned for the infamous mutiny that took place on the much-maligned Captain Bligh's ship, *HMS Bounty,* in the 18th century. The sailors chose to stay in paradise rather than return to the squalor of a sailor's life aboard a decaying wooden vessel. Since then, the island has represented the dream of escaping to a Polynesian paradise. Tahiti fits the description perfectly, because of its beautiful mountains, balmy climate, emerald and blue lagoons, and warm, inviting people. The women demonstrated their quick hip movements in the hula dance while their hand motions invited us to join them in their sensual dancing. We did and learned some basic hula moves. It didn't take long to learn the hand movements, but it took me a while to get my hips moving in the right direction. They also demonstrated how they make flower and shell leis and invited us to try. So, we all joined in and made leis. Barbara made a beautiful fragrant flower lei and I made one from small irregular sea shells. Many of the guests stayed after the show to learn how to fish the Polynesian way, but we were hungry and decided to take part in an *Alii* (King's) *Luau*, which was just beginning at the other end of the lagoon. We visited some of the Tahitian buildings on our way to the *luau* and were surprised at their similarity to some of the other Polynesian structures. The *fare* (chief's house), the large *heiva* (celebration house), and the *ututu* (kitchen) were surrounded by a plantation and gardens with a fishing hut at the edge of the lagoon. It certainly was a perfect and inviting setting for the undernourished and hard-working sailors of the *Bounty* to retreat to after many months at sea.

We followed the mixed scents coming from the *Alii Luau* and were right on the money by doing so. The sounds of drums and chanting combined with the delicious fragrance and aroma of the food being prepared led us right to the entrance. Our nut beads allowed us to bypass the lines and approach the beautiful, lightly-tanned hostess for our preferred seating as VIP guests. We were seated near the platform where the entertainment would be performed. Cousin Benny Kai, the

PCC's "Ambassador of Aloha," invited everyone by saying, "Whenever you are at a Hawaiian *luau*, you are *ohana (family).*

We accumulated other leis from the Hawaiians at the PCC and couldn't be more receptive of receiving additional fresh fragrant flowers from the ever-smiling and wriggling daughters of the Hawaiian show. To make the event more memorable, we had a souvenir picture taken of me and Barbara with some of the natives. Thirst-quenching pineapple smoothies were available and were just the drinks to get us in the mood for the King's *Luau.* Live Hawaiian music filled the air as the sounds from steel guitars vibrated throughout the palace. Cousin Benny, who was also the master of ceremony, explained the meaning of *luau* and its significance. The performers, wearing fascinating grass skirts, colorful beads, and leis, began the program by singing a *pule* (The Queen's Prayer), which was written by Hawaii's prolific song writer and last reigning monarch, Queen Liliuokalani, while she was imprisoned by the United States Government in her own palace. The song written by this very religious monarch is as follows:

"Your loving mercy is as high as Heaven and your truth so perfect. I live in sorrow, imprisoned. You are my light, your glory my support. Behold not with malevolence the sins of man, but forgive and cleanse. And so, O Lord, protect us beneath your wings and let peace be our portion now and forever more."

The performers' perpetual motion of their hips and the flowing movements of their arms in harmony with the beats of drums and chants made their entrance dreamlike. This was how the beautiful unspoiled natives conducted themselves on a daily basis, before the uninvited Europeans entered their world and altered the way they lived. We were delighted to watch them perform their most stunning routines as exhibitions, to please their guests; unfortunately, the spiritual meanings of the rituals are no longer a realistic part of their lives, but the pleasure of watching such splendor in motion still lives on and is not soon forgotten by those who are fortunate to witness such a display of beauty.

Cousin Benny announced the procession of the Royal Court into the *luau*, consisting of a ruling *Alii* (Chief) and his entourage. He explained their ranks and the significance of their traditional colorful costumes, which included many feathered headbands and long, rainbow-colored robes. The *Alii* invited everyone to partake in the evening's feast and to watch the uncovering of the *imu* (underground oven), which contained a very large pig that was cooking throughout the afternoon and was ready for consumption. The *imu* is a steam oven made up of river rocks heated over firewood at 350 degrees for several hours. When the rocks are sufficiently hot, any remaining firewood is removed, and crushed banana stumps containing lots of water are placed on top of the hot rocks, creating aromatic steam. Then the food is added and covered until cooked to perfection. Multilingual hosts and hostesses directed guests at each table for the all-you-can-eat buffet stations. Cousin Benny announced, "You shouldn't eat till you're full; you should eat till you're dizzy." The music and hula dancing continued throughout dinner and special tropical drinks made our experience all the more enjoyable. I was starting to get a little silly from the refreshing drinks, and actually got up and danced what I thought was a hula with a charming, pretty Hawaiian dancer. We were told, "Every hula tells a story. Graceful hands depict birds, waves, flowers blossoming, rainbows and mountains; while the feet move around the island and hips sway in tempo. Whether the words are in English or Hawaiian, you will understand the meaning of the song as long as you keep your eyes on the dancer's hands."

Beginning to explain what was served on the extensive *luau* buffet is best accomplished by listing the information from the Alii *Luau* Menu, and here it is:

"Poi is a traditional Hawaiian staple. It's a starch dish made by pounding boiled taro roots and mixing them with water until the mixture reaches a smooth consistency. Taro is one of the most nutritious starches on the planet; some eat their poi with salt, some with sugar and some even like it with soy sauce.

"Poke is a raw fish marinated in soy sauce with a dash of seaweed, onions, and other condiments.

"*Lomilomi* salmon: In Hawaiian, *lomilomi* means to massage, or, in this case, to break the salmon into small pieces, which are then mixed with tomatoes, onions and other small condiments, giving it a tangy taste that goes great with poi.

"*Pipi kaula* is seasoned beef jerky, which was first introduced to the islands by European sailors.

"*Kalua puaa* is roasted pork, which is steamed to perfection in an *imu* and is usually seasoned with sea salt and green onions.

"*Moa* is chicken, boiled in the old Polynesian way with Asian teriyaki sauce served over Asian bean noodles.

"Deep-fried filets of flakey, white island fish with Hawaiian sweet potatoes are mixed for a nice cold salad. Taro rolls are baked daily and have a distinctive purple color, derived from the taro flour used in the recipe.

"A variety of salads are offered: tossed greens with carrots and cherry tomatoes, spinach salad, sweet potato salad, fruit ambrosia, and cucumber carrot salad.

"Cold fruits: Ripe pineapple spears, watermelon, papaya, and other fruits in season.

"Beverages (all decaffeinated): Passion-Orange-Guava, Coca Cola, Diet Pepsi, Root Beer, Sprite, Fruit Punch, and herbal teas. (As Mormons, who are the hosts of the PCC, do not drink any caffeinated beverages; they are only served if requested by guests.)

"Desserts include *haupia,* which are sweet custard cubes made with rich coconut cream, guava cake, coconut cake, and chocolate macadamia nut cake."

I guess their menu says it all: a feast of feasts, Hawaiian music, tropical drinks, and beautiful Hawaiian dancers, male and female, performing and mingling amongst the guests. I was tempted to get a nose rub from one of the Polynesian princesses, but Barbara's ever-watchful eyes seemed to always be at my side preventing the event from happening. With full hearts and bellies, we proceeded to the 2,800-seat Pacific Theater to see the evening show, "Horizons: Where the Sea Meets the Sky."

Our VIP tickets again came in handy as we were escorted in the amphitheater to up front, center-aisle seats by a pretty Polynesian hostess, and again given soft, colorful, fragrant leis. The beautiful necklaces were starting to weigh me down, but it was worth every extra ounce around my neck to see the smiles on their stunning faces and the glimmer in their eyes as they placed the flowers over my head and around my neck. Distinguishing between the aromatic fragrances of the flowers making up the leis from the natural fragrance of the native girls was becoming difficult, but trying to make the distinction became a pleasant task for me.

The storyteller announced in a powerful god-like voice: "*Komo mai* (come in) and set your course to *Makalii* (Southern Star) and sail through the horizon to the islands of paradise." As he was speaking, the lights in the huge amphitheater dimmed and a magnificent rainbow waterfall curtain, which I thought was a fixed part of the background, rose to the sound of aggressive drums pounding Polynesian music. All that remained when the water disappeared was the fury of a volcano, making thunderous and threatening sounds.

The Hawaiians were the first to greet us with *ke alaula,* which is a contemporary hula by young girls that expresses the dawning of light and peace that accompanies the break of day. The storyteller announced:

> Here is the procession of the Royal Court. The sounds of the distinctive moan of the conch shells announces the arrival of the King and Queen, accompanied by their entourage and bearers of the feathered royal standards called *kahilis.* Notice how the members of the court are richly arrayed in brilliant capes, leis, and feathered helmets, according to their rank. *Aia La o Pele'* (There is Pele), the fire goddess of ancient Hawaii. We recall a time when man walked and talked with the ancestral gods in the *kahiko,* which is an ancient style of hula and is done to haunting sounds of drums and chants. With *kalaau'* (dancing sticks), the men remember the love found by *Kamohai Mamala,* the shoreline between Honolulu Harbor and Pearl Harbor. *Pihanakalani,* the sound of the nose flute, beckons *Halialaulani,* the maiden, to the top of the mountain on the Island of Kauai. The ceremony *of Alii no Oe* (dancing with split bamboo rattles), is done to tell how men enjoy being treated like kings. The sounding of *E Kuu Sweetie* and *Pili Mau Me oe* start the men dancing, remembering

> their sweethearts and hoping they will be together forever. *Ka anoi,* dancing with the *uliuli* (feathered gourds) and *ipu* (hollowed gourds), starts men and women dancing to honor the beautiful maidens of Kauai. *Ke alaula* (Reprise) tells of the strength of our cultural and spiritual past that leads us to the dawning of a bright new day.

As the god-like voice faded into the background, the Hawaiian portion of the entertainment ended. The dancing and chanting, harmonized with the music as the words of the storyteller, became less audible and the dream-like view evaporated.

The storyteller continued with:

> My heart dances with the joy to the rhythm of the pounding *nafa* (drums), as the dancers from the Island of Tonga perform their sensuous and energetic *maulu ulu* and *lakalaka* movements. They listen for shouts of *malie* (well done) and *lue* (move it), which increases their motion and jubilation. *Ngaahi ongo o e Nafa* calls the community together as the drummers reveal their unity and skill. *Malui a e Atakai* calls for the young men to form two opposing groups to demonstrate their skill with the *kailao* (jabbing spear), in preparation of defending their people. *Tavake taumafua* calls the young women to honor and give tribute to the royalty with their graceful movements and beautiful costumes. *Taumua kuo siumafua* beckons the community to sing and dance the *lakalaka* in celebration of their unified culture and customs and their future destiny, which lies just over the horizon.

The music, dancers, scenery, and the storyteller's voice faded, as the lights dimmed and the Tonga part of the show ended. The young girls' costumes remained in my mind, as they were not the usual hula skirts and leis, but colorful red and white knee-length sun dresses with complementary accessories of dark beads around their necks. White vertical feather headpieces and wrist flowers completed their perfect appearance as children of their Sun God.

Our storyteller continued with:

> Welcome to the land of the long white cloud, where mountains touch the sky each and every day in the island known as New Zealand. *Maori* flutes will play as the women dancers welcome everyone to their magical island of the long white cloud, as the island magically appears in the background. *Taiaha* is the challenging movements of the *taiaha* (fighting lance), which welcomes visitors to enter the *marae,* the ceremonial gathering place. *Whaka eke* is heard by the performers seeking permission to enter the dancing platform on the marae. *Haka KO Te Puru* is also heard when the men and women transform from the ancient to modern styles of dance and music. Through their actions and songs, the men and women combine to invite us to enjoy the traditions of their unique world. Young women are then likened to the grace and the voice of *tui* (beautiful indigenous bird), in the *poi* ball dance. Their last dance is the *Titi Torea.* It is a stick dance that teaches flexibility, rapid reflexes, and quick coordination to prepare everyone for life's constant surprises.

The performance was fast, aggressive, and somewhat scary when you consider the Maori warriors' threatening facial tattoos, fierce swinging poi balls, their extended distorted tongues, and grimacing facial expressions, while yelling and howling their traditional invitations to fight or flee. Fortunately, they were the first to fade into the night scene, leaving an image of the beautiful *Aotearoa* women in my mind as their performance ended.

Intermission time introduced us to "Pineapple Deelites," which consist of half a pineapple with ice cream and island fruits with a colorful umbrella on top. Just what the doctor ordered to refresh us after a long day of enjoying the Hawaiian sun and the exciting Polynesian activities.

The storyteller continued as colorful natives filled the stage:

> I hear my ancestors call me; they speak through the voice of the *lali* (log drum). Come back to my beautiful Island of Fiji. *Vakamalolo,* the chief and his young men welcome you with tokens of acceptance and respect. *Vakarorogo Noda Tuaga* is an aggressive chant and dance telling of warriors who have encountered and fought the enemy and fiercely and courageously defended their people. Through the fan dance, *Raude,* they express gratitude for the land and its beauty, as ancestors who have departed to the land of the spirits are remembered and revered. The Fijian men use their colored war fans and the women their bamboo *derua* to bid farewell to us with a vibrant and energetic music score written for the Polynesian Cultural Center. When Elvis Presley filmed *Paradise Hawaiian Style* at the center in 1965, he had the song arranged in English as 'Drums of the Islands.' Come and sing along with us:
>
> Drums of the islands, you're beating in my heart.
> You're with me no matter where I roam . . .

The scene slowly faded as the performers and the musical number disappeared out of sight and sound.

The storyteller continued:

> The exotic fragrance of the *tiare* flower on the night air, the soft glow of the black pearl, the pulsating drums to the rhythm of the *tamure,* and the magic of a Polynesian moon all whisper: Tahiti. Out of the mist, the sun breaks through and now we are on the mystical Island of Tahiti. Villagers are led by torchbearers and join in a wedding ceremony as Hinakura and her mate, Tane Nui, are united by the chief in marriage. *Otea Amui*—the marriage celebration begins; villagers rejoice in expressing their hopes of youth and love through a traditional dance, the *Otea.* Young maidens join Hinakura, dancing the *Aparima* with poise and

> elegance, followed by the young men and *tane nui* dancing with lively exuberance. Hinakura, through the *Otui* (solo dance), shares her radiant beauty, while Tane Nui shows his strength and agility. *Otea* is the final demonstration of energy, color, and excitement of traditional Tahitian dances at times of celebration.

The handsome, muscular Tahitian men serenading the gorgeous women of their romantic island are idyllic in every sense. The island, which rightly is associated with "Escaping to Paradise," reflects that mysterious image, as these harmonious people ended their affair with the audience by throwing flower petals and kisses, which I actually felt, across the theater.

The storyteller continued with his final narration:

> When the Polynesian demigod Maui, who is known in all the islands, captured the sun, he discovered the power of fire and shared it with the people of Samoa. As the Samoan women come on stage, they begin dancing the *Mauluulu,* which encourages the young men to look toward the future by working hard for a better life. Their motions of the Salsa dance demonstrate the many activities that must be completed in preparation of an important celebration. With rhythmic energy, the young men burst into a traditional slap dance that dazzles the eye and delights the ear. The men accept a challenge to conquer fear by playfully extinguishing fire. Their princess then appears and does a solo dance; she is the daughter of the high chief and invites the villagers to sing, clap, and dance around her to show their happiness and love. They chant and dance, inspired by the volcanic eruption in the background that reminds us that adversity is part of life and that strength comes from unity in the face of danger. Our warriors always show strength and bravery as they perform the traditional Samoan fire knife dance.

The fires from their sticks, swords, and knives diminished with their quick movements, and as they extinguished the flames, the show came to a delightful end.

The extravaganza ended with the entire cast of over 100 performers entering the stage, fully dressed in their various native costumes. A god-like voice reminded us that, "Happiness is here in paradise and beyond the horizon . . ." What an end to a glorious day!

I convinced Barbara to join me in what was becoming my morning ritual of running full speed ahead into the ever-so-sweet turquoise-blue saltwater at the edge of my children's property. What a delightful way to start our day. We decided to spend the day just relaxing and maybe going for a ride to see some of the local sights, but nothing too strenuous, as we planned on returning to the Palladium Dance Hall in the evening for more ballroom dancing. Steve suggested that we visit some of the North Shore's beaches, and hopefully see some world-class surfing. We agreed, and after breakfast, Steve, who is a bit of a historian, gave us some history about the beaches in the area. "The North Shore of Oahu is world renowned as the surfing capital of the world. During the winter months, gigantic swells generate in the North Pacific to produce the most reliable surfing waves on the planet. The two most popular surfing spots are Banzai Pipeline and Waimea Bay, where the Hawaiian Triple Crown is held during December, and transforms the peaceful and quiet area into a world-class championship location, with people from around the world flocking in to witness or participate in the daring sport and unique Hawaiian spectacle. During the summer months, the ocean is placid and safe for swimming, snorkeling, boogie-boarding, diving, and rather safe surfing." Our first stop was the Banzai Pipeline in Ehukai Beach Park, which probably has the most treacherous waves on earth that form a giant tube when they move from deep water on to shallow coral reefs. On days where the waves are ten feet or more, they break in six feet of water, which is challenging and dangerous even to the world's most experienced surfers. The pipeline is "an expert only" area in the winter, but is rather peaceful and safe in the summer months. Our visit was in the summer and I was very pleased to see that many surfers were enjoying themselves riding high, sideways, and then forward on their small tubes. It seemed like many of them were practicing under safe conditions, preparing for the more grueling challenges during the winter season when they search for the "perfect wave." I was surprised that the only hotel nearby was the Turtle Bay Resort, which has a renowned Sunday brunch with panoramic ocean views. We were considering spending our next trip at the hotel, but although it's an incredible resort and near our kids, with many amenities, including a world-class golf course, it was too far from Waikiki and the Palladium Dance Hall at the Ali Wai Country Club for us to seriously consider. I did, however, make a mental note about the Sunday brunch and the golf course for our next visit. Steve's next stop was Waimea Beach Park, another legendary surf spot, where waves reach 30 feet in the winter and is also an expert-only surfing area in season. We spread our blankets on the beach, as we couldn't resist the temptation to stretch out and relax, and then try the inviting soft waves that beckoned us to come and play. And play we did; the water was so soft and cool that spending the day in it was tempting and not out of the question. I was beginning to get a clear picture of what Paradise must be like, soft white sand, soft turquoise-blue water, soft white clouds pasted onto a soft blue sky, a soft tropical drink, and a soft beach towel. Add them together and we had the closest thing to Paradise that I could imagine. The picturesque scene of people parasailing, surfing, paddle boarding, and just horsing around was part of what makes the site a candidate as a contender for being Paradise on earth.

We arrived at the Palladium Dance Hall a little late, and found that the hall was divided in half by a portable partition hosting two different dances. I was surprised to see the "Hawaii Federation of Square Dance Clubs" occupying one of the halls to full capacity. We were coaxed to join them and sign up for their "Annual Aloha State Square and Round Dance Festival," which takes place in January. It is attended by square dance aficionados from around the world who compete for many of the championship levels, which are very similar to ballroom dance championships. We were tempted to join the "squares" (as they are called), for a dance lesson, but decided instead to enter the other half of the hall to join the "Hawaiian Ballroom Dance Association" (HBDA) for some good ballroom dancing. I took some of their brochures for future reference, and to remind me to look into the square dancing activities when we returned in the winter, time permitting.

We were greeted by some of the same people we met on our previous visit to the dance hall and were made to feel right at home. We sat next to an American, Jack, and his Japanese wife, Mieko, from Tokyo, who were recently married and on their honeymoon. She told us that it was her life-long dream to honeymoon in Hawaii and that she was waiting to wake up from her dream, as she couldn't believe she was at the dance with her handsome American husband. It seems that many Japanese women have the same dream, due to the good weather and beaches. But I think an underlying reason was the buying power of the Japanese yen, which makes Hawaii a buyer's paradise for them. She told us that in addition to her luggage containing her personal items, she came to the island with two empty suitcases, and had already started filling the second with goodies. If need be, she said, "I can always buy more suitcases, they are so cheap."

We danced the night away, enjoying the spaciousness of the dance floor, the incredibly good music, and the companionship of our newfound friends. We asked one of the locals if there were any other places to dance in the immediate area and were surprised to find several nearby. There was Salsa Hawaii at the Acqua Club in the Hawaiian Regent Hotel and the Rumours nightclub at the Ala Moana Hotel, just to name a couple. We couldn't wait to return in the winter and visit those "Hot Spots," as the locals referred to them. On the way out, we peeked in on the "squares." The energy from their dancing and the colorful western outfits were mesmerizing; it drew us in and we found ourselves dancing along. Even though we didn't have much experience in square or western-style dancing, we were able to do a West Coast swing and one country western two step.

Finally, our last day was upon us. After a morning dip in the ocean, the consensus was to just hang around and spend time on the beach and do a little barbequing. Steve said he needed to do some shopping at the Army PX (Post Exchange) and asked if we would like to come along; we immediately said yes. I always get a special feeling of pride when entering a military post. In my four years in the U.S. Air Force, the only more pleasant feeling that I can remember was leaving for furlough. The feeling was still the same as we entered the Schofield Barracks entrance gate. The facility is enormous, some 18,000 acres in Central Oahu. It was established in 1908 to provide mobile defense for Pearl Harbor and the entire island by the Army's 25th Infantry Division (Tropic Lightning Division). It houses almost 15,000 people in approximately 3,000 households. It lies adjacent to Wheeler Field, which in December of 1941 put it in the path of the Japanese warplanes who were headed for that airfield to destroy the two pursuit fighter groups of P-36s and P-40s. Although the attacking planes passed through the mountains that run along KoleKole Path, which runs through Schofield Barracks, they only strafed Schofield Barracks and the installation sustained just minor damage. Their main objective on that infamous day was to destroy as many planes and ships as possible. Steve took us to an observation area that had a monument and information about the attack that took place over the Barracks, while the Japanese warplanes passed on the way to their kills. In the darkness of that day, when Pearl Harbor, Wheeler Field, Hickam Field, Bellows Field, and many other military and civilian facilities were demolished, there is a story that brings some light into that most horrific day in American history. The Japanese also launched five, two-man mini-submarines against Pearl Harbor to complete the destruction of the American Naval Fleet in the harbor; all were sunk except one, which drifted out to Bellows Field and grounded on a reef. The Air Force personnel captured the surviving seaman, Ensign Kazuo Sakamaki, and then dragged the mini-submarine onto the beach, recording the first WWII prisoner of war captured by American forces and our first war prize.

Steve filled his car with gas, at a very reasonable price, and then took us to the PX. I always enjoyed shopping at the military stores when I was in the service. The variety of items for sale exceeds anything found in our major department stores and at more moderate prices. Steve bought some steaks, spareribs, and all the goodies that go along with a delicious BBQ. Steve and Donna invited some of their friends over for a farewell outing and we again enjoyed the beach, swimming, great food, wonderful singing, and the camaraderie of our children and their friends. What a wonderful way to end an evening and a splendid way to end our second visit to Hawaii. Our last thoughts were of returning in the winter and meeting our first grandchild.

* * *

Trip Three to Paradise: Meeting Grandchild Number One

We began planning our trip back to Hawaii as soon as we boarded our flight to New York. We had seven months before returning, and Barbara figured if we used only our American Express card for purchases, we would have enough frequent flyer miles to pay for two coach tickets. She was right; in a few months we did have enough frequent flyer miles to buy two tickets, which I immediately upgraded to first class by paying an additional fee, which would make the long flight a lot more comfortable. Our next challenge was choosing a hotel in Waikiki Beach that was centrally located. There seemed to be literally hundreds of hotels that would serve our purpose, but we chose the Hyatt Regency on Kalakaua Avenue, which is across the street from the breakwater at Waikiki Beach. It's also a short distance from the International Marketplace, Waikiki Aquarium, Honolulu Zoo, and Kapiolani Park. With the "blink of an eye" it was January 1999, and we were on our nonstop flight, from JFK to Hawaii. Or so we thought. We boarded an American Airlines airplane and settled in for the takeoff, but there was a mechanical problem and we had to exit the plane and wait for a replacement. Fortunately, as first-class passengers, we had the use of their Admiral's Club Lounge, which made things a little more tolerable. We boarded the next plane and were informed that it didn't have the fuel capacity to take us nonstop to Hawaii, and that we would have to land in Los Angeles to refuel. To make a very long story short, our 12-hour flight took 16 uncomfortable hours. When we landed in Hawaii, we were exhausted and totally annoyed at the whole experience; what else could go wrong? We soon found out. I can't explain the gruesome feeling I had while waiting for our luggage to arrive on the carousel. There was no baggage left on the arrival conveyor belt. There we were, standing by the carousel, flat footed, totally exhausted from the long flight, and not knowing what to do next. We went to the American Airlines' office and waited in line with about 20 other people. Some of the people in line were frantic, as they had to catch other flights out of Honolulu and were totally baffled as to what to do. We finally filled out the appropriate forms and explained our dilemma to a very sympathetic young lady, who assured us that the luggage would be found within a few days. Ugh! I couldn't imagine being without our personal belongings for that period of time. What was most upsetting, however, was that we had lots of presents for our new grandson in our baggage.

Seeing beautiful Waikiki Beach again had a calming effect on me and eased my frustration, somewhat. Seeing the Hyatt Regency's two forty-story towers also recycled my anger and made me a little more comfortable. The final comforting scene was the three-story, open-air atrium with orchids, palm trees, and cascading waterfalls, plus, to Barbara's delight, more than sixty oceanfront shops surrounding the atrium. We had been using the Hyatt Regency in Washington D.C. on our winter car trips to Florida and were card-holding members of the chain, which gave us another welcomed surprise, a free room upgrade that included breakfast. We got a room on the 38th floor that was very spacious, with a furnished balcony facing the ocean, a view to die for! A nice feature was a pillow-top mattress draped beneath earth-toned duvets and fine linens. The oversized bathroom featured granite countertops and was stocked with Portico toiletries, which Barbara wasted no time in adding to her international collection. There was also a laptop-size safe, which accommodated my computer easily, with room to spare. We were exhausted from the day's mishaps and jet lag, so we immediately jumped into bed to get some much-needed sleep and to get rid of some of the stress that was weighing us down.

Thank God we woke up to a whole new sunny day, a much-relieved attitude, and famished. The breakfast buffet was still open, so we showered and made a beeline straight to the dining hall. What a pleasant surprise! The buffet was endless, with an overwhelming smell of pineapple and bacon filling the room. I didn't waste any time getting an omelet with mushrooms and ham and a large glass of pineapple juice. Barbara went to the Japanese food section and came back with an assortment of sushi and a large glass of pineapple juice. The Hawaiian

Kona coffee was delicious beyond words, and after we finished off a pot, the day began to look brighter. If we were lucky, after breakfast, our luggage would be waiting in our room. Another pleasant experience was our waitress; a beautiful tan-skinned, bright smiling *wahine* (girl) named Lois. She brought sunshine into the room and lightened our table when her colorful flowered, red, and white dress appeared before us. She asked, in a soft, bubbly voice, if there was anything she could get us? I couldn't take my eyes off the Plumeria flower inserted on top of her ear. Barbara also couldn't stop admiring it and we told Lois so several times. Our day really started to perk up a bit after the wholesome breakfast and meeting the beautiful daughter of Hawaii, Lois. We had no luck with our baggage arriving, so we prepared for the 45-minute drive in our rented Buick Regal to see our new grandson with only a couple of presents that we had packed in our carry-on luggage.

There he was, our seven-pound, nine-day old, bundle of chubby joy. We couldn't stop kissing Donna and Ian Charles Bivona while telling them how happy we were with the new addition to our family. Steve, our little baby, all six-foot-two of him, was smiling so hard I thought that his smile was going to continue around to the back of his head. We spent the day holding, cuddling, and kissing Ian Charles's small body until it was time to change his diaper. At that point, I turned him over to the girls, who seemed to get a special delight from changing diapers "the right way," whatever that means. Steve prepared another of his wonderful BBQs that we so enjoyed eating previously on their expansive lawn, while watching the surf capturing the sand and replacing it in different locations along the beach. We were anxious to return to our hotel to see if any of our baggage had been discovered, which made our return drive seem a lot longer than the morning trip. No luck, no luggage. We asked the kids to join us for breakfast at the hotel and to spend the day with us enjoying the amenities of the pool and spa. We decided to buy some swimsuits so we could at least enjoy the pool when the children arrived. The hotel had a nice beach clothing store, so we didn't have any difficulty finding suits that were very tropical looking, with lots of flowers and colorful designs.

The kids arrived for a late breakfast buffet at the outdoor Terrace Grill, which overlooked the ocean. They were thrilled to be out of their house and at a place that felt like vacationland. It was just what the doctor ordered after spending several weeks isolated while preparing for and giving birth to our little Ian Charles. Barbara and I couldn't get over how delicious the Hawaiian Kona coffee tasted. The kids were already Kona fans, but said that they thought the brew at breakfast was exceptionally good. We spent the day hanging around the rooftop pool, which was bordered by two spa tubs and overlooked Waikiki Beach. I took advantage of the hotel's diversified cardiovascular exercise equipment in their state-of-the-art gym. Exercising had become a part of my new lifestyle since my heart bypass surgery in 1993, so I was looking forward to using their sophisticated equipment. We told the kids that we would watch their new package (Ian Charles), if they got the urge to wander around on their own. Before I could get the last word out of my mouth, they were gone. What a pleasure to be babysitting again; we haven't had that pleasure for over 20 years and enjoyed every moment of it. We told the kids to take their time and to enjoy themselves; they returned in the late afternoon, which was perfect, as it gave us a good part of the day to play and show off Ian Charles to the other hotel guests. We decided to have dinner at one of the local Japanese restaurants and had a choice of several along the main strip. It was a new experience for us to be spending time not only with our children but with our new grandson, who required lots of attention and soft soothing sways to keep him happy. After dinner, the kids left and we returned to our room anticipating finding our baggage, but no such luck. Numerous telephone calls to the airline were to no avail. They reassured us that, in time, they would locate and forward our luggage to us, but we just didn't believe them. We knew our baggage was somewhere in Davey Jones's Locker, and that our personal belongings were being sold somewhere on the black market.

Our telephone rang early the next morning and, lo and behold, our luggage had arrived. They were brought up to our room; I had had an overwhelming urge to hug and kiss the suitcases on sight. We examined all the bags and found that everything was intact, just slightly bruised due to their long journey to God knows where and back. I wondered, where does lost luggage go? Is it left at the airport? Is it left on the airplane in some dark corner? Is it put on the wrong airplane? Is it put on the wrong carousel? Is it put aside and looked into for possible theft? There are so many possibilities, so I decided to just be content with the fact that they were returned to us. We headed for our children's home with lots of presents for Ian Charles and a couple of niceties for our kids. After enjoying an outdoor lunch provided by our expert chef Steve, Donna suggested that, being that we were captivated by the aroma of pineapples in the air, that we should go to the source and pay a visit to the Dole Plantation Pineapple Museum, which was just a few miles away in the town of Wahiawa. It was a great idea, so we went post haste to the quaint town.

Upon entering the plantation, we were immediately drawn to the world's largest maze that has eight rest stations in an area occupying more than two acres, with paths in excess of three miles. It consisted of over 11,000 colorful Hawaiian plants, including hibiscus, heliconia, croton, panax, and pineapple. The center of the maze was in the shape of a huge pineapple, which was made up of croton and had a crown of *agapanthus* (blue lilies). There is an ongoing contest for adventurers to search for the eight secret stations on their way to solving the mystery of the labyrinth. In each station there were maze cards directing participants to possible paths to the next station; eventually, if interpreted correctly, the cards, and the adventurer's ability will lead them to the exit. The winner for the day is the person that has the shortest exiting time, and is rewarded by having their name placed on the entrance and receives a special prize, usually pineapple related. The best time had been recorded at seven minutes, while the average was between 45 minutes to one hour. Well, we all entered at the same time and eventually took our own paths through the network; Steve exited in about 15 minutes, with Donna right behind him. Barbara exited in about 25 minutes, while I was dead last at 45 minutes. I got so lost I couldn't believe it. How can an accountant get lost in a maze when it's such an integral part of his professional life? Oh well, it was lots of fun, although slightly embarrassing for me, especially the ribbing I took when I exited and found everyone pretending to be asleep. We then took a two-mile jitney tour around the plantation that showcased the legacy of the pineapple and its impact on Hawaiian agriculture. There were several acres of diversified farming that included specimens of lychee, banana, mango, papaya, cacao, and coffee. Along the route, we were treated to views of the Koolau and Waianae mountain ranges that monopolized the background and added to the overall splendor of the plantation.

A brochure at the center explained the purpose of this one-of-a-kind museum:

"The plantation blends the traditional elements of Hawaii's plantation life and the early pineapple industry with the new breed of diversified agriculture currently being grown on the North Shore of Oahu. It's dedicated to perpetuating the agricultural heritage of Hawaii, its place in history, and the progress of the islands and its people. The founder, James D. Dole of the Dole Food Company, came to Hawaii in 1899, after graduating from Harvard University, with $1,200 in his money pouch. He single-handedly began the pineapple industry in Hawaii with 60-acres of rich red dirt on the site of today's Dole Plantation Museum."

In addition to learning about the wide variety of fruits, vegetables, Hawaiian plants, and tropical flora, we participated in pineapple planting and picking. We learned how to pick the fruit, as well as how to safely and properly slice it for consumption. The museum center began as a fruit stand on the 60-acre Dole Plantation in 1950, and now has become a first-class museum telling the story of how pineapple impacted the Hawaiian Islands and its people. The plantation center featured "Made in Hawaii" items, including a variety of goods and handicrafts from local merchants, and including Dole logo items and pineapple-themed baked goods, such as snacks, Waialua chocolates, and delicious Waialua coffee. Antique tables, baskets, and traditional wooden bins displayed items reflecting Hawaii's plantation stores of days gone by. The objective was to present a traditional marketplace, a country store, and a series of building facades reminiscent of the Town of Haleiwa on Oahu's North Shore, which at one time was the center of the pineapple industry. We had a late lunch in their restaurant that featured a "Crown of Hawaii" menu and enjoyed their Teri Chicken, Kalua Pig, Mahi sandwiches, salads featuring ingredients from the islands, and, of course, our drink of choice, freshly made pineapple juice.

We invited the kids over the next day to again enjoy the hotel's facilities and just hang around at the pool or, if they preferred, the calm section of Waikiki beach, which was just across the road from our hotel. We dropped them off at their home and gave our new bundle of joy kisses and squeezes; then returned to our hotel anxious to revisit the Palladium Dance Hall for some ballroom dancing.

We were pleasantly surprised to find that the Hawaii U.S. Amateur Ballroom Dancers Association (HUSABDA) was holding their weekly dance. We showed our Florida USABDA cards and were given a hero's welcome. We were invited in at no charge, and were shocked that an announcement was made over the public address system stating that: "Our friends and members of USABDA from Florida and New York are joining us tonight, please welcome Mike and Barbara Bivona." We received applause and cheers. All night long people came over to greet us with the famous Hawaiian *Aloha.* Of course, for the entire evening, people were watching us dance. At first this made us very uncomfortable, but as all ballroom dancers like to show off a little, we ended up totally enjoying the experience while doing our special and well-learned routines. We were surprised that a small crowd gathered around us when we did a cha-cha and praised our performance when we finished. I never considered it one of our better dances, but accepted the accolades with a great smile and receptive heart. The evening ended with our saying goodbye to many of our new comrades, and to my delight, a very young, pretty, flower-smelling *wahine,* named Joanna, actually gave me a sweet nose rub.

The kids joined us for a Sunday brunch at the Terrace Grill. The overwhelming aroma from pineapples and the view of the ocean from the outdoor restaurant were a perfect setting for what was becoming, for me, a realization of a fantasy vacation comes true. It was wonderful to have a choice of whatever food my palate desired; a view of Waikiki Beach's surf; my beautiful and pleasant wife Barbara at my side; my good-natured and excellent chef-son-Steve, smiling at his wonderful masterpiece, Ian Charles; and my beautiful daughter-in-law and mother of our new bundle of joy; all of this together in one place. It was, without a shadow of a doubt, the realization of my perfect fantasy come true. We split the day between the pool and beach. It was winter, which is the time of year that the surf gets pretty rough and the waves high. Steve and Donna took advantage of some high waves and did some neat surf boarding, while Barbara, who is a very strong swimmer, swam out to meet some of the smaller waves and came back arms extended while riding the crests toward the beach. In the meantime, I got myself a Mai Tai and just lounged around on my beach blanket, enjoying the view of all the athletic souls challenging the elements. The kids left after an early dinner. I couldn't get over how quiet Ian Charles had been all day, not at all like his father who, at that age, was quite a handful and required a lot of attention. I guess Steve and Donna are just plain lucky; they certainly deserved it after long tours of duty with the Army outside of the U.S.A.

We had the next day to ourselves, as Donna and Steve had to go to Schofield Barracks. Donna had a doctor's appointment for a checkup and Steve had some meetings to attend. So we decided to finally pay a visit to Pearl Harbor, which I was avoiding, as I do not handle seeing the results of destruction and its resultant gravestones very well. Until this day, although I live only a short distance from New York City, I haven't been to see the remnants of the destruction at the Twin Towers on September 11, 2001, or its reconstruction. But, I just couldn't avoid visiting Pearl Harbor as it meant so much to all of us growing up during that period of time. Hopefully, in the near future, I will gather enough courage to also visit the Twin Towers Memorial in my hometown, New York City.

I had my laptop with me, so I decided to go on the Internet and do some research on the events that led to that "Infamous Day" on December 7, 1941. Growing up at that time, any information available was spoon fed to us to serve the immediate purpose of its authors. But, now that almost 60 years have passed, much of the data has been carefully studied by historians and eyewitnesses, and hopefully clarified. The United States government was certainly not unprepared for the war; it developed contingency plans for an eventual conflict with Japan as early as the 1920s and began preparing Pearl Harbor for the transfer of our Pacific Naval Fleet and Headquarters from San Diego to that location. As a matter of fact, our own military conducted a surprise attack on Pearl Harbor in the 1930s to determine the adequacy of our defenses; the attack succeeded and our defense was deemed inadequate. In the early 1930s, Japan invaded Manchuria and began to expand into China, Indochina, and the oil-rich Dutch East Indies. This expansion into the "Southern Resource Area" (the Japanese term for the East Indies and Southeast Asia in general), caused U.S. Pacific bases and facilities, including Pearl Harbor and the Philippine Islands, to go on practice alerts many times before the attack of December 7, 1941. Our factories were already geared and producing military armament for our defense, and shipping a multitude of equipment to many of our soon-to-be allies. There we have it; how can a country that was expecting an attack from Japan get caught "flat footed?" There is ongoing controversy, due to allegations made by many historians, that some members of our government had advance knowledge of the attack and ignored the information in order to gain public and Congressional support for the U.S. to enter WWII. Whatever the case may be, when Emperor Showa gave Admiral Isoroku Yamamoto his approval to attack Pearl Harbor, it was up to our military to have been prepared and to ward off any assault, which they failed to do. Looking back at the event, there was a combination of mismanagement and unfortunate circumstances that made the attacks devastating for us. In my opinion, one of the main problems was that on Sunday in the land of Paradise, most servicemen were in town having a good time, with only skeleton crews remaining to man the military installations. The Japanese knew this, and therefore, chose that day to launch their attack. Subsequent events became academic; we had the equipment to ward off an attack, but there were not enough personnel to man the defensive positions on land or sea. In addition to our ships being exposed and lined up like sitting ducks in a pond in Pearl Harbor Bay, we made our aircraft easy targets on the airfields by lining them up wing to wing. Why did we do this? Because the "brains" in the Navy were afraid that the Japanese living in Hawaii might sabotage them. This act alone undoubtedly supports the theory that we certainly were preparing for an attack of some sort from the Japanese Empire. The Japanese pilots' prayers were answered, and came upon targets on land and sea and sophisticated defensive military equipment unmanned.

So it happened: on Sunday, December 7, 1941, aircraft and midget submarines of the Imperial Japanese Navy began their "alleged surprise attack" on the U.S. facilities in Hawaii from six aircraft carriers. Prior to the attack, two reconnaissance aircraft were launched from Japanese's cruisers to scout over Oahu to report our fleet's composition and location. Another four scout planes patrolled the area in order to prevent their task force from being caught by a surprise counterattack from us. So there were six aircraft flying over our military installations, all unseen electronically or by the human eye, or, if they were detected, effectively, nothing was done to alert our military. At approximately 8:00 A.M., the first wave of 183 planes attacked our ships in the harbor concentrating on the large battleships. Air bases across Oahu were attacked, simultaneously, starting with Hickam Field, the largest, and Wheeler Field, the main Army Air Force fighter base. One hour later, the second wave of 171 planes attacked the Army Air Corps' Bellows Field and Ford Island's airfield. Of the 402 American aircraft in Hawaii, 188 were destroyed and 159 damaged. None were ready to take off to defend the military installations or to protect our servicemen; they were not properly positioned on the airfields to take off, and, in addition, most of the pilots were in town on weekend passes. The attack lasted 90 minutes and when it was over, 2,387 Americans were dead and 1,139 wounded. Eighteen ships were sunk, including five battleships. Nearly half the Americans killed were on the *USS Arizona*, when its forward magazine exploded after being hit by a bomb.

If there are any bright sides to that horrific day, it would be that our ships sunk or captured all five midget-submarines before they could do much damage, although the Japanese reported that one did get into the harbor and successfully launched a torpedo at its target. A tactical error was made by Admiral Yamamoto in cancelling a planned third strike by Japanese aircraft to destroy our repair facilities and oil reserves. This enabled us to begin repairs to the damaged vessels immediately and to put them back in service. The valuable oil reserves were used to quickly supply our aircraft carriers with fuel so they could pursue the Imperial Fleet, and ultimately engage them successfully in battle.

With all this information, we were prepared to visit the heart-wrenching memorial with a somewhat better understanding of how countries are drawn into wars. At the entrance to the Visitor Center was the Arizona's 19,585-pound anchor. Upon entering the center, we passed one of the battleship's two bells, and were very surprised at the size and complexity of the hall. It hosts the Pearl Harbor Museum, dual theaters, restrooms, a snack bar, and the Pearl Harbor Memorial Exhibit, complete with wartime memorabilia. The central room featured seven large open windows on the walls and ceiling commemorating the date of the attack. We sat through an orientation film explaining the events leading up to the December 7th attack and the massive restoration that subsequently took place. I was anxious to see the USS Arizona Memorial, so we skipped the rest of the Center and went directly to that site. We were lucky to find a docent, Johnny, who was a survivor of the attack, to guide us through the Memorial. He pointed out oil bubbles that were still surfacing from the ship (two quarts a day), that are dramatically called "Black Tears" or "Tears of the Arizona," in memory of the 1,000-plus sailors that were left buried in the ship and are considered by the U.S. Navy to have been buried at sea. It is at this opening that visitors are permitted to pay their respects by tossing flowers and leis into the water in honor of the fallen sailors. The *USS Arizona's* deck lies six feet below the water line, with a pole attached to its mainmast flying an American flag and protruding skyward from a 184-foot-tall Memorial that encompasses the vessel. Every day a new flag is flown and the former one is folded in a triangular shape and given to a special person, sometimes a lucky visitor. The ship was built in the early 1900s and had a rather relatively uneventful history up until that horrific day. The ill-fated ship arrived at Pearl Harbor on December 6, 1941, the day before the attack, and had the honor of having the Battle Ship Fleet Commander Admiral Isaac Kidd (known as Captain Kidd) pay it an inspection visit. The ship and the Admiral both became history on the next day, but Captain Kidd put up a gallant fight; he gathered and organized his ships and men to give whatever resistance they could to the oncoming slaughter. He was awarded the Congressional Medal of Honor posthumously for his heroic conduct, and subsequently had three destroyers named after him. Unfortunately, he was never asked why his battleships were all in port at the same time and lined up in such a precarious formation. A choking experience was when Johnny took us to the marble shrine that bears the names of the seamen that went down with their ships. There were several men Johnny's age standing before the wall, hats in hand, heads bowed, and crying, while others searched the list for lost comrades and relatives. Scenes such as these always have a profound effect on me, as I find it difficult not to join in their sorrow and shed a tear with them. Leaving the Memorial was bittersweet; I was glad to pay my respect to those fallen Americans, but sad that hostility seems to be the only solution to many of the world's problems.

Next to the battleship USS Arizona Memorial is the battleship USS Missouri Memorial. Looking at the two structures reminded me of a mechanical vise: the *Arizona* being the fixed part of the vise and the *Missouri* (Big Mo) the parallel jaw that moves back and forward. It was on this ship that the unconditional surrender of the Imperial Empire of Japan was signed. *Big Mo* represents the power of the United States that squeezed the energy and resources from the infamous Empire like a vise and brought it to the peace table with hat in hand to sign an unconditional surrender. The *Big Mo* overshadowed its counterpart in size, which perfectly represents the overwhelming might of the United States once it entered the war against Japan. It is 887 feet long, 209 feet from keel to mast, and has a 108-foot beam. It had speeds in excess of 30 knots (35 mph) and is 279 feet longer and 11 feet wider than its sister ship. The *Big Mo* was the most formidable ship of its day, and the last U.S. battleship to be commissioned. In addition to its massive firepower capabilities, she possessed thick steel armor plating from between 13.5 to 17 inches. It fought in most of our wars and conflicts: WWII, Korea, Vietnam, and Desert Storm. She secured her place in history when the unconditional surrender documents were signed between Japan and the Allied Forces on September 2, 1945, on her deck. The image is etched in my mind of the Supreme Allied Commander, General Douglas MacArthur, signing the Formal Instrument of Surrender, which ended the final hostilities of WWII, and then handing the historic pen to General Wainwright, as a sign of redemption for his being a prisoner of war throughout the struggle. Wainwright's heroic efforts in the Philippine Islands in resisting the Japanese attacks won him a fourth star and the Medal of Honor.

Unfortunately, he spent three years of the war in various prisoner of war camps, ending up in Manchuria before his release.

We took a guided tour of the enormous ship with Jason, a Korean War veteran who served on *Big Mo* during that conflict. He was one of 2,700 officers and men who served honorably on the ship that had nine 16-inch guns, which are approximately 67 feet long, and was used effectively in sinking enemy ships and in support of our ground troops. There was a group of young children, 11 to 14 years old, in an overnight Encampment Program. They were allowed to live aboard the ship, like real sailors, sleeping in the crew's berthing areas, storing their gear in navy lockers, eating Navy-style meals on the ship's mess deck, and using the restrooms and showers as if they were real seamen. What an exciting overnight camp-out for those young people. The satisfaction and the experience of being a sailor were clearly reflected in their beaming smiles and faces. We moved along with Jason through the bridge admiring the sophisticated electronic equipment that the ship required to effectively perform its duty: radar, sonar, GPS, LORAN, electronic compasses, autopilot, plotting equipment, and a multitude of computers. It is amusing that with all the state-of-the-art equipment, they still have old-fashioned manual steering and magnetic compasses on standby just in case of an unforeseen happening that could disable their electronics. The big guns were frightening; they have the capacity of delivering shells of up to 2,700 pounds to their targets. In addition, the ship's rocket launchers made the ship an impressive aggressive and defensive weapon.

The crew's quarters on large ships have always startled me; the closeness of the living conditions certainly requires patience and a great deal of tolerance in human behavior. My favorite place on naval vessels has always been the kitchen, especially if they are serving their delicious vanilla cake with chocolate icing, which they were. It seems that it is a tradition on all naval ships to have that wonderful cake available for their crews and visitors; I was able to take a second helping of the delicious cake with the blessing of the chef. We thanked Jason for his informative guided tour and left the enormous ship to visit her neighbor, the *USS Bowfin* Submarine at the Submarine Museum and Park.

The museum featured the world of submarines, both past and present. A 10,000-square-foot building exhibited an impressive collection of submarine-related artifacts, such as weapon systems, photographs, paintings, battle flags, original recruiting posters, and an incredible collection of submarine models. An outstanding exhibit displayed a Poseidon C-3 missile; we were allowed to examine the inner and outer workings of the deadly projectile, but very carefully; although it was disabled, it still looked threatening. In the park stands a public memorial honoring the 52 American submarines and more than 3,500 submariners that were lost during WWII. We were given electronic docents to guide us through the *Bowfin*. "The submarine was built on December 7, 1942, and was immediately nicknamed 'the Pearl Harbor Avenger' because it was launched exactly one year after the ill-fated day in 1941. The submarine is 312 feet long with a 27-foot beam, and carried 24 torpedoes manned by 80 submariners. It lived up to its nickname as 'the Avenger' as it sunk 44 enemy ships during its nine extraordinary war patrols." The crew's quarters were exceptionally small compared to the accommodations on *Big Mo.* I could never understand how men could live in such tight quarters without becoming claustrophobic or at least ornery. Everything on the vessel was scaled down compared to other ships, but the kitchen was unique as it acted as a meeting place and a compact restaurant. They also had the delicious vanilla cake with chocolate icing laid out for guests, and I didn't waste any time eating another large slice. The most fascinating part of the boat was the torpedo room. The large shiny torpedoes made the hair on the back of my neck stand out as they were so threatening in their appearance and size. I was glad to leave the stuffy area and go for a walk on the topside where the air was crisp and clean. WWII submarines are small and cramped for space compared to the spacious modern atomic subs of today. It's eerie that the small vessel successfully carried out its missions, with 80 crewmembers aboard, into the deep waters of the Pacific for extended periods of time, searching for enemy ships, and returned to tell their heroic stories. They were all alone and for a good deal of the time submerged in the deep waters of the ocean on and off for months on end; still, they gallantly carried out their almost-suicidal missions. God bless those brave men.

The next morning, we rushed to the breakfast buffet where we were greeted by Hawaii's beautiful daughter, Lois, whose captivating smile and presence brought the morning sunlight deep into my soul. She presented Barbara with a beautiful, white gardenia-type Plumeria flower that she grew in her garden; the beautiful specimen emitted a sweet tropical floral aroma that perked up my day. It matched the head garland she was wearing, which had a mix of colorful flowers that were also grown in her garden, which she proudly displayed on her shiny silk-like black hair. What a sweet gesture from a more-than-sweet *wahine.* What a great way to start our day.

Off we went to visit our speechless, toothless, chubby, cuddly little bundle of happiness. We found the kids enjoying their beach and didn't waste any time changing into our bathing suits to join them. Steve had snorkeling gear ready for us to use, so we donned the masks and mouthpieces and went pell-mell into the water. After a few minutes, Donna, who was knee deep in the water, picked up a two-by-three-foot piece of white coral to show us; what a surprise when a green sea cucumber, which is a sea urchin and is in the starfish family, jumped off from underneath the coral. It was about 15 inches long with tiny legs and looked like a giant, fat, wriggly green worm. She put the coral back ASAP and did a quick turn towards the beach, with us close behind.

I asked Steve if we could revisit Banzai Pipeline to see the winter surfers challenging the large waves we had heard so much about. He agreed and said it would also be a good opportunity to play some golf at the Turtle Bay Resort, which was not far from the Pipeline. What a sight to see—expert surfers riding the giant tubes of water that slowly turn into tsunami-type waves. What is spectacular to watch is their paddling out on their boards to what they anticipate are good locations to begin their journey back on crests of what they hope are "perfect waves." The name *Banzai* (suicide) Pipeline is certainly an appropriate name for the beach that attracts so many of the world's surfing daredevils. It was surprising to see the large number of surfers challenging the waves and the great number of people spread out on beach towels, picnicking, while observing the daredevils in action. Needless to say, none of the spectators ventured into the surf, including us.

We drove over to Turtle Bay Resort in time for their famous cornucopia brunch. The resort is located on Turtle Bay; its brochure says it all:

> It's located on an 880-acre oasis on the North Shore of Oahu, set among swaying palms, quiet coves and rolling surf. The beauty of this tropical paradise can be seen from one of the 443 magnificent beach cottages and guest rooms. The resort features two lushly landscaped pools, one overlooking the azure Pacific, two championship golf courses, ten tennis courts, horseback riding, hiking and mountain bike trails, a surfing school, world-class dining, and upscale shopping. The Palmer course is an 18-hole championship golf course designed by Arnold Palmer and Ed Seay and hosts the PGA Champions Tour Event in October. The course has five tee locations: Black, Blue, Gold, White, and Red. The smaller George Fazio Course hosts the LPGA Tour's Hawaiian Open and was the site of the first Senior Skins Game, which included Arnold Palmer, Chi-Chi Rodriquez, Gary Player and Sam Sneed.

Talk about being intimidated; I wanted to play the smaller Fazio Course, but Steve insisted that we play nine holes on the Palmer Course. I gratefully acquiesced being that he was treating me and I didn't want him to feel that I was unappreciative. Steve and I rushed through our brunch; we left the girls and Ian Charles in the Palm Terrace Restaurant so they could finish their meal and then go on to explore the Resort's facilities, especially the upscale shops.

Steve brought an extra set of clubs for me, which we checked at the baggage drop-off and proceeded to the check in for some real quality golf time. There were several Japanese men in front of us at the cashier; I couldn't believe how much they paid for a round of golf. I told my son it was too much to pay for a few hours of relaxation, but he said, "No sweat, Dad, everything is under control." I've heard him use that phrase many times when he was a youngster and immediately began to sweat. Little did I know that the military received a large discount and paid about a third of the going price. He paid for the nine holes and away we went. We had a choice of playing the front nine, which is nearly devoid of trees and shrubs and has lots of sand, water, wind, and rolling terrain, or the back nine, which is a forest of ironwood pines and offers no less than nine craggy bunkers surrounding the landing area and extending all the way up to the green. We decided on the front nine, as it seemed a little easier; we teed off from the white marker, which was 5,574 yards versus the black, which was 7,199 yards. My first shot was heavenly, about 180 yards right down the middle of the fairway. Steve hit his about 200 yards a little to the right. Unfortunately, those were our best shots for the day. I certainly was the more experienced player as I knew the most important rules of the game, which distinguishes a seasoned player from a novice. I knew all the reasons why I missed opportunities, such as, the club is bent, the grass is wet, the greens are wavy, unexpected winds, etc., etc., etc. The course was mind-boggling and we were way over our heads as golfers, but we did spend some quality time together and did lots of laughing as we pretended to be serious players.

We found the girls strolling around the shops and decided it was time to join them for drinks in the Lei Lei Bar and Grill. We spent a couple of hours relaxing and wandering around the spacious resort, admiring the views of the turquoise-blue Pacific Ocean from our chaise lounges while nursing tropical drinks. Steve and Donna said they wanted to take us to a small restaurant in the town of Haleiwa, located only a few minutes from their home, to enjoy some local food. They hadn't had an opportunity to dine in their favorite restaurant since the arrival of Ian Charles.

We had some time before dinner so we walked around the quaint town of Haleiwa. There was an abundance of surf shops selling snorkeling equipment, surf boards, skin-diving gear, and every imaginable type of aquatic equipment that anyone might need. The town boasts that it is the surfing capital of the world and rightfully so, as it is the first stop that the world-renowned daredevils visit before seeking the "perfect wave" at the largest and most beautiful beaches in the world. There were some nice antique shops, which we visited and admired some of the photographs of Hawaiian scenes and natives. We couldn't resist buying a beautiful 8x12-inch photo of a beautiful *wahine* with her mate, expressing their love story through a peaceful hula dance on a beach; today, the photo hangs in my office at home and its presence brings comfort and serenity to the room. One of the antique shops had French music playing that was so beautiful that I asked the owner if I could sit a spell and listen to some of the songs. He was delighted and told me, in his French accent, to come back after dinner; he said he would have a surprise for me at that time. He spoke English with a very heavy French accent, a Maurice Chevalier-type voice that was friendly and sincere and reminded me of that great French singer/actor.

The town had an old plantation character and was a throwback to the beginning of the 20th century. The building facades were quaint and there were many town folks sitting on benches outside the stores, as if they were permanent fixtures, rocking away and passing the time of day in conversation. On the North entrance to the town was the white twin-span "Rainbow Bridge" that got its name from the shape and the rainbows it seems to attract during the rainy season. Children were diving off the lower part of the bridge, about 20 feet, into the Anahulu River, swimming to the rocky shore, and then repeating the exercise. Another distinction that the town has is that on December 7, 1941, the only fighter plane that managed to scramble against the Japanese took off from the now-abandoned Haleiwa Airfield. There were many tee shirts for sale in town honoring that historic event.

We had dinner in Haleiwa Joe's, and chose to sit in the lanai so we could enjoy the view of the water and the setting sun. We all ordered Caesar salads and Mai Tai drinks, which was a perfect combination; after a couple of those tropical drinks, everything seemed to "hang loose." We kept track of the number of drinks we had by the umbrellas that were accumulating on the table, which were inserted into the pineapples garnishing our hour-glass-shaped drinks when they were served. The presentation of the drinks was so glamorous that it was difficult to disrupt their appearance, at least that's how it felt before having the first drink; after that, it became a lot easier. The girls ordered steamed lobsters that were caught in local waters and came fresh off the Haleiwa fishing boats. They were served with lemon, butter, sautéed vegetable, and steamed white rice. Steve ordered a pound of Alaskan king crab legs, served with steamed white rice, sautéed vegetable, and drawn butter. I chose the fresh wild Atlantic salmon, grilled and topped off with a zesty dill sauce. It was served with sautéed vegetable and my favorite, garlic mashed potatoes. We devoured the meals as if they were our last suppers and would have probably stayed for seconds, but Ian Charles was starting to get restless. By the time we finished, the sun, which seemed magnified, was setting and cast an orange-red glow over the whole area, bringing sounds of delight from all of the restaurants' patrons, except for our little baby, who was starting to make some strange baby sounds. We went back to the antique shop to visit our French friend, Rene, who greeted us with double-cheek kisses and a hug. He presented me with a copy of his tape that I had enjoyed listening to that afternoon. There were songs by Edith Piaf, Maurice Chevalier, Josephine Baker, Jean Gabin, and Fernandel. I couldn't stop thanking him for his kindness and for the considerate act and gave him an extra hug and handshake. We exchanged names and addresses, promising to visit each other if ever the occasion would arise. We drove the short distance back to the children's home listening to the French songs that were graciously supplied by our new French/Hawaiian friend. We reminded the kids that they were spending the next day with us at Waikiki Beach and then continued our long drive back to our hotel, humming along to the beautiful French music.

We spent the next day hanging around the pool and enjoying the hotel's facilities. Steve and I took the opportunity to work out at the gym and then we babysat while the girls spent some quality time at the spa. We had a poolside lunch of hamburgers and hotdogs and enjoyed the onsite Hawaiian band's music, especially the Hawaiian Wedding Song, which was written by Charles King in 1926. The song is one of my favorite; the lyrics go something like this:

> "This is the moment, I've waited for. I can hear my heart singing, soon bells will be ringing . . ."

What a way to spend a day: a relaxing pool, the sun shining and bringing warmth to our bodies, delicious tropical drinks served by beautiful *wahines,* tropical music filling the warm air, coos coming from our chunky grandson, and my family at arms' reach. The kids had to get back early to prepare for a big BBQ that they were having in our honor the next day. So we had an early dinner at a quaint Japanese restaurant a couple of blocks away and then returned to our room to dress for another visit to the Palladium to join our Aloha Dance Club friends.

We heard that at sunset there would be a torch-lighting ceremony across the street from our hotel on Kuhio Beach, at the foot of the statue of the island's champion surfer, Duke Kahanamoku. The detour was worth the time, as a procession of Hawaiian dancers and torch lighters sang and danced to the rhythm of the drums while lighting the torches and paying homage to the great surfer. No matter how many times I see hula dancing by the beautiful, pleasant Hawaiians, I'm overwhelmed with the showmanship and sensuality of their performances, and just enjoy watching while breathing the same fragrant air as they do. I was surprised at the large number of people that gathered to watch the event. Many came with beach blankets and refreshments and seemed prepared to spend the evening at the site. We became so relaxed that we decided to order a couple of exotic rum concoctions from a beach vendor and enjoy the festivities. Soon several Hawaiians struck up conversations with us; their big question was; "How do you like our place in the sun?" We were the right people to ask; we couldn't stop telling them about our Hawaiian-born grandson, the beautiful beaches that we enjoyed, the beautiful Hawaiians that we met, and when we told them it was our third visit to the islands, they ordered drinks for us and baptized us Hawaiians. Between the drinks, the camaraderie, the cool air, and the swaying tropical music, we lost track of time and never got to go dancing at the Palladium. So we called it a night, and went back to our room for some well-deserved sleep.

Although we had two more days to spend in Hawaii, it was the last day that we were spending with our kids, as they had to report back to duty the following day. We decided to hang around their beach house and just coast along for the day, enjoying the expansive lawn, palm trees embracing a multitude of coconuts, the soft sandy beach, swimming, and our little joy bundle, Ian Charles. The guests started arriving in the late afternoon, 12 in all, carrying their contributions to the BBQ, which was gratefully accepted by Donna and placed on ice for future enjoyment. Steve lit the half-dozen torches scattered throughout his lawn to ward off any uninvited flying visitors, which set the stage and tropical mood for the afternoon. A couple of ukuleles and a guitar appeared and the music and singing began. Some of the girls actually did some exotic hula dancing, which was spoiled when the guys tried to show them the right way to wriggle around and move their hairy arms and legs, while puffing on smelly cigars. Steve's barbequed spareribs were amazing, as were his hamburgers. I think the fact that he loves to cook adds flavor to his cuisine. He picked some coconuts from the trees, split them, and made coconut juice tropical drinks, with lots of rum. Fresh coconuts are one of the most delicious fruits I can think of, especially when spiked with a little rum or crème de cacao. Saying goodbye was not easy. The quality time we spent with the children was over and after many kisses, hugs, and special squeezes for Ian Charles, we said *adieu*, hoping that we would see them in the very near future back in the States. Another trip to Hawaii was not out of the question. As a matter of fact, the thought of returning to Paradise for a fourth time was a tempting possibility, especially since we were now Hawaiians.

We had the next day to ourselves and mapped out our itinerary so we could put every minute of our last day to good use. First, we decided to visit the Punchbowl and then go to the Hilton Hawaiian Village Resort to see one of our favorite performers, actress-singer-comedian-guitarist, Charo. After her show, we would go over to the Hawaiian Regent Hotel and spend the rest of the evening dancing some hot salsa at their Acqua Club. The Punchbowl is the United States' National Memorial Cemetery of the Pacific and includes the Honolulu Memorial. It covers approximately 116 acres in the extinct Puowaina Crater; *Puowaina* means "Consecrated Hill" or "Hill of Sacrifice." It was the site of many royal burials and also the place where certain religious offenders were sacrificed to the Gods. By the end of WWII, there were many temporary cemeteries scattered throughout the Pacific, which included 776 casualties from the December 7, 1941, attack on Hawaii. They were the first to be interred at the cemetery, and thereafter, 11,597 identified and 2,079 unidentified WWII soldiers were gathered from Guadalcanal, China, Burma, Saipan, Guam, Okinawa, and Iwo Jima and from prisoner of war camps in Japan, and laid to rest at this site. The cemetery is now filled to capacity with 33,230 gravesites, which includes soldiers from WWII to the Vietnam War. The remains are of soldiers killed in action and whose next of kin decided not to have their bodies returned to the U.S. mainland. There is only one other hallowed burial place for WWII soldiers in the Pacific, the Manila American Cemetery and Memorial, Fort Bonifacio, Manila, in the Philippines.

Viewing the gravesites was just too much to bear. The heart-wrenching experience was overwhelming and exhausting and demanded lots of soul searching, especially when trying to rationalize why so many lives are always sacrificed in the fight for freedom. To compound the deep uneasiness of viewing the gravesites is the Honolulu Memorial, which features eight marble courts containing the names of 26,280 Americans missing in action from WWII and the Korean War. Two additional areas list the names of 2,503 soldiers missing from the Vietnam War. At the top of the marble staircase stands a towering 30-foot statue of the woman, Columbia, with a laurel branch in her hand, representing peace and liberty. Cradled on each side of the statue were walls etched with maps of the many military campaigns in the Pacific, including Pearl Harbor, Wake Island, Coral Sea, Midway, New Guinea, the Solomons, Iwo Jima, the Gilbert Islands, Okinawa, and Korea. Many of the names brought back memories of my brother Victor, who was in the Marines during WWII and fought in many of the battles listed. At the center, behind the statue, is an interdenominational chapel, which is available for those visitors who require time to reflect on the human race's inability to refrain from wars that produced these two memorials representing over 60,000 missing and dead soldiers. I had the same bittersweet feeling there that I experienced at the Pearl Harbor memorials: pleased to be honoring our fallen heroes, and disappointed and frustrated that mankind has not found a more sane and humane way to resolve disputes.

When we got back to the hotel, we made a beeline straight to the rooftop bar and had Mai Tais to take the edge off of the disturbing sights we had seen at the memorials. We dressed and revisited the Hawaiian Village Resort, where we spent time on a previous trip enjoying a native *luau* while participating in some ceremonial dances. The hotel was as beautiful as we remembered, right on the beach with its own lagoon, probably one of the most beautiful of the beautiful hotels in Waikiki. While we waited for Charo's show to begin, we ordered more Mai Tais to erase the day's scenery from our minds and to put us in the right mood to enjoy this one-of-a-kind entertainer. I made good use of my laptop computer in the hotel and did some research on the Spanish, chameleon-type goddess:

> She was born in Murcia, Spain, in either 1941 or 1951, as Maria del Rosario Pilar Martinez Molina Baeza, the daughter of a lawyer who fled the country to Casablanca during Francisco Franco's dictatorship, while his wife remained behind to raise the family. She had a passion as a young child for classical guitar music and proudly claims that the world-renowned Andres Segovia was her instructor. She took lessons from him and other teachers beginning at age nine, and as a result of her training and skill, she was named the 'Best Flamenco Guitarist' in *Guitar Player Magazine's* readers' poll twice. As a young entertainer, she was discovered by the famous Latin bandleader Xavier Cugat and soon became his fifth, but not last, wife in 1966 at Caesars Palace in Las Vegas. They were married for 12 years and upon separating, she gave him a Rolls Royce to express her gratitude for his guiding her successful career. Her talents were in such demand that she commanded the same salaries as Frank Sinatra, Ray Charles, and Dean Martin when she entertained in Las Vegas.

I remember her so well on the Johnny Carson show where her complete lack of fluency in the English language had him and his partner, Ed McMahon, rolling on the floor laughing, especially when she did her *cuchi-cuchi* routine. She was called the *cuchi-cuchi* girl from that time on. People would roar laughing at her attempts to speak the English language, starting the rumor that she learned English from the comedian Buddy Hackett. She made her entrance singing in Spanish and playing her famous flamenco guitar. The audience stood up and applauded and howled at her flamboyant stage presence and provocative outfit. Her voice was magical due to the way she whined and sighed while expressing her love or grief and expertly playing flamenco music on her oversized guitar. The arrangements made her performance a truly artistic and passionate one. Her attempt at the English language was so out of sync with its cadence that many in attendance had tears rolling down their faces from the spontaneous laughter that her words brought, including Barbara and me. The highlight of the evening was when she sat on my lap as she sang, in her unique English, "you do me something" or "you do something to me," while running her fingers through my diminished hair and pulling on my pony tail. I still have pleasant nightmares about that incident, which always puts a smirk and then a very large smile on my face. In one of her recent interviews, she expressed that she would love to be a contestant on *Dancing with the Stars*—wouldn't that be earth shattering?

We wandered over to the Hawaiian Regent Hotel to hear Roland Sanchez and his "Salsa Hawaii Band" perform their musical magic. He had been playing at the hotel for three years and was instrumental in organizing and participating in many Latin Festivals in Hawaii. He has been featured on TV shows and music videos in Hawaii and Tahiti. The dance floor was small but it didn't stop us from doing some great salsa, mambo, meringue, and cumbia dancing. Fortunately, most Latin dances do not require lots of room, as they are done in place without moving around the dance floor, so the small dance floor worked out very well for our purpose. Half the fun was just listening to the great maestro and enjoying the last of our Mai Tais before we left Paradise. *Con Mucho Gusto.*

We never returned to Hawaii as Steve, Donna, and Ian Charles soon returned to the mainland. Although we loved the "Islands of Paradise," there are many other destinations that we are determined to remove from our "Bucket List" of things to do before we "kick the bucket." We plan on doing more traveling before I begin my follow-up book, *Traveling Around the World with Mike & Barbara Bivona, Part Two.*

So long until then . . .